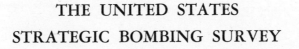
THE UNITED STATES
STRATEGIC BOMBING SURVEY

The Effects

of

Strategic Bombing

on

Japan's War Economy

Appendix A B C

OVER-ALL ECONOMIC EFFECTS DIVISION

December 1946

For sale by the Superintendent of Documents, U. S. Government Printing Office
Washington 25, D. C. • Price 65 cents

This report was written primarily for the use of the U. S. Strategic Bombing Survey in the preparation of further reports of a more comprehensive nature. Any conclusions or opinions expressed in this report must be considered as limited to the specific material covered and as subject to further interpretation in the light of further studies conducted by the Survey.

FOREWORD

The United States Strategic Bombing Survey was established by the Secretary of War on 3 November 1944, pursuant to a directive from the late President Roosevelt. Its mission was to conduct an impartial and expert study of the effects of our aerial attack on Germany, to be used in connection with air attacks on Japan and to establish a basis for evaluating the importance and potentialities of air power as an instrument of military strategy for planning the future development of the United States armed forces and for determining future economic policies with respect to the national defense. A summary report and some 200 supporting reports containing the findings of the Survey in Germany have been published.

On 15 August 1945, President Truman requested that the Survey conduct a similar study of the effects of all types of air attack in the war against Japan, submitting reports in duplicate to the Secretary of War and to the Secretary of the Navy. The officers of the Survey during its Japanese phase were:

Franklin D'Olier, *Chairman.*
Paul H. Nitze, Henry C. Alexander, *Vice Chairmen.*
Harry L. Bowman,
J. Kenneth Galbraith,
Rensis Likert,
Frank A. McNamee, Jr.,
Fred Searls, Jr.,
Monroe E. Spaght,
Dr. Lewis R. Thompson,
Theodore P. Wright, *Directors.*
Walter Wilds, *Secretary.*

The Survey's complement provided for 300 civilians, 350 officers, and 500 enlisted men. The military segment of the organization was drawn from the Army to the extent of 60 percent, and from the Navy to the extent of 40 percent. Both the Army and the Navy gave the Survey all possible assistance in furnishing men, supplies, transport, and information. The Survey operated from headquarters established in Tokyo early in September 1945, with subheadquarters in Nagoya, Osaka, Hiroshima, and Nagasaki, and with mobile teams operating in other parts of Japan, the islands of the Pacific, and the Asiatic mainland.

It was possible to reconstruct much of wartime Japanese military planning and execution, engagement by engagement, and campaign by campaign, and to secure reasonably accurate statistics on Japan's economy and war production, plant by plant, and industry by industry. In addition, studies were conducted on Japan's over-all strategic plans and the background of her entry into the war, the internal discussions and negotiations leading to her acceptance of unconditional surrender, the course of health and morale among the civilian population, the effectiveness of the Japanese civilian defense organization, and the effects of the atomic bombs. Separate reports will be issued covering each phase of the study.

The Survey interrogated more than 700 Japanese military, government, and industrial officials. It also recovered and translated many documents which not only have been useful to the Survey, but also will furnish data valuable for other studies. Arrangements have been made to turn over the Survey's files to the Central Intelligence Group, through which they will be available for further examination and distribution.

TABLE OF CONTENTS

INTRODUCTION

The present volume attempts to gauge broadly the effects of air power on the Japanese economic potential and to appraise the role of our attack against the Japanese war economy in the 4 years of our struggle in the Pacific.

It is not so much a summary of individual reports on specific branches of the Japanese economy,[1] as an effort to present an integrated account which describes the extent of Japan's economic paralysis caused by our military operations and the role of the economic disaster in the final outcome of the conflict.

To accomplish this task, the economic components of the Japanese war potential had to be viewed against the social and political background of modern Japan. This is the subject matter of the introductory chapter, which sketches briefly the events which led Japan into war and summarizes the results of the Survey interrogations concerning Japanese war plans and strategy. An analysis of the Japanese economy in 1941 assesses the initial economic position of Japan on which she based her decision to enter the war.

The development, the up's and down's of the Japanese war economy, is described in some detail in chapter II. Analyzing systematically its strength and weaknesses, the chapter pictures the target which our air and naval forces were directed to destroy.

The actual course of these destructive assaults is traced in chapter III, while chapter IV gives an account of the damages inflicted upon the Japanese economy.

Chapter V gives a short narrative of the final stage of the war and tentatively delineates the role which air power, the destruction of the enemy's economy, and other factors played in forcing Japanese surrender.

The considerations underlying our target selection during the war are examined in the sixth and concluding chapter in the light of the information secured by the Survey in Japan. The conclusions drawn point to some lessons which may be of use for the formulation of the future military policy of the United States.

Three appendices contain material which was deemed unsuitable for inclusion in the report but which may prove valuable to workers in the field of Japanese economic intelligence:

A. Allied economic intelligence: Analysis and comparison.

B. Gross national product of Japan and its components.

C. Statistical sources.

This report is the result of collective work undertaken by the Over-all Economic Effects Staff of the United States Strategic Bombing Survey (Pacific). In their research, the members of the staff relied heavily on other divisions of the Survey. It may be appropriate, however, to list the following, who carried the major responsibility for the completion of this volume:

Mr. Milton Gilbert, Chief, Over-all Economic Effects Staff.

Mr. Paul A. Baran, deputy chief.

Mr. Thomas A. Bisson.

Lt. Russell Dorr, USNR.

1st Lt. Seymour J. Wenner and Sgt. Walter E. Sanford, Jr., responsible for appendix A.

Mr. Lawrence Bridge, responsible for appendix B.

Mr. Jerome Stoner, responsible for appendix C.

---

[1] For detailed information, consult the reports prepared by the industrial divisions of the United States Strategic Bombing Survey.

CONCLUSIONS

ECONOMIC EFFECTS OF THE STRATEGIC BOMBING OF JAPAN

By July 1945 Japan's economic system had been shattered. Production of civilian goods was below the level of subsistence. Munitions output had been curtailed to less than half the wartime peak, a level that could not support sustained military operations against our opposing forces. The economic basis of Japanese resistance had been destroyed.

This economic decay resulted from the sea-air blockade of the Japanese home islands and direct bombing attacks on industrial and urban-area targets.

The contribution of the blockade was to deny Japan access to vital raw materials on the mainland and in the South Pacific area. Japan's dependence on these sources was crucial in the case of oil, bauxite, iron ore, coking coal, salt, and, to a lesser extent, foodstuffs. Heavy merchant ship losses began to cut raw material imports as early as 1943. As the blockade was tightened by submarines, the mining program, and airpower imports were almost completely stopped. Munitions production reached its peak in the fall of 1944; thereafter output began to decline, due to the shortage of raw materials. Thus, before the large-scale bombing of Japan was initiated, the raw material base of Japanese industry was effectively undermined. An accelerated decline of armament production was inevitable.

The program was transformed from one of slow strangulation to a relatively quick knock-out by strategic bombing. It was initiated in November 1944, though the main weight of the attack came between the months of March and August 1945.

The precision attacks on industrial targets were of major consequence in the case of the aircraft industry. The decline in aircraft output initiated by lack of essential raw materials, was greatly accelerated by the bombing attacks which caused severe damage to production facilities and necessitated the dispersal program. In addition, a carrier plane strike on the Hokkaido-Honshu rail ferries virtually severed this transportation artery. Other precision attacks, in which oil refineries and arsenals were the major targets, accomplished a considerable amount of physical destruction, but had less effect upon production either because material shortages had already created so much excess capacity or because plants were already idle, due to dispersal.

The urban-area incendiary raids had profound repercussions on civilian morale and Japan's will to stay in the war. Sixty-six cities, virtually all those of economic significance, were subjected to bombing raids and suffered destruction ranging from 25 to 90 percent. Almost 50 percent of the area of these cities was leveled. The area raids interrupted the normal processes of city life to an extent that interfered seriously with such production as the shrinking raw material base still permitted. Destruction of living quarters, disruption of food distribution, and curtailment of public services resulted in the migration of a large part of the urban population, thus increasing absenteeism and inefficiency to paralyzing proportions. So concentrated were the attacks, both in weight and time, that they overwhelmed Japan's resources for organizing either defense or recuperation. The economic disintegration caused by the blockade was finished by the bombers.

The influence of the bomber offensive was not solely dependent on the volume of arms it may have denied to Japanese military forces. Japan's production of munitions, at its peak, was only about 10 percent of United States output. With about one-third of its mobilized strength deployed in the Pacific, the United States had decisive superiority. Air, sea, and ground engagements preceding the bombardment of the home islands, had sealed Japan's doom. American armed forces could have gone on to Tokyo at great cost in American lives, even had there been no attack on Japan's industrial structure. Blockade and bombing together deprived Japanese forces of about 4 months' munitions production. That production could have made a substantial difference in Japan's ability to cause us losses had we invaded but could not have affected the outcome of the war.

It was the timing and the manner of surrender which was largely influenced by Allied air supremacy in Japanese skies. The bombing offensive was the major factor which secured agreement to unconditional surrender without an invasion of the home islands—an invasion that would have cost tens of thousands of American lives. The demonstrated strength of the United States in the B–29 attacks contrasted with Japan's lack of adequate defense made clear to the Japanese people and to the government the futility of further resistance. This was reinforced by the evident deterioration of the Japanese economy and the impact it was having on a large segment of the population. The atomic bomb and Russia's entry into the war speeded the process of surrender already realized as the only possible outcome.

The effectiveness of strategic air attack was limited by the concepts of its mission. Had the purpose of strategic air attack been primarily to force an independent decision rather than to support a ground force invasion in November 1945, there would have been no occasion to attack oil, tetraethyl lead, arsenals or, after March, aircraft. Effort could have been concentrated against food and fuel supply by attack on internal transportation and against urban areas, thus striking solely at the main elements upon which continued Japanese resistance was based. Moreover, a part of the bombing effort merely duplicated results already achieved by blockade. Attack on the rail transportation system would have secured full coordination with the blockade program. The railroads were overburdened, defenseless, and had only limited ability to replace rolling stock or major installations. This target system was about to be exploited by the AAF as the war ended; it could have been given an earlier priority with distinct advantage.

Chapter I

THE ROAD TO PEARL HARBOR

THE POLITICAL SETTING

Even a fleeting appraisal of the Japanese war potential raises immediately the question of the rationale behind Japan's decision to initiate hostilities with the United States. The dividing line between erroneous calculations and adventurous irrationality in the conduct of national affairs is always difficult to draw. Considering retrospectively the policies which ultimately led Japan to the catastrophe of 7 December, it would be tempting to dismiss them summarily as expansionist megalomania of the Japanese war lords and to abandon all search for a rational scheme which could have guided the Japanese military and economic planners.

Yet such an attitude would be wholly inappropriate. It would render an understanding of Japan's strategy impossible and would obscure the nature of the enemy whom we were fighting for almost 4 years. That grave mistakes were committed by the rulers of Japan during the last 15 years is beyond doubt. That the gravest of these mistakes was the war against the United States can also be regarded as demonstrated. Nevertheless it was not "insanity" which drove them into disaster, nor can the fault be attributed solely to specific individuals in responsibility—it was a considered national policy whose pitfalls, however, were insufficiently appreciated—whose chances of success were inadequately gauged.

THE ROOTS OF EXPANSIONISM

The origins of Japanese expansionism date as far back as the days of the Meiji restoration. It was in this turbulent period of industrial revolution that the political structure of the Japanese society was adjusted to the necessities of its economic growth. The terms of this adjustment were all-important. They did not involve a complete breaking of the feudal grip on the country, nor did they destroy in any essential sense the position of the landed gentry. Japan went the "Prussian way". Its newly emerging captains of industry compromised with the traditional feudal ruling classes. Having secured most of the institutional reforms needed for an unhampered development of a modern capitalist economy, they conceded to the feudal overlords—big and small—a practically unlimited control over the armed forces and a dominant position in the national administration.

The result of this arrangement was a unique system of "checks and balances" which transformed national policy into a process of permanent bargaining between the old and the new controlling interests. The imperial institution became the unifying factor in the struggle of opposing forces. While each decision was a complicated deal concluded by shrewd political "wire-pullers", it was presented to the nation as the sovereign will of the imperial throne, beyond debate and above criticism. The elevation of the Tenno to the status of divinity, the stress placed on his impartiality, his independence of all pressure and interest groups, created in him a national symbol which lent stability and authority to a government frequently torn by internal strife.

In the midst of clashing interests, of deeply rooted political and economic conflicts, there was, however, one objective which—for different reasons—commanded unqualified enthusiasm on the part of both the rising industrial class and the older military and bureaucratic ruling group receiving favorable acceptance on the part of the population as a whole. This common goal was Japanese aggrandizement through foreign expansion, leading to a dominant position in the Asiatic family of nations.

The pressure in this direction was enormous. The overpopulation of Japan had reached disturbing proportions. The paucity of domestic resources seemed to present rigid limits to the growth of output and income. Cultivation of industrial skills and fostering of industries which would import raw materials and export processed goods appeared to be the only outlet for economic energies and the only way to prevent a continuous deterioration of the already low standard of living. To the industrial interests of Japan, the control of raw materials sources and the acquisition of export markets appeared thus to be an essential condition for the country's economic prosperity.

The military rulers of Japan readily concurred in this concept of foreign expansion. It warranted the maintenance of a large military establishment; it provided the basis for the political power of the military camarilla; it moved the leadership of the army and navy into the center of the political scene.

The spectacular success in the Sino-Japanese war, which secured for Japan the profitable control of Formosa and Korea, and the even more impressive victory over Russia in 1905, seemed to prove the fundamental soundness of this national policy. Within a few decades Japan became a world power, looming large in the economic and political struggles of the Far East.

A certain set-back was suffered in connection with the First World War. Although the economic prosperity enjoyed during the war was substantial, and the increase of international prestige was encouraging, the direct advantages secured by Japan at Versailles were disappointing. Neither important territorial acquisitions nor significant economic concessions resulted ·from adherance to the side of the victors.

This outcome of the war left a deeply rooted grudge in the Japanese ruling group. Very similar to Italian sentiments in the early 20's, the reparation of the "wrongs" endured at Versailles remained an underlying motive of Japanese foreign policy in the following two decades. Not that it changed by any means the course of Japan's national policy. On the contrary it accentuated the century-old trend toward aggrandizement and economic expansion and lent this drive the additional stimulus of moral indignation.

This expansionist ideology was largely confined, however, to the upper "policy making" strata of Japanese society. It was not until the great depression that foreign expansionism assumed the proportions of a popular movement. In this sense, the early 30's may be regarded as one of the important turning points in Japan's history. The severe economic dislocation caused by the world crisis awakened the Japanese middle classes, particularly the army officers recruited in the main from the countryside, to the necessity of some radical action which would open a way out of their economic plight. Faced with the danger of rapid pauperization and unable to see any prospect of a positive solution of the structural problems of the Japanese economic and social order, the young and energetic elements in Japanese society turned to the traditional panacea for all domestic ills—to foreign adventure.

It is a matter of definition whether the movement which developed in these years and which culminated in the May 1932 assassination of Premier Inukai should be properly called fascism. There are striking similarities with fascism, particularly the Italian brand, but also significant differences. The ideas of Hitler and Mussolini certainly contributed much to its ideological arsenal. Its aims and methods in the field of foreign relations could readily have been laid down by Ribbentrop or Ciano. It was in their domestic position, however, that the Japanese nationalists differed vastly from their European forerunners. Although perhaps for the first time in 60 years large numbers of Japanese citizens transcended clique politics and tried to take active part in the formulation of national policy, although it may be approximately correct to speak of popular support of the aggressive elements in the officers corps, the militarists and nationalists who moved into the center of Japan's political events in 1931 had no organized mass support in the fascist sense of the word.

An overthrow of the government and establishment of a fascist dictatorship was thus impossible. The ascendance to power of the radical elements was, consequently, the result of a compromise with the traditional powers. While the army conducted an aggressive expansionist policy, big business, powerfully entrenched in national councils, and the old-line political leaders were assured of continuing control in domestic affairs.

The Emperor once more became the "common denominator." His immense popular standing sustained the new combination just as it sustained the previous ones. The radical elements were to a large extent "tamed" and integrated into the traditional stream of Japanese politics. What Hindenburg and Victor Emmanuel were unable to attain with respect to Hitler and Mussolini—to canalize them into the mold of "normal" bargaining—the Tenno achieved without too much difficulty. Unlike Hindenburg or Victor Emmanuel, he could not be pushed aside. In Japan, the approval by the Emperor meant mass approval, the support by the Imperial Household meant support by the broad strata of the population living in the ideology of Shintoism, governed by awe of the supreme ruler.

The resulting political and legal continuity of the Japanese Government was welcome to the ruling classes of the country. The new forces were again absorbed by the institutionalized spider web of the various pressure and interest groups, and were certain not to develop into a threat to the existing social and economic order. As a consequence, however, the drive for aggrandizement which was initiated by the newly arrived nationalists was to a large extent deprived of its original momentum and singleness of purpose. Political steps to be taken, military operations to be prepared, economic measures to be embarked upon—they all were subject to bargaining, to pushing and pulling in secret chambers, to continuous struggles among competing cliques. Japan reentered the scene of conquest as an *undecided* aggressor, with a domestic political setting which made continuous ambivalence the outstanding characteristic of its strategy and tactics.

ANNEXATION OF MANCHURIA

The expedition to Manchuria was the first enterprise of the new ruling coalition. Leaving entirely apart the ideology surrounding that move, forgetting about the professed goal to create a "national-socialist" state in Manchukuo which should inspire the old country as a shining example of justice and prosperity—the rational reasons for the Manchurian adventure were transparently clear. Strategically, the domination of Manchuria was to provide Japan with a firm base on the Asiatic continent. Whether for further operations against China or against Russia, it was to be the indispensable staging area for air power, troops, and supplies. The economic resources of the country promised to render it, fairly soon, the arsenal of Japanese expansionism. Sizable supplies of coal, steel, and nonferrous metals were expected to be the rich reward of investment. The development of Manchurian industries was to become an important outlet for the overflowing Japanese labor market. At the same time, the army hoped to acquire a stronghold which would further strengthen its domestic position.

The international situation was well fitted for the coup. China was deeply torn by civil war. Russia was in the midst of its first 5-year plan, with its military and economic strength at a low ebb. The Western Powers, preoccupied with domestic difficulties and unable to reach common decisions on foreign policy, were most unlikely to oppose forcefully Japan's unilateral move.

Militarily and politically, the venture was an easy victory. The occupation of Manchuria proceeded swiftly and without much fighting. A puppet government was set up and met with little opposition. The international complications, conspicuous as they were, hardly amounted to much. The Kwantung army, the main echelon of the militarist group, took over the country and rapidly established its exclusive domination.

Economically, however, the Manchurian experiment soon became a disappointment. The semifascist regime introduced by the Kwantung army was not such as to encourage conservative-venture capital. A closer examination of the Manchurian investment opportunities disclosed at an early date that returns could only be expected after a long stretch of time. A considerable amount of railroad construction, road building, and other essential improvements had to precede the economic exploitation of the province. Japanese capitalists, accustomed to relatively quick returns of international trade, were little inclined to sink substantial funds into long-range Manchurian projects.

What is most important, however, is that it soon became evident that Japan had little surplus capital available for overseas investment. The rather common belief among Japanese economists and political planners that Japan had reached the stage of capital-exporting imperialism and was in need of outlets for foreign investment proved to be a fallacy. What Japanese business wanted was markets for export articles and supplies of cheap raw materials rather than opportunities for long-range foreign developments. As a matter of fact, they were looked upon unfavorably as a source of potential competition.

Nor was the government itself in a position to provide the necessary investment. Participating only half heartedly in the aggressive undertakings of its imperialist wing, influenced strongly by its big-business and traditional bureaucratic components, the Tokyo cabinet did not pursue a determined policy of economic expansion. The first 5 years of Manchurian occupation thus hardly resulted in any significant economic advantages to Japan. Whatever was done was largely organized by the Kwantung army which, living off the land, began developing its own supplies of military equipment. Japanese big business moved very reluctantly, if at all, into Manchurian industrial enterprises. Some entrepreneurs, like Aikawa and his Nissan group, assumed the pioneer function. They were frowned upon by the banks and the business community. Treated as newcomers and intruders, they found it increasingly difficult to finance their commitments and to secure the necessary management, fixed capital, and materials.

Nonetheless, the Manchurian expedition lived up to the political expectations of the radical wing. The Kwantung army—and, correspondingly, the army as a whole—became an increasingly important factor in the determination of Japan's national policy. The control of Manchuria placed at the disposal of the Army a mighty political machine and a vast system of patronage. In addition to the direct beneficiaries of army rule over Manchuria, thousands of small businessmen, traders, and dealers of all kinds, established themselves under the wings of the military and furnished powerful support to its claim to power. Many a politician, originally cautious and doubtful as to the wisdom of the expansionist drive, became swayed by the political advantages of close cooperation with the army. The "political climate" in Tokyo became markedly influenced by the radicals and their numerous fellow travelers. The slogan "Greater East Asia Co-Prosperity Sphere" became the official motto of Japan's national policy. Outstanding representatives of the "old line" political leadership, like Prince Konoye, associated themselves with leagues and committees whose aim was to prepare the ground for Japanese penetration of further territories selected for membership in the "Co-Prosperity Sphere." It is significant, also, that the improvement of business conditions in Japan, which was worldwide in years 1933–1937, was interpreted widely as a direct result of the expansionist initiative.

THE NEXT STOP: NORTHERN CHINA

By 1936 the stage was set for the next move. The international situation was increasingly promising from the Japanese point of view. The Chinese civil war, dragging on for more than 10 years, rendered China militarily impotent. The instability of the Kuomintang government made it apparent that it would be unable to withstand a combination of domestic opposition and foreign pressure. The reaction of the Great Powers toward Japan's Manchurian undertaking and toward similar moves by Germany and Italy warranted the assumption that no serious anti-Japanese action would be taken should Japan advance further in its expansionist drive.

Thus, as was confirmed by many Japanese officials interrogated by the Survey, the 1937 thrust into northern China was not expected to develop into a major war. Those responsible for national policy at the time were fully confident that the Chinese government would yield quickly to Japan's demands and adjust itself readily to the position of a Japanese puppet. A full military conquest of China was considered to be neither necessary nor desirable. Troops were sent to China not to force a military decision but to serve as symbols of Japanese power. Negotiations—or rather intimidations—were to accomplish the rest.

While the motivations for the drive into China were similar to the ones which led Japan into Manchuria, the immediate interest of the army was even more pronounced. A large contingent of the army was anxious to secure foreign "grazing grounds" which would provide a lavish "master race" existence. Once more large numbers of petty merchants, importers, and exporters swarmed into the newly acquired territories, to form the political and economic machine of the high command. The control of northern China became, thus, the basis of continuous well-being of a large strata of politically influential and vociferous Japanese.

The Chinese enterprise reached, however, an impasse at a very early stage. To lead the Chinese campaign to a victorious conclusion was militarily—and what is more important—politically impossible. For a military domination of 400 million Chinese—if such could at all be envisaged—Japan had neither the manpower nor the material resources. Even if feasible, a military subjugation of China would defeat its purpose. Japan could not conceivably substitute its own administration for the Chiang Kai-shek regime, which would have necessarily collapsed in the case of China's outright defeat. What Japan wanted was monopolization of Chinese markets—a hostile, probably communist-dominated, and guerrilla-ridden China would hardly be an attractive outlet for Japanese economic energies. The only arrangement which would have assured success of the Japanese scheme would have been a Chinese government sufficiently popular with the masses and at the same time willing to cooperate with the invader.

The striving for such a solution determined entirely Japan's strategy in the China war. It never contemplated an all-out military effort to crush Chinese resistance. It was much rather a series of discontinuous blows intended to intimidate the Chungking government, each followed by a period of attempted or actual negotiations. Those negotiations proved unsuccessful throughout. For domestic and partly international reasons Chiang's government refused to yield. The creation of a puppet regime in Nanking aggravated the situation. Powerless as it was, it forced Chiang even more strongly into an intransigent position. The China affair dragged on without any prospect of a conclusion.

At the same time, a withdrawal from China was politically impossible. The political standing of the army was predicated upon the maintenance of the Chinese stronghold. The equilibrium of political power in Japan was predicated upon the standing of the army.

ENTRY INTO THE WORLD CONFLICT

It was not until the outbreak of the European war in September 1939 that there appeared some hope of a settlement of the Chinese conflict. Not only did the European conflagration divert the Western Powers' attention from Far Eastern events, but the possibility of Chiang's swinging over to the victorious Axis combination was regarded as considerable.

Under the circumstances, it was self-evident to all groups of the ruling coalition that the European conflict had to be used to further Japan's drive for aggrandizement. Only the method and the timing of the appropriate move were at issue. The fall of France rendered French Indochina the most convenient target. After having blackmailed the Vichy government into concessions with respect to northern Indochina in September 1940, the Japanese proceeded to establish military bases in southern Indochina by the "agreement" concluded with Petain in July 1941.

Interrogation of Japanese officials and perusal of documentary evidence show that this undertaking was again not expected to result in major hostilities. The driving spirts behind it were the radicals in the Japanese Navy, who regarded the possession of ample sources of oil as essential to the maintenance of Japan's power position in the Pacific. The official explanation of the move as aiming solely toward an improvement of Japan's strategic position with respect to China was clearly ingenuous. Singapore, Hong Kong, and eventually the Dutch East Indies, were the ultimate goals. Indochina was to provide the necessary bases.

The forceful reaction in Washington came as a surprise. Germany's attack and spectacular successes in Russia, the United States policy of aiding both Britain and Russia in their struggle against Germany and the extremely precarious position of the United Kingdom made it appear very unlikely that Japan's move would be seriously opposed. The freezing of Japanese assets ordered by President Roosevelt and the ensuing stoppage of American oil shipments to Japan exceeded by far the extent of retaliatory measure anticipated in Tokyo. The negotiations with the United States which had been going on for a considerable time, attained thus suddenly supreme urgency. Lacking further oil imports, the Japanese Navy began living on borrowed time. In the near future (1–1½ years) its oil stocks would be exhausted. The most important card in the hands of Japan, the possibility of naval domination of the Pacific, would be obliterated.

Thus, the Chinese impasse led to an impasse of Japanese-American relations. An understanding with the United States implied withdrawal from Indochina. This became incompatible with the prestige of the radical elements in the navy who, jockeying for domestic power with the army, could not afford to lose face in their first major undertaking. The evacuation of northern China—the other demand of the United States—conflicted with the interests of the even more powerful army. The coalition of militarist and conservative elements forming the basis of the Japanese government was unable to take a step amounting practically to a political catastrophe to its major and strongest component.

The ensuing months were filled with bargaining and anxiety on all fronts. There is good reason to believe that the conservative wing of the ruling coalition was advocating a moderate course toward the United States. Though it had indorsed each move of its coalition partners, it hoped, at each stage, that the current step would not be the breaking point leading to war. It arranged and concluded the tripartite pact with Germany and Italy and hoped that the Western Powers would be sufficiently impressed with the might and solidarity of the Axis to understand the futility of further resistance. It approved of the Indochina adventure, assuming that Japan would get away with this act of aggression as easily as with the previous ones.

When the freezing of Japanese assets and the embargo faced Japan and made it necessary for Japan "to fish or to cut bait," the political conservatives lost control of the situation. They were unable to suggest a formula which would satisfy Washington and at the same time be acceptable to their intransigent partners in the government. Though not opposed to war on principle, they believed that the time was not yet ripe. They wanted to repeat the 1914–1916 performance and enter the war on the winning side. That Germany and Italy were on the winning side did not yet appear to them as established.

In this appraisal of the military situation the conservatives differed from the radicals. The spectacular successes of Germany in Poland, the low countries, France, and particularly in Russia, created among Japan's Nazi sympathizers the myth of Germany's invincibility. The defeat of Russia seemed only a matter of months in the fall of 1941 and German victory over Russia was believed tantamount to Axis victory in the war. That Great Britain and the United States would then, at last, recognize Germany's dominant position in Europe was regarded as self-evident. If Britain still refused to listen to reason, Germany could then easily invade the isles and dictate its terms in London.

Japan's policy had to be adjusted to such an exigency. While the ideological affinity of the Japanese "expansionists" to Hitler and his movement was very important in cementing German-Japanese collaboration, it also accounted for a profound distrust of the German fellow-imperialists. Tokyo was acutely aware of the possibility that Hitler might attempt to obtain a settlement with Great Britain and the U. S. at Japan's expense. Germany's frequent offers to respect and to protect the integrity of the British and the Dutch empires were clearly contrary to Japan's expansionist ambitions. To experience another Versailles and to leave the coming peace conference empty-handed was a distasteful prospect to Japanese nationalists. This could be avoided only if, instead of depending on Hitler's good graces, Japan would seize whatever territories it wished to annex as its share of the future war booty.

This line of reasoning was predicated upon expectation of an early German victory. Germany's foreign minister von Ribbentrop and the Japanese ambassador to Berlin, Oshima, did everything in their power to bolster such hopes with optimistic reports on the German-Russian war. While not necessarily bent on war, the radical wing of the Japanese government did not feel that Japan needed to make any concessions under international conditions as favorable as those. They certainly refused to consent to any agreement which, by yielding on the Indochina or northern China issues would jeopardize their domestic political standing. The conservative group played its usual game. It hoped to the very last that it would be able to secure everything which the radicals demanded by skillful diplomacy. It negotiated with the State Department, it suggested conferences between the President and Prince Konoye, it dispatched special envoys to Washington—it was unable, however, to devise a single proposal which would meet to any extent the American viewpoint and at the same time have a chance with the radical, fascist wing of the coalition.

The radicals took over when the decision to go to war was finally reached. The Imperial Household accepted this decision as it had accepted, previously, all decisions presented to it as the outcome of bargaining between the various political factions. True to century-old tradition, the formula adopted was announced as the best considered resolve of the Emperor himself. Whatever the preceding struggles may have been, the 7th of December was the day of unity between the groups and cliques forming the Japanese ruling coalition.

JAPAN'S WAR PLAN

Japan's decision to go to war with the United States and the war plan upon which it counted to achieve its objectives can be understood only in the light of the background sketched above. The tradition of success with limited commitments, the imminence of Germany's victory on the European Continent—these counted for more in the minds of Japan's war planners than any careful balancing of Nipponese and American war potentials.

Above all, they biased the thinking of the high command toward the notion that the war would not be a lengthy enterprise. Total war, annihilation of the enemy, and occupation of the United States never entered the planning of the Japanese military. One or two crucial battles were expected to determine the outcome of the conflict. The Pacific war was to follow the pattern set by the Russian-Japanese hostilities in 1905. A terrific blow at Pearl Harbor would inflict a disastrous Cannae on the American Pacific fleet. Combined with Russia's defeat and England's inevitable doom, this would assure American willingness to enter peace negotiations. A settlement satisfying most Japanese demands would be in sight within 6 months.

A less exuberant appraisal of the war prospects anticipated a somewhat lengthier struggle but was equally confident as to its ultimate success. By the surprise attack on 7 December, Japan would deprive the United States of a major part of its naval strength. The supremacy in the Pacific gained thereby would be used to occupy the strategically important Pacific islands, and to establish a "Pacific wall," impregnable to all American attacks. This chain, properly fortified, would be indefinitely defended. Japan's war potential was regarded as sufficient to sustain such a defensive operation. The impossibility of breaking through the system of Japanese island defenses would soon become obvious to the United States. After some unsuccessful attempts to force a military decision, the United States would be willing to consider a compromise agreement. In return for an unconditional recognition of the "Greater East Asia Co-Prosperity Sphere" and the American acquiescence to some territorial annexations, Japan would be prepared to restore some of its initial conquests.

The early successes in the South Pacific were expected to strengthen Japan immensely for the possible American siege of the "defensive perimeter." Raw materials in short supply, particularly oil and bauxite, would be obtainable in large quantities from the southern resources area. The Japanese navy would not have to fear exhaustion of its meager oil reserves. A genuine war of attrition, in which the United States would turn the tables and stage an all-out offensive against Japan proper, was considered unlikely. The international situation, the "degeneracy" of American democracy, and the demoralization of the United States, which would follow disastrous defeats and vain attempts at a come-back, were expected to prevent Washington from continuing, very long, a hopeless struggle.

Comparisons of American and Japanese economic potentials were drawn up but could be readily dismissed. What mattered was not superiority in the long run, but supremacy in the immediate future. Even if the American capacity to produce the sinews of war was many times larger than that of Japan, it would be too long before that capacity could play a role in the impending conflict. By the time the United States would be able to develop and deploy its war potential, the international factors would have decided the war in Japan's favor.

For the bold stroke scheduled for 7 December, Japan had the military wherewithall. The immediately deployable striking force on land, at sea, and in the air was formidable, assuring the success of the initial operation. This operation was expected to determine the outcome of the war. This was the only kind of war Japan was able to fight. The national economy was just strong enough for a commitment of this magnitude. It certainly could not support anything larger.

THE ECONOMIC POTENTIAL

Although, in the first 5 years, the possession of Manchuria contributed but little to Japan's economic and military potential, the indirect repercussions of the expansionist initiative were very considerable. Japan was suddenly thrown into a state of national emergency, and the economic life of the country soon felt the impact of the mobilization effort.

The government embarked upon a large armament program. An increasing part of the budget was earmarked for military purposes, and a fiscal deficit lifted the economic system rapidly to high levels of output and income. Similar to what took place almost simultaneously in Hitler's Germany, the prosperity thus attained determined to a large extent the course of the country's national policy. It cemented firmly the union between the conservative, big business wing of Japan's political life and the aggressive, radical elements of the army and navy. It imbued the ruling coalition with a strong awareness of Japan's growing military might which was to provide the basis for future aggrandizement.

The increase of military capabilities in the 30's was, no doubt, overrated by the enthusiastic imperialists. This optimism is, however, readily comprehensible in the light of the sensational growth experienced in this period by the Japanese economic potential.

The rise in national production at the rate of about 5 percent a year was in itself a very encouraging phenomenon. Its military significance becomes obvious if the source of the increases is considered. Due almost entirely to a rapid broadening of the industrial base of the Japanese economy, the upward trend of output was most pronounced in the militarily crucial heavy industries.

TABLE 1.—*Relative growth of industrial and agricultural output 1930–42*

[Million yen]

Year	Industrial output (A)	Agricultural output (B)	A/B [1]
1930	5,960	2,400	2.5
1937	16,360	4,040	4
1942	32,130	5,700	5.6

[1] Since prices of industrial products were rising more than those of agricultural commodities, these ratios exaggerate somewhat the relative growth of industrial output.

The shift toward heavy industries is strikingly shown by the data in table 2.

TABLE 2.—*Composition of industrial output, 1930–42*

	1930	1937	1942
	Percent	*Percent*	*Percent*
Heavy industries	38.2	57.8	72.7
Light industries	61.8	42.2	27.3
	100.0	100.0	100.0

The industrial effort which resulted in this spectacular development and in the vast increase of Japan's war potential involved a number of almost equally important economic programs: (1) The volume of plant and equipment had to be markedly increased in order to provide for an enlarged flow of armaments; (2) the raw material basis of the industrial economy had to be deepened by both development of current supplies and accumulation of emergency stocks; (3) a sizeable output of finished munitions had to be maintained in order to support current military commitments (Manchuria, China); (4) the shipping potential had to be expanded to assure a sufficient flow of raw materials; and (5) the relative allocation of manpower had to be shifted from agricultural pursuits to industrial occupations.

Whether the economic planners of Japan were able to attain the optimum distribution of resources between these partly competing purposes, is a hardly answerable question. It is beyond doubt, however, that remarkable accomplishments marked the "expansionist" decade.

(1) No data are available to measure the size of investment in fixed plants and equipment. The information contained in the tables presented above and in the reports on individual industries prepared by various economic divisions of the Survey indicate, however, that the construction of industrial facilities in the years 1930–42 assumed—for Japanese conditions—gigantic proportions. Almost the entire aircraft industry, producing more than 7,000 planes annually by 1941; a tank and an automotive industry were constructed during this period.

(2) This industrial expansion was based and dependent on the availability of raw materials. Considerable quantities of structural steel, coal, and lumber were needed for the construction of plants and equipment. Still larger quantities of these and other materials were required to assure continuous production. Immense efforts were devoted to the increase of raw material output in the home islands. In some respects, significant successes were achieved. Coal production, for instance, rose, within Japan proper, from 28 million tons in 1931 to 55.6 million tons in 1941. Domestic mining of iron ore also made significant progress. Nevertheless, no country could have been further from self-sufficiency with respect to raw materials than was Japan. Supplies from the continent of Asia became the key to the armament program. The development of Manchuria and Northern China became almost the central issue of Japan's economic policy.

By 1936 the preparatory moves toward a systematic exploitation of Manchuria's natural resources reached a degree of completion. The 5-year plan of Manchurian economic development, based to a large extent on preliminary work accomplished in the province in the years 1932–36, envisaged sizeable shipments of Manchurian raw materials. Together with Northern China, Manchuria became an exclusive source of some critical materials and an important contributor to the insufficient home output of others. In addition, food deliveries (in particular soybeans) from the continental possessions of Japan became important factors in maintaining Japan's food balance. By the end of the decade Japan's salt requirements were met largely from Northern China and Manchuria, while an increasing variety of nonferrous metals and ferro-alloys were supplied by Manchuria and Korea.

The Japanese iron and steel industry depended on Northern China for its major supply of good coking coal. From 1938 to 1941, coal output rose from 10 million to 24 million tons in North China-Mongolia, and from 16 to 24 million tons in Manchuria. Pig iron production in Manchuria increased from 500,000 tons in 1934 to 1,417,000 tons in 1941 and ingot steel from 137,000 tons in 1935 to 573,000 tons in 1941. Exports of Manchurian pig iron to Japan rose from 383,000 ton in 1935 to 557,000 tons in 1941. In 1937, China supplied 14 percent of Japan's iron ore imports; in 1941 it supplied 50 percent.

Although the progress made in Manchuria and China helped significantly to alleviate Japan's raw materials shortage, insufficiency of raw materials continued to be the most important limiting factor on Japanese industrial output. With respect to some materials, the Continental possessions of Japan failed to enhance Japan's position. Neither oil nor bauxite sources exist in appreciable quantities within the "inner zone". The output of aluminum ingots had risen from 19 tons in 1933 to 71,740 tons in 1941, of which 90 percent was produced from bauxite. Plans to develop a synthetic oil industry or to exploit the existing low grade substitute aluminous materials failed to attain significant results.

Pending seizure and economic exploitation of the oil and bauxite resources of the Southern Pacific, stockpiling these vital materials was unavoidable. The situation was similar in the supply of certain ferro alloys, such as nickel, and of such nonferrous metals as lead and zinc. A considerable accumulation of bauxite and oil was accomplished. By the end of 1941 bauxite stocks totaled about 250,000 tons, sufficient for somewhat less than 9 months supply at the current rate of utilization or 6 months at the actual 1942 rate.

At the same time, 9,200,000 kilolitres of oil were stored in Japan, 2,300,000 kilolitres more than the combined imports and production during the war.

(3) The expansion of industrial facilities and of the raw material supplies for Japan's home industry were used almost exclusively for a substantial increase of military output. By December 1941, Japan was producing over 550 planes monthly and had accumulated an air force aggregating some 7,500 units of all types. The naval building program reached unprecedented proportions. In 1941–42, 331 naval vessels, aggregating just short of 450,000 tons, were added to the fleet. Ammunition on hand in January 1942 totaled nearly 5 years production at the 1942 rate, while land weapons exceeded 6 years production. At that time, there were 81,000 motor vehicles on hand, or well over 5 years production at the 1942 level, while the tank park of 1,180 vehicles slightly exceeded 1942 output.

The war industries centered around aircraft production and shipbuilding. The development of the automotive industry was very slow. Heavy tanks were not produced at all. Japan's armament program was directed toward a fight among the islands of the Pacific and not toward mainland warfare. Such ground operations as were conducted on the Asiatic mainland were to a large extent supported by the Manchurian industries themselves.

(4) The necessity of enlarging Japan's merchant fleet to handle the vastly increased turn-over of supplies between Japan and the outside world was a major aspect of the prewar armament effort. During the decade as a whole, the shipping potential had expanded by one-third, with 2,136,245 gross tons constructed. Peak construction occurred in the years 1937–39, when 1,027,514 tons were built, while in 1940 and 1941, 491,886 tons were added to the merchant fleet.

In spite of this serious attempt to provide a merchant fleet which would be able to cope with Japan's foreign trade, the country remained dependent on foreign shipping for its normal import and export activities. Of 18,490 ships, aggregating 62,230,000 gross tons which entered Japanese harbors in 1938, only 11,456 ships (36,659,000 gross tons) were flying the Japanese flag. The remainder were foreign bottoms chartered by Japanese shippers or negotiated on foreign account.

(5) The expansion of manufacturing activities

during the thirties involved a considerable increase in the industrial labor force. The total number of males in manufacturing rose from 4.4 million in 1930 to 6.1 million of 1940, while during the same period, the number of women increased from 1.4 to 2 million. This additional labor force was almost entirely provided for by the growth in population. The number gainfully employed in agriculture—14.1 million people—declined by on'y 0.5 million during the decade. In spite of the industrialization process, Japan still remained essentially an agrarian country in which roughly half of the population was engaged in feeding the nation. It was necessary to import from 10 to 20 percent of the food supply. At the same time there was a considerable manpower "cushion", consisting of "hidden unemployed", which prevented manpower from becoming a limiting factor in spite of the considerable requirements of the armed forces.

Considering the economic performance of the decade, one is impressed with the intensity of the effort and the magnitude of the results. Without them, the Japanese war planners would not have even thought of a military operation like the one undertaken during the months following Pearl Harbor.

Nonetheless, Japan remained with serious economic weaknesses. Depending for an essential margin of food, for most important basic materials, for the lifeblood of a modern industrial nation—oil—on overseas imports, Japan was desperately vulnerable to blockade operations. Having a comparatively small, newly developed war industry, it had to work without much of a cushion of excess capacity. Having had little experience with munitions production or other lines of mass output, the country was not able to build up a large force of industrially and mechanically trained personnel. This meant later shortage of skills, shortage of ingenuity and little ability to improvise when the economy was under the stresses and strains of large-scale warfare.

Being essentially a small and poor country with an industrial structure dependent upon imported raw materials, Japan was wide open to every type of modern attack. Living from hand to mouth, the Japanese economy had no reserves with which it could maneuver in a case of an emergency. Crowded in primitively constructed wooden cities, the Japanese population had no dwelling possibilities in case of the destruction of their homes.

The economic potential could support a short war of limited liability. The accumulated stocks of munitions, oil, and ships could be thrown into action and produce a devastating effect on an unmobilized enemy. It could be done only once. When this unique blow failed to result in peace, Japan was doomed. Its economy could not support a protracted campaign against an enemy even half as strong as the United States.

Chapter II

JAPAN'S ECONOMY UNDER THE STRESS OF WAR

THE PATTERN OF ECONOMIC MO- BILIZATION

The economic expansion which had been achieved in the thirties, and the degree to which Japan's economy was already functioning to meet the requirements of war, determined Japan's economic mobilization in the early phase of the war.

A thorough planning for total economic mobilization appeared unnecessary. Contemplating a short war and counting heavily on the initial advantages enjoyed by Japan, the Japanese planners failed to consider Japan's economic potential in relation to a protracted war of attrition. They examined only the economic requirements of their immediate war plan. They did not plan to lift the total level of output. They planned only to make good certain obvious deficiencies of their economy and to supply little more than the replacement needs of the military forces.

The contrast with the kind of economic mobilization sought in the United States is striking. The plans worked out in the second half of 1941 and put into effect by President Roosevelt's first war budget were based upon achieving maximum total output in order to allow the largest possible flow of war material. Elimination of unemployment, drawing new workers into the labor force, increasing capacity of basic industries, multiple-shift operation of industrial facilities, and shifting resources to more productive uses were all counted upon in setting the sights for total production and munitions output.

Japan, on the contrary, concentrated on limited objectives. It was essential that sources of basic raw materials—particularly oil and bauxite—be secured in the southern resources area. In addition, it was necessary to increase the output of munitions in conformity with the military operations being contemplated.

As a consequence of this limited program, the over-all production of Japan remained relatively stable in the fiscal years 1941 and 1942. From a level of 39.8 billion yen in fiscal 1940 the real gross national output, shown in table 3, rose to only 41 billion yen for fiscal 1942. This stability is the more surprising since that period includes 16 months of war with the United States. That it was due to inadequate planning and not to the inherent limitations of the Japanese economy is clear from the expansion that was secured both before 1940 and after 1942.

TABLE 3.—*Gross national product, fiscal years 1940–44*

[Billions of 1940 yen]

	1940	1941	1942	1943	1944
Gross national product	39. 8	40. 3	40. 6	45. 1	49. 3
Government	8. 0	10. 1	13. 2	18. 0	24. 1
Central government	6. 0	8. 0	11. 6	16. 2	22. 2
Nonwar	1. 3	1. 4	1. 7	1. 7	2. 0
War	4. 7	6. 6	9. 9	14. 5	20. 2
Pay, travel, and subsistence	1. 2	1. 5	1. 8	2. 3	3. 4
Munitions	2. 7	3. 5	4. 9	8. 6	12. 2
Other	.8	1. 6	3. 1	3. 5	4. 6
Local government	2. 0	2. 1	1. 6	1. 8	1. 9
Private gross capital formation	5. 1	4. 2	3. 6	4. 7	6. 4
Net exports	.2	−. 6	(1)	−. 6	1. 0
Residential construction	.4	.5	.2	.2	.1
Plant and equipment	4. 5	4. 3	3. 4	5. 1	5. 3
Munitions industries	----	2. 8	2. 5	4. 5	4. 9
Nonmunitions industries	----	1. 5	.9	.6	.4
Consumer expenditures	26. 7	26. 0	23. 8	22. 4	18. 8
Food and tobacco	15. 5	14. 8	18. 9	13. 3	11. 7
Clothing and furnishings	3. 5	3. 5	2. 9	2. 7	1. 4
Other	7. 7	7. 7	7. 0	6. 4	5. 7
War expenditures abroad	1. 0	2. 2	2. 5	3. 4	7. 1

1 Less than 50 million yen.

Source: Appendix B.

While thus, total production increased imperceptibly, a strong effort was made to expand war output. This manifested itself in a sharply rising trend of government war expenditures during the period. From a level of 4.7 billion yen in fiscal

1940, this segment of output increased to 9.9 billion in 1942, after adjustment for rising prices. While the percentage change was large, the total of war supplies secured, even in 1942, was hardly consistent with the size of Japan's military commitments. Indicative of the assurance of the ruling group during the early phase of the war, and its appraisal of the probable length of the war is the fact that plant and equipment expenditures in the munitions industries were actually allowed to decline between 1941 and 1942.

As total output was not rising, the increased flow of war output in these 2 years was secured by a gradual restriction of the civilian sectors of the economy. This occurred not so much as a result of a well-rounded policy of eliminating nonessentials but rather of the increasing encroachment of government war purchasing upon civilian sources of supply. While the conversion of civilian plants to munitions production was not extensive during this period, the greater share of food and clothing going to the military meant that less was available for civilians. Other consumers' goods declined to a lesser extent, though by 1942 the shortages of basic materials were felt. Consumers' services generally tended upward—a reflection of the expansibility of this type of output as well as the lack of real tightness in the labor market.

The most noticeable curtailment came in the field of nonwar capital outlays. Real expenditures of local government units declined as the channeling of materials prevented new construction and even normal replacement and maintenance work. The same factor reduced the volume of residential construction and plant and equipment outlays in civilian goods industries. In the latter field the restriction of processing materials tended also to make plant expansion unnecessary.

The entire pace of Japan's economic mobilization during this period of confidence can be seen in the relation of war expenditures to total gross product. The percentage of total production accounted for by government war expenditures and capital outlays in the munitions industries rose from 17 in 1940 to slightly over 30 in 1942.

The United States raised its war outlays from 2.6 percent of total production to 33.5 percent over the same period—at a time when total output was substantially increased.

The spectacular and easy military successes of the first half-year of the war seemed for a time to

TABLE 4.—*Percentage of war expenditures to gross product, Japan and the United States*

	Japan [1]	United States
1940	17. 0	2. 6
1941	23. 1	11. 2
1942	30. 5	33. 5
1943	42. 1	45. 0
1944	50. 9	46. 0

[1] Includes private capital outlays in munitions industries.

justify the prevailing notion of Japan's wartime economic requirements. Loss of the battle of Midway was attributed to lack of radar, not to any extraordinary recuperative powers of the United States Navy. The shock of the Guadalcanal campaign, however, forced a fundamental reappraisal of Japanese economic and military plans. While this defeat was laid to over extension of Japan's outer perimeter and was not taken as a foreshadowing of eventual disaster, it did demonstrate conclusively that the United States was preparing to take the initiative much more quickly than Tokyo had assumed. In addition, the Allied invasion of North Africa and the German defeat at Stalingrad blasted all hope of an early Axis victory in Europe. Thus, it became evident that the entire Japanese conception of the war was no longer tenable. There would not be a negotiated peace without large-scale fighting. The test of strength in the Pacific had already begun.

Allowing for inevitable administrative reorganization and the time lag between planning and performance, recognition of the true military situation was quickly translated into an all out effort in the economic sphere. Economic objectives were recast during the winter of 1942–43, and during the spring and summer of 1943 definite progress was made in giving effect to the new program. A very substantial increase in new production facilities was projected and extensive conversion of civilian goods plants was undertaken. Economic controls over materials and manpower were tightened. The sights of virtually the whole munitions program were raised to the limits of the Japanese economic potential, with particular emphasis on aircraft and ships. The civilian economy was pared to the minimum of subsistence, with all luxuries eliminated and neither replacements nor maintenance of civilian facilities allowed for. Total war was made the order of the day.

TABLE 5.—*Comparison of the dynamics of "real" gross national product, Japan and the United States, selected years 1930–44*

[1940=100]

	Japan	United States
1930	57	[1] 89
1936	84	86
1940	100	100
1941	101	118
1942	102	136
1943	113	158
1944	124	165

[1] 1929.

Given the inherent limitations of the Japanese economy with respect to basic resources and technological skills, given the delay of over a year before the need for a supreme effort was recognized, and given the fact that mounting ship losses interfered with the production drive, the performance of the economy in 1943 and 1944 was very creditable. A large expansion of total production was achieved and the percentage of output devoted to war purposes was sharply increased.

After the relative stability of the previous 2 years, the real gross product rose from a level of 41 billion yen in 1942 to almost 50 billion in 1944. This increase was concentrated in the war production segment. Government war outlays, after allowance for price changes, more than doubled over the period, rising from 9.9 billion yen in 1942 to 20.2 billion in 1944.

The increase in the output of munitions was made possible, in part, by the large expansion of plant facilities. Capital outlays in the munitions industries were increased from 2.5 billion yen in 1942 to 4.5 billion in 1943 and even exceeded that level in the following year. Approximately 70 percent of this industrial expansion program was in facilities to produce finished war goods, planes, ships, and ordnance. Plant investment had to yield quick returns in terms of military output as it was no longer feasible to spare men or materials to expand the basic industrial capacity of the nation. It is ironic that this effort was partly abortive since the growing shortage of materials made some of the facilities excess capacity by the second half of fiscal 1944. This was particularly the case with shipbuilding facilities, which in the expanded program of 1943–44 had been allotted the largest increase in new construction.

The extent of Japanese economic mobilization during this period can be seen by the growing absorption of resources into production for war. Government war outlays and capital expenditures in the munitions industries rose from 31 percent of gross output in 1942 to about 51 percent in 1944. At the peak of its war effort, the percentage for these war expenditures in the United States was 46. In view of Japan's much lower productivity, involving a much lower standard of living, the difference between the two figures is a wholly inadequate measure of the greater intensity of Japan's war effort.

In the years 1943 and 1944 all nonwar activities were sacrificed to the greatest possible extent. This is not fully revealed by the statistics in table 3 because of difficulties of classification. What are listed as nonwar government expenditures rose, for example, only because they include certain home defense activities. Capital outlays in nonmunitions industries were cut to an average of a half billion yen in the 2 years. The most substantial restriction of civilian output shows up, however, in consumers expenditures. From just under 24 billion yen in 1942, this component dropped to less than 19 billion in 1944, representing a decline from the 1940 level of 30 percent. The deterioration of the standard of living was so great that by the end of the period shipping had to be diverted from vital war purposes to the importation of food.

In point of time, the peak of the Japanese war economy came about the middle of the fiscal year 1944. By then the Allied attack on Japanese shipping had so reduced the importation of raw materials that not only was a further rise of total output impossible but a downward trend was initiated. Thus, the decline of Japan's war making powers started before her home island industries were subjected to the main weight of the bombing attack during the months of March to August 1945.

Complete data for this period were not obtainable but available evidence shows that there was widespread disruption of the economic mechanism. It may be estimated roughly that the level of the gross product for the whole of this period—the first half of the fiscal year 1945—was 20 to 25 percent below that of fiscal 1944. This drop could not have been regarded as a temporary decline. It represented, obviously, a breaking point. Complete disintegration of the entire economy could already be foreseen.

With this general pattern in mind, the wartime developments in the key sectors of the economy can now be traced in detail.

THE FIRST YEAR

The occupation of the southern areas accomplished in the first year of the war corrected certain of Japan's basic raw material deficiencies, but added little new strength to Japan's over-all economic potential. The major accomplishment was the seizure of certain indispensable raw material resources of which the inner zone was basically deficient. Oil and bauxite were the crucial items. Of the two, contrary to popular opinion, the Japanese position in bauxite was the more critical. Processing capacity, however, in these territories was negligible, contrasting markedly with the gains made by Germany in taking over countries such as France and Czechoslovakia.

At the end of 1941 Japan's stock pile of some 43 million barrels of crude petroleum and refined products was adequate for nearly 2 years at the estimated consumption rate. Refining capacity totaled 35,000,000 barrels annually in the inner zone, but production of crude and synthetic oil amounted to little more than 5 million barrels. The first imports of crude oil from the south began in the spring of 1942, and had amounted to 6,213,-000 barrels by the end of the calendar year. An additional 9,395,000 barrels of southern crude oil and refined products were consumed in the south during calendar 1942.[1] Under these conditions total stocks declined no faster than anticipated, and the outlook for 1943 was favorable.

In the case of bauxite, the stock pile of about 250,000 tons held on 7 December 1941 was sufficient for 9 months' aluminum production at the current rate of utilization.[2] At the higher 1942 rate, corresponding to rising aircraft production, this supply actually covered but 6 months' requirements. During the fiscal year 1941, marked by the "freezing" regulations imposed in July, imports of bauxite had totaled but 146,711 tons, the lowest since 1937. Imports were cut off until the spring of 1942, and by the end of June 1942 stocks were reduced to 172,620 tons. During fiscal 1942, however, bauxite imports rose to 450,134 tons, the highest figure recorded up to that time. By the end of December 1942, despite the increasing utilization rate, bauxite stocks had climbed back to 209,427 tons. At this time imports of bauxite, like those of oil, were steadily increasing.

By the summer of 1942, if not earlier, such economic gains as could be expected from the southern operations had become as evident as the strategic triumph. These gains seem to have delayed realistic appraisal of the economic task which confronted Japan in the conduct of a total Pacific war. For almost a year the measures and means which had made the first conquest possible were largely assumed to be adequate for the war itself.

There could be no exact calculation of the time within which the initial advantage in mobilization would continue to operate. The speed of American conversion to war output and the degree to which Germany would absorb American military strength were unknowns. To maintain their advantage, or even to prolong it, the Japanese leaders were required to mobilize their limited economic resources with exceptional skill. The highest premium of all would derive from a correct estimate of the needs that would develop immediately upon the occupation of the southern regions. With such an estimate, made effective through speedy redeployment of resources to meet critical needs, Japan might still be able to compensate for its relatively inferior economic potential. At the very least, more time would be gained to secure the maximum benefit from the southern areas.

As shown above, the steps taken during the first year of the war did not measure up to the requirements of the situation. With few exceptions the Japanese economy continued to operate under directives laid down before the attack on Pearl Harbor. While these directives featured the continued expansion of the armament industry, they failed to lay adequate stress on greater output of certain end products, notably shipping, that rapidly assumed crucial significance. Neither the setting of higher goals nor timely readjustments in the programming of vital items, both of which would have prolonged Japan's initial military advantage, were thought to be necessary.

When the difficulties finally caught up with Japan at the end of 1942, they developed with extraordinary rapidity. In part they were the

---

[1] A negligible amount may have been "lost," presumably by sinkings.

[2] Approximately 90 percent of aluminum was being produced from bauxite, obtained almost entirely from Bintan Island (NEI), Malays, and Palau.

result of the completeness with which the objectives of the southern operation had been achieved. Strategic plans had originally called for the establishment of a relatively circumscribed Pacific defense ring, permitting a maximum concentration of available forces and supplies. But, in fact, Japan committed forces well beyond the line set up in the original plan, more especially in New Guinea, the Solomons, the Aleutians, and in operations which led to the Coral Sea, Indian Ocean, and Midway engagements. Behind these actions lay an underestimate of the prospective speed and power of the United States come-back, an overestimate of Japanese capacities for defense of the enlarged empire, and a general lack of economic planning in relation to this strategic problem. The burden of heavy supply lines, the attrition on shipping, the inability to defend widely scattered outposts—all these concrete aspects of an unfavorable situation developed with apparent unexpectedness. No previously organized measures with which to counter them seemed to exist, and economic preparation lagged well behind the emerging strategic demands.

Through most of 1942 this general problem failed to emerge with sufficient definiteness to make an impact on Tokyo. At the end of July, Japan's merchant shipping totaled 6,376,000 tons— almost exactly the amount on hand when the war began. Thus, for a period of nearly 8 months, losses from sinkings had been offset by gains from construction, capture, and salvage. The first marked reduction in total tonnage was not to occur until October. At midyear 1942 Japan could set the occupation of the southern regions, including Burma and much of New Guinea, against the one major defeat at Midway.

In August the American forces secured a position on Guadalcanal, and thereafter the picture changed rapidly. By October–November, the decisive engagements for control of Guadalcanal were being fought. In these engagements Japan's losses of all types of ships were unexpectedly heavy. In October–November over-all merchant ship losses climbed sharply to 482,000 tons. By the end of November, total Japanese merchant shipping was reduced to 5,946,000 tons, or 430,000 tons below the December 1941 and July 1942 level.

Taking these developments at face value, and discounting only the Battle of Midway, there would appear to be little reason for concern until October or November 1942. Midway was dis-

counted or explained away, but the events around Guadalcanal in October–November, combined with the abrupt rise in total shipping losses, evoked real dismay. After the war, Hoshino Naoki, who had been Chief Secretary of the Tojo Cabinet, exclaimed that the calendar of the Japanese war economy should be dated "After Guadalcanal".[3] Not until then did the full dimensions of the Pacific war's economic demands strike home to Japan's leaders. The entire Guadalcanal campaign lasted from 7 August 1942 to 9 February 1943, but the handwriting on the wall had become plainly visible in mid-November 1942.[4]

This date, 11 months after the Pearl Harbor attack, marked the end of the first phase of Japanese economic development in the Pacific war. With November 1942 began the really energetic effort to raise over-all production sights and to adopt a selective approach involving a fundamental redeployment of facilities and materials. The previous willingness to "coast" on the military achievements of the early months, however, was reflected in production levels of the entire fiscal year 1942. In many cases, therefore, analysis of the economic data for the first period can be projected into the early months of 1943.

DIFFUSED ADMINISTRATIVE RESPONSIBILITY

During this period there was no centralized responsibility for the planning and execution of economic mobilization. The Cabinet Planning Board had been established in the spring of 1937 as an agency designed to coordinate Cabinet policy in the economic sphere. In October 1937, mainly as a result of problems created by the China war, its statutory powers and functions had been enlarged. Even so, it was far from being an effective agency of central planning and control. Its schedules were most important in relation to mobilization of basic materials, but it had little influence on the programming of key munitions products such as ordnance, aircraft, and shipping. The planning board, moreover, possessed no executive powers. It could only lay its plans before the Cabinet for approval and enforcement. Thereafter each of the Ministries carried through, in its own sphere, the approved directives.

Primary executive responsibility was thus vested

[3] USSBS interrogation No. 505, p. 36.
[4] Marked by the sinking of 16 Japanese warships and 4 transports in the Battle of Guadalcanal, 13–15 November.

in the Cabinet. This responsibility, however, was exercised not so much collectively as Ministry by Ministry. The Ministries of Commerce and Industry, Agriculture and Forestry, Railways, and Communications exercised an essentially exclusive authority over their respective spheres of economic administration. In addition, the Army and Navy Ministries dominated policy affecting ordnance, aircraft, and shipping. The different ministers were supreme in their own spheres and jealously guarded their jurisdictional prerogatives. They were not amenable to the orders of the Prime Minister, who functioned more as the chairman of a group of Ministers than as controlling head of the government.

Centralized planning and control was further handicapped by the industrial control associations established in 1941–42. These associations, comprising the great industrial monopolies of Japan, were responsible for the organization of production on the operating level. They were dominated by the *Zaibatsu* executives who had previously headed the cartels in iron and steel, coal, machinery, light metals, and other industries, but were imperfectly controlled by the various Ministries to which they owed jurisdictional allegiance. Most of the control associations were responsible to the Ministry of Commerce and Industry, but others were responsible to the Army, Navy, Communications, and Railways Ministries. On the operating level, the associations tended to work along lines set by the business leaders while, administratively, not even the Premier could overstep the rigid lines of jurisdictional authority set by the Ministries.

Virtually no changes were made in this administrative system during the first year of the war. In 1942 it was possible to ignore or discount the lack of centralized control in the mobilization of war production. The limited goals set for aircraft and shipping did not require a large-scale reallocation of facilities and materials. In administration, as in other respects, the Japanese leaders were content to accept the existing system.

SUPPLY OF BASIC MATERIALS

During this period the level of basic industries, which sharply limited the capabilities of the Japanese war economy, was not significantly changed. In 1942, except in the case of iron

ore and aluminum, there was but slight improvement in the domestic output of basic materials.

In absolute amount, the output of aluminum was still relatively small, despite the increase recorded in 1942. Even more significant was the fact that, of the total primary ingots distributed, only 62 percent was channeled into aircraft production. Owing to considerable leakage of aluminum into prohibited uses this figure overstates the percentage flow to aircraft. As far as aluminum ingots were concerned, a more energetic expansion of aircraft production would have been possible in 1942. Large-scale additions to plant capacity were not made an emergency requirement until late in the year, with full results delayed until 1944.

TABLE 6.—*Production of basic materials, Japan proper, fiscal years 1941–42*

[Thousands of metric tons]

	1941	1942
Coal	55, 602	54, 178
Coke [1]	4, 567	4, 773
Iron ore [2]	6, 625	7, 669
Pig iron [3]	4, 982	5, 184
Ingot steel	6, 837	7, 099
Finished steel	5, 120	5, 166
Alumina	152	226
Aluminum ingot	72	103

[1] Excludes gas and chemical company products.
[2] Includes domestic production of iron sands, delivers of pyrite sinter, and imports of iron ore.
[3] Includes imports.

The low production of iron and steel was a prime limiting factor for the whole war economy. An ambitious program of capacity expansion for this industry dated from 1937–38 and continued up to the last year of the war. In level of output, however, the Japanese iron and steel industry fell far below capacity.[5] During the first half of the war, there existed a cushion of excess capacity, which was gradually used up in meeting operating problems created by poor quality refractory materials and prefabricated linings.

At the outset of the war, the necessary raw materials such as iron ore, coal, and ferro-alloys were available in quantities adequate for normal operations. Even at this early stage, however, signs of the ultimate crisis in materials supply

[5] See Table 6. The capacity is that assigned to the furnaces under Western operating conditions. It advanced from 10,721,000 metric tons in 1941 to 13,665,000 tons in 1944.

were present. Both in 1941 and 1942, substantial drafts were made on the iron ore stock pile, to the extent of 1,207,000 and 1,206,000 tons respectively. By April 1943 this stock pile totaling 2,605,000 tons at the end of 1941, had been reduced to 1,399,000 tons. Little iron ore was received from the south, due to the shipping stringency.[6] Over-optimistic expectations as to raw materials supply were nevertheless prevalent during both 1942 and 1943.

In its own context Japanese basic industry was doing fairly well during the first year of the war. The point is, however, that more was required. Operation was not characterized by an energetic effort to raise production levels. In this period, for example, the Japanese were stiffening the specifications for finished steel, thereby increasing rejections. Ingot steel output increased by only 262,000 tons, and finished steel by 46,000 tons.

MUNITIONS PROGRAM

Finished armament output rose about 30 percent from 1941 to 1942 with substantial relative increases evident in merchant ships, ordnance and aircraft production. However, these increases give an exaggerated impression of the achievements in this field. The absolute level of munitions output in 1942 was surprisingly small for a nation engaged in a major war. Despite the existence of an already organized munitions industry in 1941, Japan devoted only an additional 5 percent of its total output to armaments in 1942.

Besides the inadequacy of the over-all output, there was also maldistribution of end products due to poor evaluation of emerging war requirements. The southern operations were launched at a time when ordnance priorities, a key directional factor in industrial mobilization, were pointed toward assuring the items needed for the continental war in China. On the 1941 priorities list, the A ratings were given, in order, to tanks and tractors, medium and small guns, large guns, car and craft radio, and large radios. For 1942, the A ratings were given to three items, in the following order: Tanks and tractors, large radios and radio detectors. The changes in the priority ratings of the accompanying list of items, all of which rapidly became vitally necessary, illustrate the slow adjustment to demands of the Pacific war.

	1941	1942	1943
Submarine locators	D3	C3	A7
Air-Force weapons	C2	B5	A1
Air-Force ammunition and accessories.	C3	B6	A2

More serious was the failure to lay due emphasis on the construction of merchant shipping. In the fiscal year 1941, which included the first 4 months of the war, the total for new ships completed fell to 241,120 gross registered tons, the lowest since 1935. In fiscal 1942, the figure rose to 358,280 gross tons, or approximately 50 percent.[7] In view of the low absolute level in both years, however, it is apparent that the Japanese plans discounted the need for merchant tonnage instead of stressing it.

The slow awakening to realities can be traced in the ship construction planning that took place in 1942. Initial plans drafted in March set a 4-year schedule for merchant shipbuilding contemplating a gradual increase from about 470,000 tons in 1942 to 820,000 tons in 1945. Nine months later, in December 1942, a drastic revision of these plans virtually doubled the original goal established for 1943, while scaling down 1942 construction nearer to the levels then being actually achieved.

Errors in planning extended also to the type of ships built. In 1940–41 no large tankers were built, while aggregate tanker construction fell to the lowest levels since the mid-thirties. For the three fiscal years 1940–42, new tankers totaled 3,928, 8,486 and 47,743 tons. This oversight in planning could not be repaired, even though by 1943–44, with the tremendous premium attached to tankers, over one-third of the total merchant-ship constructions was accounted for by this type of vessel.

Somewhat greater progress was being registered in aircraft production. Unlike shipping, a moderate expansion program had been scheduled; in addition, the demand for more planes had developed in the early months of 1942. At the beginning of December 1941, the navy had on hand 2,120 planes, while the army had 4,860. Only 1,068 of the army planes were in the first-line operational category, however. The clamor was not only for more planes but for improved models. A limited effort to step up the aircraft expansion program began early in 1942, but encountered obstacles

---

[6] As against over 3,000,000 tons supplied in the calendar year 1940, Malaya and the Philippines provided barely 150,000 tons in 1942.

[7] The dead-weight tonnage of completed naval vessels actually declined in this period, from 231,980 in 1941 to 216,416 in 1942.

such as retooling problems and shortages of heavy machinery and structural steel.

MANPOWER

The goals set for the Japanese war economy in 1942 were so limited that no special manpower difficulties arose. By December 1941 the Japanese authorities possessed all essential powers needed to control the allocation of manpower. Employment exchanges were in Government hands and labor conscription had been legalized. For several years, measures designed to prevent the uncontrolled movement of workers in essential industries had been in force. By means of the "work record passbook system," workers in designated industries could not change their occupations without having the shift approved, in effect, both by the employer and the Government-controlled labor exchange. In case of necessity the government had legal authority to "freeze" the workers in a given industry. The coercive powers were supplemented by more normal attractions, such as the higher wages and larger food allowances generally offered by the munitions industries. These various powers and inducements were comprehensive, but they were applied on a piecemeal basis without too effective over-all integration. In 1941 and 1942, mainly through the work of the labor exchanges in effecting transfers, quotas of 2.2 million and 1.9 million persons required for the more essential phases of the economy, including industry, transport, and agriculture, were successfully met. Some degree of compulsion had already become necessary, so that by 1941–42 a small, increasing segment of the working force was being conscripted. The threat of labor conscription, moreover, facilitated the work of the labor exchanges by inducing many workers, principally in commerce, to shift to an essential employment category.

* * * * *

TABLE 7.—*Total labor conscription for essential work, 1939–42*

Year	Labor conscripts	Cumulative total
1939	850	850
1940	52, 692	53, 542
1941	258, 192	311, 724
1942	311, 649	623, 385

During 1942 there was some expansion of capacity, but not of output, in the Japanese iron and steel industry. The biggest gains were achieved in the aircraft industry and primary aluminum ingot production. Even in this field, as later achievements demonstrated, the sights were set far too low. In the priority estimates for 1942, the crucial oversight was the lack of stress on expansion of merchant ship construction. Realization of the attrition to which Japanese merchant shipping was to be subjected did not come until November 1942. Here again, later achievements demonstrated what would have been possible in the first year of the war, despite the intrinsic limitations of Japan's productive structure. Within the Japanese economy of 1942 were the resources in manpower and civilian industry that were not fully converted to war production until 1943–44. They could have been harnessed to the task a full year earlier.

UNLIMITED EFFORT

The greatest achievements of Japan's war economy were registered during 1944, peak output of many essential items being reached in the early fall. Almost 3 years elapsed between December 1941 and peak industrial mobilization. The period was approximately the same as that taken by the United States. Since the Japanese economy was better geared for war at the outset, however, these equal periods actually measure an inequality in rate of achievement.

This should not be allowed to obscure the essential accomplishments of Japan's productive system in 1943–44. By an immense effort, war production was lifted to record heights, despite the basic limitations within which the Japanese were compelled to work. Large additions to plant capacity were made, resources of all kinds were shifted to a plane and ship construction, and the civilian economy was cut severely. It proved impossible, however, to raise basic industry to a level which could sustain the peak output of essential munitions products. By the time the munitions industries had reached their peak, the supply of basic materials was suffering a sharp decline. By fall of 1944 it had already become impossible to hold steel, coal, and aluminum production at the 1942–43 level, and thereafter the foundations of basic industry progressively crumbled. The Japanese war economy disintegrated at its base, even while utilization of available stocks kept the munitions output at high levels for a few additional months.

Parallel with the large-scale redeployment of resources begun in 1943, an intensive effort was made to wipe out the competing lines of jurisdictional authority which plagued the operation of Japan's war economy until the end of the war. The urgent necessity of raising production sights, finally recognized late in 1942, was the signal for a series of administrative reforms during the following year. As already noted, the possibilities of delay and friction within the administrative system existing in 1941–42 were immense. When it was proved imperative to shift labor, materials, capital, and motive power rapidly to key war industries, the need for greater administrative coordination became a primary concern of the Japanese authorities.

First efforts to deal with this problem led to the formation of an emergency Ministerial coordinating committee in November 1942. Two months later Tojo laid before the Diet sweeping proposals vesting the Prime Minister with dictatorial powers of supervision over the other Ministers and the war economy generally. In these proposals five industries—shipping, aircraft, light metals, coal, and iron and steel—were set apart as requiring special powers on the part of the Prime Minister. After an intense struggle, the Diet voted the emergency powers, and Imperial approval was given on 17 March 1943. Associated with the Premier in the exercise of his new powers, however, was an Advisory Council of seven leading Zaibatsu representatives, heading the most important of the Industrial Control Associations.

Eight months later, on 1 November 1943, the munitions ministry was formally inaugurated as the central feature in a drastic reorganization of Ministerial functions. The changes effected in November 1943 represented an attempt to provide coherent and unified direction of the war economy. Authority over transport was hitherto divided mainly between a railways and a communications ministry. The former ministry of commerce and industry, previously the central agency of control over industry, was divided. Half of it went to a new Ministry of Agriculture and Commerce, charged with responsibility for the civilian economy. Administrative control over industry as a whole was vested in the munitions ministry. Within the new Ministry, a Total Mobilization Bureau replaced the Cabinet Planning Board. This new bureau, given the executive powers formerly denied to the Planning Board, was designed to function as the general staff of the war economy. Finally, under terms of a munition company act, the vital war industries were made "designated munitions companies," and placed under the munitions ministry's direction, thus limiting the role of the Industrial Control Associations.

A full year had elapsed between recognition of the need for administrative reform and final reorganization of the cabinet structure in November 1943. Even then, the army and navy ministries were not fully subordinated to the authority of the munitions ministry. On many occasions the minister of munitions was forced into the position of arbiter between the army and navy. In the case of aircraft production, expedition of which was the primary function of the munitions ministry, the centralization of administrative authority was most complete. To the very end, however, no single and effective center of authority for the allocation of materials was established, and ultimate decisions were often the result not so much of considered combined judgment as of bitter wrangles in which the strongest voice prevailed.

THE DRIVE FOR AIRCRAFT

Formation of the munitions ministry was a direct outgrowth of difficulties experienced with the aircraft industry. By the spring of 1943, the construction of a number of new and enlarged aircraft plants was well under way. Despite substantial increases in physical plants, manufacturers were having difficulty in meeting schedules. It was clear that interservice jealousies and uncontrolled competition might well undermine the whole effort. The allocation of available materials, tools, and manpower was a constant bone of contention. During the summer of 1943, moreover, the Japanese business leaders were also engaged in a determined struggle to protect their interests in the administrative reorganization then pending. In the terms of the Munitions Company Act, as well as in the men chosen to head the munitions ministry, the Zaibatsu effectively maintained their position.[8]

In this period, aircraft became one of the largest industries in Japan. Key units were the Mitsu-

---

[8] During the period 16-28 August, the Zaibatsu leaders of the Industrial Control Associations were successively called to the palace to render an accounting to the Emperor.

bishi airframe plant at Nagoya with an area of 2,204,000 square feet and the same company's engine plant, also at Nagoya, with an area of 2,703,000 square feet. In spite of the large manufacturing areas available at assembly plants, a considerable percentage of airframe and engine subassembly manufacture was let to subcontractors, and a high percentage of the parts came from an even larger network of sub-subcontractors. Shops scattered throughout the industrial areas supplied the thousands of instruments, electrical accessories, and other bits and pieces that make up modern aircraft. These areas, and the sprawling assembly plants, presented highly vulnerable bombing targets.

In the fall of 1943 plant expansion slowed down and a great production drive was inagurated. Spurring this drive was a government demand that aircraft manufacturers produce 2.16 times as many planes and engines by June 1944 as they had in September 1943. The full effects of improved administrative coordination under the munitions ministry were not felt in airframe fabrication until the spring of 1944, however, and the highest levels of aircraft output were achieved during the spring and summer of that year.

Engine production failed to keep up in the spring of 1944 and became increasingly critical during the months when airplane output was reaching its maximum. In April 1944, the available supply of engines fell below the 1.8 engines per airplane requirement considered minimum. From then on, engine supply was a real bottleneck in the aircraft program. By cutting the spare engine allotment of 20 percent included in the normal requirement, the aircraft manufacturers were able to maintain deliveries at 80 to 85 percent of schedule until June 1944, but thereafter the position steadily deteriorated. After the first B–29 raids in November-December, dispersals from the huge Mitsubishi and Nakajima plants at Nagoya and Musashi began in earnest and the situation became hopeless. As early as the spring of 1944, a wide gap opened between actual production and production plans. A steep rise in output from about 2,400 planes in August 1944, to 5,500 in March 1945 had been scheduled by Japanese planners. As difficulties were encountered around the middle of 1944, sights were lowered to 3,200 planes monthly by June 1945. Actual production leveled off at about 2,400 planes during the 1944 peak.

Table 8.—*Aircraft and engine production, fiscal years 1942–44*[1]

	Planes	Engines
1942:		
I	1, 991	4, 131
II	2, 187	4, 250
III	2, 852	4, 778
IV	3, 206	5, 609
Total	10, 236	18, 768
1943:		
I	3, 565	6, 380
II	4, 250	7, 434
III	5, 672	9, 118
IV	6, 756	11, 952
Total	20, 243	34, 884
1944:		
I	7, 332	12, 468
II	7, 391	11, 507
III	6, 701	10, 599
IV	4, 940	5, 469
Total	26, 364	40, 043

[1] Japanese fiscal year, 1 April—31 March.

During 1942, the output of fighters and bombers accounted for roughly 60 percent of total production, while in 1943 and 1944, the proportion rose to nearly 70 percent. In the latter year, however, fighters were almost half the total, while in 1942 they accounted for only one-third.

Employment data for the aircraft industry showed a tremendous increase from 314,300 workers in December 1941 to 1,258,000 in April 1945. Of these totals 124,300 and 427,000 respectively were engaged in the manufacture of engines and propellers, with the remainder making airframes and accessories. These figures do not account for all the many direct and indirect contributors to the industry among the subcontractors. When these are taken into account, it becomes probable that 1.5 million workers were involved in the manufacture of aircraft at the end of the war. Women probably never exceeded 20 percent of the total, but high-school boys, physically substandard college students, and nonessential workers from other industries were drafted in large numbers for the aircraft plants. Skilled workers were desperately lacking, until the point came at which some key personnel, both engineers and production men, were released from the services to retake their former civilian jobs, and the Army and Navy arsenals detailed a certain number of their own skilled workers to private industry. Large numbers of soldiers, regardless of skills, were detailed for temporary duty, usually of six months duration, with aircraft manufacturers. The labor problem was never solved and contributed to the general decline in aircraft output which began in the fall of 1944 and continued to the end of the war.

The aircraft industry, during the first half of 1944, was extending output at a time when production of its critical raw material—aluminum—was beginning to decline. Imports of bauxite, which had totaled 450,134 tons in fiscal 1942, rose to a record 820,534 tons in 1943, and then dropped off to 347,335 tons in 1944. By the end of 1944 bauxite stocks had reached the vanishing point and a belated effort to transfer to the use of aluminous shales was in full swing. Conversion of the plants to the use of shale was delayed too long, however, even if the imports of shale—only 147,000 tons in 1944—had been adequate to compensate for the decline in bauxite supplies. A sharp decrease in aluminum output occurred in fiscal 1944.

TABLE 9—*Capacity and production of aluminum, 1941–45*

Fiscal year	Alumina		Aluminum ingot	
	Capacity	Output	Capacity	Output
1941	229, 100	151, 883	111, 200	71, 740
1942	313, 700	226, 181	132, 400	103, 075
1943	360, 700	318, 493	171, 600	141, 084
1944	398, 700	225, 229	159, 100	110, 398
1945	419, 300	[1] 16, 255	159, 100	[1] 6, 647

[1] First quarter only.

The decline from 141,084 metric tons of aluminum ingot in 1943 to 110,398 tons in 1944, was compensated by a much more rigid channeling of available supplies into the aircraft industry. During the last quarter of fiscal year 1943 as much as 18 percent of primary ingot was still going into other than aircraft uses. This percentage declined sharply in 1944, making it possible to scrape together the necessary supplies of aluminum for the aircraft industry. This was accomplished, how-

ever, only at the cost of an increasing utilization of processing scrap. Virgin ingot declined from 75–78 percent of the aluminum entering the aircraft pipeline during the second quarter of fiscal year 1944, to from 30–50 percent in the third quarter, and to but 20 percent in the fourth quarter. By these methods Japan was able successfully to supply the 1944–45 requirements of aircraft production, and the evidence fails to indicate that aluminum, in a quantitative sense, hindered aircraft output within the period of the war. Had aircraft production met its schedules, however, the picture might have been materially different.

Japan put immense effort into aircraft production during the war, and the results were not inconsiderable. Between December 1941 and August 1945, the industry produced a total of 65,971 planes and 103,650 aircraft engines. In view of the essential limitations within which the Japanese economy had to operate, this achievement cannot be minimized.

TABLE 10.—*Allocation of primary aluminum, 1942–45*

[Metric tons]

Fiscal quarters	Aircraft	Army	Navy	Civilian [1]	Total
1942:					
I	17, 184	4, 221	1, 216	5, 117	27, 738
II	14, 591	3, 638	1, 233	4, 635	24, 097
III	16, 100	3, 750	1, 923	4, 961	26, 734
IV	18, 339	3, 245	1, 520	5, 237	28, 341
Total	66, 214	14, 854	5, 892	19, 950	106, 910
1943:					
I	25, 961	2, 877	1, 384	5, 398	33, 620
II	25, 854	3, 117	1, 543	2, 799	33, 253
III	27, 185	2, 819	1, 571	2, 307	33, 882
IV	28, 290	2, 515	2, 555	966	34, 326
Total	107, 290	11, 328	7, 053	11, 470	135, 081
1944:					
I	33, 017	2, 175	2, 134	0	37, 326
II	34, 419	1, 037	1, 156	0	36, 612
III	16, 352	423	465	0	17, 240
IV	15, 250	0	0	0	15, 250
Total	99, 038	3, 635	3, 755	0	106, 428
1945, I	6, 500	0	0	0	6, 500

[1] Includes indirect military use.

TABLE 11.—*Japan's merchant fleet, selected months*

End of month	Total afloat	Months elapsed
	Tons	
November 1942	5,946,000	
December 1943	4,944,000	13
March 1944	3,966,000	3
October 1944	2,911,000	7
April 1945	1,961,000	5

THE SHIPBUILDING EFFORT

Behind the expansion of ship construction during 1943–44 lay an urgency as intense as that which spurred aircraft output. Table 11 shows the successive periods within which the Japanese merchant fleet was reduced by steps of roughly one million tons. The rapid deterioration in Japan's shipping position stimulated a series of upward revisions in construction plans. Major changes in plans for 1943–44, and their relation to actual production for the fiscal years are shown in Table 12.

TABLE 12.—*Planned and Actual Merchant Ship Construction. Fiscal Year 1943–44*

Planned 1943 Production as of—
March 1942	689,310
March 1943	818,880
Actual 1943 Production	1,110,553

Planned 1944 Production as of—
March 1942	675,580
December 1943	1,898,110
March 1944	2,631,250
August 1944	1,966,480
Actual 1944 Production	1,600,049

Drastic upward revisions featured the planning to March 1944. By the end of the first half of 1944, however, actual production had lagged so far behind schedule that a reduced program had to be adopted. The August 1944 plan reduced the total schedule for the year by the amount of the lag in the first half, but required production at an annual rate of 2,500,000 tons for the last half of the fiscal year.

These figures cover the planning and construction of steel ships only. In fiscal 1943, a total of 87,210 tons of wooden ships was built, and in 1944, a total of 258,733 tons. Including wooden ships, total construction for 1943 and 1944 amounted to 1,022,837 and 1,655,580 tons respectively. These totals compare with the previous record total of about 600,000 tons in 1919.

The great increase in shipbuilding in 1943 was due to the centering of responsibility in the Navy, the shift to the simplified design of the second series of standardized ships, and the substantial increase of shipyard capacity, as well as to the upward revision of the planned program. Up to February 1943 when the Navy assumed control, both steel and yard capacity had been pre-empted by the Army and Navy for purposes other than merchant ship construction. Administration of the program by the Navy provided the authority and the drive needed to eliminate the leisurely methods and general inertia characteristic of 1942. Four new yards successfully applied mass production techniques to the building of small cargo ships of 877 gross tons. For the most part, however, shipyards continued to build ships in the traditional manner, assembling hulls piece by piece, using only a limited amount of welding, and launching from single position slipways.

Additions to shipyard capacity during the war represented the most significant factor in achieving expansion of output. At the outset, Japan had approximately 15 large and 24 small yards capable of building steel ships of over 500 tons. These yards were expanded to some extent, but the building of six new large yards and seven small ones accounted for the major increase in capacity. The major additions to yard capacity came in 1943–44. When shortages in material forced abandonment of the expansion program early in 1945, several of the new yards were incomplete and a few were not yet in operation.

TABLE 13.—*Merchant shipbuilding, fiscal years 1943–44*

[Gross registered tons]

Fiscal quarters	Cargo	Collier	Tanker	Other	Total
1943:					
I	54,301	0	26,728	3,285	84,314
II	77,703	21,260	80,200	139	179,302
III	114,767	16,572	100,328	17,864	249,531
IV	233,513	21,128	154,887	12,892	422,420
Total	480,284	58,960	362,143	34,180	935,567
1944:					
I	252,674	0	110,205	5,310	368,189
II	184,002	0	154,684	9,540	348,226
III	212,259	0	138,139	18,493	368,891
IV	190,537	0	57,378	23,626	271,541
Total	839,472	0	460,406	56,971	1,356,847

During most of this period, yard capacity, and especially lack of mass production facilities, held the merchant shipping program within relatively narrow bounds. Even in available facilities, however, there was a shortage of skilled labor which became progressively worse as the war went on. And this as in other industries, conscription for the armed services was carried through with a minimum of deferments. By mid-1944, when the first cut-back in ship construction plans was made, shortage of steel had become a major limitation and soon became controlling. In fiscal 1944, 38 percent of ordinary rolled steel and 28 percent of total steel was used in ship construction.

Naval ship construction experienced a parallel expansion during these years, advancing from 256,012 dead-weight tons in fiscal 1943 to 466,208 tons in 1944. This program, however, utilized but one-third of the steel consumed by merchant shipbuilding in 1943, and one-sixth in 1944. The last battleship was completed in 1942, after which the major emphasis shifted to aircraft carriers, destroyers, submarines, and coast defense vessels.

TABLE 14.—*Production of naval ships, fiscal years 1942–44*

[Deadweight tons]

	1942		1943		1944	
	No.	Tonnage	No.	Tonnage	No.	Tonnage
Battleships	1	64,000	---	-------	-----	-------
Carriers	6	6,050	5	78,360	4	114,500
Cruisers	2	14,500	2	16,000	1	8,000
Destroyers	9	21,660	12	25,140	32	46,860
Submarines	23	28,047	41	52,565	37	53,560
Minelayers	38	18,859	27	14,609	7	4,465
Coast defense	3	2,820	34	28,420	113	86,420
Transports	---	-------	7	6,840	58	61,990
Auxiliaries	105	30,480	107	28,245	138	48,290
Landing craft	---	-------	7	5,833	1,432	30,668
Special attack	---	-------	---	-------	5,115	11,455
Total	187	186,416	242	256,012	6,937	466,208

OTHER MUNITIONS

The general trend in production of munitions, other than airplanes and ships, was toward an accelerated increase in output. This reached its peak in the early fall of 1944. A decline in output then set in, becoming disastrous by the summer of 1945. Aircraft armament, aircraft ammunition, and communication equipment, and the general category of naval ordnance production increases, to the 1944 peak, equalled or exceeded the increased production of planes and merchant ships. As this would indicate, munitions items not connected with the expansion of air power were generally neglected. Production as a whole increased, but the ratio to total war production declined through the war. This is shown by the ratio of munitions production, other than aircraft and air munitions, to total production of finished munitions items in the years 1941–1945:

Fiscal year:	Ratio (percent)
1941	67.8
1942	61.0
1943	53.2
1944	51.7
1945 [1]	48.0

[1] First four months.

The drop in the ratio of production of strictly ground-use munitions to total production of finished munitions items is even more striking:

Fiscal Year:	Ratio (percent)
1941	28.9
1942	20.5
1943	20.5
1943	12.4
1944	8.2
1945 [1]	7.5

[1] First four months.

These figures illustrate the extent to which the developments of the war changed Japanese concepts of war production requirements. As the priority of aircraft and aircraft munitions increased and the lack of raw material supplies grew more stringent, production of motor vehicles, naval guns and their ammunition, and ammunition for ground use dropped below 1941 levels. Production of tanks and ground-use artillery remained at about the same level throughout the war.

The high level of naval ordnance production, particularly machine guns and ammunition, and radio and electrical equipment, was generally sufficient to supply the naval aircraft and ships that were produced. The low technical level of part of this production—radar is a notable example—to some extent nullified this achievement.

While army ordnance production was inadequate in many items, lack of shipping and the loss of supplies through ship sinkings were the primary reasons for a shortage of Japanese Army supplies in overseas areas.

The drop in truck production (from 42,000 in the fiscal year 1941 to 20,500 in 1944 and to less than 2,000 in April–July 1945) did not have an immediate effect on the war because the Army and Navy were taking an ever-increasing share of the existing output. By the end of 1944, however, lack of replacement vehicles, lack of parts, and an increased traffic burden resulted in a deterioriation in the domestic economy which had strong repercussions on the whole war production program.

TABLE 15.—*Armament Production, Fiscal Years 1941–44*

[Millions of 1945 yen]

	1941	1942	1943	1944
Merchant ships	403	533	1,235	1,508
Navy ships	1,014	1,112	1,476	2,099
Navy surface and air ordnance	972	1,540	2,551	4,638
Army ground and air ordnance	956	1,262	1,586	2,107
Motor vehicles	691	427	307	270
Aircraft	1,081	1,843	3,687	5,024
Total	5,117	6,717	10,842	15,646

These series were derived by a summation of available quantity data for all major items of munitions output valued at 1945 prices. The coverage is not as broad as the total munitions expenditures shown in Table 3 for the latter includes purchases of miscellaneous equipment and supplies.

DECLINE OF BASIC MATERIALS

The peak level for basic industry was reached early in 1944, some months earlier than that for the munitions industries. While aircraft, shipbuilding, and ordnance were achieving record outputs in 1944, the position of the coal, iron, steel, and aluminum industries was deteriorating. Even more significant than the short-lived peak for basic industry is the fact that the increases achieved were confined within an extremely limited range. Coal production hardly changed, while ingot steel increased by only 700,000 tons in 1943 and finished steel by only 450,000 tons. A better record was made for aluminum. These results, however, were totally inadequate to provide the basic materials needed to lift Japan's munitions production to levels matching the scale in which the Pacific War was being fought.

TABLE 16.—*Production of basic materials, Japan proper, fiscal years 1942–44*

[Thousand metric tons]

Commodity	1942	1943	1944
Coal	54,178	55,538	49,335
Coke	4,778	5,158	3,980
Iron ore [1]	7,669	7,524	6,077
Pig iron [2]	5,184	4,947	3,655
Ingot steel	7,099	7,821	5,911
Finished steel	5,166	5,609	4,320
Alumina	226	318	225
Aluminum ingot	103	141	110

[1] Includes domestic production of iron sands, deliveries of pyrite, sinter, and imports of iron ore.
[2] Includes imports.

Coal production in the home islands reached its wartime peak during the last quarter of fiscal 1943—15,344,000 tons. Production in this quarter, however, but slightly exceeded that for the corresponding period of 1942, and total output for 1943 was only 1,360,000 tons above 1942. In 1944 total output declined by over 6,000,000 tons. When imports are taken into consideration the position became even more critical, with total available supply in 1944 reduced by 9,000,000 tons.

TABLE 17.—*Production and imports of coal, fiscal years 1942–44*

[Thousand metric tons]

	Domestic output	Imports	Total supply
1942:			
1st half	24,899	(1)	---
2d half	29,279	(1)	---
Total	54,178	8,748	62,926
1934:			
1st half	26,249	4,073	30,322
2d half	29,289	1,956	31,245
Total	55,538	6,029	61,567
1944:			
1st half	25,235	2,259	27,494
2d half	24,100	876	24,976
Total	49,335	3,135	52,470

[1] Not available.

Technical factors in the coal industry, as well as the rapid shrinkage of imports, rendered the underlying situation even more hopeless than the output figures suggest. Abuse and neglect had featured virtually every aspect of the operation of the coal industry throughout the war. During 1941–44 the total labor force increased from 339,000 to 416,000 but indescriminate draft procedures, inadequate maintenance and other factors had reduced annual output per miner from 164 to 119 tons in these years. Coal producers experienced increasing difficulty in securing the supplies of steel, cement, and lumber needed to maintain efficient operation. Although machinery steadily deteriorated from long and constant use, it proved impossible in most cases to get new replacements or parts needed for repairs. The cutting of new galleries essential for sustained production was also neglected. Rationalization of mining operations through the best use of the most efficient and highest quality mines was never accomplished, although the execution of such a program had been one of the tasks set for the Coal Control Association in 1941.

By 1944 the position of the iron and steel industry had become even more critical than that of the coal industry. High level imports of coking coal, iron ore, and even pig iron were requirements crucial to the full-scale operation of Japan's blast furnaces and steel mills. The decline in these imports began in 1943 and reached critical proportions in 1944.

TABLE 18.—*Production and imports of coking coal, iron ore, and pig iron, fiscal years 1942–44*

[Thousand metric tons]

	Domestic output	Imports	Total
Coking coal:			
1942	(¹)	4, 025	--------
1943	(¹)	2, 939	--------
1944	(¹)	1, 435	--------
Iron ore:			
1942	2, 789	4, 880	7, 669
1943	3, 838	3, 686	7, 166
1944	4, 409	1, 668	6, 077
Pig iron:			
1942	4, 306	878	5, 184
1943	3, 813	1, 134	4, 947
1944	2, 713	942	3, 655

¹ Not available.

The loss of good coking coal, most of which came from North China, was probably the most serious problem. Peak imports of 2,058,000 tons were reached during the first half of fiscal 1942. By early 1944, imports were down to about 40 percent of their wartime peak, and they continued to fall off drastically. To counter the severe shortage of imported coking coal, efforts were made to utilize greater quantities of the best available domestic coal. Of the coking coal used by the Yawata iron and steel plant during the first half of fiscal year 1943, 58 percent was low grade domestic. This percentage rose to 62 in the first half and to 68 in the second half of 1944.

Imports of iron ore declined at about the same rate as coking coal. The wartime peak for iron ore imports, amounting to 1,356,000 tons, was reached during the third quarter of fiscal 1942. By the first quarter of 1944, they were down to 692,000 tons, and they fell successively to 458,000, 312,000 and 206,000 in the following quarters of the fiscal year. Some compensation was had in the rising domestic output, which reached its peak in the second quarter of 1944. The last drafts on the iron ore stockpile also helped to eke out supplies in 1943, when 400,000 tons were used and in 1944 when the remnant supply of 190,000 tons was taken.

Pig iron imports held up steadily until the last quarter of 1944, then they turned sharply downward. Production declined straight through 1944, largely as a result of short supplies and inferior grades of available ore and coking coal. Several newly constructed blast furnace plants, including the Amagasaki Steel Works and Nakayama Steel Works, had to be shut down because of the shortage of raw materials.

By 1944, scrap was more plentiful than pig iron, and most of the producers returned to the high scrap to pig iron ratios they had used before the war. Nevertheless ingot steel production declined steadily and sharply through fiscal 1943 and 1944. Annual production of 5,911,000 tons for fiscal 1944 was down nearly 2 million tons from the 1943 peak of 7,821,000 tons.

Finished steel, reached its peak output during the last quarter of fiscal 1943. This supply of finished steel helped to sustain shipping, ordnance, and aircraft production for the rest of 1944. After the first quarter of fiscal 1944 there was a precipitous drop, resulting in a decline of 1,300,000 tons for the year as a whole.

TABLE 19.—*Production of finished steel, fiscal years 1942–44*

TABLE 19.—*Production of finished steel, fiscal years 1942–44*

[Thousand metric tons]

Fiscal quarters	1942	1943	1944
I	1,033	1,401	1,429
II	922	1,307	1,051
III	1,021	1,389	1,059
IV	1,076	1,512	781
Total	4,052	5,609	4,320

Throughout the war, moreover, production delays occurred as a result of faulty administration of steel allocations. Over-allocation of the limited supply coupled with over-optimistic planning led to chronic failure of scheduled deliveries. The resulting dislocation of production added to the difficulties caused by the intrinsic shortage.

The Japanese failure to develop an adequate synthetic oil industry left a vulnerable point in the war economy. At the outbreak of the war synthetic oil production, at the rate of 400,000 barrels annually, was less than 1½ percent of estimated requirements, and little or no expansion was achieved during the war years. Limitations of technical skill, and the inability of the economy to supply competing military and industrial needs for large quantities of high-grade steel and complicated equipment, combined to prevent the construction of large-scale synthetic petroleum plants in Japan either before or after Pearl Harbor. The plants that did operate, unlike those in Germany, were never an important factor in aviation fuel production. Inner Zone production of natural petroleum averaged barely 1,500,000 barrels annually during the war years, with Manchurian shale oil production supplying possibly 3,000,000 additional barrels. Combined Inner Zone production from all sources amounted to roughly 5,000,000 barrels, or about one-sixth of total needs.

Output of crude oil in the Netherlands East Indies, along with Inner Zone imports, reached a wartime peak in 1943. The situation rapidly changed, however, and by the fall of 1944 Japan was beginning to scrape the bottom of its oil barrel. Last imports of crude oil from the south were received in the final quarter of fiscal 1944. In April 1945 the remaining Inner Zone stocks fell below two hundred thousand barrels. Although Netherlands East Indies crude oil production was about 80 percent of normal in fiscal 1943, stocks in the Inner Zone declined continuously during

the war years because of inadequate shipping. A large part of the East Indies production was consumed in the south; in the 1943–44 period much of it was lost in transit. Production was also cut back because more could not be moved.

TABLE 20.—*Crude oil production and stocks, fiscal years 1942–44*

[Thousands of barrels]

Fiscal quarters	Output in NEI	Consumed in south [1]	Imports	Inner zone	
				Output	Stock [2]
1942:					
I		1,966	1,133	430	12,346
II		4,003	1,861	407	10,390
III		3,426	3,093	400	8,748
IV		6,020	2,059	453	7,677
Total	25,927	15,415	8,146	1,670	
1943:					
I		6,544	3,712	441	6,839
II		9,552	2,264	442	5,557
III		9,475	2,546	466	4,839
IV		9,555	1,326	465	3,512
Total	49,614	35,126	9,848	1,814	
1944:					
I		7,814	994	419	2,354
II		8,442	224	386	1,240
III		8,881	423	379	594
IV		6,816		401	490
Total	36,916	31,953	1,641	1,585	

[1] Includes refined products; no breakdown for losses.
[2] At beginning of period.

MANPOWER MOBILIZATION

The conversion of civilian industry provided relatively few workers to meet the war sectors' increasing demand for manpower in 1943–45. By the drastic reduction in cotton spindles after 1942, for example, only 82,000 workers were released for essential industry. Against this meager gain from one of the largest of the converted industries should be set the demands of the armed forces—roughly 5 million conscripts in the 1943–45 period. During these years, moreover, production sights were raised to unprecedented heights in aircraft, shipbuilding, and ordnance.

Weaknesses in Japan's economic structure increased the difficulties of this manpower shortage. A primitive agriculture absorbed nearly half of

Japan's civilian labor force. In February 1944, agriculture, forestry, and fishing absorbed 46.8 percent of the total civilian labor force, with manufacturing, mining, and construction taking 32.5 percent. In October 1940, the corresponding figures had been 44.3 and 26.8 percent.

Other factors added to the difficulty of securing a labor force adequate to man the munitions industries. Even in 1941 there was no longer a reserve of adult unemployed workers. Mobilization of labor thus meant, for the most part, just a shifting of workers from one occupation to another. Between October 1940 and February 1944, after adjustment for students not yet added to the labor force in the latter month,[9] there was a net gain of only 944,000 in the Japanese civilian labor force. Male workers, which show an actual decrease of about 300,000, were drained off by the military and only partially replaced by women, among whom the gainfully employed increased by some 1,400,000 in the 1940–44 period.

As mentioned above, Japan's labor force was also marked by qualitative deficiencies. There was an exceedingly small reserve of skilled workers, with insufficient attention devoted to training programs in the prewar period. When such programs were finally instituted, it was no longer possible to keep the supply of skilled workers abreast of industrial expansion. Uncontrolled military conscription, with only slight provision for deferment, also cut into the skilled labor force.

After 1942, during which year requirements were met with ease, manpower difficulties became greater year by year. By June 1943 it was evident that the early pool of nonessential civilian production workers had been largely exhausted and that new sources had to be tapped. In late 1943 and early 1944 male workers were debarred from working in 17 categories of industry. Tighter controls were established over the nation's 1.8 million day laborers, and increasing numbers of students were brought into factories for limited periods. Some prisoners of war and penitentiary inmates were placed in the labor force. The maximum age for labor conscription was advanced from 40 to 45 years. Labor conscription placed 699,728 male workers in essential industries in 1943, raising to 1.3 million the total number conscripted since 1939. Large additional numbers of workers were "frozen" to their jobs.

In 1944 the government turned largely to students and women for solution of the growing manpower problem. All remaining restrictions on student mobilization were removed in April and industry began absorbing them in greatly increased numbers. By the end of the war, more than three million students had been successfully placed in industry. A special effort to enroll women in the labor force had more limited results. The Women's Volunteer Corps, organized in March 1944, succeeded in mobilizing 470,000 women for factory work. During the last year of the war the armed services reversed their previous indiscriminate conscription policy. The military authorities, in this period, granted 850,000 permanent deferments and 1,600,000 temporary deferments, even managing to demobilize and return small numbers of skilled workers to essential plants. In 1944–45 the government also resorted to shifting workers from one essential industry to another deemed even more essential.

TABLE 21.—*Percentage distribution of civilian labor force by industry and sex, Japan proper, Oct. 1, 1940 and Feb. 22, 1944*

Industry	Oct. 1, 1940			Feb. 22, 1944		
	Total	Male	Female	Total	Male	Female
Civilian labor force__	100. 0	100. 0	100. 0	100. 0	100. 0	100. 0
Agriculture and forestry_____	42. 6	33. 5	56. 6	42. 3	30. 3	59. 0
Fishing_____	1. 7	2. 4	. 5	1. 5	2. 1	. 6
Mining_____	1. 8	2. 7	. 6	2. 5	3. 7	1. 0
Manufacturing and construction_____	25. 0	31. 3	15. 3	30. 0	39. 3	17. 0
Commerce_____	15. 0	15. 2	14. 7	7. 5	6. 1	9. 3
Transportation and communication___	4. 2	6. 2	1. 2	5. 2	7. 5	2. 0
Government and professional_____	6. 8	7. 7	5. 3	9. 2	10. 3	7. 6
Domestic service_____	2. 2	. 2	5. 3	1. 5	. 3	3. 1
Others_____	. 7	. 8	. 5	. 4	. 4	. 4

The slowing down of Japan's war economy, first evidence in basic industry during 1944, was, however, not primarily attributable to labor scarcity, the quality of the workers available, or the administration of manpower mobilization. These factors had some influence in cutting down Japan's ability to hold the mid-1944 production level, but the primary cause was the growing

---

[9] As of February 1944, Table 22 shows a total civilian labor force of 31,657,000, with 18,411,000 males and 13,246,000 females. Adding the students, to make the data comparable to October 1940, the corresponding total becomes 33,427,000, with 19,415,000 males and 14,012,000 females.

[Thousands of persons]

	Total	
	Oct. 1, 1940	Feb. 22, 1944
Agriculture	13, 842	13, 376
Marine products	543	464
Mining	598	805
Manufacturing and construction	8, 132	9, 494
Commerce	4, 882	2, 364
Transportation and communication	1, 364	1, 650
Government and professional	2, 145	2, 900
Domestic service	709	473
Others	218	131
Total	32, 436	[1] 31, 657
		[2] 33, 427
Male		
Agriculture	6, 618	5, 569
Marine products	476	380
Mining	529	681
Manufacturing and construction	6, 179	7, 243
Commerce	3, 006	1, 127
Transportation and communication	1, 214	1, 385
Government and professional	1, 515	1, 895
Domestic service	39	58
Others	154	73
Total	19, 730	[1] 18, 411
		[2] 19, 415
Female		
Agriculture	7, 223	7, 807
Marine products	67	84
Mining	69	124
Manufacturing and construction	1, 954	2, 251
Commerce	1, 876	1, 237
Transportation and communication	150	265
Government and professional	680	1, 005
Domestic service	670	415
Others	64	58
Total	12, 753	[1] 13, 246
		[2] 14, 012

[1] To make territorial areas comparable to the 1940 census, it is necessary to add about 140,000 (with 32,000 males and 108,000 females) to the total.

[2] Adjusted for students not yet enrolled in labor force, and other statistical differences between the 1940 and 1944 census.

shortage of raw materials. Imports of coking coal, iron ore, bauxite and oil, to name but the most significant commodities, had begun to fall off late in calendar 1943 and were progressively curtailed throughout 1944. For lack of these imports the Japanese economy was in effect drying up at the roots from six months to a year before the period of intensive air attack and ultimate collapse in 1945.

IMPACT ON THE CIVILIAN ECONOMY

Resources of the Japanese civilian economy were much smaller than those of most other belligerent powers. To the extent that such resources existed, however, they were drafted in 1943–44 more completely in the services of war production. The pressure of the war effort on the civilian population became progressively greater during the war years. As more and more manpower, civilian goods, productive facilities, and civilian supplies were diverted to the war machine, consumers' outlays for goods and services declined from 26.7 to 18.8 billions of 1940 yen from 1940 to 1944—a decline of 30 percent.

Although the food situation at the beginning of the war was satisfactory, Japan's dependence on imports for almost one-fifth of rice requirements, and about four-fifths for such staples as sugar and soybeans necessitated great care in the handling of food distribution. In preparation for war, a rice rationing system in the six largest Japanese cities was initiated during April 1941. Shortly after Pearl Harbor, rice rationing was made country-wide. During the war years, the food situation rapidly deteriorated due to lowered imports, the drain upon manpower, and poor crop yields. Domestic food production in 1944 was about 25 percent below the prewar average. Rice imports declined from 2.5 million metric tons in 1941 to 875,000 tons in 1944, and by the end of fiscal 1944, the rice reserve was exhausted. This decline was only partly offset by trippling grain imports from Manchuria. The supply of fish and marine products was sharply curtailed, due to manpower shortages and restricted fishing waters.

The food position became more alarming as the war went on and necessitated a tightening of the rationing system, with the major emphasis on channeling available supplies to essential workers and special segments of the population. The average caloric intake of the civilian population in 1944 was estimated to have declined about 20 percent from the not too high level of 2,250 calories per day in 1941—substantially below the minimum requirement of 2,160 calories.

Clothing supplies were affected to a much greater extent than most other nondurable consumers' goods as a result of the diversion of the major portion of the textile industry's facilities to aircraft production, and the cutting off of most imports of textiles. The large cotton spinning industry provided the greatest single resource within the civilian economy. Major reductions in this industry had begun in 1942, but the cuts went much deeper in 1943–44. The workers were mobilized for military service or the war industries, machinery was turned into scrap, and the buildings were used to house war factories.

TABLE 23.—*Reduction in the cotton industry, calendar years 1937–44*

Calendar year	Spindles	Workers
1937	12, 165, 000	208, 154
1941	11, 435, 000	164, 095
1942	8, 646, 000	115, 605
1943	4, 166, 000	80, 977
1944	3, 593, 000	56, 000

From this remnant cotton goods industry, a much greater proportion of output was usurped by the military for war use. By 1943–44, as shown in table 24, the military were taking more than half of the reduced supply instead of the minute fraction of a far greater supply taken in 1937. Much the same picture is presented by the woolen industry. The cut-down for the civilian population between these years was staggering. In 1937 the net supply of cotton cloth for civilian use had totaled 2,184 million square yards. By 1943 the Japanese civilians were reduced to 51 million square yards. Little or no additional silk or synthetic fiber was available to compensate for the loss of the cotton cloth.

TABLE 24.—*Allocation of cotton and wool cloth supply, calendar years 1937–44*

(Millions of square yards)

Calendar year	Cotton cloth			Wool cloth		
	Total	Civilian	Military	Total	Civilian	Military
1937	2, 214. 0	2, 184. 0	30. 0	259. 5	248. 9	10. 6
1941	449. 2	310. 2	139. 0	83. 1	62. 5	20. 6
1942	353. 3	182. 4	170. 9	66. 0	39. 1	26. 9
1943	283. 9	51. 0	332. 9	71. 8	43. 0	28. 8
1944	375. 3	174. 6	200. 7	54. 3	19. 3	35. 0

Civilian supplies of furniture in 1944 were only about one-half the prewar volume while most of the durable goods had almost completely disappeared from the market.

Although the supply for the medical care of civilians was maintained at fairly high levels, the nation's health was endangered by severe shortages of drugs, medical supplies, proper housing, and lighting and heating materials.

Residential construction declined approximately 75 percent from 1941 to 1944. Despite the ever-increasing demand resulting from the concentration of workers in the large industrial areas, building materials were diverted from housing to war construction. The allocation of lumber for residential construction fell from 9.7 million koku in 1941 to only 2.2 million in 1944. In addition, some 400,000 dwelling units were destroyed in early 1944 to provide firebreaks in anticipation of large-scale B–29 raids. The feeble attempts to provide government housing for war workers did little to alleviate the housing shortage.

Chapter III

THE AIR ATTACK AGAINST JAPAN'S WAR ECONOMY

In the war against Japan, as in the European struggle, a major part of the battle was carried on in the skies. The forces engaged were, until the last months of the war, much smaller than those committed in Europe, but these operations constituted a very large fraction of the total combatant effort. Starting from a virtual zero point after the initial Japanese successes in 1941 and the first half of 1942, United States air strength in the Far East [1] rose as follows:

	First line combat aircraft	Men	Tons of bombs dropped [1]
January 1943	1,622	91,060	752
January 1944	3,174	245,677	7,558
January 1945	4,911	402,307	19,055
April 1945	5,827	439,628	40,756
July 1945	7,260	467,957	50,798

[1] Does not include mines.

Naval and marine figures for the same months are as follows:

	First line combat aircraft	Men	Tons of bombs dropped
January 1943	1,915	----------	120
January 1944	8,268	----------	1,723
January 1945	13,065	----------	3,824
April 1945	14,576	----------	9,161
July 1945	14,648	----------	5,612

Data on Japanese air strength are not entirely reliable, but the following figures give the order of magnitude of Japanese forces:

	First line combat aircraft [1]	Men
January 1942	2,520	78,500
January 1943	3,200	84,500
January 1944	4,050	117,000
January 1945	4,100	184,250
July 1945	4,600	----------

[1] Includes reconnaissance aircraft, but not the 5,500 suicide planes available by July 1945.

[1] Including theaters from Hawaii as far west as India. Does not include Eighth Army Air Force which was redeployed in the Far East but did not become operational.

The total bomb tonnage used in the entire air effort against Japan was 583,962. Of this, 161,425 tons or 28 percent were dropped on Japan proper. Naval air forces accounted for 6,740 tons, Far Eastern Air Forces for 7,109 tons, and the Twentieth AF for 147,576 tons. By contrast, the total bomb tonnage in the European theater was 2,697,433 tons, of which 1,356,808 tons were dropped on Germany.

Because of the depth of the Japanese defense perimeter and the concentration of Japanese production in the home islands, it was not until the fourth year of the war that Allied air power was able to mount heavy air attacks against Japan's war economy. Although the air campaign against shipping in 1944 was of major importance, the bomb tonnage involved was comparatively small. Until December 1944, the predominant weight of air operations was devoted to direct attacks against enemy air and surface forces. Such specific military operations, by notably increasing Japanese combat wastage, had extremely significant effects on Japanese strength, particularly in the fields of shipping and aircraft. But they were not undertaken primarily for that purpose and their success was measured in terms of their contribution to current military operations.

Basic United States strategy contemplated that the decision in the Japanese war would be attained by a ground force invasion of the Japanese islands. The bomb offensive against the Japanese home islands was initiated in November 1944 with this in mind. As in Europe, prior to D-day, the measure of success set up for strategic air action was the extent to which it would weaken enemy resistance to our ground forces *at the time of landings*. This led to selection of targets such as aircraft factories, arsenals, electronics plants, and finished military goods, the destruction of which could be expected to weaken the capabilities of the Japanese armed forces to meet ours on Kyushu beachheads in November 1945, rather than of targets constituting the more basic production facilities. The possibility of attaining this result while at the same time putting pressure on the whole Japanese economic and social order by attacking the distribution of raw material, energy, and finished and semifinished goods was not actively considered until the beginning of April 1945. While it was recognized as not impossible that Japan would surrender prior to invasion, it was felt that intelligence appraisals of political and morale factors were bound to be so uncertain that target selection could safely be made only on the assumption that ground force action would be inevitable.[2]

Air operations against Japan's war economy fall into two main categories: Those that contributed to blockade (countershipping), and those that were directed against industrial and urban area targets.

COUNTERSHIPPING

Air attacks against shipping were carried on throughout the war. Until November 1943 they were undertaken almost exclusively as part of military and naval operations, first as delaying actions in the Philippines, Malaya, Netherlands, Indies, and Burma; later in support of the long offensives in the Southwest and Central Pacific. Land-based aircraft of the Thirteenth, Fifth, and Seventh Army Air Forces, and of Navy and Marine units were active both in search and attack. Carrier-based forces mainly attacked large shipping concentrations.

In the fall of 1943, attacks against two Japanese main economic overseas shipping routes—that between Singapore and Japan and that between the iron ore shipping points on the Yangtze and Japan, which had hitherto been maintained by submarines alone—were supplemented by Fourteenth AF operations from China bases. These were the first air attacks of any magnitude directed primarily against Japan's economy. They took the form of sea sweeps, bombardment of shipping and ship loading and repair facilities at mainland ports from Hainan to Shanghai, and the bombing, mining, and strafing of Yangtze shipping and ports.

In the spring and summer of 1944, effort which would have otherwise been available for this campaign was used to establish Twentieth Bomber Command bases in China and to supply B–29 operations against nonshipping targets from these bases. The limited capacity of the air supply

[2] It is to be noted, however, that in spite of the preparation-for-invasion concept of strategic air attack, a number of urban area target chosen by the field command of the Twentieth Army Air Force were more consistent with an objective of securing a decision by air power alone. See the discussion on later pages of B–29 operations from the Marianas.

operation over the "Hump" had been the limiting factor on Fourteenth AF operations from the beginning, and adequate logistic support of both air forces was impossible.

In October 1944, a task force sweep against the Ryukyus brought Japanese economic life lines for the first time under naval air attack, and with the fall of the Philippines late in the same year, land-based air power, not hampered by logistic limitations, was brought within range of the main enemy sea routes. A carrier sweep of the South China Sea against shipping concentrations at sea and in ports from Cape St. Jacques to the Ryukyus was carried out in January 1945, and until the Japanese abandoned the route in March 1945, FEAF (Far Eastern Air Forces) and land-based naval aircraft hunted down enemy shipping in the South and East China Seas and along the length of the China and Formosan coasts.

Even before the securing of Okinawa in June 1945, FEAF and long-range land-based naval air units, operating from the island, extended their countershipping activities to the Yellow Sea, the Korean Straits, and the waters around Kyushu. These activities continued until the conclusion of hostilities.

In the final months of the war, several carrier strikes were mounted against the Japanese home islands. Merchant shipping concentrations were not made a primary target, but significant shipping attacks occured incident to the main operations, particularly in the southern Hokkaido-Northern Honshu strike of July.

Beginning at the end of March 1945, the B–29's took a powerful hand in the shipping attack. An aerial mining campaign was undertaken against all still active harbors and home island shipping routes. It operated not only against overseas traffic, but against the even more important inter-island movement and in the late stages of the war was extended to the Korean ports. Approximately 6 percent of the B–29 sorties flown during this period were devoted to this effort, and more would have been flown had enough mines been available. In all, 12,000 mines were dropped on a total of about 20 target areas.

INDUSTRIAL AND URBAN TARGETS— EARLY ATTACKS

Until June 1944 there was virtually no industry of importance to the Japanese war economy within range of United States air bases. The phosphate rock mining facilities on Nauru and the Celebes nickel concentration were successfully put out of action in 1943. An attack was made on the oil-refinery and storage at Balikpapan in August 1943. With the exception of the Doolittle raid of April 1942, which was obviously in too little strength to achieve anything but a morale effect in the United States, these were the only raids on Japanese industrial targets prior to the activation of the Twentieth Bomber Command B–29 bases in China.

TWENTIETH BOMBER COMMAND B–29's

Twentieth Bomber Command operations, which, as we have noted, imposed a limitation on Fourteenth Army Air Force operations, had as their primary objective the destruction of Manchurian and northern Kyushu steel capacity.[3] Two attacks were made by the Twentieth Bomber Command on the Yawata steel plant in Kyushu and three on the Showa plant at Anshan, Manchuria, the total weight dropped on the two targets being, respectively, 221 and 550 tons. Results are discussed in the next chapter.

Toward the end of October 1944, top priority was given to aircraft targets, and between 7 July 1944 and 6 January 1945 some 500 tons were dropped on the Omura Aircraft Assembly Plant, the sole important Japanese aircraft factory within range from Chengtu.

Attacks of 36 and 56 tons, respectively, were made against the naval dockyards at Sasebo and the town of Nagasaki in July and August of 1944.

Of some 5,200 tons of bombs dropped by B–29's operating from China bases between 6 June 1944 and 17 January 1945, over 1,000 tons were dropped on a total of four Japanese targets.

Insignificant attacks with from 2 to 60 tons of bombs were made on various Chinese ports by aircraft unable to bomb their primary targets and one heavy attack, primarily for tactical purposes, was made against Hankow.

In support of the Philippines campaign, airfields and air installations targets on Formosa received some 2,000 tons of bombs from China-based B–29's.

[3] The extent to which raw material shortage in Japan had already reduced the operation of the Yawata area steel plants was unknown to United States intelligence agencies and both the output and the exports to Japan of the Manchurian steel plants were overestimated. While these facts conditioned the nature of the targets actually chosen, they were, of course, not the determining factor in the decision to base B–29's in China. Target appraisal prior to the movement had indicated that top priority should be given to shipping rather than steel plants.

Operating from India bases, the Twentieth Bomber Command, in January, February, and March 1945, mined the harbors of Singapore and Saigon, and two mining missions were flown along the Yangtze during the same months, presumably from China bases.

Burmese and Siamese railroads, Singapore and Saigon dockyards, and tactical targets in Burma and Malaya were the principal objects of the balance of Twentieth Bomber Command attacks.

MARIANAS B–29's

The air attack on industrial objectives in Japan proper did not get under way until the end of November 1944, when the Marianas B–29 bases became operational. Between 24 November and 9 March 1945, the effort was directed almost exclusively against aircraft targets. Bombing accuracy was poor, loads were light and opposition was serious.

At the beginning of March it was decided to make night incendiary attacks on the major Japanese cities at comparatively low altitudes (5,000–8,000 feet). This decision was made partly for operational reasons and in the belief that the industrial results of urban-area attacks would be far more significant than they had been in Germany, because of the greater fire vulnerability of Japanese cities and the importance of small industry to Japanese war production. It was further thought that destruction of the principal urban areas would prevent any substantial recuperation of the aircraft industry and prevent the conversion to its use of other industrial facilities, particularly machine tools. Finally, there was a strong opinion, that the will of the Japanese people and of its government to resist could be greatly weakened and perhaps destroyed by urban area attacks. Between 9 March and 16 April 1945, 53.5 square miles of the cities of Tokyo, Kawasaki, Yokohama, Nagoya, Kobe, and Osaka were burned out in low-level night incendiary attacks, and the new operating technique became firmly established.

At the end of March, B–29 operations were, as noted above, broadened to include sea mining. From that time on, about 6 percent of the total effort was devoted to this target system.

Early in April the main weight of attack was shifted back to precision targets largely because the unprecedented heavy bomb lift which resulted from lowering the operating altitude in the urban-area attacks had depleted the supply of incendiaries on hand at the operating bases. In the first half of the month, effort was again concentrated on aircraft plants which still had top priority in target directives because of the kamikaze threat and our lack of knowledge of the drop in production which had occurred as a result of Japanese plant dispersal efforts. Though some evidences of dispersal had been discovered, there was nothing in the information at hand or in the British or German experience to indicate the extent of collapse in production which had, in fact, occurred.

April also saw precision-bombing attacks on two chemical plants which were believed to be making tetraethyl lead.

During the last half of April and the first half of May, virtually the entire B–29 effort was diverted from strategic targets to the bombardment of Kyushu airfields in support of the Okinawa operation.

Beginning in May, a considerable tonnage was directed against oil targets, and from the third week in June on, about 20 percent of the available B–29 effort was so employed. The 315th Wing, with special precision radar equipment, was devoted exclusively to this target system until the close of the war.

In the latter part of June, urban area incendiary attacks were resumed and from then until the end of the war continued on an increasing scale, absorbing about 70 percent of B–29 bomb tonnage. Although an effort was made to direct these attacks toward targets the destruction of which would do damage to industrial production, the preponderant purpose appears to have been to secure the heaviest possible morale and shock effect by widespread attack upon the Japanese civilian population. To this end, the practice was adopted, in July, of broadcasting, in advance, the names of towns marked for destruction. Certain of the cities attacked had virtually no industrial importance. Others were significant only as transportation centers, but results of earlier attacks had demonstrated that incendiary bombs were ineffective against railroad targets. During this period, 55 towns were subjected to incendiary strikes. Large percentages of all these targets were burned out. In 15 cases the figures ran from 70 to 90 percent and in 14 cases from 50 to 70 percent.

In May, June, and July, airframe plants and certain other aircraft factories were a principal target for precision attack. Seven thousand and

forty-five tons, amounting to about 8 percent of the total effort during these months, were expended against these objectives.

During June, July, and August, 5,270 tons of bombs were dropped in eight precision attacks on five army and navy arsenals. The same period saw three attacks on two light metals processors (1,020 tons) and one heavy electrical equipment producer (806 tons).

FAR EASTERN AIR FORCES

The liberation of the Philippines brought Formosan targets within range of the Far Eastern Air Forces, comprising the Fifth, Seventh, and Thirteenth Air Forces. During the ensuing months, airfields, aluminum plants, power plants serving these, urban areas, railroads, ports, and shipping were subjected to attack. The distribution of this tonnage is shown in table 25.

TABLE 25.—*Distribution of 5th Air Force effort against Formosan targets*

	Tonnage total
Airdromes	4, 851
Buildings, urban areas	4, 565
Industry	1, 547
Railroads	791
Harbor facilities	1, 449
Antiaircraft positions	677
Oil storage	506
Military supplies	518
Shipping	380
Others	520
Total	15, 804

The primary mission of the operations against Formosa was a tactical one, the neutralization of enemy air strength on the island in support of United States campaigns in the Philippines and Okinawa. Two thirds of the available bomb tonnage was directed at Formosan urban areas, ports, railroads, and industry on the theory that this would assist the ground campaign in Luzon by affecting resupply of Japanese ground forces.

Seven thousand one hundred tons of bombs were dropped on Japanese targets by the Fifth and Seventh Air Forces between June 1945 and the end of the war. The distribution of this tonnage among target systems is set out in table 26.

TABLE 26.—*Distribution of tonnage by Fifth and Seventh AF between June 1945 and end of war*

	Tons	Percentage
Tactical	2,242	31.5
Countershipping	1,287	18.1
Ships, 629		
Ports, 640		
Naval installations, 18		
Land communications	1,103	15.5
Urban areas	1,514	21.3
Miscellaneous (principally industrial)	507	7.1
Unidentified	458	6.5
Total	7,111	100.0

TABLE 27.—*Distribution of bomb tonnage by Naval Aircraft on Japanese targets*

	Tons	Percentage
Airfields	3,176	47.1
Warships	1,282	19.0
Military targets	442	6.6
Countershipping	1,095	16.2
Merchant ships, 834		
Harbors, 261		
Industry	603	8.9
Transportation	142	2.1
Total	6,740	99.9

It will be noted that over half of the countershipping effort and 9 percent of the total was expended against port installations, although, at this stage of the war, the merchant fleet had been so reduced that these facilities were used to only small fraction of capacity. Over 35 percent of the effort was scattered over urban areas and industrial targets of minor significance. The railroad attack, amounting to 15 percent of the tonnage, was centered on the rail net serving the rural areas of southern Kyushu.[4]

IWO-BASED FIGHTERS

P-51's were based on Iwo primarily to provide escort for B-29's. Strafing attacks were carried out mainly against airfields and railroads, but the distance from base was too great to permit any substantial weight of attack.

NAVAL AIRCRAFT

Carrier strikes were made against the Japanese islands in 1945. The main effort was expended against operational aircraft, airfields, and naval vessels already rendered inoperative by lack of oil. Attacks were also made on several aircraft plants, on oil depots, harbors, and shipping. The tonnage was distributed among targets as follows in Table 27.

[4] One mission scheduled against the Kammon Tunnel entrance was frustrated by foul weather and this particular target was later specifically assigned to other forces. There remained, however, at least four vital rail yards in the area, Moji, Shimonoseki, Hatabu, and Tobata, as well as bridges and yards on the Sanyo-, Kagoshima, and Chikuho lines which were essential to the movement of Kyushu and Ube district coal.

Over one-third of the effort against airfields was expended in support of the Okinawa campaign. Of the balance, the bulk, particularly in the early strikes, was part of the expense of conducting the operation and was to a large extent for the purpose of gaining control of the Japanese air.

Of the countershipping effort, about one-quarter was expended against harbor facilities, of which, as noted in the discussion of Far Eastern Air Force attack, the enemy had a plethora.

Long-range land-based naval aircraft from Okinawa flew shipping search and attack missions over the East China and Yellow Seas and Korean Straits. The effort of this force and that of FEAF, against shipping, supplemented each other. These naval aircraft also attacked the main Korean rail lines.

TENTH AIR FORCE

The mission of the Tenth AF was tactical support of the ground forces in Burma. The bulk of bombardment was directed against Burmese railroads and river traffic in support of ground operations. Techniques of attack and tactical target selection appear to have been highly developed. Use of air power as a means of large scale transport and supply of ground troops was a prominent feature of the late stages of the operations of this air force.

ELEVENTH AIR FORCE

This air force was based in the Aleutians. During the period of active fighting in this area its mission was tactical. After the recovery of Attu and Kiska, its principal targets were Japanese military installations and shipping in the Kuriles.

Chapter IV

EFFECT OF ALLIED AIR OPERATIONS ON THE JAPANESE WAR ECONOMY

In August 1945, the Japanese war economy was bankrupt. Although accumulated stocks of military supplies were still considerable, the current output of aircraft, armaments, and oil had dropped to levels insufficient to support any long-sustained defense against invasion. The destruction of a major portion of the plants in these industries rendered the possibility of recuperation negligible. While full-scale suicide effort could have been supported by the supplies on hand, they not only would have been exhausted in a few months of full-scale combat but were qualitatively inadequate, with such essential items as tanks, heavy artillery, and field-communications equipment largely lacking. A serious shortage of trucks and fuel made the Japanese army dependent on a highly vulnerable and overloaded railroad system and reduced dangerously its mobility. Overseas supplies of foodstuffs amounting to 10 percent of the national per capita subsistence requirements were cut off. Edible fish supplies had been cut 35 percent. Domestic rice crops were around 10 percent below normal and fertilizer shortages threatened to cause a severe drop in domestic food production during the coming rice year. These factors threatened famine by the summer of 1946.

About 33 percent of the urban population, which included a major fraction of Japan's industrial workers, had lost its housing, household goods, and clothing, and been driven to rely on the bounty of relatives and friends. There was no prospect of replacing these houses and goods in the immediate future.

Overseas shipping routes had been almost completely denied and vital coast-wise movement fundamentally impaired. As a result, the supplies of basic raw materials such as coking coal, iron ore, and oil, large at the beginning of the war, were exhausted and their replenishment had become impossible. The aluminum industry was at a standstill, steel production could not be expected to exceed 20 percent of its wartime peak, coal production was declining disastrously and coal distribution in Honshu would have become impossible once the threatened railroad attack materialized. Under these circumstances it was obvious that the invasion would find Japan without means for prolonged resistance, and that, even if it were initially repelled, disintegration of the entire economy would occur in a short time.

To what extent was this destruction of the economic base of the Japanese war machine the result of the operations of Allied air power as outlined in the preceding chapter?

TRANSPORTATION

Shipping

Few countries in the world have been more dependent upon shipping than was Japan during 1941–45. Her industrial activity and her food supply depended on a steady flow of shipments from abroad and between the various Japanese islands. Even at the outset of the war, as we have seen, the Japanese-owned merchant fleet was not large enough to meet the needs of the economy and to meet the logistic requirements of her forces in the Pacific areas. The original shortage of shipping space was aggravated by the counteroffensive of the United States, which resulted in ship sinking that exceeded new construction.

As will be shown presently, the deterioration of the marine transportation system had a critical effect on most aspects of the Japanese war economy. Air power played a large part in achieving this. Air attacks on shipping in the Pacific war constituted a part of the sea blockade enforced by submarines, air power, and mining. This blockade resulted in the closing, to the Japanese, of all major sea lines, including home island coastal routes. It reduced the Japanese merchant marine from a first-class fleet of around 6.6 million tons in early 1942 to a remnant of 1.5 millions, much of it inoperable and predominantly composed of slow, comparatively small and inefficient vessels.

First phase.—In the first year of the war, the contribution of air power to the blockade was secondary. The main burden was borne by the submarines which alone, during this period, had the range and ability to penetrate deeply the defensive perimeter established by the enemy.

Second phase.—During the ensuing 21 months (November 1942–July 1944), the bulk of ship sinkings continued to be made by submarines and it was their operations which caused the abandonment of such major shipping lanes outside the tactical areas as the routes along the east and south coasts of Honshu, Hokkaido, Kyushu, and Skikoku. But during this time, as advanced bases brought more targets within range of our land based air patrols, and as our carrier forces built up their strength, air power moved steadily toward a position of full partnership in the enterprise. During the first 11 months of the war, loss of only 123,000 g. r. t. (18 percent of total tonnage sunk) was caused by air attack. During the period November 1943–July 1944, however, sinkings of 897,000 g. r. t., or 29.5 percent of total sinkings for the period were the result of direct air attack on ships, or of aerial mining. In addition, Fourteenth AF bombing, strafing and mining of shipping on the Yangtze, which were the earliest important strategic air operations of the Japanese war, had, by the end of 1943, interdicted light ship traffic on this vital iron ore route, and greatly increased ship turn-about time and marine casualties. Chinese ore shipments to Japan during the January–March quarter of 1943 had amounted to 91 percent of Japanese receipts of Fe from overseas.[1] Owing largely to the attacks on Yangtze shipping, shipments declined steadily until in the January–March 1944 quarter they reached a level of only 55 percent of those for the same quarter of the previous year. By July 1944, the Fourteenth AF despite the logistic problems which always limited its capabilities, had succeeded in closing the Yangtze almost completely and imports of Chinese iron ore fell in the July–September quarter of 1944 to 25 percent of their January–March 1943 level. It is, of course, true

---

[1] Pig iron imports plus iron ore imports adjusted for iron content and an estimated 3 percent smelting loss.

that during this quarter, a drop would have occurred in any event owing to the increasing tightness of shipping. The drop in bottoms available, however, was not nearly as drastic as the drop in ore movement. Sea sweeps by the Fourteenth AF, in addition to sinking ships, had the by-product for several months of forcing Japanese shipping routes further offshore and thus increasing their vulnerability to submarine attack.

As pointed out in the preceding chapter, supply difficulties compelled the Fourteenth AF to curtail operations in the spring and summer of 1944 in order to permit China-based B–29 operations. In addition, the Japanese, stung by the results of the 14th's attacks, undertook a major land campaign in China which resulted in November 1944 in the capture of those bases from which operations could best be conducted against the Singapore-Japan sea lanes.

Third phase.—In the final 12 months of the war, air power played a decisive part in the blockade. The capture of the Philippines and later of Okinawa, meant that, for the first time during the war, fully supplied land based aircraft could be located in strength at points from which the principal shipping arteries of the enemy—the routes from Singapore, from North China and finally from Korea—were readily accessible to sustained attack. In addition, carrier forces were able to operate in enemy waters. The ships sinkings caused by direct air attack jumped to 1,379,000 g. r. t. or to about 50 percent of the total for the 12 months. More important, the actual, and in some cases the suspected, ability of our air forces to patrol the routes to Singapore, and across the Yellow Sea and Korean Straits led to virtual abandonment of the Singapore and Yellow Sea route by March. Because of air attack, sailings in the Korean Straits were restricted to the hours of darkness in July 1945. The interdiction of the Southern and Yellow Sea routes produced a markedly more rapid effect on cargo movement than would have been achieved merely by the reduction in the number of ships available during this period.

Aerial mining also contributed largely to the sea blockade of Japan during the last 12 months of the war. Mining of the Yangtze played an important part in the reduction of iron ore shipments from China discussed above. Mining of other mainland ports such as Singapore also caused ship sinkings. The principal effort, however, was carried out by B–29's from the Mariannas bases against Shimonoseki Straits and inland Japanese sea ports. As indicated, this campaign began at the end of March 1945. By July it had reduced traffic through Shimonoseki Straits to a trickle (12 percent of the peak level), and had severely reduced the usefulness of the Japan Sea–Honshu ports which were the only ones still comparatively free from direct air and submarine threat. Sinkings due to aircraft mining during the period amounted to 353,000 g. r. t. or over 12 percent of the 12 month total. In addition, more ships were damaged than sunk, and repair of most of these became well nigh impossible since access to all but a small fraction of Japanese ship repair facilities could be gained only by passing the mine fields at Shimonoseki. Submarine attack was well maintained during this period, despite the restricted and relatively sheltered areas in which Japanese shipping operated. It accounted for 1,043,000 g. r. t. or 37.5 percent of total tonnage sunk. Together with aerial mining, it carried the blockade into the Japan Sea, the only area in which at the end of the war, Japanese shipping was not subject to direct bombing attack.

SUMMARY OF SINKINGS

The tonnage of Japanese merchant vessels sunk by submarine, aircraft and mines during the different phases of the Pacific war is set out in table 26.

1. The sinkings tabulated above constitute about 92 percent of Japanese wartime shipping losses. The balance were marine casualties. Some of these were due to increased hazards imposed by Allied countershipping action. Contributing to such casualties were inadequate ship maintenance caused by shortage of bottoms, running without lights, use of more dangerous routes (often at night) and the like. No quantitive value can be attached to such factors, but they were significant.

2. After 1942, mining was almost entirely an aircraft activity. Land based air patrols could establish and maintain continuous interdiction. The limited time during which it was felt advisable to hold a carrier force in a given area prevented complete and continuous interdiction. Where the loss of the last available ports was threatened, the mine threat was insufficient to cause stoppage of traffic, and movement continued on a reduced scale despite heavy sinkings.

It will be observed from the foregoing discussion that it is a misnomer to speak of the "naval," "air," or "submarine" blockade of Japan, par-

TABLE 28—*Japanese merchant ship sinkings by Allied action 1941–45*

[Thousands of gross registered tons]

	Submarines		Aircraft		Mines	
	Tonnage sunk	Percent of total	Tonnage sunk	Percent of total	Tonnage sunk	Percent of total
December 1941–October 1942. (Outbreak of war to beginning of important countershipping air operations in Guadalcanal campaign)	480	71.6	123	18.3	68	10.1
November 1942–October 1943 (Guadalcanal to beginning of major 14th AF operations against shipping)	1,188	74.1	374	23.3	41	2.6
November 1943–August 1944 (Beginning of 14th AF countershipping operations to beginning of carrier strikes supporting Philippines operation)	2,150	70.6	846	27.7	51	1.7
September 1944–August 1945 (Philippine campaign to Japan Surrender)	1,043	37.6	1,379	49.7	353	12.7
Entire war	4,861	60.1	2,722	33.6	513	6.3

ticularly in the light of the important role played by interdiction of routes. Each arm, each weapon played a significant and indispensable part. The submarine predominated at the start and in the middle period, carrier- and land-based aircraft at the end.

THE ALLIED OFFENSIVE

In weighing the effect of submarine and air attack against the Japanese merchant marine, the wastage of Japanese shipping caused by the requirements of the military establishment must be kept in mind. The Japanese strategic plan had called for the immediate release of a large tonnage of Army and Navy operated vessels as soon as operations in the Dutch East Indies and Malaya were concluded. The inception of the allied counter offensive in the late summer of 1942 and the maintenance of pressure against Japanese peripheral positions continuously thereafter prevented release of substantial amounts of Army and Navy merchant vessels for cargo movement until all the outlying positions had been lost. Throughout 1942 and 1943, no more than 50–55 percent of the total merchant tonnage could be made available solely for cargo carriage and it was not until December 1944, when the South was virtually cut off and all of the outlying positions were lost, that more than 62 percent could be utilized for purely economic purpose.[2]

Our military and naval operations diverted shipping from cargo transportation. They also brought Japanese shipping within easy range of our air forces, both ashore and afloat, and of our submarines, exposing it to severe losses. The heaviest and most concentrated ship casualties of the war were inflicted on the Japanese in connection operations against the Marshalls and the Philippines. In the course of these campaigns, around 2 million tons were sent to the bottom by air, submarine, and mining attack.

The attack against Japan's shipping and shipping routes have, for convenience, been referred to in this report as "blockade". In fact, it was not a true blockade in the sense of the slow economic strangulation applied to the Confederacy in 1861–64 or to Germany in 1914-18, but rather, an active fighting campaign in which the infantrymen and marines in the Solomons, Gilberts, Marshalls, New Guinea, Marianas, and Philippines not only secured the bases necessary for the operations of the naval and air arms, but in a very real sense shared with the men who dropped the bombs and aimed the torpedoes, the credit for the sunken wrecks strewn around the harbors and along the bottom of the Pacific from Cape Esperance, Rabaul and Truk to Manila Bay.

Land Transportation

Blockade forced a shift of a constantly increasing portion of coastwise traffic to the rails after the early months of 1943. This additional burden increased the vulnerability of an already heavily laden railroad system. No systematic air attacks exploited this weakness. A single carrier-based air attack in July 1945 struck the rail ferries

---

[2] It is, of course, true that on occasion Army and Navy ("A" & "B") ships carried commercial cargo. Aside from oil, however, the amount of cargo moved by such vessels was small.

between Hokkaido and Honshu with brilliant success. Out of 12 ferries, 10 were destroyed completely and 2 damaged. The capacity of the link, over which 30 percent of Hokkaido's coal shipments moved to Honshu, was reduced by 82 percent, with no prospect of recovery for 9 months. Other strafing attacks and naval bombardments had inconsequential results. The urban fire raids, while hampering local transport, were ineffective against freight movement, whether through direct damage, destruction of rolling stock, or effect on labor supply. There is no evidence that, as a direct result of any urban attack, the railroads were unable to handle any freight offered for transport. Physical damage was minor and consisted principally of the destruction of transit sheds and perhaps one-half of 1 percent of the freight car pool.

A more important factor, in limiting Japanese economic capabilities, was the state of local transportation. Urban area attacks, which destroyed a considerable number of vehicles, at the same time increased the demand for local transport. Manufacture of motor vehicles, however, had been declining from the outset of the war because of diminishing steel allocations. Though only a single 4,000 pound experimental bomb was dropped on a truck plant in June 1945, a panicky dispersal effort shut off any hopes for further manufacture of vehicles.

It should be noted, however, that in July the decision was made to concentrate strategic air effort against the railroads. A program of systematic attack had been worked out and the first operation in pursuance of it took place on the last day of the war. The Japanese statements that in case of such attacks they would have been unable to continue food distribution probably assess the situation correctly. The chapter of this report entitled "Postscript on Target Selection" attempts to assess the required effort and probable results of such a program.

BASIC COMMODITIES

Steel

The inadequacy of the Japanese steel industry to support a war against a major industrial power has been repeatedly pointed out. The history of Japan's war economy, even before the blockade affected her position, is largely of an attempt to make up for the loss of supplies of iron from overseas and to spread a limited steel supply over a number of competing and ever-increasing needs. Nearly all the deficiencies in plants, raw materials, and military supplies which so seriously plagued the enemy's war effort can be traced to these causes. Limitations of electric steel capacity were at times a further disturbing factor.

The blockade exploited and greatly aggravated these weaknesses. From April 1943 on, imports of iron, in ore and pig form, began to decline. Steel production cuts were staved off, however, for over a year, since stockpiles provided a cushion and even permitted an expansion of output during the period.

By June 1944, the day of reckoning could be postponed no longer. Iron ore stockpiles in the home island, amounting to about 2.6 million tons in December 1941, had dwindled to 800,000 tons. Chinese iron ore accounted in 1943 for 89 percent of the Fe contents of iron ore imports to Japan. This movement dropped from an average of 374,-000 tons per month in the period January–June 1943 to 252,000 tons for the following 6 months and by December 1944 to a mere 37,000 tons. The loss was principally the result of 14th Air Force bombing, mining and straffing of Yangtze shipping, but was also contributed to, particularly in the later months, by the submarine and air attacks against shipping. After June 1944, the drop in iron ore imports was closely paralleled by a drop in ingot steel production. Even before stockpiles of ore were exhausted, blast and steel furnace operations were reduced and production was allowed to fall below plan without apparent regard to the effect on scheduled production of finished goods.

In the July–September quarter of 1944 a reduction in imports of pig iron, ingot and rolled steel from Manchuria was added to the results of attack on iron ore transportation. The decline in Manchuria pig iron shipments was 28 percent from the previous quarter. In the next 3 months there was further 5 percent drop. Ingot and rolled steel exports to Japan were also reduced.

This was primarily due to the 20th Bomber Command attacks on Showa Steel, at Anshan, in July and September 1944 and secondarily to 14th AF and Chinese guerilla operations against Chinese railroads, which reduced the movement of North China coking coal to Anshan.

As a result of all these factors, monthly average finished steel production for the second half of fiscal 1944 dropped to 64 percent of the monthly average for January 1943–May 1944.

At the April–June 1945 rate of production, annual ingot steel output of around 1.5 million tons, or 18 percent of the war time peak, would have been possible. The naval bombardment of steel facilities in July 1945, however, would have prevented the processing of more than even a fraction of this amount. The Kamaishi and Wanishi steel plants were processing locally produced ores. In 1944 they handled 41 percent of total domestic ore supplies. These ores were smelted almost entirely by the use of Hokkaido coking coal. Naval surface vessel bombardments of these plants in July 1945 were successful.

Transportation between Hokkaido and Honshu was a bottleneck even before the carrier based aircraft destroyed the rail ferries. The already overloaded railroads of Honshu were in no position to move 700,000 additional tons of iron ore and 1.2 million additional tons of Hokkaido coal hundreds of miles to the idle blast furnaces in central Honshu and northern Kyushu. The strike, therefore, significantly reduced Japan's chances of using even her inadequate domestic resources of iron ore. At the close of the war, the prospect was that Japanese steel production for the balance of the year would hardly exceed an annual rate of one million tons.

The few air attacks directed against steel plants had little effect on Japanese steel supply. With the exception of China based B–29 operations the steel industry was subject to air attack only through transportation. The comparatively light (221 tons) air bombardment of the Yawata plant by Twentieth Bomber Command in June 1944 caused only a negligible drop in production. Plant capacity, unused because of lack of raw materials, could be pressed into service to compensate for such bomb damage as was inflicted. The three raids on the Anshan works were somewhat heavier in weight and appear to have caused a loss in production of approximately 200,000 tons of pig iron (15 percent of fiscal year 1943 output) 136,000 tons of ingot steel and 93,000 tons of rolled steel. The main impact was upon the availability of iron and steel for Manchurian consumption. The effect on supplies in Japan proper is uncertain but was clearly much smaller. Pig iron loss fell somewhere within a range of 3 to 5 percent of the total amount of pig iron available in Japan in 1944. The reduction in ingot steel supply, excluding electric steel, was not over 2 percent and in finished steel less than 1 percent.

Mariannas based B-29s did not specifically attack Japanese steel plants, although the incendiary campaign against urban areas included attacks on all principal steel manufacturing centers from Tokyo south. By the time these occurred, however, steel manufacturing operations had been so restricted by lack of raw materials that what little steel production remained was not materially affected.

Oil

Of less pervasive importance to the economy as a whole than steel, but of even more immediate concern to Japanese fighting capabilities, was the oil supply which largely depended on imports. As noted in chapter II, the Japanese synthetic oil industry was too small to be a substantial factor in her oil economy. Japan's planners attempted to provide against an oil shortage by building up, in the years immediately preceeding Pearl Harbor, a substantial stockpile. Despite withdrawals from stocks necessitated by the United States embargo in 1941, Japan entered the war with reserves of 43 million barrels. If she expected to fight beyond the time that these stocks might last, it was obvious that she would have to depend upon oil sources from Borneo south.

In the face of the blockade, such dependence proved to be a fatal weakness. Requirements mounted steeply during 1942 and 1943, under pressure of military operations on a scale beyond that anticipated by the Japanese war planners.

Although oil imports continued to follow a sharply arising trend up to the end of 1943, increases after the summer of 1942 were always outbalanced by rising consumption. Never could enough oil be shipped to Japan to close the gap between oil receipts and expenditures. In spite of the most stringent efforts to economize and to employ substitutes, inventories of crude oil declinded from 1941 on, fuel oil after 1937, aviation fuel from early in 1942, diesel oil from the beginning of 1943 and motor gas after June 1944. During the fall of 1944, motor gasoline and diesel oil consumption were reduced by 50 percent of their wartime peaks, fuel oil by 40 percent and aviation gasoline by 24 percent although requirements were more pressing than ever before.

In 1944, oil imports dropped sharply, falling in the October–December quarter about 33 percent from the same period of the preceeding year. This was caused by a drop in shipping efficiency under the impact of submarine and air attack. During the October–December quarter of 1944 the tanker tonnage devoted to hauling oil to the home islands was actually significantly higher than in the same period a year earlier. After February 1945, imports of oil to Japan ceased entirely, owing to interdiction of the shipping routes from the south, principally by air operations.

Such a state of affairs could obviously have but one end. Military pilot training was progressively reduced until in 1945 it reached a level of only 50 percent of the minimum number of hours previously thought necessary, with serious injury to the fighting ability of the Japanese air force. Reconnaissance flights and antisubmarine patrols were curtailed. In the face of a desperate need for bottoms, over 100,000 tons of oil-burning shipping in the home island coastal trade was laid up early in 1945. Even military trucks were converted to the use of charcoal gas. Despite these and other drastic measures which prevented further widening of the gap between receipts and consumption, oil tanks all over the industrial areas of Japan were running dry and tankage was being town down for scrap. By April 1945, naval stocks were so low that of five battleships left afloat, only one, the *Yamato*, was able to sortie against our forces invading Okinawa. The balance, along with lesser naval units, were left with skeleton crews as floating antiaircraft and coast defense batteries at the bases of Kure and Yokosuka. Later these were sunk or put out of action at their moorings by our carrier based aircraft.

By the third week in June 1945, when B-29 attacks on refineries began in earnest, stocks of crude oil had been virtually exhausted and the refineries almost entirely shut down. Only a minor fraction of the small finished products stocks still in Japanese hands were located at the points attacked and such destruction of those materials that occurred did not materially affect enemy strength. The following data give an indication of the importance of the stocks destroyed:

	Inventory as of 1 April 1945	Inventory destroyed by bombing
Aviation gasoline	1, 538, 000	61, 473
Fuel oil	1, 840, 000	125, 309
Diesel fuel	308, 000	37, 047
Motor gasoline	719, 000	12, 498
Lubricating oil	346, 000	29, 009
Crude oil	195, 000	[1] 103, 785
Other products		101, 257
Total	[2] 3, 948, 000	470, 378

[1] While this represented more than 50 percent of the remaining crude inventory the latter was sufficient for only 1.7 days of capacity operation.
[2] Incomplete.

It appears from the above that the oil attack was almost superfluous. Production had very nearly ceased before the attack, and the destruction of stocks was not significant. The gasoline required for the Ketsu Kamikaze air operations against invasion was dispersed when the B–29 and carrier attacks were made. The potentialities of the Ketsu operation remained thus undiminished.

Nor were the attacks on tetra-ethyl lead production in April 1945 more significant. The drop in TEL supplies which began in September 1944 was attributable only to a negligible degree to air attack on producing facilities. In any event, it merely paralleled the decline in aviation fuel supply resulting from blockade and had no independent effect on enemy strength.

Coal

It has been noted that Japanese coal supplies followed a rising curve through 1940, declined slightly through 1943, sharply in 1944 and then plummeted abruptly to collapse levels in 1945. The decline in 1941–43 was attributable almost entirely to reduced imports resulting from competing demands for shipping. Domestic production was sustained though "high grading" the mines but at severe cost to the capital equipment of the industry which, because of the pressing needs for armaments and ships, was not allotted sufficient steel for maintenance.

In 1944 the influence of blockade became predominant. Imports from China, the prime source of high grade coking coal, were cut to 58 percent and those from Karafuto and from Korea about 50 percent. While the drop in North China coking coal imports did not prevent smelting of the also dwindling supply of iron ore, it affected the quality of the steel produced and increased fabricating difficulties and rejections.

During this year, the blockade began also to effect domestic production. Equipment maintenance was further impaired by the increasing steel shortage and undermaintenance of earlier years, coupled with scarcity of trained manpower, began to cut into production.

The year witnessed collapse of the Japanese coal position. January saw the virtual end of Chinese coal shipments and the beginning of an almost equally rapid drop in movement from Manchuria. Domestic production was maintained until July, but shipments from Kyushu to Honshu by sea dropped sharply from April on and those from Hokkaido to Honshu from June on, primarily as a result of the mining campaign. The percentage drop exceeded the drop in total bottoms available.

The fleet carrier strike which sank 10 out of the 12 Honshu-Hokkaido rail ferries and damaged the other 2, cut movement of Hokkaido coal to Honshu by nearly 40 percent. The same strike also sank numerous cargo vessels which had been carrying about 65,000 tons of coal a month to Honshu. At the other end of the home islands, FEAF attacks on noncoal targets in the Miike area resulted in incidental but severe reductions in the output of the Miike and Takashima fields, causing a loss of about 500,000 tons.

Domestic production fell to 2,712,000 tons in July and to 1,617,000 in August.

Until the end of the war, the major direct effect of the declining coal supply was upon the steel industry. The loss of Chinese high grade coking coal impaired the quality of such steel as could be manufactured from vanishing inventories. Incidental loss of capacity in the steel industry itself was also significant. While the over-all excess capacity was ample to handle the relatively small amount of raw material available for processing, the drop in efficiency meant that some Hokkaido and north Honshu ores could be used only by moving them at least as far south as Tokyo on the already overloaded railroads.

The decline in coal supply had other significant effects. The decrease in coke-oven operation which was caused by both decreasing coking coal supplies and the exhaustion of iron ore stocks reduced supplies of benzol and toluol severely.

During the second half of the calendar year 1944, toluol production dropped 50 percent from its early 1944 peak. By July 1945 production was down to 15 percent of the highest 1944 month. Corresponding figures for benzol are 36 percent and 35 percent respectively.

The drop in toluol output threatened explosives production but apparently did not actually affect it until May 1945. Benzol constituted only a small fraction of the liquid fuel resources but production at peak levels would have been of marked usefulness in supplementing dwindling aviation fuel supplies. As a very rough measure of significance it can be noted that peak benzol production exceeded 200,000 barrels per month while peak monthly aviation fuel consumption was 500,000 barrels. In June 1945 the Japanese army belatedly requested the steel industry to operate all coke ovens at full capacity, regardless of coke demands, in order to provide benzol and toluol. The falling production of coal, however, prevented this program from being carried out on any substantial scale.

Increasing difficulty in coal production and transportation contributed significantly to the 33 percent drop in cement output between 1943 and 1945, which hampered dispersion and reconstruction efforts after air attack. Limited domestic coke supplies, which continued until the end of the war, would apparently have become a limiting factor even on high priority production. Given continuance of the war, the further severe declines in coal output which were in prospect for the next 6 to 9 months would, by themselves, have seriously threatened the whole economic structure.

d. Light Metals

Japan depended upon imports of war materials for aluminum and magnesium production. Beginning in 1944 shipment of these materials to Japan was seriously curtailed by the blockade and by the end of the year bauxite imports were completely interrupted. Attempts to substitute aluminous shale, mined in North China, for bauxite were not commenced early enough nor prosecuted vigorously enough to yield any substantial amount of alumina. By spring 1945 Japan's aluminum resources therefore consisted almost entirely of scrap and finished and semi-finished material in the hands of fabricating and aircraft plants. The magnesium situation was

somewhat less difficult, since the Korean and Manchurian sources of supply were not cut off until the allocation of shipping to the hauling of food supplies occurred in April 1945. Within a few months, the position would have been parallel to that of aluminum.

The aircraft industry was the only important consumer of magnesium and aluminum. Had Japanese aircraft fabricating capacity been greater, limitations on light metal supply would have prevented full attainment of planned production schedules in 1944. As it was, other factors discussed later in connection with aircraft production intervened to prevent raw material supply from being a production bottleneck in the industry during this year. In 1945 the impending stringency in aluminum supply lead to some substitution of other metals, seriously impairing the durability of some types of aircraft. The curtailment of aluminum and magnesium supplies in this year would have forced a substantial cut in production, but would not have reduced it to the levels to which it was forced by air attacks.

c. Chemicals

Ship sinkings and interruption of shipping routes had important repercussions in the Japanese chemical industry. They consisted mainly of reduction of the coke oven operations and of shortages of steel necessary for the maintenance of high pressure equipment. The only high priority basic chemicals (aside from those important to the oil industry) were synthetic nitrogen, methanol and toluol. In the case of other basic chemicals such as caustic soda, soda ash, and sulphuric acid, the Japanese seem to have been content to accept declines in production from the very beginning of the war, since the civilian economy was their main consumer.

The trend of synthetic nitrogen production was downward from April 1944 but fell off particularly seriously from July 1944—declining 50 percent between the latter date and June 1945. The impact of the decline seems to have been felt almost entirely by fertilizer production. Output of ammonium sulphate was virtually parallel with that of synthetic nitrogen from the first quarter of 1942 until the end of the war. Nitric acid production, allocated mainly to explosive manufacture, was reduced somewhat in 1944 but not severely curtailed until April 1945. The decline in nitrogen output from the very beginning of the

war reduced the supply of nitrogenous fertilizer with the results which are noted later in the discussion of food supply. Explosive production was not significantly effected until April 1945.

The curtailment of synthetic nitrogen manufacture appears to be principally attributable to the lack of maintenance material for the very high pressure equipment used in the industry. This was the result of the limitations of Japanese heavy industry and technology and, during 1944 and 1945, of the blockade caused steel shortage.

There is no evidence that air operations, aside from their large contribution to the blockade of iron ore movement, affected the supply of synthetic nitrogen or its two most important derivatives: fertilizer and explosives. While a number of fertilizer plants were destroyed in the urban area attacks, comparison of ammonium sulphate and synthetic nitrogen supply curves indicate that lack of raw material rather than of processing facilities was the limiting factor in fertilizer output. Had not synthetic nitrogen availability already been reduced, air attack would, however, have cut ammonium sulphate manufacture during the second half of 1945 by around 60 percent.

The effect of air attack on explosives production is somewhat obscure. Nitric acid output dropped by 80 percent between April and August 1945. Explosives production followed the same general trend during this period. The percentage reduction was 50 to 65 percent, army and navy arsenals were hit in urban areas and precision raids, but the extent to which this accelerated the already established trend cannot be determined from the data available.

MUNITIONS

Aircraft Production

The building of military and naval aircraft was given top priority in the organization of the Japanese war economy and had first call on materials and manpower from the outset of the war. The limiting factors in production to the fall of 1944 were those inherent to the size and organization of the Japanese economy. In 1942 necessary plant expansion was hampered by lack of steel and machine tools but this was before the blockade had begun to cut steel production and was attributable to the intrinsic limitations of the Japanese steel and machine tool situation.

In 1942 and 1943 the failure to integrate army and navy programs and facilities held back production until Munitions Ministry control began in November 1943. Raw material supply was not a retarding factor during this period. However, planning of alloy material requirements during the war did not take into account increases in aircraft production and consequent increases in demand, so that, as early as 1943, it was necessary to alter the specifications of alloy steels so as to spread the supply over the rising demand.

A very considerable increase in airframe production was realized in 1944. September output was about 175 percent of the 1943 average monthly figure. Production fell far below plan, however, due mainly to shortages of alloy steel and labor. No restriction on output was imposed by the aluminum supply though this would have been limiting, had the Japanese been able to approach planned output. The increase in production occurred in spite of the mounting success of the blockade and the consequent drop in the general level of all basic industrial activity. The series of strikes by China based B–29s on the integrated plant at Omura beginning in July 1944 may have cost Japan about 50 aircraft, but were not sufficient to check the upward trend of production.

Combat airframe production reached a peak in September 1944. It fell off in October and November but even during those months was maintained at or about pre-September level. In December production dropped 7 percent from the November level. Non-combat-aircraft production decreased sharply after June 1944, principally because of a declining need for trainer aircraft, the tight fuel situation having forced a curtailment of training.

Engine output was irregular in trend and failed to keep pace with the increase in air frames. Through November 1944, however, it was far higher than for the previous year. (The average for eleven months was 164 percent of the 1943 average.) Peaks were reached in March and June 1944. After June, engine production declined irregularly through September, recovering in October and November to a level around three-quarters of the June peak. Total output still exceeded total installation requirements but there were difficulties with a new engine which delayed the equipping of some aircraft.

An important factor in the failure to sustain

peak production of engines was the alloy steel situation which combined with labor inefficiency and absenteeism to limit output. Planning mistakes, in 1942 and 1943, had resulted in a failure to sufficiently expand the supply of alloy materials available in Japanese controlled areas.

True, the Japanese did erect a nickel concentrator in the Celebes in 1943 but they failed to develop available tungsten and chromium resources in China and the Philippines respectively. The shipping attack, particularly in 1942 and 1943, cannot be blamed for this. Two or three shiploads a year of tungsten concentrates would have provided a large stockpile. As for chromium, army and navy controlled ships were returned from Manila with partial cargos, while chromium was left on the piers. Peak ferro-chrome output could have been doubled by movement of about 100,000 tons of ore. Even had all shipping been used to capacity this would have required a shift of less than 1 percent in the pattern of ship usage. Changes in alloy specification created problems in machining and increased rejections about six months after the changes were initiated. These difficulties were, however, met and production increased sharply through June 1944. Further declines in ferro-alloy availability occurred in 1944, as supply, which had up to then increased, took a down turn. This was attributable to several factors. Molybdenum and vanadium were available in Japan and Korea only in small quantities and the supply in Burma was inaccessible because of air operations in that country. Cobalt did not exist within Japanese controlled territories, except for the Bawdwin mine. Nickel was cut off by air attacks on the Celebes concentrator in the fall and winter of 1943 and by the interdiction of shipping from the Celebes by the Fifth AF. Chromium and tungsten were available in the Philippines and China respectively, but, as noted above, were not exploited for reasons other than the shipping shortage.

Decreases in ferro-alloy increased aero engines production difficulties seriously in the fall of 1944 and led the Japanese to substitute, to an increasing degree, high carbon steel to the detriment of output volume and quality. Increases in aluminum capacity more than matched increases in aircraft requirements and during the middle period of the war, the material was actually in surplus supply, as far as the aircraft industry was concerned. However, the attainment of the sharply increased aircraft goal in 1944 would have required more aluminum than could have been produced from the raw materials available.

The blockade cut deeply into bauxite imports from the beginning of 1944, and by the end of the year, had virtually cut off new supplies. This fact, together with the inability of the aluminum industry to process shale from North China, to any substantial extent, led to a 66 percent drop in aluminum output between May and December 1944 and indiated that the end of the production of metal aircraft in Japan was in sight. Continued production at a level of around 1,500 units a month could probably have been maintained until June 1945, and at perhaps a third of that level for the balance of the year by the fabrication of unused material still in the production pipe line, eked out with scrap and the few thousand tons a month which could be secured from aluminous shale and domestic raw material.

Such production never actually took place. B–29 operations from the Mariannas began on 24 November 1944 and for the next three months were directed primarily against the aircraft industry. Production during these months nose-dived (engines 55 percent, from 3819 to 1695 per month, airframes 37 percent, from 2220 to 1391) Frantic measures to disperse the industry, undertaken immediately and continued to the end of the war, contributed even more heavily to the loss of output than did the direct effects of bombardment. From March 1945 on, incendiary area attacks were added to direct attack on plants in maintaining pressure against the industry, particularly in the case of components manufacture. At the end of hostilities, output of engines sank precipitously to around 600 per month or 16 percent of the pre-attack rate and of airframes to about 500 per month or 21 percent of the pre-attack level. Direct attacks in a few cases struck plants which had already been abandoned under the dispersal program.

b. Ordnance

Japanese production of army and naval ordnance and vehicles was conditioned primarily by the inherent limitations of the Japanese economy analyzed in Chapter I and II.

During 1941, 1942 and 1943 these limitations were principally important in restricting the construction of new facilities. Existing plants were generally used to capacity, except in the case of combat and motor vehicles. Production of these latter items was awarded relatively low priority, compared to plant construction and other ordnance items and was consequently limited by the amount of steel allocated.

Allocations of steel to nearly all armaments were substantially higher in 1943 than in 1941 and in every case higher than in 1942. In these years, steel output held up and, in 1943, even expanded slightly at the expense of the raw material stockpiles. Countershipping operations had no immediate direct effect on arms production. There were already important indirect effects of the Allied counteroffensive, however. The pressure of Allied military operations and ship losses incident thereto compelled the Japanese to award merchant shipbuilding a priority claim on basically limited steel supplies—second only to aircraft—severely reducing the amount available for expansion of armaments output.

The drastic reduction in iron ore imports during 1944 under the impact of the air interdiction of the Yangtze, of general blockade and the attendant sharp drop in ingot and finished steel supply has been noted above in connection with the steel discussion. Allocation of steel to army and navy ordnance reacted promptly. Ordinary steel allotments fell sharply from the first quarter of 1944 on. By March 1945, allocations of ordinary steel had dropped in terms of their peak level to 28 percent in the case of the Army, 52 percent in the case of the Navy, and 63 percent in the case of the Air Forces. Cuts in the consumptions of special steel were less severe, but substantial.

The effect of the 1944 drop in steel supply on ground force armament was concentrated on artillery, ammunition, and combat and transport vehicles. Motor vehicle manufacture, which had been held to 60 percent of its peak in 1942 and to 44 percent in 1943 to conserve steel for other uses, was cut, in the first three calendar months of 1945, to 23 percent. The measure was undertaken despite a critical shortage of local transportation in Japan and an extremely low stock of army vehicles in the home islands. The pattern of artillery production was altered to reduce the output of field and heavy pieces. Army chiefs outside the home islands were told, in the spring of 1944, that heavy artillery manufacture was being discontinued. Ammunition production was cut, and an order was issued early in 1944 practically forbidding the use of ammunition for train-

ing purposes. Output of the principal categories of combat vehicles was also reduced in 1944, as a direct result of the steel situation. Light tanks were virtually cut out and medium tanks and armored cars reduced severely.

Manufacture of electrical and communications equipment and aircraft armament was maintained at a high level through March 1945 despite the blockade. Production of ordnance as a whole, however, reached its peak in August and September 1944 and thereafter declined irregularly through March 1945 by a total of 18 percent.

A major effect of the countershipping attack on armament supply was the sinking of a large percentage of finished material enroute to the fighting zones. Losses mounted from 160,000 tons (3 percent of material shipped) in 1942, to 1,390,000 (17 percent) in 1942 to 1,405,000 (33 percent) in 1944. In the latter year half of the supplies sent to the crucial area of the Philippines were lost. In 1945, the 340,000 tons sunk amounted to nearly 50 percent of the supplies shipped.

The period of air attacks on Japan proper saw ordnance output plunge to disastrous levels. There was a break of 11 percent between March and April and of 14 percent between May and June. In July production was only 50 percent of its 1944 peak and 61 percent of its March level.

The bulk of the loss is attributable to other factors than damage to producing facilities which ranged from 3 to 30 percent for various categories but for all averaged only 17 percent. In certain instances, qualitative differences greatly increased the significance of the damage. Destruction of a gun sight factory in Tokio, for example, held up artillery production in other cities. In general, however, it was the disruptive effect of the urban area attacks on local transportation and, to a lesser degree, the absenteeism which such attacks induced which cut arms output to the levels it reached in June 1945.

As suggested earlier, electrical and communications equipment constituted a special case in the armaments picture. Strategic air attack was an even more important factor than it was in regard to other ordnance, because of the industry's relatively low response to the effect of countershipping operations. Despite high priorities given to this type of equipment and a considerable wartime expansion of manufacturing capacity, the industry had never been able to meet demands. All arms of the service were underequipped.

There was insufficient skilled labor in Japan to operate available plants on a two-shift basis. Had there been enough such labor, supplies of raw materials, which were always sufficient only for a single shift, would have restricted two-shift operations of some plants. Lack of raw materials within the Japanese controlled sphere compelled use of inferior substitutes and resulted in declines in performance and durability. However, the drop in steel production resulting from attacks on shipping did not affect this industry, because of its low consumption of steel and its high initial stockpiles of copper. The difficulties that had affected the industry prior to area attack were primarily technological ineptitude, a shortage of skilled labor, lack of silicon steel, and absence of such rare materials as diamonds, quartz crystals, cobalt, tantlum and columbium. Production increased throughout the war and was at a high level in March 1945. At this time, the area attacks struck the main centers of concentration of the industry: Tokyo, Kawasak, Osaka, Kobe and Nagoya. The communications equipment manufacturers depended upon subcontractors in these urban areas for 60 percent of their parts. Other sections of the industry were less vulnerable in this respect but many suffered direct damage and all were affected almost immediately by government orders to disperse their plants to the mountain regions. Between dispersal, direct damage, absenteeism caused by area attacks, and damage to subcontractors, production was reduced to almost negligible levels. While many dispersals were eventually carried out, it appears that no significant production could have been reestablished before 1946.

In August 1945, the communications equipment industry was subjected to a precision bombing attack by carrier-based aircraft. This attack was effective in damaging the structures against which it was directed but had no substantial effect on production because of what had previously been accomplished by incendiary attacks and dispersal.

Naval Shipbuilding

Of Japan's naval construction of about 1.5 million deadweight tons between 1930 and August 1945, 65 percent was completed during the war years. The completion peak came in the summer of 1944. The blockade, by limiting steel supply, exerted a relatively early effect on naval construction. Completions in the major categories in the peak year of 1944 amounted to only 72 percent of plan; the plan for 1945 was set at only 15 percent of the 1944 figure.

Because of the steel shortage direct damage and labor absenteeism due to air attack was of negligible importance in naval construction.

Merchant Shipbuilding

Initial underestimates of requirements and attrition and, during 1943, organizational and administrative difficulties conditioned the size and degree of accomplishment of the Japanese shipbuilding program through the first two years of the war.

After the Guadalcanal compaign, the Japanese war planners allotted to shipbuilding a priority second only to aircraft, and programs were stepped up successively until March 1944. Actual launchings always lagged behind plans, but between April and December 1944 averaged about 150 percent of the 1943 rate. May and June 1944 saw the greatest output and production was maintained until the end of the year. It then dropped substantially and by March reached 61 percent of its 1944 average. The failure to achieve the hoped for increase was the result of the decline in steel output which, as already noted, had begun to fall sharply at this time. By August 1944, it had become necessary to revise production schedules downward from 2.5 million tons. Actual production up to March 1945 was at the rate of only 71 percent of the revised plan.

In April 1945, a new plan was adopted, apparently in the light of the now irretrievable overseas shipping and steel situation. The amount of steel allocated in shipbuilding was cut drastically and the program was reduced to slightly over half a million gross tons for the next year. A "secondary goal" of an additional 660,000 tons was set. The rapidly deteriorating supply of steel plus the effects of area raids, which at some yards caused a permanent loss of as much as 50 percent of the labor force, caused the industry to fall short by 15 percent, during the months of March–June, of fulfilling even the final plan. It is doubtful if more than a minor proportion of this drop was due to the direct incendiary raid damage since there was already at least 60 percent idle capacity in the industry. The smaller establishments, particularly wooden shipbuilders, suffered most heavily and a considerable number of small marine engine builders were burned out.

MANPOWER

The demands of the armed forces were the primary factor conditioning the labor supply up to the spring of 1945, both in regard to quality, and in 1944 and 1945, in quantity.

Air attack by intensification of the blockade contributed to a reduction of the productivity of the Japanese labor force. Blockade operated on the labor force by curtailing food supplies, particularly from early in 1944 on. This caused absenteeism due to foraging and, to a lesser extent, poor nutrition. The inadequacy of the diet also combined with other factors, such as excessive hours, depreciation of capital equipment, and difficulties in processing inferior raw materials, to reduce labor efficiency.

The Japanese did not maintain accurate records showing labor productivity and it is therefore impossible to make a precise statement regarding the over-all extent of the drop in productivity. Such qualitative evidence as could be gathered indicates that the decline in output per man-hour in industries important to war production was felt, prior to air attack, principally in coal mining and to a lesser extent in armaments, electrical equipment, and aircraft.

Falling labor productivity would have increased the difficulty in shifting labor from the processing and fabricating to the domestic extractive industries, if the Japanese had attempted to make up for declining imports by more intensive exploitation of home resources. There is no evidence, however, that the Japanese ever considered it possible to redress the balance of their economy in this manner.

Lack of accurate statistics on absenteeism compel reliance on estimates and general statements for an appraisal of the effect of bombardment on manpower resources. It is clear that air-raid alarms and air attacks caused substantial man-hour losses and greatly increased absenteeism. Estimates for some industries, such as electrical equipment, run as high as 50 percent. There were numerous instances of labor being permanently driven from its normal place of employment by urban attacks, particularly in the Tokyo and Kobe-Osaka areas. The devastating attacks on Hiroshima and Nagasaki failed rather surprisingly to accomplish this.

On the whole, the effect of urban area attack on Japanese industrial manpower was significant against construction, electrical and communications equipment industries and, in some cases, against ordnance and aircraft plants.

Air attack created a large new labor demand, principally in the construction field. The Japanese hastily attempted to disperse high priority war production, beginning in December 1944, and attempted to put a large fraction of the aircraft industry underground. Limited labor supply seriously hindered the carrying out of the dispersal program and, thereby, reduced the production of aircraft, ordnance, and electrical equipment.

CIVILIAN SUPPLY

Foodstuffs

Japan's total 1941 food supply allowed for average caloric intake only 6.4 percent above a subsistence minimum. This supply was maintained only by intensive exploitation of domestic resources (Japan's rice yield per acre was the highest in the world and virtually all the land that could be farmed was double cropped); by large-scale fishing, both coastal and deep sea; by imports of food amounting to 15 percent of the total; and by lavish use of fertilizers of which the phosphatic and potasic elements were imported. Stocks on hand were not in excess of the normal carry-over.

From the beginning of the war, forces became operative which impaired this precariously balanced position. Naval and military needs for patrol, escort, small transport, and landing vessels led to requisitions of fishing craft which continued throughout the war. Important deep-sea fishing grounds had to be abandoned because they were within range of the United States action. Synthetic ammonia plants had to allot a larger share of their production to explosives manufacture and less to fertilizer. Nitrogenous fertilizer consumption dropped 68 percent between 1941 and 1945. About half the drop occurred after August 1944. Farm labor was drafted, and with the qualitative decline in agricultural labor supply came abandonment of marginal land, which more than offset government attempts to increase the total area under food cultivation.

These influences, which would have been felt in any event, made the Japanese even more vulnerable to the results of Allied attack. Phosphatic fertilizer supplies were denied in 1943 by air bombardment of facilities on Nauru, one of the earliest strategic air operations of the Pacific war. As early as 1943, ship sinkings incident to tactical operations began to reduce the amount of food imports, consisting mainly of rice shipments from the South. Japan took no effective steps to lessen her dependence on southern rice supplies by shifting consumption to the more readily accessible and higher food value Manchurian soybeans but maintained the rice ration by running down stocks until, by November 1944, they fell below an adequate working level. In the late fall of 1944, food shipments from the south were virtually cut off and domestic food production in the 1944 rice year was but 93 percent of the 1930-1940 average.

Meanwhile, requisition of fishing vessels for naval and coastwise cargo purposes and of fishermen to replace lost merchant and naval crews, as well as lack of fuel which limited the range and operating time of fishing craft, accelerated the drop in fish supply. Consumption of fish, for food, fell by 1945 to 65 percent of its 1939 level and the drop in fertilizer was more than 20 percent greater.

As a result of these events, Japan, despite the rapidly deteriorating supply of raw materials for war production was, in April 1945, compelled virtually to abandon the import of nonfood items from the mainland. The entire program was shifted to the movement of grains, soy beans, and salt from Manchuria and Korea. By August, the blockade had been practically achieved and even food shipments had dropped to insignificant levels.

Beginning in March 1945, urban area attacks, which destroyed large sections of the principal cities of Japan, increased the food shortage. About 25 percent of the emergency rice stocks in the hands of thousands of retail distributors were destroyed and normal distribution of food supplies interfered with. Millions of persons migrated to small towns outside the larger cities. While this meant greater proximity to the source of that part of the food supply which had to be secured on the black market, it increased the difficulty of distributing the official rations. All these factors aggravated the effects of the basic situation.

Further severe declines in the food supply were in prospect. The impairment of nitrogenous fertilizer manufacture had not occurred early enough to reduce crop yields seriously through the summer of 1945 but threatened to do so

during the rice year 1945 (beginning in October). The close approach of Allied air power from the south meant further heavy cuts in the fish supply through inhibiting operation even in local waters. Even if domestic food production had been maintained by unusually favorable weather, the normal carry-over was so greatly impaired that only by going on starvation rations could the supply be stretched until the rice harvest in the fall. Such an expedient would be possible only on the assumption that organized distribution of food within the home islands could be continued. The Japanese, themselves, expected that air attack on the railroads, which was about to start when the war ended, would prevent even this.

b. Clothing and Shelter

During the war years, severe decreases in an already meager standard of living occurred in Japan as a result of the scarcity of shipping. Even before Allied attack had cut materially into the merchant fleet, war demands on marine transport had cut imports of goods for civilian consumption (other than food) to very low levels. By 1942, the imports of cotton and wool raw materials fell to 7 percent and 8 percent, respectively, of the corresponding imports for 1937. War production demands removed plants and manpower from industries working on civilian supplies, and allocations of basic materials were either eliminated or reduced to a fraction of the prewar level. The productive plants of many civilian goods industries, notably textiles, were, to a considerable extent, broken up for scrap or converted for war purposes.

Pressure on the raw materials and internal transportation positions resulting from the blockade constantly accelerated the downward trend. As imports of raw materials were cut off, the over-all production of textiles declined from 2½ billion square yards in 1943 to 400 million in 1944. In the period January 1941 to August 1945, the ratio of actual production to estimated minimum civilian requirements fell to the following levels: cotton cloth 24 percent, wool cloth 19 percent, and silk cloth 30 percent.

Early in 1944, the fear of air attack led to the destruction, for firebreak purposes, of several hundred thousand dwelling units and to the evacuation, under government auspices, of 2.1 million persons from 12 major cities. A second

and voluntary wave of evacuations occurred after the fall of Saipan. Owing to scarcity of building materials, no attempt was made to furnish these evacuees with new housing. They were either quartered upon friends, relatives or in public buildings.

The urban area raids which began in March 1945, reacted upon this situation with decisive force. About 13 million people were driven from their homes by the destruction of around 2.6 million dwelling units and a substantial additional number were affected by the burning of factory dormitories. The economy had been stretched too tight and Japanese organizing ability had been too poor to permit the orderly rehousing and feeding of these millions and the replacement of even a basic minimum of household goods and clothing. Hordes were driven from the cities into the surrounding towns and rural areas, on a virtually unplanned basis. At the same time, what meager stocks of civilian goods were still available, were reduced by fire, and factories making such goods suffered severely. The air raids are estimated to have directly destroyed 2 billion square yards of cloth and, in addition, to have demolished 18 percent of the capacity of the cotton industry. Coupled with the food shortage already discussed, the housing and civilian supply situation made the plight of Japan's civilian population at the end of the war difficult indeed.

Chapter V

SURRENDER [1]

The war against the United States took a course distinctly at variance with the original assumptions of the Japanese war planners and after Midway and Guadalcanal became obvious, even to the optimists in the Tokyo Government. The severe losses suffered by the Japanese Navy in both engagements exceeded by far the anticipated costs of the defense of the perimeter and rendered the feasibility of this defense itself subject to grave doubt. The initial advantage secured at Pearl Harbor, which was supposed to assure Japan's naval superiority in the Pacific and to lay the foundation for a speedy termination of the war, dissolved itself into an illusion. The United States soon proved a formidable foe—far from disheartened or defeatist.

The military engagements from Midway to Saipan, from Saipan to the Philippines and on to Okinawa was an uninterrupted series of Japanese defeats. In spite of the high quality of the Japanese fighting men, one Pacific outpost after another was wiped out by superior American forces. The "Pacific wall," not unlike the Maginot Line, the Atlantic wall and other systems of fixed fortifications, proved to be a liability rather than an asset. In spite of the large investment of forces, the necessity of defending the entire island chain limited the strength of every link. As the German Ambassador to Japan, the experienced General Ott remarked, it was entirely up to the American High Command which island it chose to attack. None was able to withstand the power which could be concentrated against it. Whichever sector of the outer perimeter was singled out for the American attack soon became a graveyard of Japanese ships, men and supplies.

These graveyards were bottomless. All efforts of the Japanese economy to live up to the demands of the military establishment produced only a fraction of the actual requirements. As soon as American war production overcame the hurdles of conversion and assumed proportions commensurate with the country's economic potential, the military doom of Japan became only a matter of time. It may be very difficult to specify the point in calendar or in geography at which Japan actually lost the war. There is much to be said for Midway or Guadalcanal. It could be argued, however, that if a miracle had enabled Japan to multiply its military output at that time, the catastrophe could have been prevented. Yet, after Saipan was lost no miracle could have helped the empire of the Rising Sun. Within reach of the B-29s, subject to ever-tightening blockade and facing an early air offensive against the home islands, Japan could have thrown in the sponge without fear of foregoing any serious chances of victory.

But while defeat in a war is a military event, the recognition of the defeat is a political act. The timing of the political recognition of the military realities is only partly determined by the actual situation on the fronts. The international situation, the domestic balance of power, the interests and antagonisms of relevant political groups— they all weigh heavily when the grim realities of the armed contest have to be translated into the blunt language of capitulation.

The attempts to draw conclusions from the military failure and to negotiate peace date as far back as the fall of Saipan. At that time (July 1944), the conservative elements in Japan's ruling coalition began plotting to overthrow the Tojo government and to find a way toward some conclusion of the war. The fascist wing, however, was far from ready to accept defeat. Vividly aware of the close relationship between their power position in the country and the continuation of the war, the army and navy leadership were clinging desperately to whatever hopes the objec-

[1] For a detailed account of the history of Japan's surrender, as established by survey interrogations and research, the reader should consult the special paper "Japan's Struggle to End the War," prepared by the chairman's office of the USSBS.

tive situation may have left. The fact that Germany was fighting and that Hitler made dark suggestions of powerful secret weapons was importantly positioned on the otherwise cloudy international horizon.

The notion that an actual victory by the United States could be obtained only by an outright invasion of the Japanese home islands and that such an invasion was bound to be very hazardous and costly was widely accepted in the Japanese army circles. Preparing to repulse landing attempts with all the fighting powers of the Japanese soldier and to render the American sacrifice prohibitive by a large scale employment of Kamikaze tactics, the military leadership hoped that there was still a large gap between Japanese defeat and American victory. Independent of such calculations, the reluctance on the part of the fascist wing of the Japanese ruling coalition to admit complete bankruptcy of its policies, which were forced upon Japan during an entire decade, was the most important single force preventing the recognition of defeat. The substitution of Koiso for Tojo symbolized the victory of the intransigent group. An army general like Tojo, Koiso disappointed the conservative wing and actually followed all the policies of his predecessor. It was a change in name, not in direction.

Popular sentiments did not materially aid the "surrender party". Exhausted and disheartened by long privations and strains of the war, the population was hardly aware of the extent of the adversities suffered by Japanese arms. The fear that a sudden announcement of a debacle might have a shock effect which would endanger the stability of the social and political system was seriously entertained by the conservative wing of the Government and strengthened markedly the position taken by the military. The front had to move nearer to the homeland and the nation had to have immediate *experience* of the war before the capitulation would be accepted as an inevitable result of overpowering circumstances.

The bomber offensive against the home islands accomplished this task—it brought the war home to the Japanese. The reverses on the distant islands of the newly created Japanese Empire, known to the populous only from hearsay, became tangibly evident in the air raids on Tokyo, Nagoya and Osaka. The inability of the Japanese air force to stave off the American bombers and the resulting defenselessness of the Japanese

cities made the magnitude of the disaster obvious to the man in the street. While public morale may have never reached an ebb which would have rendered the prosecution of the war impossible, incessant bombardment and continued shortage of food, clothing and shelter created ever increasing popular despair. The possibility of such despair expressing itself in rioting and violent actions was not discounted by the Government.

The decline of war production, which set in in the fall of 1944 and which assumed disastrous proportions in 1945, rendered the possibility of supporting anti-invasion operations of the Japanese army very problematical. The tightening of the blockade made possible by American acquisition of nearby bases strangled, further, the meager flow of basic materials. The wholesale destruction of shipping clearly signaled the day on which stocks of raw materials would be entirely exhausted. The break-down of dispersal and repair operations reduced Japanese manufacturing capacity to a level at which significant output of military supplies was out of question. Possibilities of a recovery were not visible. In spite of the availability of sizable stocks of military supplies, defense of the home islands against an American amphibious assault based on a vast array of ships, planes and supplies, appeared to be a fantastic undertaking. The best that could be expected was "death in honor" with comparatively large costs to the American forces.

While the army radicals were inclined to accept the last ditch fight, the only alternative being ignominious defeat and probably apprehension for war crimes, the conservative elements in the Japanese ruling coalition refused to sacrifice all chances of Japan's ultimate survival for the sake of the army's "honor." Determined to bring the war to an end, the forces around Suzuki, who became the symbol of the entire conservative group, maneuvered only to improve, somewhat, the terms of unconditional surrender.

These maneuvers were speeded up and intensified after the capitulation of Germany. May 8, 1945, the day of Germany's official departure from the war, was, in full corroboration of the grand strategy adopted by President Roosevelt, the decisive date in the history of Japan's internal struggle for termination of the war. Whatever illusions may have existed in Tokyo prior to Germany's surrender evaporated after the Allied victory in Europe. Japan, drained of all power of resistance, was ready to capitulate, though a formula that would take a little of the sting out of unconditional surrender was still being sought.

The atomic bomb dropped on Hiroshima made it clear that the United States was prepared to enforce by overwhelming means the Potsdam ultimatum. Further delays would mean only larger sacrifices without the slightest hope of improvement of the peace terms. The increasing threat to the Japanese internal transportation system rendered the prospects of mobility of the Japanese anti-invasion forces well-nigh negligible and promised increasing disaster to the civilian population. The continuation of the war was nothing short of irrational and Russia's declaration of war and advance into Manchuria added to the pressure by threatening a ground army disaster. The army, which thus far suffered only limited defeats in the Philippines and in Okinawa, faced a supreme test of strength. Difficult as it was to conceive of supplying adequately the forces charged with the defense of the home islands, to support simultaneously a large scale campaign on the Continent of Asia was an entirely hopeless undertaking. The industries of Manchuria, not strong enough to provide the Kwantung Army with the limited wherewithal of the North China campaign, could not possibly serve as a basis for protracted fighting against an enemy as powerful as the Russians. For the first time during the war, the Army, itself, faced the prospect of inescapable doom.

There is little point in attempting to impute Japan's surrender to any one of the numerous causes which, jointly and cumulatively, were responsible for the disastrous outcome of the nation's greatest military undertaking. The time which lapsed between the military decision and the political acceptance of the inevitable might have been shorter had the political structure of Japan permitted a more rapid formulation of national policies. As it was, the struggle between the different forces dominating Japan's society had to reach a point at which the Fascist, intransigent wing, could be subdued. The partnership between the conservatives, big business and military radicals had to result in bankruptcy before the groups which led Japan into war could be ousted from the political saddle.

While the outcome of the war was decided in the waters of the Pacific and on the landing beaches of invaded islands of the outer and inner perimeter, well in advance of the strategic bomber offensive against Japan's home islands, the air offensive against Japan proper was the major factor determining the timing of Japan's surrender. Without strategic bombing, a landing on Japanese shores would have been costly, in spite of all the weaknesses of the defending forces. The victory actually gained was cheaper and earlier than that which would have been gained in the absence of strategic bombing. The importance of this contribution of strategic air attack and its implications for the future cannot be overestimated.

Chapter VI

POSTSCRIPT ON TARGET SELECTION IN BOMBING OF JAPAN

FAR EASTERN AIR FORCES

The primary mission of these forces during the summer of 1945 was preparation for operation Olympic, a troop landing in southern Kyushu, scheduled for November 1945. It was apparent that the strength of the ground opposition to be experienced by U. S. forces would depend mainly upon the troops and supplies which the enemy could move into southern Kyushu from the main garrison, depot, and production areas in Honshu. Any troops or supplies which the enemy succeeded in moving from the mainland, in the face of the mine blockade, could be expected to be landed in Honshu, on northern Kyushu, and moved thence to southern Kyushu by rail. The main producing and depot facilities on Kyushu itself were located in the extreme north, in the Moji and Fukuoka areas.

It was also clear that the available military supplies and equipment would play a much larger part in Japanese defense than the comparatively small additional amounts which might be produced between June and November 1945.

The logic of these facts indicated that Japanese railroads would be the most effective target for preparatory air operation. It was suggested that the initial operations be undertaken in the Shimonoseki Straits, western Honshu, and northern Kyushu areas, with later operations developing into central and southern Kyushu, after the northerly facilities were neutralized. It seemed likely that attack in these northern areas would stop the large coal traffic originating in extreme northern Kyushu and, to a lesser extent, in western Honshu, which was vital to continued railroad and industrial operation in Kyushu and in Honshu, from Nagoya west.

The facts developed by investigation in Japan bore out this analysis. It developed that prior to June, only a small fraction of the forces and equipment which Japan planned to deploy in opposition to the Olympic operation were actually in Kyushu. During June, large movements of troops and supplies from Honshu to Kyushu were accomplished. Though these were not interfered with by FEAF, whose counter-railroad operations were confined to southern Kyushu, they were of sufficient magnitude to affect economic traffic as far east as Osaka. Even heavier movements were in store for coming months, if the planned deployment was to be accomplished.

It also developed that current munitions production was not of major importance to Japanese strength. Stocks of finished equipment and supplies amounted to over 2 years' production at rates current in the first fiscal quarter of 1945. It was clear that Japanese resistance on the beachheads was primarily dependent on the extent to which the material *in existence* could be deployed. The consequence was, of course, that transportation was more significant than new production.

As noted in chapter III, however, the air effort of FEAF, which resulted in the dropping of some 7,100 tons of bombs, was distributed over a half dozen target systems. Only 15 percent of the effort was directed against railroads and 9 percent against shipping. The tonnage against railroads was expended in the south and central regions of the island, which permitted military traffic originating in Honshu to accomplish the major part of its journey to the prospective battle fields without hinderance.[1]

Nine percent of the FEAF tonnage was directed at harbor installations, despite the fact that the reduction in the merchant fleet and the mining operations had created a great excess of such facilities and that, in any case, the physical vulnerability of such installations was very low.

More important was the expenditure of 21 percent of the tonnage against urban areas and 13 percent against miscellaneous industrial and

---

[1] For example, the most successful operation was that against a bridge in southwest Kyushu, only a few miles back of one of the projected beachheads.

unidentified targets. Much of the urban area tonnage consisted of high-explosive bombs, which were known to be of low effectiveness, compared to incendiaries, against this type of target. Neither the industries nor the cities were of major importance to the defense of Kyushu in November, since neither contributed any substantial production of immediate use to Japanese forces. The effort employed in these attacks was, on the other hand, excellently adapted to attack on railroad yards and bridges, since a high proportion of the aircraft involved were fighters and medium bombers. Consistent attack on as few as 10 rail targets (5 yards and 5 bridges), would have severely hampered both military and economic rail traffic between Honshu and Kyushu.[2] The build-up of strength in Kyushu would have been substantially smaller and very serious effects on Honshu and Kyushu coal supplies would have been caused. Nothing comparable was accomplished by the FEAF operations actually undertaken.

CARRIER-BASED AIRCRAFT

The pattern of carrier-based aircraft attack has been set forth in chapter III. It will be recalled that the largest single block of effort (47 percent) was against airfields and falls largely into the tactical category. These airfield strikes aided the Okinawa invasion and weakened Japanese kamikaze capabilities to some extent.

There is no evidence that the attacks on military installations, which absorbed 6.6 percent of carrier delivered tonnage against Japan, would have materially weakened the resistance to the Olympic or Coronet operations in the fall of 1945 and the spring of 1946.

Nineteen percent of the carrier-borne tonnage was directed against enemy naval units and installations, mainly in July and August. Entirely aside from the fact that such units had been immobilized for lack of fuel since April, the Iwo and Okinawa operations had amply demonstrated that the remnants of the Japanese Navy were powerless to interfere with amphibious operations, even when carried out practically at Japan's front door. Under these circumstances, the carrier attacks on fleet units at Kure and Yokosuka were merely redundant demonstrations of the capabilities of aircraft against surface vessels which had

already been proved at Pearl Harbor, off Malaya and Ceylon, among the Solomons, in the Sibuyan Sea, and north of Okinawa. They contributed virtually nothing toward weakening Japanese naval power to resist, since that power had already been wiped out.

About 9 percent of the carrier-based effort was directed against industrial targets, principally aircraft factories. The tonnage employed contributed somewhat to the decline in aircraft production.

Only 12 percent of the carrier effort was directed against merchant shipping in Japanese home waters. The small fraction of effort devoted to this target system included the highly successful and useful attack on the Hakodate-Aomori rail ferries and shipping concentration at Hakodate in July 1945, the important effects of which have been noted above. This attack was another demonstration of the devastating effectiveness of carrier aircraft attack on shipping which had been proved repeatedly from Truk through Palau and Manila to Formosa, the Ryukus, and the South China Sea, but which was hardly employed against Japan proper despite the fact that photo-reconnaissance often disclosed the presence of concentrations of 60,000–100,000 tons of shipping at Shimonoseki, Osaka and Kobe.

Only 143 tons were directed against railroad installations, aside from the rail ferries, although the high precision attack of which carrier air-craft are capable is particularly suited to such targets as bridges. While it is true that carrier-based attack was not large enough in volume or of a sufficiently sustained character to have accomplished a decisive stoppage of Japanese rail traffic, it appears, in retrospect, that concentrated attack resulting in virtually complete destruction of four or five long bridges on the Hokkaido main line would have been well within carrier task force capabilities and would have severely reduced Japanese rail freight movement. Transportation was already a limiting factor on armaments production in the spring of 1945 so that a substantial result would have been achieved by such reduction. More important, it now seems that such a traffic reduction would have considerably increased the shock effects of urban area attacks and done more to reduce, immediately, food availability outside rural areas than any other form of attack.

[2] Even if it had proved impossible to do serious damage to the Kammon tunnel which had been designated as a target for special weapons. Responsibility for its destruction had been shifted to the B-29's.

TWENTIETH BOMBER COMMAND

Target appraisals available at the time that the first B–29 units were being moved to China in 1944 stressed the paramount strategic importance of Japanese shipping. The evidence secured in Japan reinforces this conclusion and strongly suggests that Japan's position in early 1945 would have been considerably weaker had an even stronger attack been mounted against her shipping lanes in 1944. The ineffectual nature of the attacks which could be undertaken against Japanese industrial and urban targets, from inadequately supplied China bases, has been pointed out. In retrospect, it appears that India based aerial mining operations of the character later undertaken against Japan, directed against Singapore, Palembang, Bangkok, Saigon, Hainon, and such China ports as were within range would have afforded an opportunity to gain the necessary B–29 operating experience and at the same time permitted a more effective attack on the principal strategic target within reach.[3]

TWENTY-FIRST BOMBER COMMAND— TWENTIETH AF

As noted in the discussion of the effects of air attack on Japan's oil supply, it appears that the tonnage expended against oil and tetraethyl lead produced little effect on Japanese military capabilities or will to resist. To a lesser extent the same is true of attacks on nonurban area targets after April 1945.[4] The pattern of B–29 operations against such targets was conditioned by the limited conception of the role and capabilities of air power inherent in the basic United States war plan of reducing Japan by ground invasion.

EFFECT OF TARGET SELECTION THEORY ON THE AIR CAMPAIGN AGAINST JAPAN PROPER

The purpose of the strategic bombing campaign was, until the last weeks of the war, the reduction of the armed strength with which the enemy could be expected to oppose a landing by our ground troops in November 1945. Carrier-based and FEAF operations had the same fundamental end in view. The evidence suggests that definition of the air mission in these limited terms somewhat delayed the termination of the war. The larger mission of achieving a decision without invasion does not appear to have been recognized as the major objective until almost the end of the conflict and then only by part of the air forces engaged. Urban fire raids had, of course, begun on a large scale as early as March, but these appear to have been initially undertaken largely for operational reasons, as an easier way, than precision bombing, of getting at war production and of preventing its recuperation from precision attack. It was not until incendiary attacks were scheduled against urban areas of minor industrial importance, advance announcements of urban area raids made to the enemy and the atom bombs were dropped, that the primary mission of securing an independent decision was explicitly accepted for the B–29's. It was never accepted so far as the Far Eastern Air Forces and carrier forces were concerned.

Although a decision was in fact obtained without invasion in the Japanese war, perhaps partly because United States forces were ready to invade in the immediate future, adherence to the limited concept of the role of strategic power caused a scattering and division of effort which probably delayed this result. As noted in chapter III, B–29 strategic effort from December 1944 on was distributed over seven different main types of targets. About 70 percent was directed against urban areas and may be said to have achieved both the limited and the broader strategic objectives. The balance was distributed over such targets as oil, ordnance, and aircraft and did not put much pressure directly on the Japanese social organization. It was also expended in sea mining which tended more toward external than internal blockade and was by that time less conclusive.[5] The carrier-based aircraft directed almost their entire effort toward reducing enemy first-line air, naval, and military strength rather than the foundations of the Japanese economy. FEAF scattered its effort over transportation, urban-area, and industrial targets of distinctly secondary importance while passing up targets upon whose

---

[3] Fourteenth AF countershipping operations would also have been facilitated by the better logistic support which it would have been possible to provide had the competition of the B–29's been removed.

[4] As noted, the fuel position was such that the enemy could not have operated a substantially larger number of aircraft had these been available. Neither would the ordnance output at preattack levels have substantially increased enemy capabilities.

[5] The volume of overseas traffic in early 1945 does not appear to have exceeded a rate of about 9 million tons a year, or 5 percent of a rail movement of around 180 million tons. The qualitative importance of this traffic was no greater.

continued functioning large segments of the social organization were dependent. Had the effort of all these forces not needed for the immediate support of the Okinawa campaign been directed exclusively against targets, destruction of which tended independently to force a decision as well as to weaken enemy front lines, it seems probable that the war could have been won earlier.

Action against war production is relevant to forcing a surrender only insofar as it is backed up by the threat of armed invasion. Action which threatens the subsistence of large sections of the population and at the same time, through restricting communications, menaces the continuance of centralized and integrated social control, can exert powerful pressure toward termination of a war, even though invasion is not in the offing. A government unable to feed its people and to maintain mobility and cohesion of its forces cannot long survive. By April 1945 the threat to subsistence posed by the reduction of imports, fishing, and fertilizer, as well as by urban area casualties and disorganization, had become substantial. Nevertheless, the railroads were free to move the main bulk of living requirements and internal communication remained open. The process of disintegration remained slow.

Had attention been directed towards spectacular increases of pressure rather than toward facilitating invasion, the railroads would have presented a promising target. Railroad attack would have carried with it an almost immediate threat of starvation, not only for the major urban concentration but for the entire deficit food areas, such as western Honshu, and would have placed a severe restriction on internal communications. In view of the already overstrained truck, motor fuel, and shipping positions, the dependence of the railroads themselves on the continuance of coal traffic over only four lines [6] and the importance of food shipments from Hokkaido, there is very good reason to believe that an effective railroad attack might have brought about a very rapid capitulation.[7]

[6] Next to the steel industry, the railroads were the largest single consumer of coal in Japan and, from early in 1945, their coal stocks amounted to no more than 2 or 3 weeks' supply.

[7] When questioned on this point, Hoshino, cabinet secretary and economic planner to Tojo, stated that had coal and food from Kyushu and Hokkaido been cut off by interruption of the railroads, further resistance would have been impossible, as the population would have starved. Lt. Col. Iwakeshi, Japanese Imperial General Staff, Supply Officer, said that the General Staff had been surprised at the failure of the United States air forces to attack the railroads instead of factories; surrender would have come earlier.

It would have been possible by concentration of effort, from April on, to drop, say, 10,000 tons of HE a month on railroad targets, without materially weakening the urban area attack.[8] From experience in Europe and the relative size and vulnerability of the Japanese system it might have been expected that under a bombardment of this magnitude, traffic would have been reduced to disastrous levels within about 2 months.[9] Use of high-precision forms of air attack, particularly carrier-based aircraft, at the two vital bottlenecks at the extremities of the island of Honshu would have strengthened the campaign out of all proportion to the relative effort.[10]

The undertaking of this program would not have detracted from the accomplishment of the more limited objective of reducing Japan's front line military strength but would have increased the chance of its attainment. It seems that the effect on virtually all top priority production would have been decisive. After March 1945 either dispersal, lack of transportation, absenteeism, or lack of raw materials was the limiting factor in such production. Rail attack would have severely aggravated all those problems. In addition, virtually all production centers were remote from coal and dependent on rail movement for a large part of their food. Finally, a large part of

[8] Substantial diversions from the urban attacks to reinforce the rail program would have been justified in the event that the tonnage shifted from other targets proved insufficient. Since the spillage from bombardment of major rail yards would have resulted in serious urban damage the shifting of tonnage to rail targets would not have resulted in a proportional weakening of the urban attacks. Moreover, denial of rail transportation of the major urban areas would have greatly aggravated the effects of the urban area attacks since the accomplishment of evacuation and the provision of emergency food supplies would have been rendered most difficult. Finally there appears to have been substantial overbombing of urban targets so that in some cases a large diversion of tonnage would have effected only a minor change in result.

[9] Day and night bombardment principally by heavy bombers in a weight of about 20,000 tons a month directed against 90 French railroad yards, during 2½ months in the spring of 1944, reduced economic traffic to 13 percent of its preattack level in the area under attack although the rail system was working at only a fraction of capacity. Even if weather conditions had prevented the use of the more efficient method of line interdiction rather than yard attack, not over 30 yards would have had to be attacked in Japan to take out a larger proportion of capacity than was attained in France. In Japan, unlike France, the railroad system was heavily overloaded. There were a number of outstanding bottlenecks and, except in the urban areas, only two or three alternate routes for the main traffic flow. The Japanese system was relatively small and weak. Compared to the French it had but 58 percent of the route mileage, 10 percent of the multitrack mileage, 40 percent of the locomotives, and 25 percent of the freight cars. And a considerable portion of the Japanese facilities were in Hokkaido and Kyushu and would have been unavailable once the bottlenecks at the Kammon tunnel and the Amori-Hakodate rail ferries were plugged.

[10] About 12,000 tons of bombs dropped by fighter and medium bombers were sufficient to interdict virtually all railroad traffic in the Italian peninsula for 6 weeks in the spring of 1944. This was about the tonnage of bombs dropped on Japan by carrier forces and FEAF. While the geography and railroad system of Italy resembled that of Japan far more closely than did that of France and Germany, the Italian network was at least 50 percent denser than the Japanese.

the movement of semifinished goods such as steel plates, shapes and bars, light metal ingots, plates and shapes, chemicals, and so forth, had to be moved to fabricating plants by rail and to a considerable extent from distant plants in Hokkaido, northern Honshu, and Kyushu. The results of rail attack would therefore have been more devastating than direct plant attack.[11]

More important, greater prospect of success in achieving the limited strategic objective of weakening enemy forces at the Kyushu beachheads would have attended this form of attack than any other. Not only would additions to strength through new production have been prevented, but the mobility of existing strength could have been severely hampered. The main stocks of military supplies and material were located in Honshu. Large movements of troops and supplies from Honshu to Kyushu were accomplished by rail during the

month of June. Even larger movements were scheduled at the time the war ended. Because of the difficult truck and ship position of Japan, these movements could not have been accomplished without use of the railroads.[12]

The evidence available indicates that a concentration of air attacks exclusively on railroads and urban areas, at least from March 1945 on, would in all probability have led to an earlier surrender and would at the same time have more successfully reduced enemy military capabilities to oppose a landing.[13]

---

[11] German experience seems to collaborate this conclusion.

[12] The Japanese army had in the home islands at the end of the war but 8,900 trucks. There were, it is true, a considerable number of civilian trucks which, at a serious cost to war production, could, theoretically, have been requisitioned. As a practical matter, such requisitions on a large scale seem to present insuperable difficulties in the provision of drivers, fuel and repair echelons. The Germans in France in a similar situation secured little benefit from truck requisitions.

[13] It should be repeated here that, in July 1945, a command decision was made awarding top target priority to Japanese railroads and that this was about to be implemented when the war ended.

Over-All Economic Effects Division

Appendixes A, B, and C

Appendix A

U. S. ECONOMIC INTELLIGENCE ON JAPAN
ANALYSIS AND COMPARISONS

General Discussion

Two opposing views characterized United States estimates of Japan's wartime economy. The first was that Japanese production was at a low level. The second was that her productive capacity was large and that stock piles and imports were sufficient to support capacity production. The latter view was more widely held. However, USSBS findings indicate that the lower estimates were more accurate.

It may be argued that it is always safe to overestimate the enemy. But if one accepts this view, precise intelligence is unnecessary; a conservative bias could replace skilled judgment. Moreover, overestimates can be as dangerous as underestimates. Overestimates of German potential in many cases guided diplomatic dealings with Germany during the years before the war. Failure to realize that Japan's productive machine had come to a standstill in 1945 might have led us unnecessarily to undertake Operation Olympic, an invasion that could have cost an enormous number of lives. There is no security in being "conservative."

I

Analysis suggests three major causes of error in the various estimates of Japanese production: lack of basic data, failure to consider the over-all situation in making estimates for individual items, and the omission of administrative, cultural and psychological factors.

In making estimates, it is generally necessary to set up a base year and to measure changes from this base. In ascertaining Japanese production during the course of the war, it would have been most helpful to have had a good knowledge of production, capacity, and stock piles as of Pearl Harbor. However, data to establish such indices were generally lacking. The Japanese had forbidden the publication of statistics on most industries since 1929. Information on Japanese shipyards, docks, and harbor facilities was obsolete and very little was known about some of the most important shipbuilding and repair yards. Moreover, we had failed to secure much information that was readily available, such as all the published registers of Japanese merchant ships. A great deal of the research effort expended during the war was devoted to compiling this kind of basic prewar data. Thousands of man-hours were used to ascertain the number, type, and tonnage of ships available to the Japanese at the outbreak of the war. To determine the stock pile of oil in Japan at the time of Pearl Harbor, information was being sought as late as 1945, on American shipments of oil to Japan from 1929 through 1941. There were instances of a surprising lack of elementary data. For example, the koku is a Japanese unit of volume used to measure rice and other foods. USSBS found that the Japanese were using a conversion factor of 6 koku per ton of brown rice, whereas research analysts used a factor of 6.838, causing an error of 12 percent for part of the food estimates.

Partly as a result of this dearth of information, Japan's stock piles of raw materials in 1941 were generally overestimated. Most agencies placed her oil reserves at 75 to 80 million barrels, enough to sustain a 2 years' war. The lowest estimate was that of MIS,—JFEOC,[1] 57 million barrels. The actual figure was 43 million barrels. Bauxite reserves were assumed to be 500,000 tons, when they totaled only 250,000 tons. Instead of

---

[1] The following abbreviations will be used: JFEOC for Joint Far East Oil Committee; EOC for Enemy Oil Committee; MIS for Military Intelligence Service; FEA for Foreign Economic Administration; BEW for Board of Economic Warfare; OSS for Office of Strategic Services; ONI for Office o. Naval Intelligence; COA for Committee of Operations Analysts; JTG foe Joint Target Group; and JANIS for Joint Army Navy Intelligence Service.

building up her stocks of iron ore during 1941 as supposed, Japan had been forced to draw upon them to the extent of 1,207,000 tons, leaving only a 4 months' reserve.

The second cause of error was that some of the estimates for particular products were made without adequate consideration of the over-all situation. FEA, for example, made excellent estimates of the capacity of various Japanese industries and of the requirements for their products. However, a study of the FEA reports for 1944 indicates that the estimates for production in these various industries are not in consonance with any reasonable estimate of the total supply of available raw materials. In December 1943, FEA predicted production at capacity for most industries. At this time, the shipping section of FEA estimated shipping available to the Japanese at approximately 4,800,000 tons. A year later it was known that losses in merchant ships had been even greater than anticipated and tonnage available was correctly placed at 2,500,000 tons. Nevertheless, the FEA steel report issued in November 1944 again estimated steel ingot production at capacity, 13,690,000 tons, stating, "Equipment * * * being utilized at its full operating capacity. * * * Ample raw materials are available for such operations." The coal section's estimate was also the same as the preceding year, 68 million tons, "sufficient to meet essential requirements." Analogous views of "capacity production", or "sufficient to meet essential requirements" were expressed by the other research sections at FEA. A similar attitude, though less extreme, characterized some of OSS estimates.

Curiously, the FEA shipping section was alert to the danger of the shipping shortage. In December 1943 it warned, "The situation will probably be considerably more serious than the figures indicate . . . the Japanese shipping situation is already serious, and is deteriorating at a rate which will either limit industrial production or restrict military activity before the end of 1944. Any substantial increase in shipping losses would precipitate a situation that is already developing. There is very little slack left in the Japanese economy." The "general conclusion section" of the 1943 FEA's "Japan's War Economy" also refers to "difficulties already encountered in supplying enough raw materials to utilize fully the capacity already at hand." Nevertheless, as noted above, the individual sections of FEA

blithely disregarding the warnings of their own shipping section, estimated capacity production for their respective industries late in 1944.

Most other agencies did not realize how early in the war, even in 1942 and 1943, lack of raw materials due to shipping shortages was limiting Japanese production. Thus, in November 1943 the COA wrote: "Continuation of the present rate of sinkings, . . . would result in a serious, though not critical, reduction in Japan's military and economic strength."

In this report the COA found the major weakness in Japan's economy to be that "she lacks the excess capacity, often found in other countries, in the basic industries essential to war." Prodding from MIS and the Far East Target Section of A–2, particularly their joint dissenting opinion to the 1944 COA subcommittee report on iron and steel, induced some change in the COA opinion, expressed in its report of October 1944: "The present view of Japan's coke, iron, and steel position differs materially from that held in November 1943. Shortage of ore, rather than open hearth and rolling mill capacity, now limits iron and steel output." However, even at this stage, the COA did not fully appreciate the desperate straits to which Japanese industry had been reduced by shortages of raw materials.

An over-all view would have suggested that at all stages of the war Japan's industry was almost entirely dependent on imports for her supply of raw materials, and that the declining Japanese merchant fleet could not bring in enough to continue to supply all industries. Yet many research sections appear to have shared the notion that the Japanese would provide enough raw materials for the particular industry they were interested in developing as a target.

The MIS approach was to appraise the general situation on the basis of raw materials on hand at each stage in the war, which was in turn considered a function of the shipping section. Estimates for each industry were then made in the light of the raw materials which the general picture indicated were currently available for this purpose. Capacity was regarded as an outside limit which was not significant because of the stringency of almost all materials. This method proved the most reliable.

That the capacity-requirements method could be used successfully, if coupled with an over-all view, is shown by the 1943 report of the Far East Target Section of A–2, "North China Coal." This report accepted the FEA requirement figures, but instead of assuming that sufficient coal was available to meet this need, made an independent analysis of available shipping and concluded that "the present scale of war effort means an annual coal deficit of 10 million tons for Japan proper," an estimate which erred somewhat on the low side.

It is interesting to note that throughout the war, the Japanese broadcast and published annual estimates of national income, the total value of goods and services produced. These estimates were analyzed by OSS and used in their study of Japanese national income, which was revised by the State Department in a reparations study. There is a high correlation between these revised estimates and the USSBS findings. These national income estimates, considered in conjunction with published information on Japanese consumer income, would have suggested that the Japanese economy could not support the sum of the estimates for individual products. So far as is known, these national income estimates were never used to evaluate the individual estimates, either at OSS or any other agency.

Each item in an industrial system is interconnected with the whole. The vice of making estimates in separate compartments is that each analyst makes his estimate by assuming "other things being equal". But the crux of the Japanese situation was that other things were not equal; the production of each item was a function of what materials were being used for "other things". All of Japan's economy depended on water transportation, overseas and coastwise, and the making of isolated estimates resulted in various groups using the same space on the same ships at the same time for different commodities.

The third cause of error was the failure to give sufficient weight to administrative, social, and technological factors. The analysis in many of the estimates was almost wholly concerned with economic and statistical matters. Other elements which were not subject to quantitative measurement were often rejected as subjects for discussion. But these factors could not really be exorcised. Although they were not deliberately taken into account, they appear in the conclusions as hidden assumptions.

Most agencies did not adequately study the question of how well the Japanese could handle large scale industrial enterprises requiring much organization and widespread technical skill. It was known that the Japanese were acquainted with the most advanced industrial processes, and on this basis, they were generally credited with success in many fields of production. What was assumed by most estimators, however, was that knowledge on the part of a few engineers could be translated into large scale developments. "The Japanese have the know-how * * *", FEA wrote in 1944. JTG, knowing that the Japanese had successfully operated small plants for making alumina from aluminous shale, concluded that "conversion of the Japanese alumina industry to non-Bayer plants had been virtually completed by June 1945." Similar views of success in this field were entertained by FEA. In fact, the Japanese failed completely to attain substantial production by this method because they lacked sufficient personnel with the requisite technical skill to supervise operations. All estimates of synthetic oil production were based on the premise that the Japanese would be fairly successful in utilizing complex chemical processes on a large scale. These estimates varied from 16 million to 20 million barrels for the years 1942–44. USSBS findings show that total synthetic production from 1937, when it was introduced, through July 1945 amounted to only 5,500,000 barrels. Remarkably accurate estimates were made of the number of ships available to the Japanese. But estimates of what materials could be imported with this fleet were too high because the Japanese managed their ships less efficiently than was generally supposed; loading and unloading times were excessive; cargo was often poorly selected; ships sometimes returned empty; army and navy quarrels delayed convoys unnecessarily.

A skeptical view of Japanese technological ability was taken by the Far East Target Section of A–2. Referring to "claimed exploitation of Manchurian aluminous shales," it observed that "any substantial achievement along those lines would be dependent . . . upon remarkable technological progress. . . ." However, no specific estimates were made in the air objective folders, which were primarily area studies.

One of the few instances of adequate treatment of Japanese technology appears in the BEW's "Japan's War Economy" of March 1943. Ten of the 20 pages of the chapter on combat armament are devoted to a discussion of "the technical efficiency of Japanese industry and its effect on the production of combat armament." Limitations were considered to arise from the fact that "although remarkable progress has been made from the low levels of 15 years ago, Japanese industry is not as yet abreast of western industry in methods or efficiency. . . . It is not that the techniques cannot be mastered but that several years must elapse before they are completely mastered." Major obstacles to the development of large-scale production were seen as: difficulty in learning the techniques necessary for the production of new alloy steels; limited number of precision quality single purpose machine tools; inexperience in mass production techniques; shortcomings of industrial personnel. Under the latter section it was stated: "The Japanese are skillful artisans and under able supervision become efficient industrial workers. Facilities for training new workers . . . are limited and in the absence of a tradition of mass production, the difficulties are magnified. . . . There is an essential shortage of supervisors at the shop foreman level. Moreover, the supervisory class as a whole is less efficient and less competent than are the workers. . . . The strict caste system prevailing in Japanese industry constitutes another obstacle. . . . Management is frequently uninformed on technical problems. There is a wide gap between the technical and practical sides in the management of Japanese industries." With these limitations in mind, the BEW estimated production of airplanes engines at 18,000 for 1942 and 28,000 for 1943. The actual figures were 17,000 and 24,000, respectively—a good estimate considering the paucity of information available early in 1943.

In the main, the USSBS findings corroborate the more cautious views. In the later stages of the war, the Japanese succeeded in applying mass production methods in a few industries, shipbuilding and aircraft. A small segment of their industry was successful in producing high-precision instruments. But on the whole, they were markedly inferior to the American standards with which many estimators credited them.

Similarly, no extensive inquiry was made as to whether the Japanese could plan and direct the vast intricate industrial-governmental complex which is necessary for modern war. Estimators had opinions on this matter, snap judgments pro or con Japanese administrative ability being made on the basis of an anecdote, an isolated instance, or on the surprising extent of Japan's victories early in the war. "Management and over-all

planning are excellent" the COA reported in 1943. The BEW included a chapter on Problems of War Time Economic Administration in its "Japan's War Economy." This discussed the development of wartime controls, the resistance to such controls by the industrial leaders, the internal stuggles between competing groups in Japan and suggested that "these serious limitations on efficient administration" might have had adverse effects on war production. Referring to the establishment of what was to become the Munitions Ministry, it pointed out that "the centralization of authority over economic administration should materially increase efficiency of production during the coming year." These observations were in the right direction, but the degree to which administrative difficulties were interfering with Japanese production was not fully appreciated, even by the BEW. OSS made a short study of the Japanese civil service system in "Civil Affairs Handbook," a section on government and administration, prepared for the military government. This is a descriptive study only, listing the various titles, grades, promotion rules, etc., in the Japanese civil service. It does not discuss the administrative ability of the civil service, except for one sentence to the effect that it is "honest and efficient." The chapter in the BEW report is the only attempt to determine the influence of administration on production. Nowhere was any systematic study made of the habits, attitude, and competence of Japanese administrative agencies.

USSBS findings indicate that the practices and psychological attitudes of the Japanese administrative group were factors in the decline of Japan's economy. Until the end of 1942 they coasted along, lacking a sense of urgency. They did not anticipate the need for substantial increases in production and as a result did not make vigorous enough attempts to import raw materials from the southern areas. Although they had acquired a vast overseas empire and were completely dependent on imports which had to run the gauntlet of Allied submarines, ship construction plans for 1944, made early in 1942, were only 700,000 tons, in contrast to the 1,600,000 tons they were able to produce in 1944 when aroused to their peril. Stocks of scarce materials were wasted, expanding industries in which there was already excess capacity. Even after aircraft production was ostensibly unified under the Munitions Ministry in 1943, the testimony of its chairmen, Fujihara

Genjiro, shows that this control was not effective, branches of the army and navy continuing to grab materials and tools from manufacturers to whom they had been assigned. Accounting practices were so poor and the official language so ambiguous that control agencies were never able properly to regulate the distribution of materials. Scarce commodities leaked into the black market throughout the war. Materials were sometimes channeled into low priority industries because the only way to keep peace between the army and the navy was to give each 50 percent of available supplies. Real power rested in the hands of committees which seldom agreed on definite action. Faced with a catastrophe, the bureaucracy was unable to change its stereotyped routine. The exuberance of yesterday's victories was replaced by the depression of present defeat. No one, dared to assume individual responsibility when group control was shattered. All of this behavior had adverse effects on the economy and was a substantial contributing cause of the decline in industrial output.

II

Many agencies worked in Washington [1] on problems connected with estimating Japanese production. Joint Intelligence Committee (JIC) made special studies for the joint chiefs of staff. Navy groups included the Far Eastern section of ONI, OP 16 VA, Pacific Strategic Intelligence Service (PSIS). Army agencies were the Far East Target Section of A–2 and Military Intelligence Service. Civilian agencies were the Office of Scientific Research and Development (OSRD), Office of Strategic Services and the Foreign Economic Administration.

It is sometimes said that these agencies were wastefully competing and duplicating each other's work. Examination indicates such a view is exaggerated and omits certain facts:

1. Some agencies specialized in types of research which they were peculiarly equipped to do. For example, OSRD studied physical damage from various types of explosives and incendiaries; ONI confined its strategic intelligence to certain phases of shipping, lending personnel to other agencies engaged in research on other subjects.

2. Several committees to coordinate the work of the various agencies were formed, the Com-

mittee of Operations Analysts (COA), the Enemy Oil Committee (EOC), which was replaced by the Joint Far Eastern Oil Committee in 1945 sponsored by MIS. These committees issued their own reports after considering the views of each agency.

3. Joint Target Group was formed in 1944 through the merger of Far East Target Section of A–2 and the target Section of OP 16 VA to supply target intelligence for the Army Air Forces and the Navy. Personnel for JTG were also drawn from OSS and FEA. Joint Army-Navy Intelligence Service (JANIS) took over activities which had previously been done independently by the Army, Navy, Marine Corps and OSS. The Joint Army-Navy Assessment Committee reviewed claimed ship sinkings and its findings were accepted by all services.

4. There was a great deal of useful collaboration among the agencies. Much basic work on the capacity of Japanese industries was done by FEA. Other groups accepted these capacity figures but applied their own methods for ascertaining the rate of production. After 1944, PSIS and MIS exchanged information, MIS taking over the economic estimating. During 1945, MIS frequently briefed sections of JTG and other agencies on the results of its findings. JANIS concentrated on area studies, adopting OSS's industry analyses.

5. There was also a great deal of unofficial cooperation, interchange of data and ideas among the operating personnel of the various agencies.

The existence of several agencies permitted publication of different opinions. This study indicates that the point of view of the estimator on the general Japanese situation was an important factor in determining estimates for particular items. Had there been a single agency, a unified but erroneous point of view might have led to the suppression of dissenting opinions. The country was not so poor in research talent that it could not afford some duplication. The advantage of providing a forum for the free expression of varying views outweighed the slight waste.

However, within the limits of security, information and data possessed by one agency should be available to others with a legitimate interest. Occasionally, military personnel did not appreciate that certain tactical information had an important bearing on economic intelligence. For example, in the early stages of the war, the Navy

---

[1] Joint Intelligence Group Pacific Ocean Area (JIGPOA) and several others operated in the Pacific Ocean area but are not included in this study. They concentrated on tactical and operational intelligence.

was reluctant to keep research divisions, including its own OP 16 VA, fully informed of the progress of Japanese ship sinkings. Japan's merchant fleet was regarded too exclusively as a target, and there was not sufficient understanding of the relation of shipping to the economic situation. As the war progressed, this attitude was somewhat changed. Cominch, for example, screened its tactical reports for economic data and this was exchanged with MIS.

A considerable degree of cooperation finally prevailed among the various agencies at the close of the war. However, there is evidence of poor coordination between research agencies and field operation centers. Planners, not appreciating the time required for careful research, sometimes failed to notify research agencies of proposed operations early enough for them to prepare strategic data. For example, because of late notice, some JANIS studies of New Guinea and the Marshall Islands were not ready until after invasions of these areas had taken place. This situation appears to have been improved by the latter stages of the war.

Difficulties for research analysts were also caused by some operational reports which were written from a "press release" viewpoint without sufficient regard for accuracy. On the other hand, research analysts sometimes devised target systems without adequate consideration of operational limitations, such as weather, visibility, possible target accuracy, etc. Conflicting reports were sometimes sent to field target officers. In considering the oil attack, the target section of the Twentieth Air Force received four different estimates from four different agencies concerning the Japanese oil position. It has been suggested above that it is not disadvantageous to have several agencies studying economic intelligence. But so far as possible, information should be coordinated before being sent to the field.

Some agencies were alert to the importance of getting the results of their research into the field quickly. MIS had its studies mimeographed and flown to Guam. A special channel was arranged for prompt radio communication. When it was found that printing delayed distribution, JANIS had 25 copies of each of its studies mimeographed and flown overseas with instructions that printing copies would follow.

Perfectionism about unessential trivia caused tragic delays in the publication of JTG's studies.

Target sheets were reprinted two and three times, multicolored mosaics were made when photostats of a crayon drawing would have been adequate. Sample checks reveal that the average time consumed in printing was over 2½ months. Delays were also caused by modifications in the presentation of material. The air objective folders had been made on an area basis, industrial data being given for each area. This format did not adequately indicate the economic vulnerability of the various industries. To remedy this, JTG made its first studies on an industrial basis, but unfortunately, this method proved unsuitable for use at operational centers because it did not sufficiently locate the targets. In the spring of 1945, JTG began redoing its studies to combine a functional and a geographical analysis. This proved to be an excellent system. However, as a result of these delays, most JTG target data arrived in the field after the target had been bombed.

To make proper use of strategic research, a well-manned field intelligence staff is required to evaluate it in the light of operational intelligence. The target section of the Twentieth Air Force was badly understaffed. During the most important stage of operations it consisted of a lieutenant colonel, a first lieutenant, and a private first class. For short periods they secured the loan of a civilian, a signal officer, and two Navy language officers. While the understaffed target section of the Twentieth Air Force was slaving away in midnight sessions improvising target material, JTG personnel were demoralized with the realization that their completed research came frequently too late to be of any use.

III

We have seen that, throughout the war, there persisted two views of Japan's economy, one that it was weak and starving, the other that it was powerful and well stocked, retaining a substantial residuum of strength till very late in the war. These divergent views led to different estimates of particular items. In general the lower estimates were more accurate because to a greater extent than the others, they were based on a truer picture of the over-all situation.

Most American intelligence agencies overestimated Japan's economic strength, and the error was, in the main, caused by improper evaluation of two factors:

1. A misunderstanding of the over-all position of Japan's economy. Completed preparations were assumed to represent minimum war potential. Only a very few realized that, right from the start of the war, Japan's industries were starved for raw materials.

2. Failure to consider sufficiently the effects on the war economy of the administrative ineptitude of the Japanese in industry and government.

Strategic economic intelligence must be based on a wider set of factors than those generally considered in statistical analysis. It requires the collection of all relevant facts about a country, including the level of education and the social organization and customs of the people, as well as their industrial and natural resources. It must use the methods of all the social sciences, even if they be still in the qualitative stage. Though no precise quantitative assessment can be made for some factors, they must still be given weight.

Specific Studies

Coal Estimates [1]

The Japanese Government issued no statistics on the coal industry after 1936. The various United States intelligence agencies were, therefore, confronted with the twofold task of determining the rate of expansion of coal production within Japan proper and the occupied countries during the period from 1936 to Pearl Harbor, and the effect of the war on the output of coal in Japan proper and on imports.

In general, two approaches to the problem were utilized. The first, which might be called the requirements method, assumed that Japan's key industries were operating at full capacity. The output of coal in Japan proper was then estimated. It was then further assumed that the coal required to make up the deficiency was being imported.

The 1943 FEA-COA report illustrates this technique. This survey placed coal production in Japan, during 1943, at 52 million metric tons; the actual figure was 55.5 million tons. It also estimated that Japan's general industrial activity was at capacity rate, consuming 68 million tons. Therefore, coal imports were calculated at 16.6 million tons.

In its 1944 report, FEA again assumed requirements of 68 million tons. Believing that domes-

[1] This section is based on a special memo by First Lt. Raymond Burnes.

tic production had risen 2 million tons to 54 million, it inferred "Japan proper will have to import by water shipment about 14 million metric tons to meet essential war needs." The report further high-lighted the importance of water transportation by estimating that in addition to the 14 million tons of water borne imports, about 10 million tons of coal produced in Japan proper would have to be shipped from point of production to a point of consumption wholly, or in large part, by water. Nevertheless, the report concluded, "The 1944 coal supply should be sufficient to meet essential requirements."

MIS adopted a substantially different technique. An appraisal of the rate of general industrial operations was made in terms of the available supply of raw materials, particularly imports. Attention was focused on shipments of coal and available shipping from the occupied areas to Japan proper. Revisions in estimates were made periodically, in the light of the rapidly shifting shipping situation.

Using this approach, MIS concluded in December 1944 that Japan was facing a general coal shortage, and that the iron and steel industry was suffering from a lack of coking coal. Japan's coal imports were estimated at 4.5 to 5.2 million tons, including coking coal, from the mainland. In July 1945, a second study concluded that Japan's industries were receiving coal at the rate of 42.25 million tons per year; the actual rate in June was 42.8.

The tables below indicate that the COA-FEA estimates of coal production in Japan proper compare favorably with the actual output. The basic weakness of the COA-FEA approach was the assumption that the Japanese economy was operating at close to full capacity through 1944. As late as November 1944, FEA estimated that Japan's industries would consume 68 million tons of coal. Total 1944 consumption did not, in fact, exceed 50 million tons. The MIS production estimate of 50.5 million tons on the other hand, was a result of its view of a much lower rate of general industrial activity.

The COA-FEA assumption that Japan could import the coal needed to maintain capacity operations in key industries during 1943 and 1944 was also unfounded. Actual imports were dictated by her deteriorating shipping position rather than by industrial needs and fell substantially below their estimates.

The table below indicates the estimates of coal available in Japan compared with the USSBS figures.

APPENDIX TABLE A-1.—*Coal available in Japan proper, 1943-45*

Year	USSBS	MIS	JANIS OSS	COA-FEA	A 2
1943	61. 5			68	[1] 58
1944	52. 4	50. 5	57	68	
1945	42. 8	42. 25			

[1] 10,000,000 tons deficit figure based on FEA requirements figure.

Source: MIS, report of December 1944 and July 1945; JANIS report of May 1945; COA adopted FEA report in 1943; FEA, Japan's War Economy, December 1943 and November 1944; A 2, North China Coal, May 1943.

Steel Estimates

Two different approaches were used to estimate Japanese iron and steel production. The first, typified by FEA, attempted to determine capacity and then applied a rate of production to that capacity. The second, exemplified by MIS, attempted to determine the amount of raw materials available and then applied conversion factors to this amount of raw materials. All analysts, of course, realized that the upper limits of production are determined by capacity and by raw materials, as well as other elements. The first group, however, believed that in the main, capacity was the specific limiting factor, the second that raw materials were the bottleneck in Japanese production.

In 1942, the BEW began its studies of Japanese steel capacity. Available information was collected and analyzed, and persons familiar with Japanese steel industry were interviewed. In March 1943, BEW estimated Japan's steel ingot capacity for 1942 at 9,526,000 tons. It was also believed that mills were operating at 90 percent of capacity, giving a production of 8,750,000 tons; actual production was 8,004,000 tons. Capacity was underestimated because much of the recent Japanese expansion was not yet known. The rate of production was overestimated at 90 percent of this capacity; the true rate was 75 percent of a larger capacity. The two errors compensated and the estimated production was quite close to the actual figure.

The BEW's view was: "The primary limitation on Japan's steel production is processing capacity * * * raw materials of all essential types are available to Japan in ample quantities." The actual situation was that, even at this early date, one third of Japan's steel facilities were unused because an insufficient amount of raw materials were being imported. To maintain production in 1942, Japan had to dip into its stock pile of iron ore to the extent of 1,206,000 tons.

By the fall of 1943, evidence of recent Japanese expansion was discovered and FEA raised the estimate of Japanese capacity to 13,690,000 tons; the actual figure was 13,976,000 tons. Production was assumed to be equal to 100 percent of capacity. "Raw materials will be adequate, unless shipping stringencies are greater than previously estimated." The COA adopted this report stating: "The committee believes there are now sufficient labor and raw materials * * * for the maintenance of the above steel production." The OSS estimate for 1943 was 13,600,000 tons. Actual production was 8,838,000, leaving 5,138,000 tons excess capacity.

On the basis of new studies of Japanese imports of raw materials, MIS in April 1944, concluded that all estimates of Japanese steel production were too high. In May, MIS translated this view into an estimate of 9,500,000 tons. The Far East Target Section of A-2 had come to a similar view and a joint MIS-A-2 minority report was presented to the COA. In disagreeing with the subcommittee's calculation of 13,690,000 tons, this report stated: "a basic disagreement exists with the conclusion that availability, in the absence of confirmatory evidence, necessarily implies full utilization of steel-furnace capacity * * * it is believed that the limiting factor in Japanese production of iron and steel is the supply of iron ore." A further caution was added to this estimate of iron ore production: "This amount represents mine production and not deliveries, which will be further conditioned by transportation factors."

In June 1944, OSS, using FEA capacity figures, estimated 1944 ingot production at 11,300,000 tons. The reduction in FEA figures was based on the view that industrial activity and imports had fallen off somewhat.

In November FEA again estimated production at 100 percent of capacity of 13,690,000 tons, stating, "Ample raw materials are available for such operations."

The COA in November 1944 accepted FEA's capacity figures, but adopted the MIS-A 2 view that production did not exceed 9,500,000 tons, stating, "Shortage of ore, rather than * * * capacity now limits iron and steel * * *".

In February 1945, JTG estimated 1944 production at 7,923,000 tons. JTG accepted the FEA capacity figures. However, from a study of blast furnace and coke activity based on photos which had become available from B–29 flights, a valuable (though somewhat ambiguous) captured document, and estimates of raw material imports by MIS, JTG concluded that production was at only 54 percent of capacity.

In March 1945, MIS estimated Japan's current rate of production at 4,560,000 tons; the actual rate then was 4,300,000 tons. In June, JTG placed March production at 6,024,000 tons. An unprinted July memorandum suggested, on the basis of photo interpretation and import figures from MIS, that current production might have fallen to a rate of 2,240,000 tons.

The capacity estimates, begun by BEW and completed by FEA, were remarkably close. However, production was substantially overestimated,

partly because the Japanese were credited with greater technological efficiency than they achieved. "The Japanese have the 'know how' * * *" FEA wrote in 1944. Yet the USSBS steel report is replete with examples of improper use and care of equipment, which reduced the productive ability of equipment. The primary source of error was the assumption by some groups that Japan had an adequate supply of ore and coke. What was not generally realized was that the Japanese shipping situation was tight, right from the start of the war, becoming desperate during and after 1943. Some estimates failed to consider that, at all stages of the war, the Japanese had to adjust their imports of raw materials for steel production to the limited supply of shipping available, and to the simultaneous demands by other industries for imported materials.

The tables below compare the various estimates for steel ingot capacity and production with the USSBS figures:

APPENDIX TABLE A-2.—*Steel ingot capacity, 1942–44*

[Thousands of metric tons]

Year	USSBS	BEW	FEA	JANIS	OSS	COA	JTG
1942	[1] 12,716	9,526					
1943	13,976	9,526	13,060		13,600		
1944	15,236		15,326	13,517	13,687	14,131	13,524

[1] Extrapolated from 1941 figure of 11,456.

Source: BEW, report of May 1943; FEA, Japan's War Economy 1943 and 1944: JANIS, Japan's Resources and Trade, September 1944 and May 1945; OSS, report of June 1944; COA, 1943 and 1944 reports; JTG, reports of February and June 1945.

APPENDIX TABLE A-3.—*Steel ingot production, 1942–44*

[Thousands of metric tons]

Year	USSBS	BEW	FEA	JANIS	OSS	COA	MIS	JTG
1942	8,004	8,750						
1943	8,838	8,750	13,060		[1] 13,600	13,060		
1944	6,503		13,690	{ 10,813 / 7,550 }	11,300	9,500		{ [2] 8,940 / [3] 7,923 }
1945 [4]	4,301						4,560	6,024

[1] Revised in June 1944 to 11,600.
[2] Estimate of June 1945.
[3] Estimate of February 1945.
[4] March rate.

Source: BEW, report of May 1943; FEA, Japan's War Economy 1943 and 1944; JANIS, report from Japan's Resources and Trade September 1944; OSS, report of June 1943 and 1944; COA, May 1943 and 1944 estimates; MIS, report of April 1945; JTG, reports of February and June 1945.

Steel Consumption Pattern

Estimates of consumption of rolled and semi-finished steel were prepared by FEA and JTG. The FEA estimate was based on practices and allocations during the war years which were followed in the United States, Great Britain, and Germany. Adjustments were then made for Japanese peculiarities and known plans. These results were checked with estimated Japanese production figures of various steel-consuming industries.

JTG approached the problem somewhat differently. In 1945 it translated estimates of activity in the Japanese ship, aircraft, and railroad industries, etc., into steel requirements. This method proved more accurate but it could not be used until much more information was available on Japanese war production plans, types of weapons, etc., than had been available at an earlier date. In addition, this method demands that other groups shall have completed estimates of industries using fabricated steel. It can be used only if the steel estimators are part of a large and coordinated group.

Exact comparisons with the Japanese figures were not practicable because the Japanese included different items in the various categories than listed by the American estimators.

Urban Areas [1]

The FEA study, Mass Attack on Japanese Cities, published in February 1943, was the first complete study of the possible effects of urban area attacks on Japan. Starting with the RAF premise that "the total effect of an area raid depends primarily upon the proportion of houses rendered uninhabitable," this report was directed "solely to demonstrating the great susceptibility of the Japanese industrial economy to such profound dislocation as would result from air operation on population centers." A pioneering effort, this report is of interest as an indication of how little detailed analysis of urban attack problems existed before 1943, despite widespread popular and official interest in that subject. The report pointed out that a high percentage of total Japanese population and industrial labor had been concentrated, prior to the war, in a few large Japanese cities. British experience was drawn upon, as well as some of the available Japanese fire insurance data, to suggest Japan's high vulnerability to incendiary attack.

[1] This section is based on a special memorandum contributed by Mr. Lee Canfield.

The bulk of the report was devoted to a general description of Tokyo, Yokohama, Kobe and Osaka, using prewar census data to establish districts of highest residential density. The study did not go into attack objectives or operational methods and no attempt was made to estimate production loss or to compare the results which might be achieved with the effects of precision attacks on war industry. A brief general discussion of urban attack consequences mentioned (1) housing and consumer goods replacement, which "might mean diversion of labor and materials from war industry and have a profound effect on output," (2) temporary disruption of essential rail traffic in connection with emergency relief measures and (3) factory absenteeism.

In October 1943, the Far East Target Section of A-2 published its Japanese Incendiary Attack Data. This study may properly be regarded as the basic planning document for B-29 operations against Japanese cities. In contrast to . the primary emphasis on dehousing in the FEA report discussed above, this study stressed the possibilities of heavy physical damage to war industries, and particularly to smaller feeder plants, concentrated in the main Japanese cities. Twenty selected cities were "zoned" for incendiary attack, after a detailed study of industrial and residential construction, factory location, roof coverage, firebreaks, fire-fighting facilities, and weather factors. On the basis of tests conducted against sample Japanese structures with the various available incendiaries, the M-69 gasoline-jet bomb in aimable clusters was recommended for use against urban incendiary zones and estimates were made as to the bomb tonnages which would have to be properly distributed to overwhelm civil-defense services and cause fires of conflagration proportions in the more vulnerable districts of each key city. In the absence of large operation tests, no attempt was made to determine the operational tonnages that would be required.

Regarding the results to be expected from urban attacks, this study pointed to reduction of industrial output as the primary consequence of urban attacks—through damage to (1)—major war plants; (2) small factories supplying critical components; (3) factories producing repair and replacement items, such as machine tools, and (4) finished and semifinished military and industrial goods in storage. Dehousing and destruction of consumer goods as well as disruption of supporting public services were expected to hinder seriously the restoration of essential production. The primary impact of incendiary attacks was expected to fall upon aircraft and ordnance components, marine engines, electrical equipment, machine tools, and general machinery—much of the capacity for which was concentrated in Tokyo, Kawasaki, Yokohama, Nagoya, Osaka, and Kobe. Particular emphasis, from the standpoint of delaying recuperation, was placed on relatively complete incendiary coverage of each center in a minimum time period. Likewise, the report stressed the need for a flexible plan of operations so as to maximize the cumulative inter-effects of precision and area attacks on those end-product industrial categories of highest priority at the time operations were instituted.

The Air Objective Folders, 1944, continued the thesis that urban area attacks would cause grave economic disturbances to Japanese economy. The regional configuration of essential production and the degree of economic interdependence among cities within and without given areas was emphasized. In assessment of the importance and vulnerability of major and satellite cities, transportation problems received considerable attention.

In its 1943 report, the COA adopted the basic approach and tentative conclusion of the A-2 "Incendiary Attack" study without making any further analysis of the economic or operational problems involved. Subsequently, a COA subcommittee was set up to apply British techniques in a detailed estimate of direct and indirect production loss which might be achieved through incendiary attacks on the six major industrial cities. A report appearing in September 1944 used more restrained language in affirming the thesis of Japanese industrial vulnerability to area attack. The diffuse effects of such attacks on key war production front line strength was emphasized and production loss estimates were posted on the assumption of a relatively vigorous repair and replacement program. The revised COA report of October 1944 continued urban areas in a third priority position, urging concentration of efforts on the six major centers, with attacks heavy enough to assure successful completion within a minimum time period.

The JTG urban study materials were pointed toward economic damage resulting from the destruction of urban areas containing high concentration of industrial activity. Elaborately annotated and zoned mosaics, listing areas suitable for incendiary or radar HE attack, were prepared. However, there was considerable reproduction delay and most of it arrived in the field after the targets were bombed. Field officers did not have the benefit of JTG work on radar alternates or the large volume of detailed material on secondary cities.

Analysis by the Urban Area and other divisions of the Survey measures the accuracy of estimates on location and distribution of industrial capacity, physical damage and production loss. In general, zoning of vulnerable residential and industrial areas was confirmed by later photo reconnaissance.

Oil Estimates

Shortly after Pearl Harbor, all intelligence agencies joined in forming the Enemy Oil Committee (EOC) to study the German and Japanese oil situation—study of Japan's position being assigned to the EOC's far eastern subcommittee. Representatives of BEW, Petroleum Administration for War, OSS, Ministry of Economic Warfare, ONI, State Department and MIS were on this subcommittee. It published a series of reports until its activity was terminated by a March 1945 directive of the Joint Chiefs of Staff, which transferred responsibility for assessing the Japanese oil situation to a newly formed Joint Far East Oil Committee (JFEOC), composed of representatives of the War Department (MIS and A-2) and the Navy Department. The new committee employed a "working group" made up, for the most part, of the Oil Section of MIS; the group also included Navy and A-2 personnel.

The JFEOC made the following major revisions in the EOC estimates:

1. Japan's imports from 1929–41 were restudied and the estimates were reduced.

2. The loss in refining was increased from 10 to 15 percent.

3. Consumption estimates for the pre-Pearl Harbor period were increased by one million barrels.

4. Synthetic oil estimates were reduced.

USSBS statistics indicate that all of these changes were improvements.

EOC estimates of Japan's stockpile of oil at the time of Pearl Harbor varied from 75 million to 80 million barrels. The JFEOC estimate was 57 million barrels. USSBS findings indicate a stockpile of 42.7 million barrels. Stockpiles of oil for

July 1945 were estimated by JFEOC at 5,700,000 barrels; the USSBS figure is 2,830,000 barrels.

Estimates for synthetic oil production were high, EOC placing them at about 9,500,000 barrels for 1944 and JFEOC at about 8,000,000 barrels. Total production from 1942–1944 was only 3,900,000 barrels.

For the key item of aviation gasoline reserves available in July 1945, the JFEOC estimate was 1,037,000 barrels, the USSBS finding 1,157,000 barrels.

The Oil Division report presents a detailed estimation of presurrender intelligence.

The oil assessments were among the most difficult to make because of the paucity of data about Japanese stockpiles, consumption and technological progress.

If the JFEOC revisions had been made earlier, the stringency of Japan's oil position would have been apparent sooner. An intensive submarine and mining campaign against the Sumatran oil sources could have been undertaken in 1944, which would probably have hastened Japan's collapse. The tables below compare the estimates with USSBS findings:

APPENDIX TABLE A–4.—*Stockpiles of oil*

[Thousands of barrels]

Date	USSBS	JFEOC	EOC
1941 December	42, 696	57, 403	75, 533
1944 December	6, 434	12, 244	[1] 32, 000
1945 July	2, 836	5, 795	[2] 27, 859

[1] EOC report 76, February 1944.
[2] EOC report 86, March 1945.

Source: EOC, reports #76 and #86; MIS, report of August 1945.

APPENDIX TABLE A–5.—*Aviation gasoline stocks (inner zone)*

[Thousands of barrels]

Date	USSBS	MIS
July 1, 1945	1, 157	1, 037

Source: MIS, report of August 1945.

APPENDIX TABLE A–6.—*Synthetic production 1942–44*

[Thousands of barrels]

Date	USSBS	MIS	EOC
Total synthetic production 1942 through 1944	3, 929	16, 560	20, 692

Source: MIS, report of August 1945; EOC report #86 March 1945.

Estimates of National Income

OSS made an excellent study of Japanese national income during the war. The extimates of the Japanese Cabinet Bureau of Statistics were carefully analyzed and revised. The OSS estimates were reworked by the Foreign Economic Division of the State Department in its study, "Japan's Capacity to Pay Reparations." The findings of the State Department after removing price fluctuations from the OSS estimates are remarkably close to the USSBS findings. It is the only source that indicates the lag in Japanese production in 1942. These studies could have been very valuable as trend indicators. However, no attention was paid to them.

The following table compares the OSS State Department estimates with USSBS findings, using 1940 as an index year.

APPENDIX TABLE A–7.—*Comparison of "Real" gross national product estimates, 1940–1944*

[Indexes, 1940=100]

Year	USSBS	State Department
1940	100	100
1941	101	102
1942	102	103
1943	113	109
1944	124	125

Estimates of Airplane Production

Estimates of Japanese aircraft production were based on a few prewar studies, studies of captured planes, interrogations of prisoners, photographic intelligence and analogies from American utilization of raw materials in aircraft production.

Estimates were published by FEA in August 1944. In the summer of 1944, by agreement among British and American intelligence agencies, information on Japanese production of aircraft was centered in MIS. The first MIS estimate was made in January 1945 and the second in July 1945. Curiously, the first MIS estimate was somewhat more accurate. The reason was that the disruption caused by dispersal, after March 1945, was not sufficiently known and considered in the second estimate. These estimates, and those made by FEA in August 1944 are compared with the USSBS findings in Appendix Table A 8.

APPENDIX TABLE A–8.—*Combat airplane production, 1941-45*

Year	USSBS [1]	MIS [2]	FEA
1941	3,180	4,170	---------
1942	6,335	7,308	5,812
1943	13,406	13,794	11,134
1944	21,058	23,918	---------
1945	7,128	8,980	---------

[1] 1945, January–June.
[2] MIS as of July 1945.
Source: FEA, August 1944 report; MIS report for July 1945.

In the BEW report Japan's War Economy, March 1943, estimates of total plane production for 1942 and 1943 were 7,200 and 16,693 planes, respectively, are comparable to USSBS figures of 8,861 and 19,000 planes.

Estimates for Aluminum [1]

In estimating Japanese aluminum production, most agencies adopted the capacity-requirement method, MIS alone made independent estimates for requirements and for production.

The estimates for aluminum capacity and requirements follow below:

APPENDIX TABLE A–9.—*Aluminum Capacity, 1943–45*

[Thousands of metric tons]

Year	USSBS	COA	FEA	JTG	OSS
1943	166	120–145	-------	-------	-------
1944	184	199	199	-------	185
1945	170	-------	-------	245	-------

APPENDIX TABLE A–10.—*Aluminum requirements, 1943–45*

[Thousands of metric tons]

Year	USSBS	COA	OSS	FEA	JTG	MIS
1943	144	105	100	-------	-------	-------
1944	158 (137)	150	118	168	-------	(130)
1945	[1] 40	-------	-------	-------	154	-------

( ) Indicate fiscal year.
[1] Represents first half of fiscal year.

[1] This section is based on a special report prepared by First Lt. Arthur Freedman.

A study of the requirements estimates suggests an interesting statistical error. The requirements for aluminum were determined by estimating aircraft needs and providing some additional allowances for other uses.

Most agencies based the aircraft-aluminum relationship on American experience. However, insufficient allowance was made for differences between the American and Japanese situations, including scale of output, degree of excess inventory accumulation, rate of expansion, size of planes, loss and wastage ratios, and percentage utilization of secondary metals. The significance of expansion is illustrative. The rate of expansion of United States plane production in 1942 and 1943 was greatly in excess of the Japanese. The vice in the analogy was accented by the fact that, in contrast to American experience, Japanese requirements during the last half of 1944 and 1945 declined as their aircraft production leveled off. Consequently, figures for receipts of aluminum shapes by aircraft plants during identical periods, overweighted input per plane by the amount of the increased inventories and work in process required for the next period. The quantitive magnitude of this factor was considerable. In addition to exaggerating the total aluminum input per plane, since recovery of scrap on aluminum input came in a later period when input had increased, the effect also was to undervalue the percentage of secondary availability, further exaggerating primary requirements.

On this basis FEA, COA, and JTG calculated that input of aluminum per plane was over 7 tons. MIS using British as well as American data and making adjustments for differences, estimated input at 5.46 tons per plane. The actual figure was 5.5 tons.

These estimates, except for the JTG and MIS figures are really requirements estimates rather than those for production. The analysis runs in these terms: The Japanese will require a certain quantity of aluminum during 1943 and 1944, an amount which the capacity estimates indicate is possible. The requirements estimates are therefore taken as production estimates. So long as raw materials were available, this technique worked fairly well, but it failed when shortages became important restrictive factors on production, as bauxite was after June 1944.

The following table compares the estimates for the production of aluminum with USSBS findings:

APPENDIX TABLE A–11.—*Aluminum production, 1943–45*

[Thousands of metric tons]

Year	USSBS	COA	OSS	FEA	JTG	MIS
1943	142	105	100			
1944	{144 / 118}	150	118	168		165
1945	[1] 26				182	[2] 27

[1] Rate as of June.
[2] Based on estimate for Apr.–July, 9,000 tons.

Source: COA reports for Nov. 1943 and Mar. 1944; OSS, report of May 1944; FEA, report of June 1944; JTG, report of June 1945.

JTG's high estimate of 182,000 tons in 1945 compared with a rate of 26,000 tons in June was due to two additional errors:

1. It was assumed that the Japanese had enjoyed complete success in converting bauxite capacity to aluminous shale processing capacity. In fact, the Japanese ran into unexpected technological difficulties which severely limited production.

2. It was assumed that the Japanese had been able to import adequate supplies of shale or that there was an adequate stockpile. "There is no evidence that aluminum production has suffered from lack of imports," the report for June 1945 states. In fact, the decline in production from a rate of some 20,000 tons in June 1945 was paralleled by a decline in imports: Bauxite from 350,000 tons in 1944 to 1,800 tons in 1945; shale from 150,000 tons in 1944 to 37,000 tons in 1945. That this decline in imports caused the drop in production is shown by the virtual disappearance of the stockpile of materials during this same period.

The MIS production rate of 27,000 tons for 1945 was based on an independent estimate of imports. The actual figure for Japan proper was 18,000 tons.

All agencies overestimated Japanese technical capabilities in utilizing raw materials. Intelligence estimates were based on the inference that the Japanese would require 2 tons of bauxite or 2.5 tons of aluminous shale per ton of alumina. The actual quantities required were 2.5 and 4 tons respectively. This implies a 20 percent lower yield from given supplies of bauxite and a 38 percent lower yield from shale than estimated

Japan's stock of bauxite at the beginning of the war was overestimated, the COA-FEA figure being 500,000 tons. The actual figure was only 250,000 tons.

APPENDIX B

GROSS NATIONAL PRODUCT OF JAPAN, AND ITS COMPONENTS, 1940–45

The estimates of the gross national product of Japan for the fiscal years 1940–44, presented in this report, were prepared by the U. S. Strategic Bombing Survey from a wide variety of source materials secured by the survey from Japanese Government agencies.[1] Although official national income estimates for the war years had been prepared by the Japanese Government, these were found to be so little suited to the analysis of economic developments that it seemed preferable to begin anew with the source data than to attempt to adjust the official estimates.

The major difficulty with the Japanese estimates was conceptual. In contrast to British and United States experience, the national income data in Japan were not used as the statistical framework for over-all economic planning during the war but were, rather, restricted largely to setting the sights for the sale of war bonds. Even in this use, an eye was kept on the propaganda impact of the estimates made public. The resulting concept of national income was a cross between the American definitions of income payments, national income and gross product. In addition, the Japanese estimates did not meet the needs of the survey from the standpoint of either their geographical coverage or the breakdown of items in the yearly totals. The latter difficulty would have been particularly troublesome in deflating for the substantial price rise that occurred during the war period.

The gross product estimates prepared by the survey were designed to cover the home islands of Japan—Honshu, Hokkaido, Kyushu, and Shikoku—thereby excluding Korea, Formosa, and Manchuria, as well as all more recently acquired

territories. The concept used was in general similar to the U. S. Department of Commerce concept of gross national product. This aims to measure the value of total goods and services produced within a given time period, before allowance for depreciation of capital goods. There are, however, several differences between the U. S. concept and that used for the Japanese economy.

1. The Japanese estimates include imputed rents of owner-occupied dwelling units.

2. They exclude interest on government debt from the total gross product and from government expenditures on goods and services.

3. They exclude government subsidies to private producers from the total and from government expenditures.

4. Overseas expenditures for direct war purposes, other than pay of military forces, are not included in government war outlays or in the foreign balance. Such expenditures are shown separately from the gross product categories. It was felt that by this treatment of overseas expenditures the allocation of Japan's home resources between war and nonwar use would remain clear.

In addition, it must be noted that the Japanese estimates do not include any time for the change in business inventories. This exclusion was not a conceptual one but was due to the lack of even reasonably satisfactory data on inventory movements.

As to the general adequacy of the results of this investigation, it is believed that the estimates accurately reveal the general structure of the Japanese war economy and the significant changes that occurred during the war years. Apart from the lack of inventory information previously mentioned, more or less complete source material was found for all the component elements for the gross

---

[1] Particular mention should be made of the invaluable assistance given by Yoshimitsu Asano, assistant chief of the planning division, ministry of finance and by Professor Yuzo Morita of the Yokohama college and the bank of Japan.

national product. It may be noted, however, that in the time available to the survey staff, it was not always possible to fully trace the precise contents of the various statistical series, a task which was made the more difficult by the language barrier.

More important as a source of error in the estimates was the considerable difficulty that arose in connection with black market pricing and the deflation problem. It was quite apparent from a study of the value and quantity data for many individual components of the gross product, including goods purchased by the government, that the government's official prices were exceeded in the sales of a significant part of total output. It was, however, impossible to determine the volume of black market transactions as a whole, and thus to adjust indexes of official prices for prices on the black market. It was necessary, therefore, to build up the deflated estimates as far as possible from quantity data and for the deflation of the remaining components to use a derived price index that reflected the course of both official and black market prices. The methods used are fully explained in the technical appendix to this report.

In order to provide some historical perspective to the data for the war years, the national income estimates of the ministry of finance for the period 1930–40 were linked to the survey's gross product

data. This series was deflated by the Bank of Japan cost-of-living index for the prewar years.

The following notes will describe the statistical source material from which the gross product estimates were derived as well as the details of statistical methodology used for the various components.

WAR EXPENDITURES

The basic sources for this component were checks, paid by the Bank of Japan out of the army and navy special war accounts and expenditures by the munitions ministry, as they appear in the settled accounts of the finance ministry. The only adjustment made to these data was the deduction of discharge allowances to military personnel. (Table 1).

No estimates were available for either the purchase of existing assets or for the net prepayments on supply contracts.

In addition to the above source materials, the war and navy ministries submitted a breakdown of their total outlays by object of expenditure (Tables 2 and 3). However, only the war ministry was able to further allocate its detailed expenditures between Japan proper and the overseas empire. The geographical allocation of navy expenditures, by object, was made by the survey on the basis of Bank of Japan data on the navy ministry's expenditures by territories.

APPENDIX TABLE B–1.—*Gross national product, fiscal years 1940–44*

[Billions of yen]

	1940	1941	1942	1943	1944
Gross national product	39. 8	42. 7	52. 6	54. 7	82. 4
Government	8. 0	10. 8	19. 1	26. 7	39. 8
National	6. 0	8. 5	17. 0	24. 2	36. 7
War	4. 7	7. 0	14. 9	21. 8	33. 4
Nonwar	1. 3	1. 5	2. 1	2. 4	3. 3
Local	2. 0	2. 3	2. 1	2. 5	3. 1
Private capital formation	5. 1	4. 6	5. 0	7. 5	11. 1
Plant and equipment	4. 5	4. 7	4. 7	7. 9	10. 0
Residential construction	. 4	. 5	. 3	. 2	. 1
Foreign balance	. 2	−. 6	(1)	−. 6	1. 0
Consumer expenditures	26. 7	27. 3	28. 5	20. 5	31. 5
War expenditures abroad	1. 0	2. 5	3. 9	9. 0	41. 6

1 Less than 50 million yen.

Source: USSBS.

APPENDIX TABLE B–2.—*War expenditures, fiscal years 1940–45*

[Millions of yen]

	1940	1941	1942	1943	1944	Apr.–Oct. 1945
Total	5, 723	9, 487	18, 753	30, 787	75, 052	47, 412
Army	4, 191	6, 383	10, 368	15, 764	45, 511	20, 868
Navy	1, 532	3, 104	8, 385	13, 779	19, 069	17, 553
Munitions Ministry				1, 244	10, 472	[2] 8, 993
Japan proper	4, 441	6, 562	14, 074	20, 984	31, 601	34, 842
Army	2, 988	3, 781	6, 653	8, 611	10, 198	11, 743
Navy	1, 453	2, 781	7, 421	11, 129	10, 931	14, 106
Munitions Ministry				1, 244	10, 472	8, 993
Overseas	1, 282	2, 925	4, 679	9, 803	43, 450	12, 572
Army	1, 203	2, 602	3, 715	7, 153	35, 313	9, 125
Navy	79	323	964	2, 650	8, 137	3, 447
Korea	91	222	239	230	605	1, 433
Army	84	209	209	179	442	1, 179
Navy	7	13	30	51	163	254
Formosa	49	120	148	280	557	1, 403
Army	38	64	58	120	293	861
Navy	11	56	90	160	264	542
Manchuria	370	1, 200	1, 405	1, 661	2, 295	1, 711
Army	369	1, 198	1, 405	1, 661	2, 288	1, 711
Navy	1	2			7	
China	772	1, 062	1, 512	4, 301	27, 828	6, 837
Army	712	831	1, 123	2, 638	21, 988	4, 597
Navy	60	231	389	1, 663	5, 840	2, 240
Southern Territories	0	321	1, 373	3, 328	12, 166	1, 186
Army	0	300	919	2, 554	10, 301	777
Navy	0	21	454	774	1, 865	409
Discharge Allowances [1]	1	2	2	2	3	2, 583
Army						1, 134
Navy	1	2	2	2	3	1, 449
Net expenditures:						
Japan proper	4, 440	6, 560	14, 072	20, 982	31, 598	32, 259
Total	5, 722	9, 485	18, 751	30, 785	75, 049	44, 829

[1] All discharge allowances were paid in Japan proper.
[2] Partly estimated by USSBS.

Source: Finance ministry.

[Millions of yen]

	1940	1941	1942	1943	1944	Apr.–Nov. 1945
Total expenditures	4, 285	5, 258	8, 666	11, 570	48, 622	(1)
Japan proper	3, 057	3, 542	5, 723	7, 933	8, 973	11, 857
Pay, travel and subsistence	826	819	1, 094	1, 566	2, 661	3, 847
Pay to armed forces	172	195	278	518	1, 008	919
Clothing	319	352	482	546	924	1, 002
Food	283	216	242	393	556	600
Discharge allowances						1, 134
Other	52	56	92	109	173	192
Munitions and fuel	1, 625	1, 797	3, 267	4, 558	3, 085	3, 725
War construction	204	223	407	563	1, 067	1, 667
Other	422	703	955	1, 246	2, 160	2, 618
Overseas	1, 228	1, 716	2, 943	3, 637	39, 649	(1)
Pay, travel and subsistence	760	987	1, 444	1, 622	14, 070	
Pay to armed forces	280	345	650	624	1, 550	788
Clothing	36	34	45	83	1, 807	(1)
Food	401	550	667	829	10, 488	(1)
Other	43	58	82	56	225	132
Munitions and fuel	62	122	166	214	2, 911	(1)
War construction	164	284	468	674	4, 163	(1)
Other	242	323	865	1, 127	18, 515	(1)

1 Not available.

Source: War ministry.

The distribution of war expenditures between home and overseas and by object was required to show the approximate utilization of home resources and to permit satisfactory elimination of the influence of price changes.

The deflation procedure for these outlays in Japan proper was as follows: The changes in the physical volume index of munitions were applied to the 1941 value of munitions outlays to compute the output in 1941 yen for the years 1941 to 1944. Since the munitions index was not available for 1940, an estimate of a 10-percent increase in munitions prices from 1940 to 1941 was utilized in adjusting the derived series to the 1940 price level.

A somewhat similar method was used in reducing the pay, travel, and subsistence costs of the Japanese armed forces to the 1940 price level. This method was to move the 1940 value by the changes in the average number of the military personnel in the years 1940 through 1944.

"All other" war expenditures in the home islands were deflated by Professor Morita's wholesale price index (described below).

The deflation of Japan's overseas war outlays presented a much more difficult problem. The absence of any output data necessitated the use of a price index for deflation purposes. Despite the sharp upward movements in prices (especially in China and the southern territories) the exchange rates were held constant through the entire period. The only available price indexes were for wholesale prices in the Chinese cities of Shanghai, Peipen, and Tientsin. The latter two cities experienced a sixfold increase in price level from 1940 to 1944 while the increase in Shanghai was sixty-six times. Consultation with informed Japanese suggested that the only expedient was to use an average of prices in Peipen and Tientsin to deflate the overseas' war expenditure component as it was felt that smaller price rises in other areas would offset the fantastic rise in Shanghai. Needless to say, the margin of error of this series is considerable.

APPENDIX TABLE B–4.—*Expenditures of the imperial navy, fiscal years 1940–45*

[Millions of yen]

	1940	1941	1942	1943	1944	Apr. 1–Oct. 25 1945
Total expenditures	1, 531	3, 106	8, 386	13, 779	19, 069	18, 055
Pay, travel and subsistence	170	366	752	1, 310	3, 977	5, 499
Pay to armed personnel	39	97	235	315	554	504
Discharge allowances	1	2	2	2	3	1, 449
Other	130	267	515	993	3, 420	3, 546
Munitions	978	1, 814	5, 629	9, 114	8, 522	5, 619
Naval ships	457	906	1, 762	3, 293	4, 122	2, 189
Aircraft	460	906	3, 045	4, 092	2, 203	1, 572
Other	61	----------	822	1, 729	2, 197	1, 858
War construction	249	657	1, 131	1, 948	3, 393	2, 786
Other	134	269	874	1, 407	3, 177	4, 151

Source: Navy ministry.

APPENDIX TABLE B–5.—*Expenditures of the munitions ministry, fiscal years 1943–45*

[Millions of yen]

	1943	1944	Apr. 1–Oct. 15 1945
Total	1, 244	10, 472	8, 993
Aircraft	289	8, 528	6, 893
Other	955	1, 944	[1] 2, 100

[1] Partly estimated by USS BS.
Source: Finance ministry.

APPENDIX TABLE B–6.—*War expenditures by object, fiscal years 1940–45*

[Millions of yen]

	1940	1941	1942	1943	1944	Apr.–Oct. 1945
Total expenditures	5, 732	9, 485	18, 741	30, 785	75, 048	44, 831
Home Islands [1]	4, 740	6, 950	14, 852	21, 786	33, 448	33, 297
Pay, travel and subsistence	1, 167	1, 330	2, 145	2, 745	5, 410	4, 581
Munitions	2, 685	3, 822	8, 368	13, 501	19, 190	15, 534
Other	898	1, 798	4, 329	5, 540	8, 848	13, 182
Overseas	982	2, 535	3, 899	8, 959	41, 600	10, 634
Travel and subsistence	500	697	956	1, 384	13, 925	[2]
Munitions	119	272	1, 166	1, 414	5, 911	[2]
Others	363	1, 566	1, 777	6, 201	21, 764	[2]

[1] Includes pay of Japanese armed forces wherever stationed.
[2] Not available.
Source: USSBS, based on data from various government agencies.

CENTRAL GOVERNMENT NONWAR EXPENDITURES

Nonwar expenditures of the central government were based on actual outlays in the years prior to 1944 and on the "working budget" for 1944 (table 7). In addition to the exclusion of subsidies and interest payments—indicated in the introduction—all current accounts of government-operated public utilities were excluded.

Other adjustments made to these data in de-riving nonwar outlays for goods and services (table 8) were the elimination of duplication between the various accounts, of the purchase of existing assets, and of transfer payments to individuals.

Inability to obtain any data on government man-hours or other physical volume indicators of government's nonwar expenditures necessitated the utilization of wholesale price indexes for eliminating price fluctuations.

APPENDIX TABLE B-7.—*National government expenditures* [1]

[Millions of yen]

	1940	1941	1942	1943	1944
General account	6,174	8,657	9,319	14,400	21,836
Administrative expenses	1,831	2,259	4,475	7,006	10,827
Pensions and annuities	296	375	424	479	568
Subsidies	654	1,191	1,694	2,973	4,949
Interest on national debt	975	1,238	1,793	2,356	3,346
Reserve funds	110	340	840	1,580	2,140
War and Navy Ministries	2,304	3,250	79	2	2
Imperial household	4	4	4	4	4
Capital accounts	609	856	1,231	1,242	1,922
Investment	194	396	618	465	475
Imperial railway	346	390	503	618	1,025
Communications	69	70	110	159	422

[1] Excludes special war account.
Source: Budget Bureau, Finance Ministry. 1944 based on working budget; other years from settled accounts.

APPENDIX TABLE B-8.—*Derivation of national government nonwar expenditures*

[Millions of yen]

	1940	1941	1942	1943	1944
General account: Administrative expenses	1,831	2,259	4,475	7,006	10,827
Add: Imperial household	4	4	4	4	4
Less:					
Extraordinary military expenses	600	885	2,623	4,369	7,206
Grants to local governments	277	320	453	572	902
Assistance to soldiers' families	54	69	84	104	161
Transfer to government investment fund				12	40
Purchase of existing assets [1]				200	500
Munitions department expenditures (other than subsidies)				247	72
Equals: Expenditures for goods and services	904	989	1,319	1,506	1,950
Capital accounts, total	609	856	1,231	1,242	1,922
Less:					
Transfers to general account	100	240	230	189	150
Transfers to special war account	67	80	230	180	467
Equals: Expenditures for goods and services	442	536	771	873	1,305
Total expenditures for goods and services	1,346	1,525	2,090	2,379	3,255

[1] Compensation for property destroyed in preparation of air-raid firebreaks.
Source: Finance ministry and USSBS.

LOCAL GOVERNMENT EXPENDITURES

The basic data on local government expenditures (table 9) supplied by the ministry of home affairs consisted of the "settled accounts" for 1940 and 1941 and the budgets for 1942 and 1943. Budgetary data were available for prefectural governments only in 1944—and these data were used for extrapolation of the 1944 municipal and village expenditures.

The adjustments, shown in table 10, and the deflation procedure for this component were similar to those used for central government non-war expenditures.

APPENDIX TABLE B-9.—*Local government expenditures, fiscal years 1940–44* [1]

[Millions of yen]

	1940	1941	1942	1943	1944
Total	3,114	3,494	3,172	3,557	4,375
Education	600	709	695	818	1,100
Public works	341	375	293	339	375
Sanitation	109	74	125	162	250
Subsidies	292	325	201	247	300
Social services	79	84	85	81	125
Police and civilian defense	161	229	226	297	375
Town planning	61	64	102	126	100
Gas and electric	163	222	163	128	125
Water works	78	98	117	136	175
Interest on local bonds	488	473	445	460	650
Reserve fund	45	50	29	38	25
Motor bus operation	34	33	64	43	25
All other	663	758	627	682	750

[1] Excludes electric railways' accounts.

Source: Department of Home Affairs and USSBS, 1940–41 are actual expenditures; 1942–43 based on budgets; 1944 estimated by USSBS on basis of trend in prefectural government budgets.

APPENDIX TABLE B-10.—*Derivation of local government expenditures, fiscal years 1940–44*

[Millions of yen]

	1940	1941	1942	1943	1944
Total expenditures	3,114	3,494	3,172	3,557	4,375
Less:					
Subsidies	292	325	201	247	300
Interest	488	473	445	460	650
Public service enterprises	275	353	344	306	325
Reserve fund	45	50	29	38	25
Equals:					
Purchases of goods and services	2,014	2,293	2,153	2,506	3,075

Source: USSBS based on appendix table 9.

PLANT AND EQUIPMENT OUTLAYS

The source of these data for 1942–44 was the authorizations under the Emergency Funds Control Act. Under this legislation, all expenditures for new plant and equipment by companies with capitalization of more than 200,000, and expenditures of 50,000 or over by smaller companies had to be approved and authorized by the Finance Ministry.

The Ministry in cooperation with the Bank of Japan was able to adjust this information for timing and unused authorizations. Purchases of existing assets, other than land were excluded. It was believed that most expenditures on land were for improvements rather than direct purchases. These estimates were available by type of machinery in 1942 and by industries for 1943 and 1944. The data were available in somewhat modified form in 1940 and 1941 and permitted a rough allocation between munitions and other industries in the latter year.

The allocation of capital expenditures into

89

munitions industries and nonmunition industries, shown in the gross national product tables and appendix table 11, is only intended as an approximation. Outlays in the mining, metal refining and fabricating, and the chemical industries were included in the "munitions" category while capital expenditures in all other industries were classified as "nonmunitions" (see table 11). Even though outlays of the latter group were quite small by 1944, it is probable that they, too, were rather directly related to the war effort by that time.

RESIDENTIAL CONSTRUCTION

The estimates of the value of residential construction were based on the monthly construction statistics collected by the Ministry of Industry and Commerce from 1937 to mid-1943 (at which time the series was discontinued). These data covered

APPENDIX TABLE B-11.—*Private plant and equipment expenditures, fiscal years 1941-44* [1]

[Millions of yen]

	1941	1942	1943	1944
Total	4, 615	4, 743	7, 904	10, 125
Munitions Industries	2, 965	3, 506	7, 019	9, 371
Aircraft		1, 551	1, 076	1, 701
Ordnance			1, 941	2, 402
Shipbuilding		443	1, 835	1, 873
Wooden ships	1, 800		523	404
Railway cars and locomotives		17	7	11
Motor vehicles		39	24	5
Iron and steel		473	295	832
Light metals	500	107	234	534
Chemicals	175	204	262	680
Machine tools		96	96	130
Other machinery and tools	190	152	142	129
Coal mining		254	270	368
Mining other than coal	300	170	314	302
Nonmunitions industries	1, 650	1, 237	885	754
Cement	25	25	14	39
Electric power	525	453	242	146
Food			32	17
Textiles			37	13
Gas	1, 100	759	24	24
Agriculture and forestry			68	51
Other industries			468	464

[1] Includes small amounts for purchases of land.

Source: 1942-44, Finance Ministry. 1941, USSBS based on loans for new plant and equipment authorized under the Working Capital Regulation Act.

APPENDIX TABLE B-12.—*Derivation of residential construction activity, fiscal years 1940-44*

[Expenditure data in millions of yen]

	1940	1941	1942	1943	1944
1. Expenditures in 21 leading cities [1]	238	300	158	na	na
2. Total expenditures (1) × 1.65 [2]	393	495	260		
3. Lumber allocated to residential construction (thousand koku) [1]	8, 460	9, 720	4, 992	3, 864	2, 166
4. Lumber allocation index	169	194	100	77	43
5. Wholesale price index of construction materials [3]	92	97	100	105	122
6. Index of average wages [4]	82	97	100	111	138
7. Construction cost index [5]	87	97	100	108	130
8. Estimated construction expenditure index (4) × (7)	147	188	100	83	56
9. Total expenditures	393	495	260	220	145

na—not available.

[1] Department of Industry and Commerce.
[2] See technical notes for derivation of this multiplier.
[3] Bank of Japan index.
[4] Cabinet Bureau of Statistics.

[5] Arbitrary assumption that materials and labor costs have equal weight. The attempt to economize on materials during the war probably introduces a downward bias in this cost index.

Source: United States Strategic Bombing Survey.

21 of the leading cities of Japan. The cities, all of more than 100,000 population, represented (according to the 1940 census) approximately two-thirds of the urban population and one-fourth of the total population. This sample, for the years 1940 through 1942, was blown up by 65 percent to arrive at a nation-wide total. This factor rests upon the assumption that the sample was representative of the entire urban population and that rural outlays for housing were about 10 percent of urban outlays. Judging by American experience these assumptions may result in some overestimation.

This series was extrapolated to 1943 and 1944 by use of an index based on lumber allocation, construction material prices, and wage rates. The annual changes in this index corresponded closely to those of the value data in the overlapping 1940–42 period (table 12).

The price variations in the residential construction series were removed by use of the index of lumber allocations to residential housing.

FOREIGN BALANCE

The Finance Ministry supplied complete data on the balance of international payments apart from military expenditures that were not made through ordinary controlled channels, invasion currency, and locally arranged bank credits. These financing methods are believed to account for the bulk of overseas military expenditures. The major difficulty was the separation of accounts between Japan proper and Formosa and Korea. In some cases it was impossible to remove the transactions of the latter territories, but it is not felt that this shortcoming introduced any significant error into the net balance.

The foreign balance (current account) series, shown in table 13, was not adjusted for price variations.

APPENDIX TABLE B–13.—*Balance of international payments, fiscal years 1939–44*

[Millions of yen]

	1939	1940	1941	1942	1943	1944
Exports:						
Merchandise	3,891	4,219	2,888	2,010	1,778	1,321
Shipping	41	107	70	18	15	15
Insurance	23	31	42	49	43	19
Interest and dividends	74	104	126	218	247	229
Tourists' expenditures	19	21	33	50	49	181
Government receipts	464	640	741	748	1,028	1,774
Miscellaneous services	260	369	411	559	814	1,069
Total	4,772	5,491	4,311	3,652	3,974	4,608
Imports:						
Merchandise	2,654	3,087	2,198	1,477	1,607	1,161
Shipping	60	79	54	37	50	74
Insurance	27	32	21	31	27	29
Interest and dividends	57	42	31	9	3	106
Tourists' expenditures	19	26	19	45	66	127
Government payments	1,479	1,688	2,219	1,919	2,582	1,778
Miscellaneous services	217	347	359	125	256	327
Total	4,513	5,301	4,901	3,643	4,591	3,602
Net balance on current account	259	190	−590	9	−617	1,006
Investment of foreigners in Japan	61	85	103	677	505	285
Withdrawal of overseas' investments	100	154	184	167	219	239
Total	161	239	287	844	724	527
Investment of Japanese in foreign countries	1,176	1,290	1,614	1,640	1,760	1,274
Withdrawal of home investment of foreigners	135	106	79	119	85	255
Total	1,311	1,396	1,693	1,759	1,845	1,529
Net balance on capital account	−1,150	−1,157	−1,406	−915	−1,121	−1,002
Other transactions and residual	891	967	=1,996	906	1,738	−4

Source: Finance Ministry.

CHANGE IN INVENTORIES

As it was impossible to obtain any quantitative data on the levels of business inventories, no series is included in the capital formation estimates. There is no doubt that there was continuing liquidation of consumers' goods stocks, starting in 1937. It is believed that these stocks had already reached a rather low level by 1940. On the other hand, Finance Ministry officials were of the opinion that there was a substantial accumulation in each war year of inventories in the munitions industries. It was believed, however, that a very substantial part of the increase would be accounted for by finished munitions that had been rejected as unusable by the military authorities.

CONSUMERS' EXPENDITURES

The estimation of consumers' purchases was made by the Ministry of Finance by the means of the following data:

1. Consumption tax data.
2. Production statistics adjusted for nonconsumer flow, exports, imports, and stocks. These physical volume series were valued at official prices.
3. Government revenue data for such items as transportation and communication.
4. Special government inquiries and other miscellaneous sources.

Most estimates of food expenditures were based on investigations of the Department of Agriculture and valued by use of the official price series.

Two comments that should be made in considering the detailed data on consumers' expenditures (table 14) are that they probably include a sizable amount of second-hand items toward the end of the war and that in all probability some minor items of consumers' expenditures may have been excluded.

Wherever possible, production and civilian supply data were used in removing the effects of price fluctuations. In other cases, relevant components of the cost of living index were used for deflation purposes.

CHANGES IN PRICE LEVEL

As has been mentioned previously, current value data expressed exclusively in terms of official prices could not be obtained for all component elements of the gross national product. Many elements were derived from source material on actual transactions, in which prices were known to be substantially above the official level. When such value series could not be matched with comparable quantity data, it was necessary to deflate for price changes by means of a price index which reflected extralegal pricing. The most appropriate index of this sort that could be secured was that computed by Professor Morita of the Commercial College of Yokohama.

In general, this index was a derived series obtained by comparison of the available quantity data on production and trade with a comparable transactions aggregate. While any method of this sort is not without serious pitfalls, it may be noted that the results obtained for the period 1936 to 1940, when the official price index was representative of actual price changes, are in line with the Bank of Japan index. Professor Morita was of the opinion that his index might well understate the price rise during the war years but that a bias towards overstatement was very improbable. A comparison between Morita's wholesale price index and that of the Bank of Japan is shown in table 15.

Other price data are shown in subsequent tables.

APPENDIX TABLE B-14.—*Consumer expenditures, 1940–44*

[Millions of yen]

	1940	1941	1942	1943	1944
Total expenditures	21,554	27,153	28,423	30,422	31,371
I. Food and nonalcoholic beverages [1]	13,155	12,300	11,341	12,214	13,857
A. Grain and grain products	5,475	5,218	4,277	4,945	4,935
1. Rice			3,560	4,260	3,941
2. Barley			126	142	170
3. Rye			171	175	238
4. Wheat			119	98	222
5. Flour			146	133	153
6. Bread			63	53	74
7. Other cereals and products			92	84	137

See footnotes at end of table.

	1940	1941	1942	1943	1944
I. Food and nonalcoholic beverages—Continued					
B. Spices	1, 140	1, 120	1, 018	935	874
1. Salt			18	19	19
2. Sugar			365	269	156
3. Soy			327	294	327
4. Other spices			308	353	372
C. Tea and candy [4]	1, 740	1, 433	1, 306	1, 212	891
D. All other	4, 800	4, 529	4, 740	5, 122	7, 157
1. Fruits and vegetables			1, 703	2, 311	3, 336
a. Beans			158	207	308
b. Potatoes			203	217	274
c. Sweetpotatoes			358	464	558
d. Other			984	1, 423	2, 196
2. Meats and animal products			633	679	586
a. Beef and pork			262	305	220
b. Chicken			177	159	173
c. Milk			120	127	111
d. Other			74	88	82
3. Fish and fish products			1, 873	1, 806	2, 945
a. Fish and shells			1, 060	824	1, 873
b. Dried fish			415	428	295
c. Seaweeds			398	554	777
4. Manufactured foods			531	326	290
a. Vegetable oil			55	38	23
b. Condensed and powdered milk			32	27	30
c. Refrigerated foods			64	64	86
d. Ice			23	23	23
e. Canned and bottled food			196	59	52
f. Dairy products [2]			23	23	23
g. Dried seaweed [2]			25	25	25
h. Ham and bacon [2]			8	8	8
i. Bean curd			105	59	20
II. Liquor [2]	998	1, 239	1, 667	1, 368	1, 510
III. Tobacco and tobacco products [1]	510	570	870	1, 265	1, 445
IV. Restaurants, hotels, geisha houses, etc.[2]	858	1, 140	1, 694	1, 920	1, 374
Tax (included above)	128	200	482	751	554
V. Clothing and furnishings	3, 464	3, 786	3, 329	3, 326	1, 979
A. Clothing excluding footwear	3, 128	3, 403	2, 962	2, 728	1, 454

See footnotes at end of table.

	1940	1941	1942	1943	1944
V. Clothing and furnishings—Continued					
B. Other [2]	336	383	367	598	525
1. Tax	29	46	52	159	241
2. Footwear			129	135	64
a. Shoes			48	40	15
b. Clogs			34	48	24
c. Rubber-soled socks			47	47	25
3. Hats, canes, umbrellas			60	72	48
4. Bags			34	48	27
5. Miscellaneous leather goods			2	2	0
6. Needles			4	3	3
7. Fans			2	5	11
8. Shoe polish			7	7	3
9. Baby carriages			7	33	30
10. Thermos bottles, etc			4	4	3
11. Jewelry			24	20	9
a. Watches			18	14	5
b. Precious metals			1	1	1
c. Jewels, feathers, etc			5	5	3
12. Other personal equipment			42	110	86
VI. Lighting and heating materials [1]	1,286	1,126	1,052	995	750
1. Matches [2]			51	56	70
2. Coal			62	50	49
3. Coke			7	5	3
4. Firewood			535	572	309
5. Charcoal			320	252	251
6. Candles			18	2	2
7. Kerosene			2	2	1
8. Other fuel substitutes			57	56	65
VII. Household utilities [1]	394	442	478	488	480
1. Water supply	51	56	60	71	71
2. Gas	63	64	76	58	35
3. Electricity	280	322	327	344	362
4. Tax on electricity			15	15	12
VIII. Furniture and furnishings [2]	435	498	662	727	616
1. Wood furniture			231	231	173
2. Bamboo articles			41	41	45
3. Screens and lanterns			2	5	4
4. Lighting fixtures			31	34	19
5. Electric bulbs			37	40	31
6. Indoor ornaments			21	28	12
7. Metal goods			34	4	4
8. Plate glass			10	10	16
9. Marble, etc			8	4	1
10. Cutlery			15	2	2
11. Tea sets			2	3	3
12. Pottery and lacquerware			28	50	23

See footnotes at end of table.

	1940	1941	1942	1943	1944
VIII. Furniture and furnishings—Continued					
13. Heaters			0	0	0
14. Ice boxes			4	3	2
15. Sewing machines			56	34	7
16. Radio sets			39	33	9
17. Other			9	11	8
18. Tax	45	76	94	194	257
IX. Housing	1,590	1,590	1,831	1,864	1,864
1. Rented dwellings [5]	611	611	703	716	716
2. Owner-occupied dwellings (imputed)	979	979	1,128	1,148	1,148
X. Health and personal care	1,040	1,241	1,551	1,702	1,895
A. Drugs and sundries	580	679	829	666	533
1. Medicines [1]			360	216	187
2. Soap [1]			165	133	71
3. Toilet goods [2]			108	104	72
4. Tonics [2]			112	112	112
5. Insecticides [2]			36	36	36
6. Tooth powder [2]			16	20	11
7. Shampoos [2]			13	17	13
8. Incense [2]			3	5	8
9. Bandages [1]			1	2	3
10. Razors [2]			8	8	7
11. Thermometers [1]			4	4	4
12. Medical instruments [1]			3	9	9
B. Medical and personal care [2]	460	562	722	1,036	1,362
1. Medical care			461	612	811
2. Bath houses			261	424	551
6. Barbers and beauty parlors			150	199	264
b. Tax	0	0	0	78	112
XI. Miscellaneous goods [2]	661	752	799	951	869
A. Paper products and stationery	213	237	563	635	443
1. Printing and binding [1]	213	237	248	302	203
2. Paper and paper products			295	277	214
3. Stationery, pens, pencils, etc			20	56	26
B. Photographic equipment			37	36	16
1. Cameras			10	8	2
2. Other			27	28	14
C. Sporting goods			11	15	8
1. Fishing tackle and supplies			4	4	5
2. Other			7	11	3
D. Art and literary products curios			58	61	7

See footnotes at end of table.

APPENDIX TABLE B–14.—*Consumer expenditures, 1940–44*—Continued

	1940	1941	1942	1943	1944
XI. Miscellaneous goods—Continued					
E. Musical instruments and supplies			24	16	8
1. Musical instruments			8	4	2
2. Gramophone disks			15	11	6
3. Gramophone			1	1	0
F. Flowers			6	11	24
G. Fireworks			11	1	1
H. Other			17	18	18
I. Tax	36	59	72	158	280
XII. Amusement [2]	255	294	377	415	394
1. Spectator amusements	207	231	249	257	240
2. Tax	23	33	93	122	118
3. Radio listeners' charge	25	30	35	36	36
XIII. Private education and religion	30	37	50	67	78
1. Private education [2]			30	40	43
2. Religion [4]			20	27	35
XIV. Passenger transportation	1, 149	1, 268	1, 606	1, 667	2, 354
1. Government railway [3]			725	886	1, 111
2. Government railway tax [3]	23	23	76	90	143
3. Local transit [4]			365	365	694
4. Automobile and parts [4]			237	154	144
5. Other [4]			203	172	262
XV. Other transportation and communications	117	122	157	179	218
1. Freight transportation [3]			41	56	60
2. Communications [3]			116	123	158
XVI. Miscellaneous professional and domestic services [2]	612	748	959	1, 274	1, 688

NOTES: The following footnotes apply in all cases to the years 1942–44 and, in the case of service items, to 1940 and 1941 as well. Expenditures for goods in 1940 and 1941 are based on production data exclusively.

[1] Based on production data adjusted for changes in inventories, exports and imports, and nonconsumer flow—valued at official prices.

[2] Based on consumption taxes.

[3] Based on government revenues.

[4] Other methods.

[5] Based on 1940 ratio of the number of owner-occupied dwelling units to rented units.

Source: Finance Ministry.

APPENDIX TABLE B–15.—*Wholesale prices in Japan*

[Indexes, 1936=100]

	Morita's series	Bank of Japan
1936	100	100
1937	119	121
1938	126	127
1939	145	141
1940	171	158
1941	184	167
1942	236	180
1943	267	191
1944	325	214

Appendix C

STATISTICAL SOURCES

The collection and collation of economic statistics which would provide an accurate picture of the economic development of Japan prior to and during the war was one of the foremost tasks of the U. S. Strategic Bombing Survey. It was much more difficult to accomplish than one might have thought. The coverage as well as the quality of economic statistics in Japan are highly unsatisfactory. Japanese statistics are contradictory, based on unreliable raw material, and the method of collection of basic information is greatly deficient.

There is no single agency which would be responsible for the entire field of statistical information. Government bureaus, industrial control associations, individual company records, had to be consulted in order to obtain a set of figures depicting the most important events in Japan's war economy with reasonable accuracy. The Cabinet Planning Board, the Cabinet Bureau of Statistics, and the Total Mobilization Bureau of the Munitions Ministry, all made attempts to secure the data needed for governmental planning—most of those attempts failed.

The statistics used by the Survey had, therefore, to be built up from scratch. They represent a considerable advance over what has been done in that field by the Japanese themselves. The reports of the individual divisions of the Survey present the time series relating to their specific fields. The following set of statistical tables covers the most relevant aspects of Japanese economic development in the last decade. They should prove useful to students of Japan's economic problems.

In the following tables, unless calendar year is explicitly stated, fiscal year should be understood. The Japanese fiscal year runs from 1 April to 31 March and almost all statistical series begin on 1 April of each year. When fiscal year is used, first quarter means April, May and June of that particular year. Last, or fourth quarter of 1943, for example, when on a fiscal year basis, would be January, February, and March of 1944. The rice year runs from 1 November to 31 October, while the fertilizer year extends from 1 August to 31 July. A "koku" is a measure of volume roughly equivalent to 5.12 bushels. A "kan" is a measure of weight equal to 3.75 kilograms or 8.27 pounds. A "sho" may be either a measure of volume in which case 100 sho equal 1 koku, or it may be a measure of area in which event it is equivalent to 2.45 acres. A "picul" is a unit of weight equal to 60 kilograms or 132 pounds.

APPENDIX TABLE C–1.—*Population, armed forces, and civilian labor force by sex and activity, Japan proper, 1 Oct. 1930, 1 Oct. 1940, 22 Feb. 1944*

[In 1,000's]

	1 Oct. 1930			1 Oct. 1940			22 Feb. 1944		
	Total	Male	Female	Total	Male	Female	Total	Male	Female
Total population	64,450	32,390	32,060	73,114	36,566	36,548	[1] 77,044	[1] 38,605	38,439
Armed forces	243	243		[2] 1,694	[2] 1,694		[3] 3,980	[3] 3,980	
Civilian population	64,207	32,147	32,060	71,420	34,872	36,548	[4] 73,064	[4] 34,625	[4] 38,439
Unoccupied	34,830	13,360	21,470	38,937	15,142	23,795	[5] 41,267	[5] 16,182	[5] 25,085
Civilian labor force [6]	29,377	18,787	10,590	[7] 32,483	19,730	12,753	[5] 31,797 [8] (31,657)	[5] 18,443 [8] (18,411)	[5] 13,354 [8] (13,246)
Agriculture and forestry	14,131	7,735	6,396	13,842	6,619	7,223	13,376	5,569	7,807
Fishing	568	515	53	543	476	67	464	380	84
Mining	316	271	45	598	529	69	805	681	124
Manufacturing and construction	5,876	4,428	1,448	8,132	6,178	1,954	9,494	7,243	2,251
Commerce	4,906	3,406	1,500	4,882	3,006	1,876	2,364	1,127	1,237
Transportation and communication	945	907	38	1,364	1,214	150	1,650	1,385	265
Government and professional	1,762	1,369	393	2,195	1,515	680	2,900	1,895	1,005
Domestic service	802	92	710	709	39	670	473	58	415
Miscellaneous	71	64	7	218	154	64	131	73	58

[1] Sum of civilian population (census) and armed forces (estimated). This overstates size of population of Japan Proper since armed forces include some persons recruited from territories outside Japan Proper.

[2] Information obtained by census takers from closest civilian relative. Adjusted on the basis of information obtained by USSBS from Army and Navy ministries. Separation into those in Japan Proper and those overseas has not proved feasible.

[3] Estimated from data supplied by Army and Navy ministries. Includes all members of Japanese armed forces, due to impossibility of segregating those from outside Japan Proper. Also includes some females (numbers unknown).

[4] Figures are subject to revision, since final figures have not yet been prepared by Japanese census authorities. Several differing sets of statistics have been drawn from the 1944 enumerations by various Japanese Government agencies using differing principles of coverage, classification, etc., without adequate explanation reconciliation of these differences, and of certain internal inconsistencies, must await a recomputation of the basic returns. The figures presented here are considered the most reliable of the various versions. It should be noted in comparing 1944 with other years, that the 1944 Census officially excluded from the count the population of certain administrative subdivisions of Tokyo-To and Hokkaido; the population of these districts in 1940 was approximately 24,000.

[5] The figures for the Labor Force and the Unoccupied in 1944 are subject to a bias relative to the corresponding figures for 1930 and 1940. See table 2 where the bias is discussed and adjustment is attempted.

[6] The break-down of the Civilian Labor Force by activity has been done in terms of the industry to which an individual is attached (Sangyo-betsu).

Unemployed workers were considered as attached to the industry in which they were last employed.

[7] Excludes a group officially designated as "foreigners," numbering about 40,000 in the civilian population.

[8] Figures in parentheses are a total of the industry subdivisions below them. The total is somewhat smaller than the figures for the labor force given on the line immediately above, due to the exclusion of certain civil divisions of Japan Proper, primarily Okinawa. Part of Karafuto, not included in previous census counts, is included.

Sources: 1930—All data from census enumerations as submitted by Japanese Cabinet Bureau of Statistics.

1940—Total population from census enumerations as submitted by Japanese Cabinet Bureau of Statistics.
Armed forces estimated from census data and data submitted by officials of Japanese Army and Navy ministries. Civilian population and labor force from census enumerations as submitted by Labor Bureau, Ministry of Welfare.

1944—Total population estimated (see note [1]).
Armed forces estimated from data submitted by officials of the Japanese Army and Navy ministries. Civilian population and labor force from census data submitted by Cabinet Bureau of Statistics. Industrial classification of labor force from census data submitted by Labor Bureau, Ministry of Welfare.

APPENDIX TABLE C-2.—*Civilian population, labor force and unoccupied, by age and sex, Japan proper, 1 Oct. 1930, 1 Oct. 1940, 22 Feb. 1944*

[In 1,000's]

1 OCTOBER 1930 [1]

Age	Civilian population			Labor force			Unoccupied		
	Total	Male	Female	Total	Male	Female	Total	Male	Female
0–14	23, 579	11, 895	11, 684	1, 072	483	589	22, 507	11, 412	11, 095
15–19	6, 540	3, 319	3, 221	4, 595	2, 605	1, 990	1, 945	714	1, 231
20–24	5, 531	2, 815	2, 716	4, 048	2, 585	1, 463	1, 483	230	1, 253
25–29	4, 835	2, 480	2, 355	3, 499	2, 399	1, 100	1, 336	81	1, 255
30–34	4, 214	2, 175	2, 039	3, 129	2, 131	998	1, 085	44	1, 041
35–39	3, 585	1, 857	1, 728	2, 722	1, 823	899	863	34	829
40–44	3, 286	1, 688	1, 598	2, 513	1, 652	861	773	36	737
45–49	3, 046	1, 525	1, 521	2, 295	1, 479	816	751	46	705
50–54	2, 831	1, 411	1, 420	2, 065	1, 344	721	766	67	699
55–59	2, 217	1, 086	1, 131	1, 508	998	510	709	88	621
60 and over	4, 786	2, 139	2, 647	2, 174	1, 531	643	2, 612	608	2, 004
Total	64, 450	32, 390	32, 060	29, 620	19, 030	10, 590	34, 830	13, 360	21, 470

1 OCTOBER 1940 [2]

Age	Civilian population			Labor force			Unoccupied		
	Total	Male	Female	Total	Male	Female	Total	Male	Female
0–14	26, 367	13, 324	13, 043	925	426	499	25, 442	12, 898	12, 544
15–19	7, 337	3, 646	3, 691	5, 261	2, 822	2, 439	2, 076	824	1, 252
20–24	5, 010	1, 965	3, 045	3, 528	1, 747	1, 781	1, 482	218	1, 264
25–30	5, 278	2, 463	2, 815	3, 670	2, 375	1, 295	1, 608	88	1, 520
30–34	4, 855	2, 415	2, 440	3, 537	2, 361	1, 176	1, 318	54	1, 264
35–39	4, 392	2, 230	2, 162	3, 320	2, 186	1, 134	1, 072	44	1, 028
40–44	3, 820	1, 963	1, 857	2, 964	1, 923	1, 041	856	40	816
45–49	3, 200	1, 642	1, 558	2, 506	1, 599	907	694	43	651
50–54	2, 882	1, 452	1, 430	2, 200	1, 386	814	682	66	616
55–59	2, 559	1, 240	1, 319	1, 809	1, 125	684	750	115	635
60 and over	5, 681	2, 510	3, 171	2, 763	1, 780	983	2, 918	730	2, 188
Total	71, 381	34, 850	36, 531	32, 483	19, 730	12, 753	38, 898	15, 120	23, 778

22 FEBRUARY 1944 [3]

Age	Civilian population			Labor force			Unoccupied		
	Total	Male	Female	Total	Male	Female	Total	Male	Female
0–14	26, 107	13, 222	12, 885	[4] 113	38	75	[4] 25, 994	13, 184	12, 810
15–19	7, 837	3, 822	4, 015	[4] 4, 784	2, 371	2, 413	[4] 3, 053	1, 451	1, 602
20–24	5, 227	1, 782	3, 445	3, 939	1, 570	2, 369	1, 288	212	1, 076
25–29	4, 625	1, 823	2, 802	3, 068	1, 757	1, 311	1, 557	66	1, 491
30–34	4, 716	2, 036	2, 680	3, 217	1, 991	1, 226	1, 499	45	1, 454
35–39	4, 475	2, 170	2, 305	3, 274	2, 134	1, 140	1, 201	36	1, 165
40–44	4, 200	2, 130	2, 070	3, 193	2, 095	1, 098	1, 007	35	972
45–49	3, 604	1, 855	1, 749	2, 805	1, 817	988	799	38	761
50–54	2, 968	1, 524	1, 444	2, 295	1, 475	820	673	49	624
55–59	2, 647	1, 318	1, 329	1, 946	1, 236	710	701	82	619
60 and over	6, 381	2, 827	3, 554	3, 023	1, 927	1, 096	3, 358	900	2, 458
Total	72, 787	34, 509	38, 278	[4] 31, 657	18, 411	13, 246	[4] 41, 130	16, 098	25, 032

[1] Differs from totals of civilian population and labor force in table 1 since data in this table for 1930 includes armed forces which numbered 243,000.

[2] Differs from totals in table 1 as a result of exclusion of a group officially designated as "foreigners" numbering about 40,000 in civilian population.

[3] Differs from totals in table 1 as a result of exclusion of certain civil divisions of Japan proper, primarily Okinawa; but includes part of Karafuto. The latter was not included in the census counts of earlier years.

[4] The break-down of these age groups into civilian labor force and unoccupied is subject to a bias as described in appendix table 2. An adjustment of this bias has been computed from a more detailed age break-down and results in the following net additions to be applied to the 1944 labor force in the table above:

Age 0–14: 803,000 (385,000 males; 418,000 females),

Age 15–19: 827,000 (587,000 males; 240,000 females),

Total civilian labor force: 1,630,000 (972,000 males; 658,000 females).

A corresponding decrease in the unoccupied should be made.

Source: Census data submitted by labor bureau, Ministry of Welfare.

APPENDIX TABLE C–3.—*Percentage distribution of civilian labor force by sex and activity Japan proper, 1 Oct. 1930, 1 Oct. 1940, 22 Feb. 1944*

	1 Oct. 1930			1 Oct. 1940			22 Feb. 1944		
	Total	Male	Female	Total	Male	Female	Total	Male	Female
Civilian labor force	100.0	100.0	100.0	100.0	100.0	100.0	100.0	100.0	100.0
Agriculture and forestry	48.1	41.2	60.4	42.6	33.5	56.6	42.2	30.3	59.0
Fishing	1.9	2.7	.5	1.7	2.4	.5	1.5	2.1	.6
Mining	1.1	1.5	.4	1.8	2.7	.6	2.5	3.7	1.0
Manufacturing and construction	20.0	23.6	13.7	25.0	31.3	15.3	30.0	39.3	17.0
Commerce	16.7	18.1	14.1	15.0	15.2	14.7	7.5	6.1	9.3
Transportation and communication	3.2	4.8	.4	4.2	6.2	1.2	5.2	7.5	2.0
Government and professional	6.0	7.3	3.7	6.8	7.7	5.3	9.2	10.3	7.6
Domestic service	2.7	.5	6.7	2.2	.2	5.3	1.5	.3	3.1
Miscellaneous	.3	.3	.1	.7	.8	.5	.4	.4	.4

Source: Based on table 1.

APPENDIX TABLE C–4.—*Percentage distribution of males and females in civilian labor force by activity, Japan proper, 1 Oct. 1930, 1 Oct. 1940, 22 Feb. 1944*

	1 Oct. 1930			1 Oct. 1940			22 Feb. 1944		
	Total	Male	Female	Total	Male	Female	Total	Male	Female
Civilian labor force	100.0	64.0	36.0	100.0	60.7	39.3	100.0	58.2	41.8
Agriculture and forestry	100.0	54.7	45.3	100.0	47.8	52.2	100.0	41.6	58.4
Fishing	100.0	90.7	9.3	100.0	87.7	12.3	100.0	81.9	18.1
Mining	100.0	85.8	14.2	100.0	88.5	11.5	100.0	84.6	15.4
Manufacturing and construction	100.0	75.4	24.6	100.0	76.0	24.0	100.0	76.3	23.7
Commerce	100.0	69.4	30.6	100.0	61.6	38.4	100.0	47.7	52.3
Transportation and communication	100.0	96.0	4.0	100.0	89.0	11.0	100.0	83.9	16.1
Government and professional	100.0	77.7	22.3	100.0	69.0	31.0	100.0	65.3	34.7
Domestic service	100.0	11.5	88.5	100.0	5.5	94.5	100.0	12.3	87.7
Miscellaneous	100.0	90.1	9.9	100.0	70.6	29.4	100.0	55.7	44.3

Source: Based on table 1.

APPENDIX TABLE C–5.—*Labor force, mining and manufacturing and construction, by sex and industry, Japan proper, 1 Oct. 1930 and 22 Feb. 1944* [1]

[In thousands]

	1 Oct. 1930			22 Feb. 1944		
	Total	Male	Female	Total	Male	Female
Mining	316	271	45	805	681	124
Metal	46	41	5	[2] 159	133	26
Coal	226	189	37	[2] 540	461	79
Oil	5	5		[2] 12	10	2
Other mining	3	3		[2] 36	29	7
Stone and earth quarrying	36	33	3	[2] 58	48	10
Manufacturing and construction	5,876	4,428	1,448	9,494	7,243	2,251
Metals	399	380	19	836	720	116
Machinery and tools	217	207	10	[2] 936	757	179
Shipbuilding	100	99	1	[2] 693	638	55
Aircraft and parts [3]	9	9		[2] 1,988	1,574	414
Vehicles and conveyances	90	89	1	[2] 194	171	23
Ordnance [4]	34	33	1	[2] 496	395	101
Precision Instruments [5]	57	54	3	[2] 85	65	20
Chemicals [6]	301	164	37	613	428	185
Textiles [7]	1,960	844	1,116	824	251	573
Ceramics, earth and stone	210	180	30	232	170	62
Lumber, woodworking	652	583	69	372	309	63
Printing, publishing	266	230	36	110	77	33
Food products	496	396	100	364	227	137
Gas, electricity and water	122	118	4	157	139	18
Construction and civil engineering	963	956	7	1,075	1,026	49
Miscellaneous	100	86	14	519	296	223

[1] See note (f) of table 1.
[2] Estimated from census data covering only those aged 13 to 60 to include all those in labor force.
[3] Assembling of aircraft, manufacturing of aircraft body, engine propeller, special parts, and aircraft ordnance.
[4] Manufacture of ordnance for aircraft is classified under aircraft and parts.
[5] Measuring instruments for aircraft is classified under aircraft and parts.

[6] Includes synthetic rubber and oil.
[7] Includes apparel.

Sources: 1930 data are adapted from the 1930 census, final report, table 47; industrial distribution 1944 data are adapted from census enumeration data submitted by labor bureau, Ministry of Welfare and cabinet bureau of statistics.

APPENDIX TABLE C–6.—*Workers in the labor force, aged 14–59, manufacturing and construction, Japan proper, 1 Oct. 1940 and 22 Feb. 1944* [1]

[In thousands]

	October 1940	February 1944	Difference 1940–1944	Percent change 1940–1944
Total manufacturing and construction	6, 981	7, 814	833	12
Male	5, 271	5, 936	665	13
Female	1, 710	1, 878	168	10
Metal	594	695	101	17
Male	550	610	60	11
Female	44	85	41	93
Machinery, Tools,[2] etc	1, 800	3, 681	1, 881	105
Male	1, 633	3, 067	1, 434	88
Female	167	614	447	268
Chemical	475	471	−4	−1
Male	347	321	−26	−7
Female	128	150	22	17
Utilities (gas, electricity, water)	82	94	12	15
Male	79	89	10	13
Female	3	5	2	67
Ceramics and earth stone	256	188	−68	−27
Male	205	134	−71	−35
Female	51	54	3	6
Textiles [3]	1, 497	717	−780	−52
Male	533	178	−355	−67
Female	964	539	−425	−44
Lumber and wood products	431	294	−137	−32
Male	399	243	−156	−39
Female	32	51	19	59
Food products	368	284	−84	−23
Male	249	166	−83	−33
Female	119	118	−1	−1
Printing and publishing	116	85	−31	−27
Male	98	57	−41	−42
Female	18	28	10	56
Engineering and construction	825	885	60	7
Male	809	850	41	5
Female	16	35	19	119
Miscellaneous	537	420	−117	−22
Male	369	221	−148	−40
Female	168	199	31	18

[1] Workers (Sagyosha) are those actually engaged in productive processes other than technicians.
[2] Includes aircraft, shipbuilding, transportation equipment, and ordnance.
[3] Includes apparel.

Source: Labor Bureau, Ministry of Welfare.

APPENDIX TABLE C–7.—*Labor conscription into essential industries, Japan proper, 1939–1945* [1]

	New conscripts			New conscripts	
	For the year	Cumulative total		For the year	Cumulative total
1939	850	850	1944	229, 448	1, 552, 559
1940	52, 692	53, 542	1945 [2]	47, 771	1, 600, 330
1941	258, 192	311, 734			
1942	311, 649	623, 383	Total	1, 600, 330	1, 600, 330
1943	699, 728	1, 323, 111			

[1] Labor conscription, as used here, was confined solely to males who entered essential industries because of government compulsion.
[2] Up to 15 August 1945.

Source: Welfare Ministry.

APPENDIX TABLE C-8.—*Survey of resident Koreans, by industry and occupation, Japan proper, 31 Dec. 1941*

In labor force	777, 023
Agriculture and fishing	9, 480
Mining	94, 320
Manufacturing	208, 338
Metal, machinery and tools	102, 648
Chemical	47, 053
Fiber	43, 953
Electrical	6, 488
Other manufacturing	8, 196
Construction and civil engineering	220, 969
Communication and transportation	15, 754
Stevedore	26, 982
General workers	32, 830
Other workers	66, 084
Hotel and restaurant	4, 751
Trade	60, 430
Professional	5, 116
Other employed	31, 630
Unemployed	339
Not in labor force	692, 207
Total Koreans	1, 469, 230

Source: *Plans for carrying out 1943 National mobilization*, Cabinet planning board, Tokyo , 14 June 1943, p. 128.

APPENDIX TABLE C-9.—*Number of Korean contract workers brought into Japan proper annually by type of work assigned, 1939-45*

Year [1]	Total number	Type of work assigned		Construction and civil engineering	Other work including factory
		Coal mining	Metal mining		
1939	38, 700	24, 279	5, 042	9, 379	
1940	54, 944	35, 431	8, 069	9, 898	1, 546
1941	53, 492	32, 099	8, 988	9, 540	2, 865
1942	112, 007	74, 576	9, 483	14, 848	13, 100
1943	122, 237	65, 208	13, 660	28, 280	15, 089
1944	280, 304	85, 953	30, 507	33, 382	130, 462
1945 [2]	6, 000	1, 000		2, 000	3, 000
Total 1939-45 [3]	667, 684	318, 546	75, 749	107, 327	166, 062

[1] Fiscal year begins on Apr. 1 and ends Mar. 31 of following year.
[2] Estimated for first quarter of fiscal year (April through June).
[3] Total number brought into Japan. Number of Koreans leaving Japan or transferring from previously assigned industry not available.

Source: Labor Bureau, Welfare Department.

APPENDIX TABLE C–10.—*Survey of Korean and Chinese workers previously introduced in groups and prisoners of war among regularly employed workers in factories and mines, Japan proper, 30 June 1944* [1]

	Total regular workers	Total Korean, Chinese and POW workers	Korean workers	Chinese workers	Prisoners of war
Factory workers	7,790,273	82,650	69,119	3,602	9,929
Male	5,512,896	80,745	67,222	3,594	9,929
Female	2,277,377	1,905	1,897	8	------------
Mine workers	633,754	148,935	140,788	2,328	5,819
Male	527,918	148,566	140,419	2,328	5,819
Female	105,836	369	369	------------	------------

[1] This survey covers only group movements of Korean and Chinese workers into Japan proper. Koreans and Chinese who migrated to Japan individually before the war are not included. Figures also do not include day workers.

Source: Cabinet Bureau of Statistics.

APPENDIX TABLE C–11.—*Students mobilized for work by school and type of work, Japan proper; October 1944, February 1945, and July 1945* [1] *(in thousands)*

OCTOBER 1944

School and sex	Total	Type of work			Miscellaneous
		War production and research	Food production	National defense and evacuation	
University, technical, and normal schools	126	85	26	12	[2] 3
Male	99	66	20	11	2
Female	27	19	6	1	1
Middle school	1,149	761	280	108	------------
Male	638	386	165	87	------------
Female	511	375	115	21	------------
Primary school	723	129	560	34	------------
Male	[3]	[3]	[3]	[3]	------------
Female	[3]	[3]	[3]	[3]	------------
Total	1,998	975	866	154	[2] 3
Male	[3]	[3]	[3]	[3]	2
Female	[3]	[3]	[3]	[3]	1

See footnotes at end of table.

APPENDIX TABLE C–11.—*Students mobilized for work by school and type of work, Japan proper; October 1944, February 1945, and July 1945* [1] (*in thousands*)—Continued

FEBRUARY 1945

School and sex	Total	Type of work			Miscellaneous
		War production and research	Food production	National defense and evacuation	
University, technical, and normal schools	180	139	25	16	
Male	147	112	20	15	
Female	33	27	5	1	
Middle school	1,629	1,220	280	129	
Male	940	669	165	106	
Female	689	551	115	23	
Primary school	1,297	587	710		
Male	690	328	362		
Female	607	259	348		
Total	3,106	1,946	1,015	145	
Male	1,777	1,109	547	121	
Female	1,329	837	468	24	

JULY 1945

School and sex	Total	War production and research	Food production	National defense and evacuation	Miscellaneous
University, technical, and normal schools	195	145	31	19	
Male	156	114	25	17	
Female	39	31	6	2	
Middle school	1,603	1,046	342	176	[4] 39
Male	883	567	195	107	14
Female	720	479	147	69	25
Primary school	1,634	517	753	211	[4] 153
Male	886	304	384	113	85
Female	748	213	369	98	68
Total	3,432	1,708	1,126	406	[4] 192
Male	1,925	985	604	237	99
Female	1,507	723	522	169	93

[1] Data in this table represents the degree of mobilization on the successive dates shown. Since totals for each date do not represent successive separate mobilizations, they should not be added.

University school students are about 17 years and older. Middle school students are from 12 to 16 years of age and students mobilized from primary schools are from 12 to 14 years of age.

[2] Mobilized for medical work.
[3] Break-down by sex not available.
[4] Mobilized for communications and transportation industry.

Source: Ministry of Education.

[Monthly average 1926=100]

	Factory workers		Mine workers	
	Employment [1]	Actual earnings [2]	Employment [1]	Actual earnings [2]
1940				
January	144.0	130.1	109.6	165.5
February	143.5	130.1	109.7	168.5
March	143.7	132.2	109.4	170.2
April	149.2	129.7	109.3	171.6
May	149.3	130.6	108.0	173.2
June	148.1	132.3	107.4	175.3
July	146.8	134.6	108.1	175.5
August	146.1	135.9	108.7	177.2
September	146.4	136.4	109.6	180.3
October	146.2	138.0	109.6	183.3
November	146.8	140.6	110.2	185.8
December	146.6	146.8	113.7	185.3
1941				
January	146.0	148.7	115.3	188.6
February	145.8	147.8	117.6	194.1
March	145.8	152.2	118.3	196.0
April	152.5	147.6	116.2	193.5
May	152.8	148.8	115.0	191.8
June	152.5	149.1	114.0	193.4
July	150.8	150.8	114.1	191.9
August	149.6	151.9	115.3	191.7
September	150.1	153.5	114.3	193.8
October	150.7	155.5	112.1	195.2
November	151.6	154.9	112.4	196.9
December	153.0	161.4	114.1	197.7
1942				
January	153.6	160.6	118.6	198.4
February	154.2	160.3	119.9	202.7
March	155.6	160.7	118.2	202.0
April	165.5	158.4	114.7	200.6
May	167.6	158.7	114.1	201.1
June	168.9	162.0	115.0	203.3
July	169.7	164.2	116.3	199.2
August	170.7	163.2	117.0	206.1
September	171.7	164.1	118.1	206.8
October	171.8	168.7	117.4	210.7
November	172.4	171.6	118.2	213.3
December	173.3	179.2	120.6	215.2

	Factory workers		Mine workers	
	Employment [1]	Actual earnings [2]	Employment [1]	Actual earnings [2]
1943				
January	173.9	184.3	123.2	218.0
February	175.2	182.3	126.1	224.4
March	176.3	185.6	125.1	224.1
April	185.7	181.1	122.2	222.5
May	187.7	184.9	[1]22.7	222.0
June	188.5	185.1	122.2	224.1
July	188.8	190.8	123.1	224.4
August	189.5	194.8	122.8	224.4
September	190.3	197.6	123.9	224.3
October	193.3	206.0	124.8	227.8
November	196.3	210.6	124.7	229.4
December	200.5	218.5	127.1	231.8
1944				
January	206.4	219.1	130.4	233.7
February	210.9	220.0	133.2	236.1
March	213.3	223.5	133.5	235.1
April	225.9	221.7	134.3	243.8
May	216.2	223.7	133.4	249.2
June	216.1	234.2	132.8	257.0
July	214.0	224.0	133.1	265.0
August	211.8	219.5	133.7	271.6
September	209.9	228.5	137.1	276.8
October	209.0	236.0	140.9	276.4
November	208.0	241.7	142.7	276.3
December	206.9	245.4	144.1	281.0
1945				
January	204.0	245.0	145.1	286.7
February	200.7	239.9	146.4	290.2
March	196.0	251.8	146.4	294.7

[1] Index of employment is a chain index based on a changing sample.

[2] Index of earnings is a fixed index of actual earnings per day (average during month) per worker based on the total sums of pay, including extra allowances and bonuses. Only allowances paid on a 3-month or less basis are included.

Source: Cabinet Bureau of Statistics.

APPENDIX TABLE C–13.—*Industrial employment and productive man-hours in 45 urban areas, Japan proper, monthly, October 1943–August 1945* [1]

[In thousands]

	Employment	Productive man-hours
1943		
October	1,978	317,820
November	1,973	322,350
December	2,077	329,370
1944		
January	2,147	342,260
February	2,158	352,530
March	2,244	358,280
April	2,369	382,870
May	2,393	391,800
June	2,392	382,150
July	2,403	381,020
August	2,432	385,830
September	2,443	391,680
October	2,464	388,310
November	2,490	394,620
December	2,497	390,900
1945		
January	2,484	373,880
February	2,424	362,850
March	2,401	332,990
April	2,351	315,560
May	2,301	309,850
June	2,306	248,030
July	2,121	220,530
August	1,845	182,340

[1] Includes private and Government-owned plants employing 50 or more workers. Excludes Nagasaki and Hiroshima.

Source: Data compiled by Urban Areas Division, U. S. S. B. S.

APPENDIX TABLE C–14.—*Active strength of the Japanese armed forces, 1930–45*

Year	Army	Navy	Total
1930	200,000	50,000	250,000
1931	230,000	78,430	308,430
1932	300,000	83,822	383,822
1933	350,000	88,968	438,968
1934	350,000	97,069	447,069
1935	350,000	98,896	448,896
1936	400,000	107,461	507,461
1937	500,000	134,013	634,013
1938	1,000,000	159,133	1,159,133
1939	1,440,000	180,098	1,620,098
1940	1,500,000	223,173	1,723,173
1941	2,100,000	311,359	2,411,359
1942	2,400,000	429,368	2,829,368
1943	3,100,000	708,159	3,808,159
1944	4,100,000	1,265,000	5,365,000
1945 [1]	5,500,000	1,693,223	7,193,223

[1] August 1945.

Sources: Army, Chief, Liaison Committee, War Ministry. Navy, Chief, Liaison Committee, Navy Ministry.

APPENDIX TABLE C–15.—*Estimated movement of farm labor to industry, July 1937 to February 1944*

[In thousands]

Period	Men	Women	Total
July 1937 to August 1939	310	130	440
August 1939 to February 1940	200	100	300
February 1940 to February 1941	250	90	340
February 1941 to February 1942	220	110	330
February 1942 to February 1943	240	140	380
February 1943 to February 1944	100	80	180

Source: Ministry of Agriculture and Forestry.

Basic Materials Tables

APPENDIX TABLE C-16.—*Coking coal imports into Japan proper, and percentage by source, 1940-45*

Fiscal year and period	Total		North China	Manchukuo	Karafuto
	Amount [1]	Percent			
1940					
First half	1,842	100	72	2	26
Second half	1,473	100	91	1	8
Total	3,315	100	80	2	18
1941					
First half	1,654	100	98	1	1
Second half	1,763	100	95		5
Total	3,417	100	96	1	3
1942					
First half	2,058	100	82		18
Second half	1,967	100	93		7
Total	4,025	100	87		13
1943					
First half	1,810	100	81		19
Second half	1,129	100	89		11
Total	2,939	100	84		16
1944					
First quarter	497	100	90		10
Second quarter	420	100	70	5	25
Third quarter	317	100	88	12	
Fourth quarter	201	100	69	31	
Total	1,435	100	81	9	10
1945					
First quarter	116	100	68	32	

[1] In thousands of metric tons.

Source: Compiled from data supplied by Japan Iron & Steel Control Association (TEKKO TOSEI KAI), November 1945.

APPENDIX TABLE C–17.—*Iron ore imports into Japan proper by source, 1931–45*

Fiscal year and quarter	Total		Korea		Manchukuo		China [2]		Philippines		Malaya		Other	
	Amount [1]	Percent	Percent	Percent Fe	Percent	Percent Fe	Percent	Percent Fe	Percent	Percent Fe	Percent	Percent Fe	Percent	Percent Fe
1931	1,727	100	10	na			35	na			53	na	2	na
1932	1,634	100	9	na			34	na			54	na	3	na
1933	1,779	100	14	na			32	na			52	na	2	na
1934	2,312	100	8	na			36	na			38	na	18	na
1935	3,646	100	7	50			35	60	8	na	40	63	10	57
1936	4,023	100	6	50			31	60	14	na	42	63	7	57
1937	4,313	100	7	50			14	60	13	na	38	63	28	57
1938	3,212	100	11	50			5	60			50	63	34	57
1939	4,949	100	8	50			14	60	13	na	39	63	26	57
1940	5,719	100	8	50	1	60	20	60	21	na	36	63	14	57
1941:														
I	1,707	100	9	50	1	60	30	61	16	na	40	63	4	59
II	1,536	100	15	50	1	60	50	61	9	na	23	63	2	59
III	935	100	20	50	1	60	67	61	3	na	8	63	1	59
IV	880	100	21	50	1	60	68	61	3	na	6	63	1	59
Total	5,058	100	15	50	1	60	50	61	9	na	23	63	2	59
1942:														
I	1,054	100	15	51	4	60	79	61			2	63		
II	1,250	100	16	51	1	60	79	61			2	63	2	59
III	1,356	100	18	51			77	61	1	60	2	63	2	59
IV	1,220	100	6	51			91	61	1	60	1	63	1	59
Total	4,880	100	13	51	1	60	82	61	1	60	2	63	1	59
1943:														
I	1,268	100	5	51			89	59	4	60	2	63		
II	940	100	4	51			91	59	3	60	2	63		
III	736	100	10	51			89	59	1	60				
IV	742	100	12	51			82	59	6	60				
Total	3,686	100	7	51			88	59	4	60	1	63		
1944:														
I	692	100	29	54			71	58						
II	458	100	35	54			62	58	3	60				
III	312	100	45	54			55	58						
IV	206	100	55	54	4	59	41	58						
Total	1,668	100	37	54	1	59	61	58	1	60				
1945: I	143	100	87	54	3	na	10	na						

"na" Indicates data not available.
[1] In thousands of metric tons.
[2] Includes Hainan Island.

Source: Compiled from data supplied by Japan Iron & Steel Control Association (Tekko Tosei Kai), November 1945.

APPENDIX TABLE C–18.—*Iron ore, iron sands, and pyrite sinters supply in Japan proper, 1931–45*

[In thousands of metric tons]

Fiscal year and quarter	Domestic supply				Imports of iron ore	Total	Iron ore stock-pile period end
	Iron ore production	Iron sand production	Pyrite sinter deliveries	Total			
1931	208	1	na	(209)	1, 727	(1, 936)	na
1932	227	5	na	(232)	1, 634	(1, 866)	na
1933	320	1	na	(321)	1, 779	(2, 100)	na
1934	432	2	na	(434)	2, 312	(2, 746)	na
1935	516	6	na	(522)	3, 646	(4, 168)	3, 195
1936	619	4	na	(623)	4, 023	(4, 646)	4, 362
1937	584	13	na	(597)	4, 313	(4, 910)	4, 151
1938	766	71	na	(837)	3, 212	(4, 049)	4, 228
1939	850	52	na	(902)	4, 949	(5, 851)	3, 952
1940	993	134	na	(1, 127)	5, 719	(6, 846)	3, 812
1941:							
I	na	na	na	na	1, 707	na	....
II	na	na	na	na	1, 536	na	....
III	na	na	na	na	935	na	....
IV	na	na	na	na	880	na	....
Total	1, 334	233	na	(1, 567)	5, 058	(6, 625)	2, 605
1942:							
I	429	72	na	(501)	1, 054	(1, 555)	....
II	709	125	na	(834)	1, 250	(2, 084)	....
III	497	81	na	(578)	1, 356	(1, 934)	....
IV	424	90	na	(514)	1, 220	(1, 734)	....
Total	2, 059	368	[1] 362	2, 789	4, 880	7, 669	1, 399
1943:							
I	590	112	na	(702)	1, 268	(1, 970)	....
II	831	142	na	(973)	940	(1, 913)	....
III	669	102	na	(771)	736	(1, 507)	....
IV	618	71	na	(689)	742	(1, 431)	....
Total	2, 708	427	703	3, 838	3, 686	7, 524	792
1944:							
I	756	130	124	1, 010	692	1, 702	....
II	1, 128	160	86	1, 374	458	1, 832	....
III	886	110	80	1, 076	312	1, 388	....
IV	817	82	50	949	206	1, 155	....
Total	3, 587	482	340	4, 409	1, 668	6, 077	672
1945, I	701	91	45	837	143	980	na

"na" Indicates data not available.
"( )" Figures in parentheses indicate totals for which one or more of the constituent figures are not available.
[1] Includes only consumption at Japan Iron Mfg. Co. Yawata plant.

Source: Compiled from data supplied by Iron and Steel Control Association (Tekko Tosei Kai) and reports by individual iron and steel plants, November 1945.

APPENDIX TABLE C–19.—*Pig iron imports into Japan proper and percentage by source, 1931–45*

Fiscal year	Total		Korea	Manchukuo	China	British India	Other
	Amount [1]	Percent					
1931	494	100	19	----------	16	30	35
1932	650	100	32	50	----------	18	----------
1933	800	100	20	57	----------	22	1
1934	777	100	21	53	----------	26	----------
1935	1,093	100	12	35	----------	31	22
1936	1,095	100	11	25	----------	30	34
1937	1,131	100	12	19	[2]	25	44
1938	1,072	100	20	20	[2]	31	29
1939	927	100	24	38	----------	32	6
1940	854	100	20	50	----------	30	----------
1941	784	100	18	71	[2]	10	1
1942	878	100	15	81	4	----------	----------
1943	1,134	100	24	60	16	----------	----------
1944	942	100	26	62	12	----------	----------
1945, first quarter	51	100	60	39	1	----------	----------

[1] In thousands of metric tons.
[2] Less than 0.5 percent.
Source: Compiled from data supplied by Japan Iron & Steel Control Association (Tekko Tosei Kai), November 1945.

APPENDIX TABLE C–20.—*Scrap steel and iron supply, consumption, and stockpiles, Japan proper, 1931–45*

[In thousands of metric tons]

Fiscal year	Imports	Domestic purchased	Self-generated	Total	Consumption	Balance	Stockpiles
1931	296	800	286	1,382	1,106	276	1,389
1932	559	800	360	1,719	1,302	417	1,806
1933	1,013	1,100	479	2,592	1,906	686	2,492
1934	1,413	1,100	569	3,082	2,538	544	3,036
1935	1,692	1,100	681	3,473	3,122	351	3,387
1936	1,497	1,100	842	3,439	3,337	102	3,489
1937	2,420	1,100	1,894	5,414	4,394	1,020	4,509
1938	1,358	1,100	2,119	4,577	4,265	312	4,821
1939	2,555	890	2,185	5,630	4,660	970	5,791
1940	1,391	871	2,064	4,326	4,405	−79	5,712
1941	203	1,022	2,018	3,243	4,487	−1,244	4,468
1942	39	1,251	2,118	3,408	4,777	−1,369	3,099
1943	25	1,292	2,296	3,613	5,275	−1,662	1,437
1944	74	1,317	1,766	3,157	4,145	−988	449
1945	1	175	251	427	568	−141	308

Source: Compiled from data supplied by Japan Iron & Steel Control Association (Tekko Tosei Kai), November 1945.

APPENDIX TABLE C-21.—Ingot steel production by type, Japan proper, Korea, and Manchukuo, fiscal years, 1931-45

[In thousands of metric tons]

Fiscal year and quarter	Japan proper														Korea			Manchukuo[1]	Grand total			
	Hokkaido			Honshu				Kyushu			Total											
	OH	E	Total	OH	B	E	Total	OH	E	Total	OH	B	E	Total	OH	E	Total	OH	OH	B	E	Total
1931	na	na	13	na	---	na	849	na	na	1,021	na	---	na	1,883	---	---	---	na	na	---	na	(1,883)
1932	na	na	35	na	---	na	1,019	na	na	1,344	na	---	na	2,398	---	---	---	na	na	---	na	(2,398)
1933	na	na	77	na	---	na	1,437	na	na	1,684	na	---	na	3,198	na	---	5	na	na	---	na	(3,203)
1934	na	na	77	na	---	na	1,904	na	na	1,863	na	---	na	3,844	na	---	60	na	na	---	na	(3,904)
1935	77	(2)	77	2,303	---	190	2,493	2,082	51	2,133	4,462	---	241	4,703	97	---	97	137	4,696	---	241	4,937
1936	65	---	65	2,612	---	246	2,858	2,224	70	2,294	4,901	---	316	5,217	87	---	87	344	5,332	---	316	5,648
1937	77	---	77	2,986	---	350	3,336	2,300	85	2,385	5,363	---	435	5,798	103	---	103	451	5,917	---	435	6,352
1938	74	2	76	3,095	59	634	3,788	2,477	120	2,597	5,646	59	756	6,461	103	3	106	622	6,371	59	759	7,189
1939	81	2	83	3,058	152	780	3,990	2,514	106	2,620	5,653	152	888	6,693	94	17	111	562	6,309	152	905	7,366
1940	79	2	81	2,981	233	939	4,153	2,479	142	2,621	5,539	233	1,083	6,855	94	15	109	554	6,187	233	1,098	7,518
1941	118	3	121	2,695	333	1,053	4,081	2,470	165	2,635	5,283	333	1,221	6,837	108	49	157	573	5,964	333	1,270	7,567
1942	252	4	256	2,717	352	1,224	4,293	2,358	192	2,550	5,327	352	1,420	7,099	128	53	181	724	6,179	352	1,473	8,004
1943:																						
I	87	2	89	717	80	387	1,184	571	77	648	1,375	80	466	1,921	29	18[3]	47	214	1,618	80	484	2,182
II	102	3	105	650	81	379	1,110	556	72	628	1,308	81	454	1,843	26	18[3]	44	199	1,533	81	472	2,086
III	110	3	113	732	86	439	1,257	590	78	668	1,432	86	520	2,038	27	18[3]	45	210	1,669	86	538	2,293
IV	126	3	129	727	84	423	1,234	590	66	656	1,443	84	492	2,019	26	18[3]	44	214	1,683	84	510	2,277
Total	425	11	436	2,826	331	1,628	4,785	2,307	293	2,600	5,558	331	1,932	7,821	108	72	180	837	6,503	331	2,004	8,838
1944:																						
I	113	3	116	663	67	460	1,190	523	64	587	1,299	67	527	1,893	28	15[3]	43	207	1,534	67	542	2,143
II	92	4	96	504	49	410	962	341	45	386	936	49	459	1,444	29	15[3]	44	72	1,037	49	474	1,560
III	74	4	78	450	49	423	922	404	66	470	928	49	493	1,470	26	15[3]	41	94	1,048	49	508	1,605
IV	41	3	44	305	32	311	648	346	66	412	692	32	380	1,104	12	15[3]	27	64	768	32	395	1,195
Total	320	14	334	1,921	197	1,604	3,722	1,614	241	1,855	3,855	197	1,859	5,911	96	60	155	437	4,387	197	1,919	6,503
1945, I	na	na	40	na	na	na	466	na	na	296	435[3]	na	368[3]	803	na	na	na	na	(435)	na	(368)	(803)

"OH" Indicates open hearth.
"B" Indicates basic Bessemer.
"E" Indicates electric furnace.
"na" Indicates data not available.
"( )" Figures in parentheses indicate totals for which one or more constituent figures are not available.

[1] Anshan only. Steel is also made in a few other plants but their output is negligible.
[2] Less than 500 tons.
[3] Estimated.

Source: Compiled from data supplied by Japan Iron & Steel Control Association (Tekko Tosei Kai), Nov. 1945.

APPENDIX TABLE C-22.—*Finished steel production, Japan proper, Korea, and Manchukuo, fiscal years, 1931-45*

[In thousands of metric tons]

Fiscal year and quarter	Japan proper[1]														
	Hokkaido					Honshu					Kyushu				
	Ordinary			Special	Total	Ordinary			Special	Total	Ordinary			Special	Total
	Rolled	Cast	Forged			Rolled	Cast	Forged			Rolled	Cast	Forged		
1931	-	2	5	3	10	871	20	9	7	907	731	9	3	4	747
1932	-	3	10	6	19	1,046	30	16	12	1,104	964	10	6	10	990
1933	10	3	16	8	37	1,397	46	35	24	1,502	1,209	14	13	18	1,254
1934	10	4	16	10	40	1,667	58	39	29	1,793	1,437	18	16	19	1,490
1935	5	4	16	7	32	2,254	74	37	70	2,435	1,486	22	19	27	1,554
1936	3	6	19	8	36	2,712	84	43	90	2,929	1,557	26	20	26	1,629
1937	5	6	20	10	41	3,056	123	49	166	3,394	1,619	29	28	36	1,712
1938	4	7	21	16	48	2,985	194	68	266	3,513	1,887	33	41	46	2,007
1939	2	8	25	17	52	2,689	222	88	405	3,404	1,985	29	38	41	2,093
1940	-	6	28	15	49	2,689	201	106	411	3,407	1,843	29	39	17	1,928
1941:															
I and II	-	na	na	na	na	1,173	na	na	na	(1,173)	895	na	na	na	(895)
III and IV	-	na	na	na	na	1,164	na	na	na	(1,164)	921	na	na	na	(921)
Total	-	6	24	20	50	2,337	253	116	462	3,168	1,816	27	42	17	1902
1942:															
I	-	na	na	na	na	529	na	na	na	(529)	504	na	na	na	(504)
II	-	na	na	na	na	484	na	na	na	(484)	438	na	na	na	(438)
III	3	na	na	na	na	554	na	na	na	(554)	464	na	na	na	(464)
IV	5	na	na	na	na	595	na	na	na	(595)	476	na	na	na	(476)
Total	8	6	27	34	75	2,162	256	115	599	3,132	1,882	27	33	17	1,959
1943:															
I	6	2	9	11	28	582	68	32	180	862	479	7	12	13	511
II	7	2	8	14	31	544	67	29	171	811	432	8	12	13	465
III	9	3	10	12	34	575	76	29	204	884	435	8	13	15	471
IV	13	3	9	14	39	602	76	31	235	944	465	9	14	41	529
Total	35	10	36	51	132	2,303	287	121	790	3,501	1,811	32	51	82	1,976
1944[4]:															
I	15	4	8	20	47	555	79	31	255	920	400	10	12	40	462
II	13	3	11	18	45	376	73	27	249	725	230	8	8	35	281
III	10	3	11	16	40	331	75	26	240	672	278	9	11	49	347
IV	-	1	9	13	23	202	57	16	198	473	222	7	8	48	285
Total	38	11	39	67	155	1,464	284	100	942	2,790	1,130	34	39	172	1,375
1945[4], I	4	2	1	13	20	125	42	9	120	296	128	7	5	36	176

See footnotes at end of table.

APPENDIX TABLE C-22.—Finished steel production, Japan proper, Korea, and Manchukuo, fiscal years, 1931–45—Continued

Fiscal year and quarter	Japan proper[1]					Korea					Manchukuo[2]					Grand total[3]				
	Ordinary			Special	Total	Ordinary			Special	Total	Ordinary			Special	Total	Ordinary			Special	Total
	Rolled	Cast	Forged			Rolled	Cast	Forged			Rolled	Cast	Forged			Rolled	Cast	Forged		
1931	1,602	31	17	14	1,664											1,602	31	17	14	1,664
1932	2,010	43	32	28	2,113											2,010	43	32	28	2,113
1933	2,616	63	64	50	2,793											2,616	63	64	50	2,793
1934	3,114	80	71	58	3,323	22				22						3,136	80	71	58	3,345
1935	3,745	100	72	104	4,021	52				52	141				141	3,938	100	72	104	4,214
1936	4,272	116	82	124	4,594	57				57	303	na	na	na	(303)	4,632	(116)	(82)	(124)	(4,954)
1937	4,680	158	97	212	5,147	66				66	417	na	na	na	(417)	5,163	(158)	(97)	(212)	(5,630)
1938	4,876	234	130	328	5,568	91			1	92	480	6	2	2	490	5,447	240	132	331	6,150
1939	4,676	259	151	463	5,549	76	6		7	89	417	12	4	1	434	5,169	277	155	471	6,072
1940	4,532	236	173	443	5,384	75			7	82	433	2	3		438	5,040	238	176	450	5,904
1941: I and II	2,068	na	na	na	(2,068)	39	na	na	na	(39)	na	na	na	na	na	(2,107)	na	na	na	(2,107)
III and IV	2,085	na	na	na	(2,085)	46	na	na	na	(46)	na	na	na	na	na	(2,131)	na	na	na	(2,131)
Total	4,153	286	182	499	5,120	85	11	2	14	112	325	5	3		333	4,563	302	187	513	5,565
1942: I	1,033	na	na	na	(1,033)	24	na	na	na	(24)	na	na	na	na	na	(1,057)	na	na	na	(1,057)
II	922	na	na	na	(922)	25	na	na	na	(25)	na	na	na	na	na	(947)	na	na	na	(947)
III	1,021	na	na	na	(1,021)	27	na	na	na	(27)	na	na	na	na	na	(1,048)	na	na	na	(1,048)
IV	1,076	na	na	na	(1,076)	27	na	na	na	(27)	na	na	na	na	na	(1,103)	na	na	na	(1,103)
Total	4,052	289	175	650	5,166	103	12	2	16	133	339	13	14	9	375	4,494	314	191	675	5,674
1943: I	1,067	77	53	204	1,401	26			3	29	na	na	na	na	na	(1,093)	na	na	na	(1,430)
II	983	77	49	198	1,307	23			3	26	na	na	na	na	na	(1,006)	na	na	na	(1,333)
III	1,019	87	52	231	1,389	24			3	27	na	na	na	na	na	(1,043)	na	na	na	(1,416)
IV	1,080	88	54	290	1,512	22			3	25	na	na	na	na	na	(1,102)	na	na	na	(1,537)
Total	4,149	329	208	923	5,609	95			12	107	542	7	11	9	569	4,786	336	219	944	6,285
1944[4]: I	970	93	51	315	1,429	22			5	27	106	na	na	na	(106)	(1,098)	na	na	na	(1,562)
II	619	84	46	302	1,051	22			5	27	28	na	na	na	(28)	669	na	na	na	(1,106)
III	619	87	48	305	1,059	16			5	21	16	na	na	na	(16)	651	na	na	na	(1,096)
IV	424	65	33	259	781	8			5	13	79	na	na	na	(79)	511	na	na	na	(873)
Total	2,632	329	178	1,181	4,320	68			20	88	229	4[5]	6[5]	5[5]	244	2,929	333	184	1,206	4,652
1945[4], I	257	51	15	169	492	12				12	20[5]				20	289	51	15	169	524

"na" indicates data are not available.

"( )" figures in parentheses indicate totals for which one or more of the constituent figures are not available.

[1] Shikoku production, which in no year exceeded 6,000 tons, has been omitted.

[2] Data limited to Manchukuo Iron Mfg. Co. production at Anshan, except for year 1943.

[3] Production in Occupied China, which in no year exceeded 500 tons, has been omitted.

[4] "Special Steel Demand and Supply Regulations," 28 Jan. 1944, broadened the "special" steel category to include certain high carbon steels formerly termed "ordinary."

[5] Estimated.

Source: Compiled from data supplied by the Iron & Steel Control Association ('Tekko Tosei Kai) and by the Military Affairs Bureaus of the War and Navy Departments. Such data, insofar as they include since 1935 production in Army and Navy arsenals (which in no year exceeded 225,000 tons), are estimated for the years prior to 1940. Cast and forged steel data are limited to steel cast and forged in iron and steel producing plants.

APPENDIX TABLE C–23.—*Rolled steel production, by product, Japan proper, 1935–45*

[In thousands of metric tons]

Fiscal year and quarter	Rails	Shapes	Bars	Sheets and tin plates	Wire rods	Plates	Pipes and tubes	Other	Total
1935	367	468	1,025	484	413	713	167	108	3,745
1936	289	555	1,034	660	487	878	189	180	4,272
1937	217	728	1,207	609	447	1,063	224	185	4,680
1938	283	664	1,321	521	401	1,280	226	180	4,876
1939	361	600	1,268	423	383	1,177	270	194	4,676
1940	366	635	1,258	572	330	822	261	288	4,532
1941:									
I and II	142	305	571	266	180	390	125	89	2,068
III and IV	150	276	630	239	165	416	124	85	2,085
Total	292	581	1,201	505	345	806	249	174	4,153
1942:									
I	80	156	264	111	85	229	56	52	1,033
II	64	146	236	86	67	220	53	50	922
III	63	146	247	100	90	258	63	54	1,021
IV	55	134	245	99	97	330	66	50	1,076
Total	262	582	992	396	339	1,037	238	206	4,052
1943:									
I	48	126	251	98	92	353	64	35	1,067
II	44	115	213	93	75	349	68	26	983
III	41	124	221	90	71	366	73	33	1,019
IV	38	114	217	91	74	407	81	58	1,080
Total	171	479	902	372	312	1,475	286	152	4,149
1944:									
I	25	124	189	80	55	382	82	33	970
II	9	55	136	62	37	240	59	21	619
III	20	54	131	72	56	210	53	23	619
IV	24	33	103	49	22	139	32	22	424
Total	78	266	559	263	170	971	226	99	2,632
1945, I	10	11	83	29	20	62	26	16	257

Source: Compiled from data supplied by Iron & Steel Control Association (Tekko Tosei Kai), November 1945.

APPENDIX TABLE C-24.—*Finished steel distribution, Japan proper, fiscal years 1937–45*

[In thousands of metric tons]

Consumer category	1937				1938				1939				1940				1941			
	Ordinary rolled	Per cent	Total steel	Per cent	Ordinary rolled	Per cent	Total steel	Per cent	Ordinary rolled	Per cent	Total steel	Per cent	Ordinary rolled	Per cent	Total steel	Per cent	Ordinary rolled	Per cent	Total steel	Per cent
A. Army ground forces	224	4	[1]267	4	368	8	489	10	468	9	630	11	570	13	745	14	808	18	1,046	19
B. Navy surface forces	584	10	650	11	482	11	575	11	499	10	629	11	565	13	804	16	821	18	1,129	21
Bx. Merchant-ship building	309	5	361	6	263	6	327	7	272	5	339	6	196	5	241	5	300	7	372	7
D. Airforces	193	3	[1]215	3	208	4	264	5	214	4	280	5	250	6	368	7	342	8	483	9
Cx. Railroads	320	6	--	--	168	4	--	--	201	4	--	--	193	5	--	--	215	5	--	--
C. Industrial facilities	{1,938	33	--	--	868	19	--	--	688	14	--	--	589	14	--	--	436	10	--	--
C. Public works and construction					--	--	--	--	212	4	--	--	140	3	--	--	52	1	--	--
C. Machinery and tools	616	11	{4,666	76	616	13	{3,420	67	759	15	{3,850	67	607	14	{2,942	58	603	13	{2,425	44
C. Manufactured goods	640	11	--	--	640	14	--	--	789	16	--	--	615	14	--	--	379	8	--	--
C. Exports	785	13	--	--	814	18	--	--	935	18	--	--	522	12	--	--	386	8	--	--
C. Miscellaneous	249	4	--	--	130	3	--	--	61	1	--	--	59	1	--	--	185	4	--	--
Grand total	5,858	100	[1]6,159	100	4,557	100	5,075	100	5,098	100	5,728	100	4,306	100	5,100	100	4,527	100	5,455	100

Consumer category	1942				1943				1944				1945 (first quarter)			
	Ordinary rolled	Per cent	Total steel	Per cent	Ordinary rolled	Per cent	Total steel	Per cent	Ordinary rolled	Per cent	Total steel	Per cent	Ordinary rolled	Per cent	Total steel	Per cent
A. Army ground forces	595	16	840	17	840	20	1,148	21	348	11	598	13	76	16	106	15
B. Navy surface forces	730	19	1,120	23	822	19	1,238	22	564	18	1,059	22	71	15	150	20
Bx. Merchant-ship building	451	12	536	11	788	19	920	17	1,178	38	1,324	28	202	43	228	31
D. Airforces	307	8	485	10	357	8	559	10	360	12	961	20	44	9	138	19
Cx. Railroads	162	4	--	--	159	4	--	--	139	4	--	--	31	7	--	--
C. Industrial facilities	367	10	--	--	445	10	--	--	178	6	--	--	11	2	--	--
C. Public works and construction	52	1	--	--	13	--	--	--	2	--	--	--	--	--	--	--
C. Machinery and tools	366	10	{1,901	39	215	5	{1,691	30	110	3	{817	17	12	3	{108	15
C. Manufactured goods	489	13	--	--	379	9	--	--	151	5	--	--	18	4	--	--
C. Exports	203	5	--	--	178	4	--	--	59	2	--	--	1	1	--	--
C. Miscellaneous	84	2	--	--	94	2	--	--	20	1	--	--	3	1	--	--
Grand total	3,806	100	4,882	100	4,290	100	5,556	100	3,109	100	4,759	100	469	100	730	100

[1] Does not include special steel distribution to the Army.

Source: Compiled from data supplied by the Iron and Steel Control Association, by the Air General Ordnance and Metals Bureau of the Ministry of Commerce and Industry, and by the Military Affairs Bureaus of the War and Navy Departments.

APPENDIX TABLE C-25.—*Finished steel, balance of supply and demand in Japan proper, fiscal years, 1932-45*

[In thousands of metric tons]

Fiscal year	Supply			Demand [1]			Supply less demand
	Production	Imports	Total	Distribution	Exports	Total	
1932	2, 113	226	2, 339	2, 185	300	2, 485	−146
1933	2, 793	394	3, 187	2, 692	435	3, 127	60
1934	3, 323	364	3, 687	3, 048	596	3, 644	43
1935	4, 021	306	4, 327	3, 145	823	3, 968	359
1936	4, 594	286	4, 880	3, 761	990	4, 751	129
1937	5, 147	701	5, 848	5, 374	785	6, 159	−311
1938	5, 568	190	5, 758	4, 259	814	5, 073	685
1939	5, 549	164	5, 713	4, 793	935	5, 728	−15
1940	5, 384	181	5, 565	4, 577	522	5, 099	466
1941	5, 120	52	5, 172	5, 068	386	5, 454	−282
1942	5, 166	6	5, 172	4, 678	203	4, 881	291
1943	5, 609	----------	5, 609	5, 376	178	5, 554	55
1944	4, 320	----------	4, 320	4, 699	62	4, 761	−441
1945, first quarter	492	----------	492	728	1	729	−237

[1] For the years 1932-36, all figures include only ordinary rolled steel. For the years 1937-43, "Exports" figures include ordinary rolled steel only; exports of other steel are included in "Distribution." For the years 1944-45, exports of ordinary rolled and special steel are included in "Exports," of cast and forged ordinary steel in "Distribution."

Source: Appendix tables C-14 and 15. Import and export data are from the Iron and Steel Control Association (Tekko Tosei Kai), Nov. 1945.

APPENDIX TABLE C-26.—*Production of ferro-alloy ores, Japan proper, 1931-45* [1]

[In metric tons] [2]

Fiscal year	Chromium	Cobalt	Manganese	Molybdenum [2]	Nickel	Silicon	Tungsten
1931	9, 727	----------	12, 849	----------	----------	na	52
1932	12, 492	----------	26, 242	----------	----------	na	20
1933	19, 997	----------	43, 535	----------	----------	na	29
1934	27, 222	----------	54, 498	5, 010	----------	na	65
1935	36, 309	----------	69, 349	6, 435	----------	na	89
1936	39, 253	----------	70, 945	6, 604	----------	na	56
1937	44, 108	----------	83, 007	4, 065	----------	na	48
1938	49, 001	----------	118, 150	2, 165	----------	na	179
1939	44, 638	----------	130, 000	3, 000	----------	na	152
1940	53, 550	----------	157, 808	11, 750	----------	na	677
1941	61, 560	----------	195, 546	49, 408	----------	134, 900	957
1942	60, 989	----------	254, 254	88, 615	1, 283	167, 600	994
1943	64, 280	120	342, 884	176, 196	2, 504	179, 000	856
1944	[3] 81, 481	334	400, 679	401, 492	1, 697	194, 300	608
1945 [4]	[3] 16, 570	315	67, 017	90, 883	369	na	82

"na" Indicates data not available.

[1] No phosphorus production. Only small amounts of titanium and vanadium were produced—from iron sands.

[2] Molybdenum figures in kilograms.

[3] Data not complete; the above figures represent known production.

[4] First quarter.

Source: Bureau of Mines, Ministry of Commerce and Industry, November 1945.

Fiscal year	Chromium	Cobalt			Manganese			Molybdenum				
	Philippines (crude ore)	Burma (crude ore)	Canada[1] (crude ore)	Total (crude ore)	India (crude ore)	Philippines (crude ore)	Total (crude ore)	Korea (crude ore)	Manchukuo (concentrates)	United States (concentrates)	Total Crude ore	Total Concentrates
1931		na		na	na		na					
1932		na		na								
1933		na		na								
1934		na		na								
1935		na		na	na		na					
1936		na		na	100,000		100,000					
1937		na		na	100,000		100,000			200		200
1938		na		na	100,000	5,700	105,700			500		500
1939	13,500	na	350	(350)	150,000	23,500	173,500			5,500		5,500
1940	37,300	na	400	(400)	120,000	5,700	125,700			4,000		4,000
1941	2,000	na		na	60,000	20,000	80,000		50			50
1942	40,000	na		na		20,000	20,000		700			700
1943	50,000	100		100		20,000	20,000	198	200		198	200
1944	20,000	100		100				155	900		155	900
1945[2]								25			25	

Fiscal year	Nickel[3]										
	Australia (metallic form)	Belgium (metallic form)	Canada (metallic form)	Celebes (concentrates)	China (metallic form)	France (metallic form)	Germany (metallic form)	Great Britain (metallic form)	Korea (crude ore)	New Caledonia (concentrates)	Norway (metallic form)
1931	na	na				na	na	na			na
1932					120	100		1,100			
1933	5	7					5	1,600			
1934	340	na	300				10	1,250			750
1935			800			2		1,800		228	800
1936			400					1,050			400
1937			[4] 4,110					na			
1938			[4] 5,729					na			
1939			[4] 9,819							17,649	[4] 432
1940			[4] 458	10,432						19,363	na
1941				23,406						4,268	
1942				17,202							
1943				48,271							
1944				7,501							
1945[2]									1,211		

See footnotes at end of table.

Fiscal year	Nickel (continued)					Titanium			Vanadium				
	United States (metallic form)	Other (metallic form)	Total			Straits Settlements (crude ore)	Thailand (crude ore)	Total (crude ore)	Man-chukuo (crude ore)	Peru (crude ore)	United States (concentrates [5])	Total	
			Crude ore	Concen-trates	Metallic form							Crude ore	Concen-trates
1931	157	---------	---------	---------	(157)	---------		---------				---------	---------
1932	150	---------	---------	---------	1, 470								
1933	37	---------	---------	---------	1, 654	---------		---------					---------
1934	---------	---------	---------	---------	(2, 650)								
1935	350	---------	---------	228	3, 752								
1936	156	---------	---------	---------	2, 006								
1937	---------	[4] 1, 432	---------	---------	[4] (21, 522)				-----	[6] 100	------	100
1938	---------		---------	---------					150	[6] 200	150	200
1939	---------		---------	17, 649					500	[6]1,500	500	1, 500
1940	---------	---------	---------	29, 795	[4] (458)	---------		---------	•	500	[6] 800	500	800
1941	---------	---------	---------	27, 674	---------	1, 000	1, 000	na	---------	na	------
1942	---------	---------	---------	17, 202	---------	1, 000	2, 000	3, 000	na	---------	na	------
1943	---------	---------	---------	48, 271	---------	2, 000	[6] 2, 800	4, 800	---------			---------
1944	---------	---------	---------	7, 501	---------	---------	---------	---------	200	---------	---------	200	------
1945 [2]	---------	---------	1, 211	---------	---------	---------	---------	---------	---------	---------	---------	---------	---------

Fiscal year	Tungsten											
	Burma (concen-trates)	China (concen-trates)	Great Britain (concen-trates)	Hong Kong (concen-trates)	India (concen-trates)	Korea (crude ore)	South America (concen-trates)	Straits Settlements		Thailand (concen-trates)	Total	
								Crude ore	Concen-trates		Crude ore	Concen-trates
1931	---------	---------	---------	---------	---------	---------	---------	---------	---------	---------	---------	---------
1932	---------	---------	---------	---------	---------	---------	---------	---------	---------	---------	---------	---------
1933	---------	---------	---------	---------	---------	---------	---------	---------	---------	---------	---------	---------
1934	---------	---------	---------	---------	---------	---------	---------	---------	---------	---------	---------	---------
1935	---------	---------	---------	---------	---------	---------	---------	---------	---------	---------	---------	---------
1936	---------	---------	---------	---------	---------	---------	---------	30	•	---------	30	---------
1937	---------	---------	---------	---------	---------	---------	---------	---------	---------	---------	---------	---------
1938	---------	---------	[6] 600	---------	200	---------	---------	---------	---------	---------	---------	800
1939	---------	---------	[6] 1, 000	---------	---------	---------	1, 000	---------	---------	---------	---------	2, 000
1940	---------	[6] 100	[6] 1, 200	---------	---------	---------	1, 000	---------	---------	200	---------	2, 500
1941	---------	[6] 150	200	450	---------	---------	1, 200	---------	---------	1, 000	---------	3, 000
1942	1, 000	[6] 500	---------	500	---------	---------	---------	200	1, 200	---------	3, 400
1943	1, 500	400	---------	450	---------	1, 069	---------	---------	400	800	1, 069	3, 550
1944	500	400	---------	400	---------	77	---------	200	------	400	277	1, 700
1945 [2]	---------	400	---------	---------	---------	•	---------	---------	---------	---------	---------	400

"na" Indicates data not available.

"( )" Figures in parentheses indicate totals for which one or more of the constituent figures are not available.

[1] 30 percent cobalt.

[2] First quarter.

[3] Crude ores contained 0.6–1.4 percent nickel; concentrates, 3.26–4.34 percent nickel; metallic nickel, 98–99 percent nickel.

[4] Calendar year.

[5] Included some ores in 1939 and 1940.

[6] Estimate.

Source: Compiled from figures collected by the Bureau of Mines, Ministry of Commerce and Industry, from the Finance Ministry, the Mitsubishi Economic Research Bureau, the Mitsubishi Trading Company, and the Mitsui Products Co., October–November 1945.

APPENDIX TABLE C-28.—*Production of ferro-alloys, Japan proper, 1931-45*

[In metric tons]

Fiscal year and quarter	Ferro-manganese	Ferro-silicon-manganese	Ferro-silicon	Ferro-chromium	Ferro-tungsten	Ferro-molybdenum	Ferro-vanadium	Ferro-titanium	Ferro-phosphorous
1931	10, 637		4, 103	218	32	21			na
1932	17, 985		4, 883	1, 126	59	85			na
1933	23, 026		7, 622	1, 480	26	286			na
1934	29, 364		11, 726	2, 280	232	132			na
1935	34, 710		15, 571	4, 078	272	188			na
1936	34, 922	3, 774	15, 313	6, 424	447	199		13	na
1937	54, 080	4, 352	11, 632	8, 597	804	285	31	25	na
1938	66, 927	3, 377	20, 513	15, 141	1, 479	672	45	46	na
1939	61, 456	6, 286	30, 035	13, 966	2, 499	1, 415	578	160	na
1940	70, 728	10, 440	36, 877	14, 716	3, 274	1, 802	708	213	2, 745
1941	51, 323	17, 230	33, 388	21, 222	2, 949	988	832	125	1, 376
1942	71, 354	16, 855	25, 741	21, 664	2, 152	546	533	117	1, 547
1943:									
I	18, 903	2, 698	8, 584	10, 725	1, 012	69	89	49	363
II	15, 843	1, 516	6, 521	7, 440	853	89	84	75	274
III	12, 481	2, 376	6, 068	8, 129	755	103	95	71	374
IV	8, 056	1, 274	2, 318	5, 538	596	104	54	48	146
Total	55, 283	7, 864	23, 491	31, 832	3, 216	365	322	243	1, 157
1944:									
I	14, 444	3, 610	8, 541	6, 240	650	118	51	69	354
II	12, 257	3, 407	8, 044	5, 451	481	72	97	74	168
III	11, 757	2, 893	9, 114	5, 828	274	70	52	66	248
IV	6, 075	2, 745	4, 879	2, 479	162	77	24	69	207
Total	44, 533	12, 655	30, 578	19, 998	1, 567	337	224	278	977
1945: I and II	15, 634		4, 551	4, 273	58	65	57	31	na

"na" Indicates data not available.

Source: Data compiled by Iron and Steel Control Association (Tekko Tosei Kai) and Bureau of Mines, Ministry of Commerce and Industry, November 1945.

APPENDIX TABLE C-29.—*Summary of supply of primary aluminum in Japan proper, Korea, and Formosa, 1933-45*

[In metric tons]

Fiscal year	Production of alumina			Production of aluminum ingot	Imports [2]	Total aluminum supply
	From bauxite	From other than bauxite [1]	Total alumina			
1933		100	100	19	3, 549	3, 568
1934		2, 424	2, 424	1, 002	5, 227	6, 229
1935		7, 434	7, 434	3, 166	10, 949	14, 115
1936		13, 167	13, 167	5, 707	10, 241	15, 948
1937	24, 316	7, 181	31, 497	13, 979	13, 701	27, 680
1938	38, 656	9, 618	48, 274	20, 736	23, 847	44, 583
1939	53, 956	11, 240	65, 196	29, 559	36, 701	66, 260
1940	81, 837	15, 650	97, 487	40, 863	na	na
1941	136, 837	15, 046	151, 883	71, 740	na	na
1942	212, 558	13, 623	226, 181	103, 075	2, 000	105, 075
1943	304, 734	13, 757	318, 491	141, 084	3, 000	144, 084
1944	190, 585	34, 626	225, 211	110, 398	4, 205	114, 603
1945	1, 621	14, 598	16, 219	6, 647	1, 070	7, 717

"na" Indicates data not available.

[1] Includes production from aluminous shale, alum-clay, alunite, and scrap.
[2] 1942-45 imports obtained from Manchukuo only.

Sources: For production data, the Light Metals Control Association (Keikinzoku Tosei Kai), with minor adjustments to agree with individual plant data obtained from the Bureau of Mines, Ministry of Commerce and Industry, November 1945. Import data before 1940 were obtained from the Light Metals Control Association, and after 1941 were estimated by the Bureau of Mines.

APPENDIX TABLE C-30.—*Annual imports of bauxite to Japan proper and Formosa, by region of origin, 1935-45* [1]

[In metric tons]

Fiscal years	Palao	Bintan	Malaya (Johore and Malacca)	Indochina	Others	Total
1936		9, 192	958		14, 612	24, 762
1937		46, 663	27, 984		26, 502	101, 149
1938	3, 655	117, 269	76, 505		23, 049	220, 478
1939	13, 987	202, 081	104, 692		31, 698	352, 458
1940	22, 495	194, 729	62, 965			280, 189
1941	59, 297	58, 059	26, 140	3, 215		146, 711
1942	103, 907	274, 449	55, 831	15, 947		450, 134
1943	84, 940	594, 589	138, 555	2, 450		820, 534
1944	4, 488	287, 782	55, 065			347, 335
1945		1, 800				1, 800

[1] By wet weight 1936-41; by dry weight 1942-45. Moisture content approximately 10 percent.

Source: Bureau of Mines, Ministry of Commerce and Industry, November 1945.

APPENDIX TABLE C-31.—*Imports of north China aluminous shale into Japan proper and Korea, annually 1935-45, monthly 1942-45*

[In metric tons]

Period [1]	Japan proper	Korea	Total	Period [1]	Japan proper	Korea	Total
1935	3, 690		3, 690	1944	114, 949	32, 462	147, 411
1936	8, 360		8, 360	1945:			
1937	21, 750		21, 750	April	8, 934		8, 934
1938	26, 750		26, 750	May	25, 768	1, 188	26, 956
1939	32, 040	3, 950	35, 990	June	1, 724		1, 724
1940	37, 000	14, 710	51, 710	July			
1941	25, 465	19, 500	44, 965	August			
1942	23, 884	23, 474	47, 358				
1943	25, 811	24, 688	50, 499	Total	36, 426	1, 188	37, 614

[1] Years are fiscal.

Source: Bureau of Mines, Ministry of Commerce and Industry, November 1945.

APPENDIX TABLE C-32.—*Stocks of bauxite, aluminous shale, alumina, and primary aluminum ingot in Japan proper, Formosa and Korea, 1941-45*

[In metric tons]

Date [1]	Bauxite [2]	Aluminous shale [3]	Alumina	Primary ingot [4]	Date [1]	Bauxite [2]	Aluminous shale [3]	Alumina	Primary ingot [4]
1941 December	254, 740	3, 650	5, 500		1943 December	296, 981	19, 474	19, 331	4, 800
1942 March	191, 174	6, 520	4, 190	7, 000	1944 March	238, 471	20, 692	19, 525	3, 700
June	172, 620	1, 522	7, 293	8, 100	June	176, 241	36, 109	10, 491	9, 700
September	183, 247	8, 766	2, 051	10, 900	September	36, 196	37, 664	11, 376	6, 900
December	209, 427	9, 572	3, 002	12, 500	December	2, 651	32, 061	4, 227	4, 700
1943 March	209, 607	11, 855	2, 897	10, 400	1945 March	5, 233	38, 767	1, 543	5, 300
June	206, 287	13, 844	3, 005	8, 000	June		55, 168	998	5, 700
September	201, 648	13, 635	22, 256	5, 500	August		35, 705	4, 659	4, 129

[1] End of month.
[2] Held in Japan proper and Formosa.
[3] Held in Japan proper and Korea.
[4] Includes stocks at all reduction plants and in the hands of the Imperial Light Metals Control Company (Teikoku Keikinzoku Tosei Kabushiki Kaisha), but excludes stocks held at fabricating plants.

Source: Light Metals Control Association (Okeikinzoku Tosei Kai), November 1945.

APPENDIX TABLE C–33.—*Allotment of primary aluminum to allocation categories, by quarters, 1942–45* [1]

[In metric tons]

Fiscal periods	Aircraft [2]	Army	Navy	Indirect military and civilian	Total
1942:					
I	17, 184	4, 221	1, 216	5, 569	28, 190
II	14, 591	3, 638	1, 233	5, 062	24, 524
III	16, 100	3, 750	1, 923	5, 554	27, 327
IV	18, 339	3, 245	1, 520	5, 581	28, 685
Total	66, 214	14, 854	5, 892	21, 766	108, 726
1943:					
I	23, 961	2, 877	1, 384	5, 263	33, 485
II	25, 854	3, 117	1, 543	5, 379	35, 893
III	27, 185	2, 819	1, 571	5, 348	36, 923
IV	28, 290	2, 515	2, 555	5, 777	39, 137
Total	105, 290	11, 328	7, 053	21, 767	145, 438
1944:					
I	33, 097	2, 175	2, 134	2, 600	40, 006
II	34, 419	1, 037	1, 156	1, 638	38, 250
III	16, 352	423	465	792	18, 032
IV	16, 223	---------	---------	---------	16, 223
Total	100, 091	3, 635	3, 755	5, 030	112, 511
1945: I	10, 200	---------	---------	---------	10, 200

[1] Quantities are those allotted under the distribution program of the Imperial Light Metals Control Co. (Teikoku Keikinzoku Tosei Kabushiki Kaisha). Totals approximate total production in Japan proper, Korea, and Formosa plus receipts from Manchukuo.

[2] Quantities for 1942 and 1943 constitute estimated portion destined for aircraft of total aluminum allocated to army and navy categories.

Source: Light Metals Control Association (Keikinzoku Tosei Kai), November 1945.

APPENDIX TABLE C–34.—*Summary of Japan's magnesium capacity and supply, fiscal years 1935–45*

[In metric tons]

Year	Capacity			Production			Supply			Total magnesium supply [1] 6+7+8−9
	Japan proper	Korea, Manchukuo, and Formosa	Total	Japan proper	Korea, Manchukuo, and Formosa	Total	Secondary ingot	Imports	Exports	
	(1)	(2)	(3)	(4)	(5)	(6)	(7)	(8)	(9)	(10)
1935	1, 500	---------	1, 500	379	---------	379	---------	---------	---------	379
1936	1, 500	---------	1, 500	637	---------	637	---------	---------	---------	637
1937	1, 600	---------	1, 600	892	---------	892	---------	---------	11	881
1938	1, 900	50	1, 950	1, 114	42	1, 156	---------	1, 650	1	2, 805
1939	2, 750	100	2, 850	1, 825	111	1, 936	---------	798	1	2, 733
1940	3, 250	400	3, 650	2, 526	280	2, 806	---------	---------	1, 019	1, 787
1941	3, 365	835	4, 200	2, 193	366	2, 559	---------	---------	115	2, 444
1942	3, 627	1, 205	4, 832	2, 121	557	2, 678	66	---------	1	2, 743
1943	4, 015	3, 755	7, 770	2, 845	1, 000	3, 845	196	---------	2	4, 039
1944	4, 705	5, 735	10, 440	2, 577	2, 548	5, 125	183	---------	---------	5, 308
1945	4, 800	5, 860	10, 660	404	587	991	62	---------	---------	1, 053

[1] Stocks not included

Source: Bureau of Mines, Ministry of Commerce and Industry; Light Metal Control Association (Keikinzoku Tosei Kai); Bureau of Taxation, Ministry of Finance; November 1945.

APPENDIX TABLE C-35.—Summary of copper refining capacity, and of supply in Japan proper, fiscal years 1935–45

(In metric tons)

Period	Refining capacity [1] end of (year) (1)	Ore (copper content) [2] Production (2)	Imports (3)	Total (2+3) (4)	Blister copper Production [3] (5)	Imports [4] (6)	Total (5+6) (7)	Electrolytic copper Production [5] (8)	Imports [6] (9)	Total (8+9) (10)	Old scrap [7] (copper content) (11)	Stocks [8] (electrolytic) (14)	Exports [9] (12)	Total available [10] (10+11+12) (13)
1935	(78, 240)	(38, 414)	na	(38, 414)	(50, 772)	1, 409	(52, 181)	(54, 422)	(60, 897)	(115, 319)	na	na	18, 052	(97, 267)
1936	(78, 240)	(37, 702)	na	(37, 702)	(49, 088)	2, 518	(51, 606)	(59, 170)	(51, 709)	(110, 879)	na	na	12, 758	(98, 121)
1937	(84, 240)	(36, 778)	na	(36, 778)	(54, 796)	3, 005	(57, 801)	(63, 836)	(72, 278)	(136, 114)	na	na	12, 941	(123, 173)
1938	(84, 240)	(37, 533)	na	(37, 533)	(61, 136)	3, 587	(65, 723)	(69, 999)	(102, 306)	(172, 305)	na	na	7, 026	(165, 279)
1939	(87, 600)	(36, 742)	na	(36, 742)	(61, 389)	6, 542	(67, 931)	(70, 142)	(120, 251)	(190, 393)	na	na	8, 675	(181, 718)
1940	(134, 000)	73, 866	na	(73, 866)	92, 011	7, 997	100, 008	108, 216	(119, 392)	(227, 608)	26, 725	na	7, 765	(246, 578)
1941	(135, 000)	76, 504	[11] 11, 670	(88, 174)	91, 674	5, 352	97, 026	103, 387	(38, 486)	(141, 873)	27, 869	105, 018	4, 649	(164, 913)
1942	(135, 000)	81, 068	11, 378	92, 446	97, 302	4, 511	101, 813	105, 137	(690)	(105, 827)	14, 789	53, 086	2, 537	(118, 079)
1943	(150, 600)	94, 575	11, 508	106, 083	110, 608	4, 619	115, 227	122, 860	(2)	(122, 862)	12, 000	58, 234	996	(133, 866)
1944	(150, 600)	81, 433	5, 503	86, 936	87, 172	5, 106	92, 278	99, 205	3, 910	103, 115	8, 923	31, 554	1, 374	110, 664
1945 (first quarter)	(150, 600)	(6, 213)	------	(6, 213)	(14, 721)	554	(15, 275)	(16, 556)	------	(16, 556)	na	[12] 31,071	25	(16, 531)

"na" Indicates data not available.

"( )" Figures in parentheses indicate a total for which one or more of the constituent figures are not available.

[1] Information on all major plants not available until 1943. 1943–45 figures exclude only the capacity of plants producing electrolytic copper as a secondary product.

[2] Information 1935–39 and 1945 available only for 11 mines, contributing approximately 50 percent to the total product.

[3] Data on all companies available only for 1943–44. Estimates for 2 plants included in 1940–42 figures. 1945 figure excludes 1 plant for which data is not available and includes two plants whose data probably contains July and August production.

[4] Production of the Chinnampo smelter in Korea which was shipped immediately to the Saganoseki refinery in Kyushu. No other information on imported blister available.

[5] Data available on all major plants for 1942–44 only. Production estimates included in 1940–41 data. Data prior to 1942 excludes scrap refined on toll for the army and navy. 1942–44 on indeterminant part of such scrap is excluded. 1945 data includes 2 plants whose figures probably include July and August production.

[6] Imports 1935–41 adjusted to fiscal from calendar year data.

[7] Source: Mining Control Association (Kozan Tosei Kai). Includes only scrap suitable for direct use by foundry or rolling mills.

[8] Includes Metals Distribution Control Co. (Kinzoku Haikyu Tosei Kaisha), army, and navy stocks. Army and navy figures are estimated. Metals Distribution Control Company figure for end of year 1941 is as of 1 February 1942.

[9] Exports purport to be all shapes and fabricated products sent to points outside Japan proper. The 1942–44 planned allocations for export are much higher.

[10] Excludes stocks and an indeterminant part of production on toll for the army and navy which was not reported.

[11] Information available on imports from Formosa and China were for the fourth quarter only.

[12] Stocks on hand 15 August 1945.

Sources: Company reports; Bureau of Mines, Ministry of Industry and Commerce; Bureau of Taxation, Ministry of Finance; Metals Distribution Control Company (Kinzoku Haikyu Tosei Kaisha); Mining Control Association (Kozan Tosei Kai), November 1945.

APPENDIX TABLE C-36.—*Imports of Copper ore and ore concentrates by country of origin, Japan proper, fiscal years 1941-44*

[In metric tons of copper content]

Country of origin	1941	1942	1943	1944
Philippines	2, 336	3, 391	6, 614	1, 213
Formosa	[1] (436)	4, 537	4, 780	4, 236
China	[1] (12)	52	114	54
South America	5, 307	3, 398		
Canada	3, 579			
Total	(11, 670)	11, 378	11, 508	5, 503

"( )" Figures in parentheses indicate totals for which one of more of the constituent figures are not available.

[1] Data includes only the fourth quarter of the fiscal year.

Source: Bureau of Mines, Ministry of Commerce and Industry, November 1945.

APPENDIX TABLE C-37.—*Stocks of refined copper, Japan proper, 1941-45*

[In metric tons]

Date	Metals Distribution Control Company	Army	Navy	Total
31 March 1942	[1] 42, 518	20, 000	42, 500	105, 018
31 March 1943	8, 586	10, 000	34, 500	53, 086
31 March 1944	27, 734		30, 500	58, 234
31 March 1945	5, 554		27, 000	32, 554
15 August 1945	3, 693		27, 378	31, 071

[1] Metals Distribution Control Company as of 1 February 1942.

Source: Reports from Metals Distribution Control Company (Kinzoku Haikyu Tosei Kaisha), army, and navy, November 1945. Army and navy figures were estimates.

APPENDIX TABLE C-38.—*Imports of electrolytic copper by country of origin, Japan proper, fiscal years 1935-44* [1]

[In metric tons]

Year	Country of origin						
	America	Manchukuo	China	Canada	Chile	Others	Total
1935	59, 753	na	na	57	na	1, 087	(60, 897)
1936	47, 902	na	na	31	na	3, 776	(51, 709)
1937	54, 221	na	na	122	na	17, 935	(72, 278)
1938	72, 049	na	na	122	na	30, 135	(102, 306)
1939	117, 204	75	na	93	2, 879	na	(120, 251)
1940	104, 908	122	na	31	14, 331	na	(119, 392)
1941	21, 153	251	na	na	17, 082	na	(38, 486)
1942	152	416	122			na	(690)
1943		na	na			2	(2)
1944		1	3, 904			5	3, 910

"na" Indicates data not available.

"( )" Figures in parentheses indicate totals for which one or more of the constituent figures are not available.

[1] Years 1935-41 adjusted to fiscal from calendar year data.

Source: Bureau of Mines, Ministry of Commerce and Industry, November 1945.

APPENDIX TABLE C-39.—*Summary of Japanese total lead-producing capacity and supply, by fiscal years 1935–45*

[In metric tons of metal content]

Fiscal year	Capacity						Total supply					
	Japan proper		Korea and Manchukuo		Total		Japan proper					
							Ore and concentrates			Crude lead		
	Smelters	Refineries[1]	Smelters[2]	Refineries[3]	Smelters	Refineries	Production	Imports	Total (7+8)	Production	Imports[4]	Total (10+11)
	(1)	(2)	(3)	(4)	(5)	(6)	(7)	(8)	(9)	(10)	(11)	(12)
1935	na	(14,200)	na	na	na	(14,200)	na	na	na	na	na	na
1936	na	(19,900)	na	na	na	(19,900)	na	na	na	na	na	na
1937	na	(29,200)	na	na	na	(29,200)	na	na	na	na	na	na
1938	na	(29,200)	na	na	na	(29,200)	na	na	na	na	na	na
1939	na	(29,200)	na	na	na	(29,200)	na	na	na	na	na	na
1940	37,380	(36,400)	(13,000)	na	(50,380)	(36,400)	11,654	na	(11,654)	13,727	(10,200)	(23,927)
1941	37,380	(36,400)	(13,000)	na	(50,380)	(36,400)	15,139	na	(15,139)	15,507	(10,500)	(26,007)
1942	37,380	(36,400)	(13,000)	na	(50,380)	(36,400)	19,636	3,648	23,284	16,489	(8,200)	(24,689)
1943	37,380	53,800	(20,000)	na	(57,380)	(53,800)	22,706	142	22,848	21,236	16,100	37,336
1944	37,380	53,800	(20,000)	na	(57,380)	(53,800)	17,344	257	17,601	20,227	14,200	34,427
1945[14]	37,380	53,800	(20,000)	na	(57,380)	(53,800)	[15](2,376)	------	(2,376)	3,105	(924)	(4,029)

See footnotes at end of table.

Fiscal year	Japan proper Refined lead — Production (13)	Imports (14)	Total (13+14) (15)	Korea and Manchukuo — Crude [5] production (16)	Refined [6] production (17)	Scrap [7] production (18)	Stock piles [8] (19)	Total imports to Japan proper (8+11+14) (20)	Total production of crude lead, Japan proper and overseas (10+16) (21)	Total production of refined lead (22)
1935	7,807	[9] 90,206	98,013	(1,338)	na	na	na	(90,206)	na	(7,807)
1936	10,601	[9] 95,921	106,522	(3,143)	na	na	na	(95,921)	na	(10,601)
1937	15,813	[9] 59,235	75,048	(6,156)	na	na	na	(59,235)	na	(15,813)
1938	16,283	[9] 60,263	76,546	(5,402)	na	na	na	(60,263)	na	(16,283)
1949	14,223	[9] 100,802	115,025	(7,786)	na	na	na	(100,802)	na	(14,223)
1940	23,531	[9] 92,091	115,622	(10,294)	na	na	na	(102,291)	(24,021)	(23,531)
1941	26,734	[9] 78,532	105,266	(10,521)	na	na	na	(89,032)	(26,028)	(26,734)
1942	25,832	4,328	30,160	(8,232)	na	na	[10][11] 99,743	(16,176)	(24,721)	(30,486)
1943	32,031	10,214	42,245	[12] (18,352)	4,654	2,436	na	26,456	(39,588)	(36,638)
1944	34,930	3,136	38,066	[12] (16,229)	4,607	21,982	[13] 56,887	17,593	(36,456)	(37,138)
1945 [14]	[16] (4,099)	---	(4,099)	(924)	2,208	na	[17] 28,900	(924)	(4,029)	(4,099)

"na" indicates data not available.

"( )" Indicates a total that is not complete, because not all constituent figures are available.

[1] Capacity before 1943 does not include the Takehara refinery on which the data is not available.

[2] Estimate of Korean capacity based on charging capacity. Manchukuo data not available.

[3] Manchukuo data not available.

[4] Estimated by Japan Mining Company. Includes all Chinnampo smelter production and 80 percent of remaining production. All crude lead imports were from Korea.

[5] Manchukuo production not available. With the exception of the years 1943-44, these figures represent production of the Chinnampo smelter in Korea.

[6] Korea has no refining capacity. Manchukuo data is unavailable, except for years shown. Data for 1944 probably includes no more than 8 months.

[7] Allocated as sorted or remelted scrap. Deductions are already made on the basis of the estimate of the Bureau of Mines that 20 percent returned to the refineries and 5 percent was lost in the remelt.

[8] Sum of the refined metal stocks held by the Metals Distribution Control Company, army, and navy. The army and navy figures are estimated by those organizations.

[9] Calendar years.

[10] As of February 1942.

[11] Includes estimates of army and navy stocks for March 31, 1942, instead of February 1942.

[12] Total Korean production.

[13] As of Mar. 31, 1944.

[14] April 1-August 15.

[15] Production of the two largest mines estimated at over 50 percent of total production.

[16] Data on Saganoseki, Takehara, and "other" refineries incomplete.

[17] As of Aug. 15, 1945.

Source: Japan proper data mainly from Bureau of Mines, Ministry of Commerce and Industry, November 1945. For Korean data, Japan Mining Company, November 1945. Japanese army and navy supplied stock pile data, November 1945. For specific sources, refer to the appendix tables from which the above material was taken.

[In metric tons]

Fiscal year	Capacity[1]				Supply		
	Japan proper		Korea Electrolytic	Total (1+2+3)	Japan proper		
					Ores and concentrates (zinc contents)		
	Distilled[1]	Electrolytic[2]			Production[3]	Imports[4]	Total (5+6)
	(1)	(2)	(3)	(4)	(5)	(6)	(7)
1935	34, 200	(10, 000)	--------	(44, 200)	(18, 536)	(12, 913)	(31, 449)
1936	34, 200	13, 000	--------	47, 200	(25, 710)	(12, 079)	(37, 789)
1937	40, 200	19, 000	--------	59, 200	(30, 353)	(4, 970)	(35, 323)
1938	41, 100	19, 000	--------	60, 100	(34, 284)	(4, 162)	(38, 446)
1939	44, 100	22, 600	--------	66, 700	(30, 901)	(3, 525)	(34, 426)
1940	46, 100	22, 600	--------	68, 700	56, 679	(8, 400)	(65, 079)
1941	46, 400	22, 600	8, 400	77, 400	63, 785	(6, 815)	(70, 600)
1942	47, 800	25, 900	8, 400	82, 100	85, 305	(6, 082)	(91, 387)
1943	51, 800	38, 500	8, 400	98, 700	94, 105	8, 641	102, 746
1944	51, 800	43, 000	8, 400	103, 200	74, 939	7, 187	82, 126
1945	51, 800	43, 000	8, 400	103, 200	(10, 829)	(2, 527)	[10] (13, 356)

Fiscal year	Supply—Continued										
	Japan proper—Continued				Korea slab zinc production,[7] electrolytic	Old scrap	Stocks at year end[8]	Total slab zinc production, Japan proper and Korea (8+9+12)	Total imports to Japan proper (6+10)	Total zinc available[9] (11+12+13)
	Slab zinc									
	Production		Import[6]	Total (8+9+10)						
	Distilled[5]	Electrolytic[2]								
	(8)	(9)	(10)	(11)	(12)	(13)	(14)	(15)	(16)	(17)
1935	26, 295	(3, 912)	32, 763	(62, 970)	--------	--------	na	(30, 207)	(45, 676)	(62, 970)
1936	29, 049	(7, 919)	42, 030	(78, 998)	--------	--------	na	(36, 968)	(54, 109)	(78, 998)
1937	38, 137	(11, 649)	37, 086	(86, 872)	--------	--------	na	(49, 786)	(42, 056)	(86, 872)
1938	41, 312	(12, 891)	28, 012	(82, 215)	--------	--------	na	(54, 203)	(32, 174)	(82, 215)
1939	39, 926	(11, 330)	58, 220	(109,476)	--------	--------	na	(51, 256)	(61, 745)	(109,476)
1940	48, 341	11, 762	23, 473	83, 576	--------	--------	na	60, 103	(31, 873)	83, 576
1941	48, 548	13, 344	6, 319	68, 211	2, 103	--------	26, 285	63, 995	(13, 134)	70, 314
1942	47, 577	13, 796	3, 409	64, 782	6, 833	--------	(11, 450)	68, 206	(9, 491)	71, 615
1943	44, 827	17, 507	3, 441	65, 775	7, 452	1, 632	36, 797	69, 786	12, 082	74, 859
1944	43, 284	17, 673	671	61, 628	5, 475	820	33, 614	66, 432	7, 858	67, 923
1945	[11](8, 966)	[11](2, 947)	na	(11, 913)	[11] 1, 527	93	[12]42, 975	(13, 440)	(2, 527)	(13, 533)

"na" Indicates data not available.

"( )" Figures in parentheses indicate totals for which one or more of the constituent figures are not available.

[1] Some zinc capacity in lead and copper smelters not included, but quantities are very small.

[2] The Hibi refinery was purchased from the Showa Mining Co. by the Mitsui Mining Co. in 1943. Capacity and production data for prior years is incomplete. Refer to appendix tables 83 and 85.

[3] Prior to 1940 only production of Hosokura and Kamioka mines reported. Production from other mines, which was appreciable, not available.

[4] Prior to 1943 only imports of Mitsui Mining Co. are included, but these represent more than 75 percent of total imports.

[5] Prior to 1942 small quantities produced at lead and copper smelters not included.

[6] After 1940 principally from French Indo China. Exports of 269 tons in 1944 and 35 tons in 1945 have been disregarded.

[7] Estimated from Japan Mining Co. information for years 1941, 1942, and 1945.

[8] Stocks held by Metals Distribution Control Co. and by Japanese Army and Navy. Refer to appendix table 90.

[9] Stocks not included.

[10] First quarter of fiscal year only.

[11] First and second quarters of fiscal year except that production of certain smelters for certain months in second quarter not included. Refer to appendix tables 85 and 89.

[12] At end of fiscal year except for 1945 which was 15 August.

Source: Japan proper data mainly from Bureau of Mines, Ministry of Commerce and Industry, November 1945. Korea data from Japan Mining Co., November 1945. Stock data from Metals Distribution Control Co. (Kinzoku Haikyu Tosei Kaisha), Japanese Army, and Japanese Navy, November 1945. For other specific sources, refer to the appendix tables 83, 84, 85, 89, and 90, giving further details of above data.

[In metric tons of metal content]

Fiscal year	Capacity		Supply (production, imports, scrap, and stock piles)								
	Smelter [1]	Refinery [2]	Ore and concentrates			Crude tin production [3]	Refined tin			Scrap production [4]	Stock piles [5]
			Production	Imports	Total (3 + 4)		Production	Imports	Total (7 + 8)		
	(1)	(2)	(3)	(4)	(5)	(6)	(7)	(8)	(9)	(10)	(11)
1935	na	(2,400)	[6] (920)	na	(920)	na	[2] (2,095)	[7] 4,251	(6,346)	na	na
1936	na	(2,400)	[6] (1,516)	na	(1,516)	na	[2] (1,770)	[7] 4,718	(6,488)	na	na
1937	na	(2,400)	[6] (1,605)	na	(1,605)	na	[2] (1,600)	[7] 4,331	(5,931)	na	na
1938	na	(3,000)	[6] (1,517)	na	(1,517)	na	[2] (1,523)	[7] 8,744	(10,267)	na	na
1939	na	(3,000)	[6] (1,423)	na	(1,423)	na	[2] (1,398)	[7] 7,964	(9,362)	na	na
1940	(2,400)	(3,000)	[6] (1,463)	na	(1,463)	2,039	[2] (1,453)	[7] 10,868	(12,321)	na	na
1941	(3,600)	(3,000)	[6] (1,277)	1,636	(2,913)	4,079	[2] (1,911)	[7] 5,480	(7,391)	na	na
1942	(3,600)	(3,000)	1,917	996	2,913	3,626	3,816	11,055	14,871	na	[8] 7,322
1943	(3,600)	(3,000)	1,120	586	1,706	1,787	1,815	26,766	28,581	134	[9] 9,316
1944	(3,600)	(1,000)	380	--------	380	536	772	16,965	17,737	95	[10] 13,053
1945 [11]	(3,600)	(1,000)	[6] (49)	--------	(49)	66	(61)	3,007	(3,068)	na	[12] 10,155

"na" Indicates data not available.

"( )" Indicates a total that is incomplete because not all constituent figures are available.

[1] This represents only the Ikuno smelter of the Mitsubishi Mining Company, which is the only significant tin smelter in Japan.

[2] This represents only the Mitsubishi Copper Refinery at Osaka, which is the only large tin refinery in Japan.

[3] Includes small amounts of low grade refined tin.

[4] Old scrap estimated by the Japanese Bureau of Mines to be allocated as scrap on the estimate that 30 percent of total scrap is refined again.

[5] Sum of the refined metal stocks held by the Metals Distribution Control Company (Kinzoku Haikyo Tosei Kaisha), Army, and Navy. The army and navy figures are estimated by those organizations. The stock for February 1942 includes army and navy figures for Mar. 31, 1942.

[6] Includes only the Akenobe mine estimated at two-thirds total production.

[7] Calendar year. No imports of refined metal January–March 1942.

[8] As of February 1942.

[9] As of Mar. 31, 1943.

[10] As of Mar. 31, 1944.

[11] April 1–August 15 except for capacity which is annual.

[12] As of Aug. 8, 1945.

Source: Bureau of Mines, Ministry of Commerce and Industry; Mitsubishi Mining Company; Metals Distribution Control Company (Kinzoku Haikyu Tosei Kaisha), November 1945.

APPENDIX TABLE C–42.—*Summary of the coal position in Japan proper, fiscal years 1931–45*

[In thousands of metric tons]

Years	Production	Imports	Exports	Production plus net imports minus exports	Consumption [1]	Stocks at end of year
1931	27,987	3,110	1,983	29,114	na	1,376
1932	28,053	3,271	1,847	29,477	na	1,237
1933	32,524	4,275	2,128	34,671	[2] 31,466	944
1934	35,925	5,072	1,676	39,321	[2] 35,168	657
1935	37,762	5,381	1,765	41,378	42,707	698
1936	41,803	6,163	1,988	45,978	47,245	1,128
1937	45,258	6,360	1,904	49,714	51,157	1,038
1938	48,684	6,493	1,725	53,452	55,313	1,145
1939	52,409	8,285	1,689	59,005	61,254	1,473
1940	57,309	10,123	1,491	65,941	66,542	1,762
1941	55,602	9,585	1,739	63,448	63,055	3,326
1942	54,178	8,748	1,596	61,330	61,992	3,159
1943	55,538	6,029	1,100	60,467	59,740	3,816
1944	49,335	3,135	714	51,756	50,471	4,031
1945:						
I	10,877	188	62	11,003	9,536	4,036
II	5,238	------------	------------	5,238	5,050	3,731

[1] Attention is called to the fact that the figures in the above table do not balance and that in some years the amount consumed is actually greater than the supply available. The data used were furnished by two different Japanese agencies, the Coal Control Association and the Japan Coal Company, which, in turn, secured their statistics from many different sources. Although several interviews with responsible officials failed to reconcile the obvious discrepancies existing in the data, the officials stated that the figures on consumption undoubtedly overstated the amounts of coal actually used.

[2] Coal consumed at coal mines not included.

Sources: Compiled from data submitted by the Coal Control Association (Sekitan Tosei Kai) and the Japan Coal Company (Nihon Sekitan Kaisha), November 1945.

APPENDIX TABLE C-43.—*Coal production, fiscal years 1938–44*

[In thousands of metric tons]

Year	Japan proper	Karafuto	Korea	Manchukuo	Formosa	North China-Inner Mongolia	Central China	Total
1938	48, 684	3, 435	3, 419	15, 988	2, 199	9, 959	na	na
1939	52, 409	4, 993	5, 171	19, 496	2, 608	15, 272	na	na
1940	57, 309	6, 465	6, 096	21, 132	2, 827	17, 966	469	112, 264
1941	55, 602	6, 471	6, 803	24, 147	2, 770	23, 968	795	120, 556
1942	54, 178	4, 910	6, 645	24, 169	2, 311	24, 878	929	118, 020
1943	55, 538	4, 979	6, 574	25, 390	2, 324	21, 735	878	117, 418
1944	49, 335	2, 678	7, 037	25, 627	1, 653	20, 333	874	107, 537

"na" Indicates data not available.

Sources: Figures for Japan proper compiled from data submitted by the Coal Control Association (Sekitan Tosei Kai); figures for production in other areas compiled from data submitted by the Japan-Manchukuo Trading Company (Nichiman Shoji Kabushiki Kaisha), the Japan, Manchukuo, China Coal Federation (Nichi Manshi Sekitan Remmei), and the Greater East Asia Ministry (Dai Toa Sho), November 1945.

APPENDIX TABLE C-44.—*Coal imports into Japan proper, by source, fiscal years 1939–45*

[In thousands of metric tons]

Year	Karafuto	Korea	Manchukuo	Formosa	North China-Inner Mongolia	Indochina, etc.	Total
1939	2, 542	1, 011	848	255	3, 042	587	8, 285
1940	3, 328	1, 467	773	263	3, 800	492	10, 123
1941	3, 310	1, 078	687	39	4, 120	351	9, 585
1942	2, 198	910	642	175	4, 539	284	8, 748
1943:							
First half	1, 414	319	293	5	1, 967	75	4, 073
Second half	236	177	121	----------	1, 422	----------	1, 956
Total	1, 650	496	414	5	3, 389	75	6, 029
1944:							
April	----------	28	50	----------	185	----------	263
May	104	41	69	----------	185	----------	399
June	314	27	54	----------	193	----------	588
July	348	30	45	----------	174	----------	597
August	35	14	37	----------	128	----------	214
September	6	16	53	----------	123	----------	198
October	----------	15	56	----------	156	----------	227
November	----------	26	39	----------	127	----------	192
December	----------	10	49	----------	92	----------	151
January	----------	12	55	----------	84	----------	151
February	----------	18	41	----------	34	----------	93
March	----------	15	13	----------	34	----------	62
Total	807	252	561	----------	1, 515	----------	3, 135
1945:							
April	----------	15	12	----------	53	----------	80
May	----------	12	16	----------	35	----------	63
June	----------	5	8	----------	32	----------	45
Total	----------	32	36	----------	120	----------	188

Source: Compiled by the Japan Coal Company (Nihon Sekitan Kaisha), November 1945.

[In thousands of metric tons]

Industry	1933	1935	1936	1937	1938	1939	1940	1941	1942	1943	1944	1945 (Apr.–July)
Iron and steel:												
For coke	3,089	4,130	4,339	4,941	5,573	6,718	7,997	8,972	8,424	7,938	6,190	1,255
For fuel	975	1,129	1,790	1,698	2,413	3,339	3,442	4,199	4,891	5,764	5,051	1,165
Total	4,064	5,259	6,129	6,639	7,986	10,057	11,439	13,171	13,315	13,702	11,241	2,420
Shipbuilding	104	120	128	164	167	166	190	193	230	281	446	148
Machinery manufacture	345	408	570	699	1,111	1,514	1,780	1,931	1,966	2,178	2,179	472
Metal mining and refining	197	517	606	725	881	664	857	952	778	714	603	157
Gas and coke	1,881	2,214	2,342	2,564	3,219	3,685	3,945	4,080	3,946	3,804	3,358	506
Electric power	1,881	2,876	3,206	3,747	4,329	6,200	5,898	4,202	5,261	5,077	3,705	588
Chemical industry	2,673	2,506	3,295	3,958	4,770	6,417	7,150	6,572	5,803	6,158	4,715	1,057
Ceramics, including cement	2,871	3,686	3,949	4,287	4,261	4,114	4,665	3,779	3,457	2,929	2,029	507
Fibre and textiles	3,274	5,449	6,384	6,968	6,919	6,420	6,724	4,926	3,080	2,109	1,026	260
Foodstuffs	2,098	1,370	1,528	1,428	1,437	1,541	1,503	1,527	1,218	958	684	187
Salt	776	753	731	702	579	718	625	355	374	362	331	83
Railroads	3,408	3,722	4,008	4,126	4,442	5,076	5,568	5,105	6,300	6,960	8,086	2,716
Liquid fuel	------	------	------	------	------	64	387	603	1,012	1,234	1,573	543
Briquets	3,859	1,288	1,367	1,430	1,527	1,666	2,206	1,780	1,358	1,035	439	88
Nonindustrial heating and cooking		3,781	4,043	4,075	3,648	3,103	3,225	3,361	2,416	2,152	2,026	564
Government factories and miscellaneous		514	523	408	374	1,090	1,366	1,327	2,005	1,482	1,135	377
Army		726	659	887	1,279	1,879	2,290	3,325	1,931	1,731	1,368	430
Navy									1,830	1,833	1,480	360
Ship bunkering	4,035	4,498	4,487	4,701	4,454	3,722	3,804	2,951	2,517	2,010	1,047	241
Total	31,466	39,687	43,955	47,508	51,383	58,096	63,622	60,140	58,797	56,709	47,471	11,704

Source: Compiled by the Japan Coal Company (Nihon Sekitan Kaisha), November 1945.

APPENDIX TABLE C–46.—*Consumption of coal in Japan Proper, by industries, excluding consumption by coal mines, in percentages of total consumption, fiscal years 1933–45*

Industry	1933	1934	1935	1936	1937	1938	1939	1940	1941	1942 First half	1942 Second half	1943 First half	1943 Second half	1944 First half	1944 Second half	1945 First half
Iron and steel:																
For coke	9.8	10.8	10.4	9.8	10.4	10.8	11.6	12.6	14.9	15.0	13.8	14.9	13.2	14.0	11.8	9.8
For fuel	3.1	3.3	2.8	4.1	3.6	4.7	5.7	5.4	7.0	8.9	7.8	11.0	9.4	10.6	10.7	9.2
Total	12.9	14.1	13.2	13.9	14.0	15.5	17.3	18.0	21.9	23.9	21.6	25.9	22.6	24.6	22.5	19.0
Shipbuilding	.3	.3	.3	.3	.4	.3	.3	.3	.3	.4	.4	.5	.5	.7	1.2	1.2
Machinery manufacture	1.1	1.1	1.0	1.3	1.5	2.2	2.6	2.8	3.2	3.5	3.2	3.5	4.1	4.5	4.7	3.7
Metal mining and refining	.6	1.0	1.3	1.4	1.5	1.7	1.1	1.3	1.6	1.3	1.3	1.4	1.2	1.3	1.2	1.4
Gas and coke	6.0	5.4	5.6	5.3	5.4	6.3	6.3	6.2	6.8	7.2	6.3	6.9	6.5	7.5	6.6	5.1
Electric power	6.0	7.3	7.2	7.3	7.9	8.4	10.6	9.3	7.0	7.9	10.0	9.5	8.4	7.5	8.1	4.4
Chemical industry	8.5	9.8	6.3	7.5	8.3	9.3	11.0	11.2	10.9	9.8	10.0	11.0	10.7	10.5	9.3	8.3
Ceramics, including cement	9.1	8.7	9.3	9.0	9.0	8.3	7.6	7.3	6.3	6.4	5.4	4.9	5.4	4.4	4.1	4.1
Fibre and textiles	10.4	10.2	13.7	14.5	14.5	13.5	11.0	10.6	8.2	6.6	4.0	3.8	3.7	2.4	1.9	2.4
Foodstuffs	6.7	6.1	3.5	3.5	3.0	2.8	2.6	2.4	2.5	2.2	2.0	1.4	2.0	1.5	1.4	1.8
Salt	2.5	2.3	1.9	1.7	1.5	1.1	1.2	1.0	.6	.9	.4	.7	.6	.7	.6	1.2
Railroads	10.8	10.2	9.4	9.1	8.7	8.6	8.7	8.8	8.5	10.8	10.6	11.2	13.3	15.2	19.1	23.5
Liquid fuel	---	---	---	---	3.0	3.0	.1	.7	1.0	1.5	1.9	2.0	2.3	2.8	3.9	4.2
Briquets	---	---	3.3	3.1	3.0	3.0	2.9	3.5	3.0	2.1	2.4	1.9	1.7	.9	.9	.7
Nonindustrial heating and cooking	---	---	9.5	9.2	8.6	7.1	5.3	5.1	5.6	3.0	5.1	2.3	5.1	4.6	3.8	7.7
Government factories and miscellaneous	12.3	11.3	1.3	1.2	.9	.7	1.8	2.1	2.2	2.2	4.4	2.0	3.2	2.1	2.8	3.6
Army			1.8	1.5	1.9	2.5	3.2	3.6	5.5	3.0	3.5	3.6	2.6	3.0	2.7	3.2
Navy										2.9	3.3	3.6	2.9	3.3	2.9	2.6
Ship bunkering	12.8	12.2	11.4	10.2	9.9	8.7	6.4	5.8	4.9	4.4	4.2	3.9	3.2	2.5	2.3	1.9
Total	100.0	100.0	100.0	100.0	100.0	100.0	100.0	100.0	100.0	100.0	100.0	100.0	100.0	100.0	100.0	100.0

Source: Compiled from data submitted by the Japan Coal Company (Nihon Sekitan Kaisha), November 1945. Based on consumption reports submitted periodically by consumers.

APPENDIX TABLE C–47.—*Interisland movement of coal to Honshu, by source and type of transportation, fiscal years 1941–45*

[In thousands of metric tons]

Year	From Hokkaido			From Kyushu			Grand total		
	Water	Rail	Total	Water	Rail	Total	Water	Rail	Total
1941	7, 316	13	7, 329	13, 379	444	13, 823	20, 695	457	21, 152
1942	8, 071	117	8, 188	12, 056	1, 860	13, 916	20, 127	1, 977	22, 104
1943:									
I	1, 569	117	1, 686	2, 811	866	3, 677	4, 380	983	5, 363
II	1, 142	120	1, 262	2, 565	913	3, 478	3, 707	1, 033	4, 740
III	1, 595	129	1, 724	2, 394	1, 268	3, 662	3, 989	1, 397	5, 386
IV	1, 886	236	2, 122	2, 366	1, 355	3, 721	4, 252	1, 591	5, 843
Total	6, 192	602	6, 794	10, 136	4, 402	14, 538	16, 328	5, 004	21, 332
1944:									
April	668	77	745	762	446	1, 208	1, 430	523	1, 953
May	348	125	473	624	489	1, 113	972	614	1, 586
June	180	118	298	568	487	1, 055	748	605	1, 353
July	193	124	317	557	460	1, 017	750	584	1, 334
August	410	157	567	513	427	940	923	584	1, 507
September	340	140	480	504	459	963	844	599	1, 443
October	378	135	513	567	427	994	945	562	1, 507
November	449	141	590	647	461	1, 108	1, 096	602	1, 698
December	407	110	517	572	487	1, 059	979	597	1, 576
January	336	83	419	414	488	902	750	571	1, 321
February	326	86	412	463	459	922	789	545	1, 334
March	446	138	584	447	447	894	893	585	1, 478
Total	4, 481	1, 434	5, 915	6, 638	5, 537	12, 175	11, 119	6, 971	18, 090
1945:									
April	458	118	576	367	416	783	825	534	1, 359
May	460	135	595	260	467	727	720	602	1, 322
June	259	138	397	191	393	584	450	531	981
July	275	75	350	189	311	500	464	386	850
August	240	--------	240	86	120	206	326	120	446
Total	1, 692	466	2, 158	1, 093	1, 707	2, 800	2, 785	2, 173	4, 958

Sources: Compiled from data submitted by the Coal Control Association (Sekitan Tosei Kai) and the Japan Coal Company (Nihon Sekitan Kaisha), November 1945.

APPENDIX TABLE C-48.—*Coal mining labor force, production, and output per employee per year, in Japan Proper,[1] Great Britain,[2] and the United States,[3] 1941-45*

	1941	1942	1943	1944	1945
Employees (1,000)					
Japan:					
Japanese workers	279	273	265	266	261
Koreans and others	60	102	128	150	151
Total	339	375	393	416	412
Great Britain	698	709	708	710	na
United States	457	462	416	393	na
Annual production (in thousands of metric tons)					
Japan	55. 6	54. 2	55. 5	49. 3	32. 2
Great Britain	209. 6	206. 9	197. 6	191. 0	na
United States	466. 4	528. 7	535. 5	562. 1	na
Output per employee per year (in metric tons)					
Japan	164	144	141	119	78
Great Britain	300	292	279	269	na
United States	1, 021	1, 144	1, 287	1, 430	na

"na" Indicates data not available.

[1] Source: Coal Control Association (Sekitan Tosei Kai), November 1945. Fiscal years. Includes all employees engaged in coal mining, as of end of fiscal year, except 1945 is as of April 30. Production figures for 1945 are conversions to annual rate of production in first 6 months.

[2] Source: "Statistical Digest, Ministry of Fuel and Power", London 1944. Calendar years. Employment figures represent average number of wage-earners on colliery books. Includes saleable mined coal only, and omits government strip-mining operations. Production figures for 1944 are conversions to annual rate of production in first 6 months.

[3] Source. "Bituminous Coal in 1944, including Lignite", United States Bureau of Mines 1945. Calendar years. Employment figures represent average number of men employed at active mines. Includes bituminous and lignite mining only, omitting anthracite.

Oil and Chemical Tables

APPENDIX TABLE C–49.—*Production, consumption,[1] and imports of liquid fuels and lubricating oil, inner zone, 1931–1945*

[Thousands of barrels]

Fiscal year, quarter	Refined stocks imported	Production			Total of imported and refined stocks	Consumption	Total inventories beginning of period
		Refined stocks from crude	Refined stocks from synthetic plants	Substitute fuels (alcohol, benzol, etc.)			
1931	13, 303	4, 675	----------	52	18, 030	14, 930	17, 527
1932	14, 868	6, 245	----------	53	21, 166	18, 276	20, 586
1933	15, 077	7, 275	----------	75	22, 427	19, 422	23, 603
1934	17, 181	8, 955	----------	97	26, 233	22, 665	26, 609
1935	20, 633	10, 006	----------	127	30, 766	28, 592	28, 919
1936	18, 739	10, 337	----------	115	29, 191	27, 699	31, 095
1937	16, 651	12, 323	31	219	29, 224	29, 927	32, 595
1938	14, 044	12, 809	69	264	27, 186	27, 951	31, 891
1939	11, 818	11, 247	133	601	23, 799	25, 261	31, 156
1940	15, 110	9, 352	146	1, 308	25, 916	28, 558	29, 680
1941:							
April to June	2, 645	3, 180	255	170	6, 250	6, 174	28, 036
July to September	1, 041	3, 619	248	140	5, 048	4, 580	28, 014
October to December	1, 052	3, 850	345	123	5, 370	5, 248	28, 348
January to March	504	3, 465	316	286	4, 571	6, 646	28, 204
1942:							
April to June	265	3, 593	289	310	4, 457	5, 765	25, 883
July to September	393	3, 570	372	347	4, 682	6, 396	24, 315
October to December	899	3, 223	384	327	4, 833	6, 742	22, 495
January to March	821	3, 607	358	294	5, 080	6, 891	20, 371
1943:							
April to June	885	3, 764	288	236	5, 173	6, 420	18, 488
July to September	1, 164	3, 869	300	299	5, 632	7, 861	17, 067
October to December	1, 105	3, 663	130	346	5, 244	6, 937	14, 725
January to March	1, 498	2, 845	163	264	4, 770	6, 562	12, 924
1944:							
April to June	893	2, 330	345	191	3, 759	5, 685	11, 462
July to September	881	2, 140	324	217	3, 562	5, 316	9, 533
October to December	799	1, 764	281	296	3, 140	4, 723	7, 683
January to March	761	1, 303	166	258	2, 488	3, 677	5, 944
1945:							
April to June	----------	802	138	501	1, 441	2, 953	4, 751
July to September	----------	239	31	222	492	1, 629	2, 836

[1] Includes the following: Aviation gasoline, motor gasoline, Diesel fuel, fuel oil and lubricating oil.

Source: Japanese Army-Navy Oil Committee.

[Thousands of barrels]

Fiscal year and quarter	Imports	Indigenous production	Inventories (beginning of period)	Fiscal year and quarter	Imports	Indigenous production	Inventories (beginning of period)
1931	6, 391	1, 923	4, 919	1942—Continued.			
1932	9, 136	1, 594	3, 699	July to September	1, 861	407	10, 390
1933	10, 179	1, 419	3, 976	October to December	3, 093	400	8, 748
1934	11, 953	1, 785	4, 040	January to March	2, 059	453	7, 677
1935	12, 829	2, 214	3, 845	1943:			
1936	15, 996	2, 458	5, 001	April to June	3, 712	441	6, 839
1937	20, 231	2, 470	10, 467	July to September	2, 264	442	5, 557
1938	18, 404	2, 465	12, 465	October to December	2, 546	446	4, 839
1939	18, 843	2, 332	20, 242	January to March	1, 326	465	3, 512
1940	22, 050	2, 063	19, 901	1944:			
1941:				April to June	994	419	2, 354
April to June	3, 004	518	20, 857	July to September	224	386	1, 240
July to September		492	18, 078	October to December	423	379	594
October to December		478	14, 650	January to March		401	490
January to March	126	453	14, 492	1945:			
1942:				April to June		406	195
April to June	1, 133	430	12, 346	July to September		403	193

Source: Japanese Army-Navy Oil Committee.

[Thousands of barrels]

Fiscal year and month	Crude Oil	Aviation gasoline	Motor gasoline	Diesel fuel	Fuel oil	Lubricating oil	Total
1931	6, 391		2, 640	7, 275	3, 145	243	19, 694
1932	9, 136		2, 908	8, 589	3, 145	226	24, 004
1933	10, 179		3,·041	8, 737	3, 145	154	25, 256
1934	11, 953		3, 670	10, 748	2, 516	247	29, 134
1935	12, 829		3, 988	13, 859	2, 516	270	33, 462
1936	15, 996		4, 218	12, 093	1, 877	551	34, 735
1937	20, 231		4, 011	10, 809	1, 573	258	36, 882
1938	18, 404		3, 020	8, 634	2, 202	188	32, 448
1939	18, 843	440	1, 966	7, 760	1, 258	394	30, 661
1940	22, 050	1, 447	4, 279	7, 839	504	1, 041	37, 160
1941:							
April to June	3, 004	346	364	1, 670		265	5, 649
July to September		302	366	126		247	1, 041
October to December		566	309			177	1, 052
January to March	126	315	101			88	630
1942:							
April to June	1, 133	63	202				1, 398
July to September	1, 861	63	261		69		2, 254
October to December	3, 093	377	258	126	138		3, 992
January to March	2, 059	220	258	205	138		2, 880
1943:							
April to June	3, 712	252	158	267	208		4, 597
July to September	2, 264	465	227	220	252		3, 428
October to December	2, 546	409	163	294	239		3, 651
January to March	1, 326	849	131	292	226		2, 824
1944:							
April to June	994	440	44	94	315		1, 887
July to September	224	535	63	126	157		1, 105
October to December	423	472	63	126	138		1, 222
January to March		440	50		271		761

[1] Kerosene, gas oil, and miscellaneous products are not included.

Source: Japanese Army-Navy Oil Committee.

APPENDIX TABLE C-52.—*Japanese consumption of liquid fuels and lubricants—inner zone, 1931–45*

[Thousands of barrels]

Fiscal year and quarter	Aviation gasoline				Motor gasoline				Diesel fuel			
	Army	Navy	Civilian	Total	Army	Navy	Civilian	Total	Army	Navy	Civilian	Total
1931	145	145	6	296	377	94	3,628	4,099	38	189	7,525	7,752
1932	151	157	6	314	629	126	4,701	5,456	44	315	8,680	9,039
1933	189	189	9	387	692	126	4,795	5,613	63	315	9,013	9,391
1934	189	189	13	391	755	189	4,629	5,573	94	315	11,375	11,784
1935	201	208	19	428	881	189	6,464	7,534	94	377	14,622	15,093
1936	252	283	22	557	1,006	220	6,015	7,241	126	377	13,036	13,539
1937	315	377	22	714	1,132	220	7,522	8,874	126	440	12,080	12,646
1938	472	472	25	969	1,258	252	6,326	7,836	189	440	11,125	11,754
1939	566	503	25	1,094	1,258	252	4,595	6,105	189	503	8,970	9,662
1940	572	629	86	1,287	1,258	283	6,323	7,864	377	566	9,252	10,195
1941:												
April to June	157	126	19	302	315	94	496	905	94	189	2,434	2,717
July to September	157	126	19	302	315	94	486	895	126	220	1,024	1,370
October to December	409	377	19	805	315	63	377	755	126	220	1,144	1,490
January to March	421	377	16	814	315	94	224	633	201	315	816	1,332
1942:												
April to June	428	377	15	820	315	94	200	609	201	220	574	995
July to September	447	409	15	871	315	94	264	673	264	283	865	1,412
October to December	509	503	9	1,021	283	94	324	701	201	252	915	1,368
January to March	566	535	13	1,114	283	94	282	659	201	252	890	1,343
1943:												
April to June	579	566	9	1,154	277	126	277	680	302	283	925	1,510
July to September	654	629	9	1,292	264	126	293	683	302	315	963	1,580
October to December	667	629	4	1,300	245	94	300	639	296	315	949	1,560
January to March	749	692	3	1,444	245	101	179	525	233	220	911	1,364
1944:												
April to June	755	755	2	1,512	252	63	99	414	252	157	579	988
July to September	679	692	------	1,371	252	63	70	385	252	157	482	891
October to December	591	566	------	1,157	233	63	47	343	239	157	281	677
January to March	359	377	------	736	170	63	41	274	126	126	118	370
1945:												
April to June	239	365	------	604	283	63	50	396	113	126	113	352
July to September	101	113	------	214	94	31	56	181	38	94	94	226

Fiscal year and quarter	Fuel oil				Lubricating oil			
	Army	Navy	Civilian	Total	Army	Navy	Civilian	Total
1931	0	1, 573	124	1, 697	40	41	1, 005	1, 086
1932	0	2, 076	109	2, 185	42	55	1, 185	1, 282
1933	0	2, 390	225	2, 615	46	60	1, 310	1, 416
1934	0	2, 705	492	3, 197	54	66	1, 600	1, 720
1935	0	2, 956	552	3, 508	62	72	1, 895	2, 029
1936	0	3, 145	1, 191	4, 336	70	72	1, 884	2, 026
1937	0	3, 522	1, 994	5, 516	78	79	2, 020	2, 177
1938	0	3, 837	1, 492	5, 329	86	84	1, 893	2, 063
1939	0	4, 403	1, 064	5, 467	86	96	2, 751	2, 933
1940	101	5, 221	1, 405	6, 727	106	109	2, 270	2, 485
1941:								
April to June	38	1, 132	269	1, 439	26	24	761	811
July to September	31	1, 132	166	1, 329	27	25	632	684
October to December	25	1, 258	291	1, 574	27	25	572	624
January to March	31	3, 019	177	3, 227	32	53	555	640
1942:								
April to June	25	2, 516	292	2, 833	33	40	435	508
July to September	25	2, 579	276	2, 880	32	43	485	560
October to December	25	2, 830	247	3, 102	30	50	470	550
January to March	25	2, 893	423	3, 341	38	55	341	434
1943:								
April to June	25	2, 076	451	2, 552	45	35	444	524
July to September	25	2, 893	855	3, 773	48	52	433	533
October to December	25	2, 264	576	2, 865	47	42	484	573
January to March	25	2, 139	520	2, 684	49	33	467	549
1944:								
April to June	0	1, 950	440	2, 390	50	33	298	381
July to September	0	1, 950	398	2, 348	48	33	240	321
October to December	0	1, 950	314	2, 264	46	33	203	282
January to March	0	1, 824	252	2, 076	38	33	150	221
1945:								
April to June	0	1, 069	312	1, 381	26	28	166	220
July to September	0	755	58	813	10	19	166	195

Source: Japanese Army-Navy Oil Committee.

APPENDIX TABLE C–53.—*Japanese inventories of liquid fuels and lubricants—inner zone, 1931–45*

[Thousands of barrels]

Date of inventory	Aviation gasoline				Motor gasoline				Diesel fuel			
	Army	Navy	Civilian	Total	Army	Navy	Civilian	Total	Army	Navy	Civilian	Total
Apr. 1, 1931	272	430	1	703	126	94	172	392	-------	315	31	346
Apr. 1, 1932	268	443	1	712	126	101	191	418	-------	315	31	346
Apr. 1, 1933	286	455	1	742	126	94	212	432	-------	315	61	376
Apr. 1, 1934	291	551	1	843	126	94	248	468	-------	315	96	411
Apr. 1, 1935	281	630	1	912	126	88	306	520	-------	377	168	545
Apr. 1, 1936	278	656	1	935	189	94	342	625	-------	377	220	597
Apr. 1, 1937	288	625	1	914	189	107	620	916	-------	377	504	881
Apr. 1, 1938	274	614	1	889	189	107	418	714	-------	377	464	841
Apr. 1, 1939	240	601	1	842	232	101	428	781	-------	440	220	660
Apr. 1, 1940	323	945	1	1,269	252	107	413	772	-------	440	189	629
Apr. 1, 1941	972	1,995	2	2,969	315	94	352	761	-------	503	176	679
July 1, 1941	1,200	2,200	2	3,402	377	94	333	804	-------	516	170	686
Oct. 1, 1941	1,507	2,393	3	3,903	503	88	320	911	-------	516	182	698
Jan. 1, 1942	1,700	2,551	3	4,254	629	88	320	1,037	-------	440	179	619
Apr. 1, 1942	1,672	2,539	2	4,213	692	88	252	1,032	-------	315	164	479
July 1, 1942	1,603	2,476	2	4,081	818	82	201	1,101	63	283	170	516
Oct. 1, 1942	1,595	2,228	2	3,825	912	63	138	1,113	126	252	182	560
Jan. 1, 1943	1,581	2,157	3	3,741	944	63	75	1,082	220	189	195	604
Apr. 1, 1943	1,501	2,030	3	3,534	1,006	50	113	1,169	352	126	192	670
July 1, 1943	1,436	1,611	3	3,050	1,038	50	126	1,214	283	126	182	591
Oct. 1, 1943	1,347	1,398	3	2,748	1,069	44	109	1,222	252	94	189	535
Jan. 1, 1944	1,125	1,245	2	2,372	1,101	38	94	1,233	252	94	176	522
Apr. 1, 1944	1,107	1,227	3	2,337	1,126	31	97	1,254	239	82	170	491
July 1, 1944	1,013	771	2	1,786	989	31	75	1,095	239	63	145	447
Oct. 1, 1944	716	748	1	1,465	868	25	50	943	226	57	126	409
Jan. 1, 1945	682	640	1	1,323	723	25	47	795	220	44	94	358
Apr. 1, 1945	830	707	1	1,538	660	19	40	719	214	31	63	308
July 1, 1945	704	452	1	1,157	315	19	31	365	101	19	53	173
Oct. 1, 1945	635	376	1	1,012	196	13	23	232	-------	13	30	43

Date of inventory	Fuel oil				Lubricating oil			
	Army	Navy	Civilian	Total	Army	Navy	Civilian	Total
Apr. 1, 1931	--------	15, 929	11	15, 940	--------	63	83	146
Apr. 1, 1932	--------	18, 954	8	18, 962	--------	63	85	148
Apr. 1, 1933	--------	21, 841	22	21, 863	--------	63	127	190
Apr. 1, 1934	--------	24, 653	25	24, 678	--------	75	134	209
Apr. 1, 1935	--------	26, 688	31	26, 719	--------	82	141	223
Apr. 1, 1936	--------	28, 669	36	28, 705	--------	82	151	233
Apr. 1, 1937	--------	29, 543	69	29, 612	--------	82	190	272
Apr. 1, 1938	--------	29, 068	75	29, 143	--------	82	222	304
Apr. 1, 1939	--------	28, 582	71	28, 653	--------	94	126	220
Apr. 1, 1940	--------	26, 674	98	26, 772	--------	126	112	238
Apr. 1, 1941	--------	23, 208	73	23, 281	126	126	94	346
July 1, 1941	--------	22, 711	66	22, 777	126	126	93	345
Oct. 1, 1941	--------	22, 285	87	22, 372	252	126	86	464
Jan. 1, 1942	--------	21, 717	44	21, 761	315	126	92	533
Apr. 1, 1942	--------	19, 585	55	19, 640	302	132	85	519
July 1, 1942	--------	18, 062	50	18, 112	289	141	75	505
Oct. 1, 1942	--------	16, 424	54	16, 478	277	148	94	519
Jan. 1, 1942	--------	14, 384	53	14, 437	258	157	92	507
Apr. 1, 1943	--------	12, 559	43	12, 602	239	167	107	513
July 1, 1943	--------	11, 678	43	11, 721	214	176	101	491
Oct. 1, 1943	--------	9, 672	40	9, 712	201	186	121	508
Jan. 1, 1943	--------	8, 259	41	8, 300	189	195	113	497
Apr. 1, 1944	--------	6, 863	33	6, 896	170	207	107	484
July 1, 1944	--------	5, 736	31	5, 767	151	186	101	438
Oct. 1, 1944	--------	4, 412	32	4, 444	132	167	123	422
Jan. 1, 1944	--------	3, 054	33	3, 087	107	145	129	381
Apr. 1, 1945	--------	1, 817	23	1, 840	82	139	125	346
July 1, 1945	--------	794	19	813	84	134	110	328
Oct. 1, 1945	--------	57	16	73	--------	130	50	180

Source: Japanese Army-Navy Oil Committee.

APPENDIX TABLE C–54 (*In 3 parts*).—*Japanese production of refined oils, by type—Inner Zone, 1931–45*

[Thousands of barrels]

PART 1

Fiscal year and quarter	Aviation gasoline					Motor gasoline				
	From crude oil	From synthetic oil	Imports	From gasoline, alcohol, pine roots, benzol	Total	From crude oil	From synthetic oil	Imports	Misc.	Total
1931	305				305	1,485		2,640		4,125
1932	344				344	2,437		2,908		5,345
1933	488				488	2,608		3,041		5,649
1934	459				459	3,213		3,670		6,883
1935	451				451	3,649		3,988		7,637
1936	536				536	3,314		4,218		7,532
1937	689				689	4,624	6	4,011	31	8,672
1938	921				921	4,744	13	3,020	63	7,840
1939	1,081		440		1,521	3,891	21	1,966	220	6,098
1940	1,211		1,447		2,658	3,261	26	4,279	252	7,818
1941	2,001	1.4	1,529		3,531	1,871	152	1,140	262	3,425
1942	2,218	1.5	723		2,942	1,437	179	979	194	2,789
1943	2,073	2.8	1,975		4,050	1,645	167	679	60	2,551
1944	1,699	1.2	1,887	329	3,916	369	152	220	12	753
1945 (April to September)	94	1.3		194	289	120	29		5	154
1941:										
April to June	389	.4	346		735	432	38	364	79	913
July to September	499	.6	302		801	534	36	366	69	1,005
October to December	590	.2	566		1,156	497	41	309	66	913
January to March	523	.2	315		838	408	37	101	48	594
1942:										
April to June	560	.4	63		623	390	32	202	60	684
July to September	549	.1	63		612	335	39	261	55	690
October to December	552	.6	377		930	305	56	258	48	667
January to March	557	.4	220		777	407	52	258	31	748
1943:										
April to June	539	.5	252		791	452	55	158	21	686
July to September	521		465		986	397	44	227	19	687
October to December	509	1.3	409		919	422	34	163	14	633
January to March	504	1.0	849		1,354	374	34	131	6	545
1944:										
April to June	504	.3	440	1	945	93	51	44	4	192
July to September	455	.7	535	35	1,026	122	47	63	3	235
October to December	406		472	126	1,004	97	32	63	2	194
January to March	334	.2	440	167	941	57	22	50	3	132
1945:										
April to June	67	1.3		[1] 153	221	80	22		3	105
July to September	27			41	68	40	7		2	49

PART 2

Fiscal year and quarter	Diesel fuel					Fuel oil				
	From crude oil	From synthetic oil	Imports	Miscellaneous	Total	From crude oil	From synthetic oil	Imports	Miscellaneous including shale oil	Total
1931	476	-------	7, 275	-------	7, 751	1, 574	-------	3, 145	-------	4, 719
1932	480	-------	8, 589	-------	9, 069	1, 941	-------	3, 145	-------	5, 086
1933	689	-------	9, 737	-------	9, 421	2, 285	-------	3, 145	-------	5, 430
1934	1, 171	-------	10, 748	-------	11, 919	2, 722	-------	2, 516	-------	5, 238
1935	1, 286	-------	13, 859	-------	15, 145	2, 978	-------	2, 516	-------	5, 494
1936	1, 731	-------	12, 093	-------	13, 824	3, 356	-------	1, 877	-------	5, 233
1937	1, 797	-------	10, 809	-------	12, 606	3, 450	25	1, 573	-------	5, 048
1938	2, 952	14	8, 634	-------	11, 600	2, 603	42	2, 202	-------	4, 847
1939	1, 867	68	7, 760	-------	9, 695	2, 109	44	1, 258	126	3, 537
1940	1, 588	68	7, 839	176	9, 671	1, 992	52	504	645	3, 193
1941	4, 559	343	1, 796	237	6, 935	3, 707	667	-------	40	4, 414
1942	3, 744	1, 013	331	945	6, 033	4, 560	209	345	-------	5, 114
1943	3, 707	406	1, 073	964	6, 150	4, 940	306	925	-------	6, 171
1944	1, 687	560	346	553	3, 146	2, 785	404	881	-------	4, 070
1945 (April to September)	228	31	-------	503	762	364	108	-------	-------	472
1941:										
April to June	1, 204	30	1, 670	6	2, 730	835	187	-------	40	1, 062
July to September	1, 198	68	126	29	1, 421	874	143	-------	-------	1, 017
October to December	1, 375	40	-------	6	1, 421	924	264	-------	-------	1, 188
January to March	962	205	-------	196	1, 363	1, 074	73	-------	-------	1, 147
1942:										
April to June	797	215	-------	209	1, 221	1, 266	41	-------	-------	1, 307
July to September	1, 031	273	-------	255	1, 559	1, 118	59	69	-------	1, 246
October to December	989	273	126	249	1, 637	869	55	138	-------	1, 062
January to March	927	252	205	232	1, 616	1, 307	54	138	-------	1, 499
1943:										
April to June	908	162	267	186	1, 523	1, 392	71	208	-------	1, 671
July to September	991	184	220	246	1, 641	1, 444	73	252	-------	1, 769
October to December	1, 058	30	294	296	1, 678	1, 149	64	239	-------	1, 452
January to March	750	30	292	236	1, 308	955	98	226	-------	1, 279
1944:										
April to June	587	179	94	165	1, 025	834	115	315	-------	1, 264
July to September	523	165	126	157	971	755	111	157	-------	1, 023
October to December	372	152	126	155	805	662	98	138	-------	898
January to March	205	64	-------	76	345	534	80	271	-------	885
1945:										
April to June	156	25	-------	333	514	308	90	-------	-------	398
July to September	72	6	-------	170	248	56	18	-------	-------	74

PART 3

Fiscal year and quarter	From crude oil	Imports	Lubricating oil		Total
			From miscellaneous including reclaimed oil	From miscellaneous asphalt, solvents, liquefied gas, etc.	
1931	855	243	52	------------	1,150
1932	1,043	226	53	------------	1,322
1933	1,205	154	75	479	1,434
1934	1,390	247	97	423	1,734
1935	1,642	270	127	501	2,039
1936	1,400	551	115	663	2,066
1937	1,763	258	188	683	2,209
1938	1,589	188	201	764	1,978
1939	2,299	394	255	628	2,948
1940	1,300	1,041	235	749	2,576
1941	1,976	777	180	619	2,933
1942	2,034	------------	139	646	2,173
1943	1,776	------------	120	424	1,896
1944	997	------------	68	174	1,065
1945 (April to September)	235	------------	21	122	256
1941:					
April to June	500	265	45	131	810
July to September	514	247	42	169	803
October to December	464	177	51	155	692
January to March	498	88	42	164	628
1942:					
April to June	580	------------	41	127	621
July to September	537	------------	37	169	574
October to December	508	------------	30	175	538
January to March	409	------------	31	175	440
1943:					
April to June	473	------------	29	103	502
July to September	516	------------	34	108	550
October to December	525	------------	36	121	561
January to March	262	------------	21	92	283
1944:					
April to June	312	------------	21	89	333
July to September	285	------------	22	47	307
October to December	227	------------	13	13	240
January to March	173	------------	12	25	185
1945:					
April to June	191	------------	12	115	203
July to September	44	------------	9	7	53

Source: Japanese Army-Navy Oil Committee.

[In barrels]

Fiscal year and month	Aviation gasoline	Motor gasoline	Gas oil	Diesel fuel	Fuel oil	Total
1938		5, 850			25, 286	31, 136
1939		13, 084		13, 681	42, 262	69, 027
1940		20, 544	2, 264	68, 474	44, 149	135, 431
1941		26, 518	3, 824	67, 749	51, 641	149, 732
April	126	11, 975	2, 573	10, 008	46, 018	70, 700
May	164	12, 907	3, 818	10, 416	54, 389	81, 694
June	120	12, 830	5, 233	9, 950	86, 198	114, 331
July	157	9, 120	5, 314	34, 244	14, 278	67, 113
August	447	13, 680	1, 982	17, 913	59, 113	93, 135
September		12, 737	4, 523	12, 208	69, 642	99, 110
October		12, 468	4, 190	12, 572	63, 145	92, 375
November	113	16, 914	1, 554	12, 850	98, 212	129, 643
December	69	12, 033	4, 523	14, 299	102, 804	133, 728
January		11, 076	7, 328	60, 254	8, 648	87, 306
February		11, 781	8, 403	94, 684	12, 203	127, 071
March	164	14, 459	8, 843	50, 880	51, 905	126, 251
1942:						
April	31	7, 258	4, 404	73, 838	12, 901	98, 432
May	264	12, 605	10, 391	49, 276	11, 367	83, 903
June	151	12, 541	6, 920	91, 539	17, 178	128, 329
July	113	11, 365	7, 417	82, 997	20, 397	122, 289
August		15, 292	9, 925	85, 266	25, 468	135, 951
September		12, 542	10, 052	104, 924	13, 342	140, 860
October	188	18, 015	10, 535	117, 712	18, 298	164, 748
November	101	20, 498	5, 572	87, 821	13, 392	127, 384
December	270	17, 461	7, 528	67, 304	23, 237	115, 800
January	340	14, 964	7, 058	57, 352	20, 600	100, 314
February	50	12, 410	7, 530	81, 235	10, 706	111, 931
March		24, 582	10, 869	113, 459	22, 738	171, 648
1943:						
April	245	17, 814	11, 553	37, 156	20, 321	87, 089
May	120	11, 298	12, 070	106, 156	25, 285	154, 929
June	88	25, 538	62, 616	18, 900	25, 530	132, 672
July		19, 267	12, 443	70, 416	25, 600	127, 726
August		12, 931	11, 883	104, 093	22, 750	151, 657
September		11, 554	7, 667	9, 271	24, 179	52, 671
October		13, 128	9, 083	12, 543	18, 561	53, 315
November	629	9, 843	7, 622	9, 013	18, 682	45, 789
December	635	10, 662	8, 498	8, 825	27, 129	55, 749
January	598	10, 127	8, 561	10, 825	30, 576	60, 687
February		11, 164	7, 014	8, 788	31, 311	58, 277
March	422	12, 309	8, 636	10, 157	36, 425	67, 949
1944:						
April	252	16, 077	12, 693	59, 856	37, 426	126, 304
May		17, 462	12, 404	63, 001	31, 362	124, 229
June		17, 053	8, 819	56, 081	46, 093	128, 046
July	667	18, 543	10, 455	54, 036	34, 049	117, 750
August		15, 165	7, 422	54, 774	32, 751	110, 112
September		13, 574	8, 303	56, 685	45, 301	123, 863
October		11, 208	8, 970	54, 729	24, 776	99, 683
November		9, 844	8, 296	49, 358	31, 646	99, 144
December		10, 498	9, 403	47, 873	41, 426	109, 200
January		7, 000	6, 164	21, 701	22, 964	57, 829
February		6, 522	7, 121	17, 895	19, 329	50, 867
March	226	8, 434	11, 366	24, 255	37, 872	82, 153

APPENDIX TABLE C–55.—*Japanese production of synthetic oil, inner zone, 1937–45*—Continued

Fiscal year and month	Aviation gasoline	Motor gasoline	Gas oil	Diesel fuel	Fuel oil	Total
1945:						
April	962	6, 604	3, 144	8, 661	31, 218	50, 589
May	189	6, 498	3, 623	10, 384	27, 814	48, 508
June	107	8, 283	3, 176	6, 277	30, 500	48, 343
July		3, 736	1, 856	5, 485	13, 637	24, 714
August		3, 195		390	4, 202	7, 787

Source: Imperial Fuel Industry Co.

APPENDIX TABLE C–56.— *Production of lubricating oil from rubber, Japan proper, 1943–44*

[In barrels]

Fiscal year and month	Nippon Oil Co.		Showa Oil Co. Kawasaki	Toa Fuel Industry Co., Shimizu	Imperial Fuel Industry Co., Ube	Total
	(Akita)	(Niigata)				
1943:						
September	315	642				956
October	195	2, 371	466			3, 032
November	1, 296	2, 069	799			4, 164
December	742	2, 308	755			3, 805
January	988	2, 227	943	1, 635	201	5, 994
February	1, 415	2, 233	371	717	635	5, 371
March	1, 793	3, 585	1, 082	6, 604	1, 340	14, 404
1944:						
April	1, 874	3, 598	981	7, 680	912	15, 045
May	1, 264	4, 000	2, 183	9, 643	1, 289	18, 379
June	4, 648	4, 460	1, 214	6, 422	1, 837	18, 581
July	2, 679	2, 711	629	7, 435	2, 271	15, 725
August	2, 390	2, 767	2, 076	7, 504	2, 057	16, 794
September	1, 899	2, 868	2, 277	7, 454	1, 271	15, 769
October	1, 629	3, 460	1, 208	2, 069	2, 107	10, 473
November	3, 277	2, 963	931	1, 132	1, 818	10, 121
December	2, 566	3, 252	459	1, 214	1, 032	8, 523
January	2, 554	2, 516	0	1, 371		6, 441
February	0	1, 887	560	2, 459		4, 906
March	868	2, 220	522	2, 158		5, 768

Source; Imperial Fuel Industry Co.

APPENDIX TABLES C–57.—*Production of explosives, Japan proper, 1931–45*

[In tons]

Fiscal year and month	Smokeless powder	Organic high explosives	Explosives	Fiscal year and month	Smokeless powder	Organic high explosives	Explosives
1931	624	1,932	2,556	1944—Continued			
1932	1,188	3,576	4,764	June	1,800	3,441	5,241
1933	1,332	4,308	5,640	July	1,957	3,391	5,348
1934	1,764	5,112	6,876	August	1,966	3,596	5,562
1935	1,824	4,320	6,144	September	2,050	3,336	5,386
1936	2,148	4,116	6,264	October	2,077	3,921	5,998
1937	5,232	14,688	19,920	November	2,201	3,910	6,111
1938	12,252	31,524	43,776	December	2,088	3,858	5,946
1939	12,768	24,828	37,596	January	2,277	4,100	6,377
1940	13,632	26,328	39,960	February	2,344	4,022	6,366
1941	14,208	36,756	50,964	March	2,256	4,279	6,535
1942	18,408	43,656	62,064	1945:			
1943	20,952	44,880	65,832	April	1,526	2,570	4,096
1944:				May	1,731	2,579	4,310
April	1,808	3,257	5,065	June	1,805	2,292	4,097
May	1,813	3,362	5,175	July	1,369	1,720	3,089

Source: Chemical Industry Control Associations, War and Navy Ministries.

APPENDIX TABLE C–58.—*Organic high-explosives production in Japan and the United States, 1940-45.*

[Thousands of tons]

	Japan	United States		Japan	United States
1940	26	21	1943	45	978
1941	37	103	1944	44	1,143
1942	44	625	1945 (4 months)	9	551

Source: Japan—Chemical Industry Control Association, War and Navy Ministries; U. S.—War Production Board.

APPENDIX TABLE C–59.—*Process efficiency in explosives production in Japan and the United States—1944*

	Point yield (lbs. of product per 100 lbs. of starting material)		Time of cycle		Production of each line (lbs. per 24-hr. day)		Man-hours per ton	
	Japan	United States	Japan	United States	Japan	United States	Japan	United States
Single base smokeless powder					8,800	140,000	1,012	5.5
TNT	185	208	11 hours	40 minutes	4,400	120,000	272	10
Tetryl	200	210	32 hours	2¼ hours	166	7,500	1,178	67
Hexogen	100	116	Continuous		2,200	30,000	1,025	20

Source: Japan—Chemical Industry Control Association; U. S.—War Production Board.

[In tons]

Fiscal year and quarter	Inventories (beginning of period)	Production	Imports [1]	Total	Consumption			Inventories (end of period)
					Food	Industry	Total	
1931	(2)	574, 600	520, 100					
1932	(2)	630, 800	604, 000					
1933	(2)	695, 400	1, 082, 200					
1934	(2)	745, 500	1, 278, 200					
1935	(2)	666, 300	1, 259, 100					
1936	(2)	571, 900	1, 560, 500					
1937	440, 900	590, 800	1, 920, 200	2, 951, 900	982, 100	1, 557, 500	2, 539, 600	412, 300
1938	412, 300	533, 500	1, 930, 100	2, 875, 900	1, 070, 300	1, 627, 000	2, 697, 300	178, 600
1939	178, 600	701, 100	2, 050, 300	2, 930, 000	1, 134, 300	1, 553, 100	2, 687, 400	242, 600
1940	242, 600	632, 300	1, 901, 200	2, 776, 100	1, 170, 600	1, 494, 700	2, 665, 300	110, 800
1941	110, 800	429, 200	1, 659, 500	2, 199, 500	1, 110, 000	1, 025, 100	2, 135, 100	64, 400
1942	64, 400	524, 000	1, 694, 500	2, 282, 900	1, 144, 200	867, 500	2, 011, 700	271, 200
1943	271, 200	457, 000	1, 556, 400	2, 284, 600	1, 213, 600	782, 600	1, 996, 200	288, 400
1944	288, 400	395, 700	1, 132, 100	1, 816, 200	1, 021, 800	650, 400	1, 672, 200	144, 000
1945, April to September	144, 000	135, 600	470, 600	750, 200				
1945 (estimated)		181, 900	999, 800	1, 181, 700				
1942:								
April to June		152, 200						
July to September		185, 300						
October to December		113, 600						
January to March		72, 900						
1943:								
April to June		143, 400						
July to September		150, 000						
October to December		110, 500						
January to March		53, 100						
1944:								
April to June		119, 000						
July to September		125, 700						
October to December		86, 000						
January to March		65, 000						
1945:								
April to June		70, 600	235, 300					
July to September		65, 000	235, 300					

[1] From Formosa, China and Manchuria.
[2] No data.

Source: Chemical Industry Control Association.

APPENDIX TABLE C-61.—*Production of chemical fertilizers in Japan, 1937-44*

[In metric tons]

Fertilizer year (Aug. 1 of year specified to the next July 31)	Nitrogenous fertilizers	Phosphatic fertilizers	Potash fertilizers	Total
1937	1, 901, 000	1, 522, 000	251, 000	3, 674, 000
1938	1, 951, 000	1, 507, 000	170, 000	3, 628, 000
1939	1, 593, 000	1, 496, 000	163, 000	3, 252, 000
1940	1, 805, 000	1, 378, 000	121, 000	3, 304, 000
1941	1, 653, 000	950, 000	48, 000	2, 651, 000
1942	1, 346, 000	879, 000	3, 000	2, 228, 000
1943	1, 117, 000	544, 000	3, 000	1, 664, 000
1944	541, 000	86, 000	3, 000	630, 000

Source: Ministry of Agriculture and Forestry.

APPENDIX TABLE C-62.— *Nitrogen balance, Japan proper, 1940–45*

[In tons]

Fiscal year and quarter	Production of nitrogen										Total
	Synthetic ammonia	Percent	Calcium cyanamide	Percent	Byproduct ammonia	Percent	Total	Percent	Imports ammonium sulfate only	Percent	
1940	309,516	76.0	49,163	12.1	22,216	5.4	380,895	93.5	26,482	6.5	407,378
1941	341,016	79.5	52,690	12.3	22,856	5.3	416,562	97.1	12,464	2.9	429,026
1942	306,275	80.5	44,312	11.7	22,436	5.9	373,023	98.1	7,176	1.9	380,199
1943	269,902	84.3	35,714	11.1	14,784	4.6	320,400	100.0	0	0.0	320,400
1944	198,400	81.0	34,281	14.0	12,098	4.9	244,779	99.9	213	0.1	244,992
1945 through June	24,685	73.9	6,393	19.1	2,324	7.0	33,402	100.0	0	0.0	33,402
1940:											
April to June	76,673	69.7	15,102	13.7	5,554	5.0	97,329	88.4	12,803	11.6	110,132
July to September	72,306	74.8	10,803	11.2	5,554	5.8	88,663	91.8	7,932	8.2	96,595
October to December	79,250	79.5	11,574	11.6	5,554	5.6	96,378	96.7	3,283	3.3	99,661
January to March	81,287	80.5	11,684	11.6	5,554	5.5	98,525	97.6	2,465	2.4	100,990
1941:											
April to June	90,099	77.1	16,204	13.9	5,714	4.9	112,017	95.9	4,820	4.1	116,837
July to September	82,383	79.9	12,787	12.4	5,714	5.5	100,884	97.8	2,266	2.2	103,150
October to December	85,888	80.9	13,117	12.4	5,714	5.4	104,719	98.7	1,392	1.3	106,111
January to March	82,646	80.3	10,582	10.3	5,714	5.5	98,942	96.1	3,986	3.9	102,928
1942:											
April to June	82,539	77.6	14,991	14.1	5,609	5.3	103,139	97.0	3,145	3.0	106,284
July to September	73,580	79.8	12,125	13.2	5,609	6.1	91,314	99.1	852	0.9	92,166
October to December	80,154	82.0	9,700	9.9	5,609	5.7	95,463	97.6	2,339	2.4	97,802
January to March	70,002	83.4	7,496	8.9	5,609	6.7	83,107	99.0	840	1.0	83,947
1943:											
April to June	78,112	84.5	10,582	11.5	3,696	4.0	92,390	100.0	0	0.0	92,390
July to September	64,566	83.2	9,370	12.0	3,696	4.8	77,632	100.0	0	0.0	77,632
October to December	66,586	84.6	8,377	10.7	3,696	4.7	78,659	100.0	0	0.0	78,659
January to March	60,638	84.6	7,385	10.3	3,696	5.1	71,719	100.0	0	0.0	71,719
1944:											
April to June	68,527	81.8	12,456	14.9	2,791	3.3	83,774	100.0	0	0.0	83,774
July to September	47,100	79.1	9,149	15.3	3,334	5.6	59,583	100.0	0	0.0	59,583
October to December	45,630	78.5	8,818	15.2	3,439	5.9	57,887	99.6	213	0.4	58,100
January to March	37,143	85.3	3,858	8.9	2,534	5.8	43,535	100.0	0	0.0	43,535
1945: April to June	24,685	73.9	6,393	19.1	2,324	7.0	33,402	100.0	0	0.0	33,402

APPENDIX TABLE C-62.—*Nitrogen balance, Japan proper, 1940–45*—Continued.

Fiscal year and quarter	Nitric acid [1] civilian production	Percent	Nitric acid Army-Navy production	Percent	Domestic consumption of nitrogen								Total
					Ammonium sulfate	Percent	Calcium cyanamide	Percent	Miscellaneous [2] nitrogen	Exports, percent	Acid only	Nitric, percent	
1940	18,426	4.5	1,349	0.3	257,983	63.3	48,502	11.9	80,738	19.9	380	0.1	407,378
1941	20,395	4.8	2,165	0.5	283,348	66.2	51,148	12.0	71,922	16.5	48	----	429,026
1942	24,308	6.4	2,506	0.7	246,995	65.0	42,217	11.1	64,060	16.8	12	----	380,098
1943	26,718	8.3	2,355	0.7	210,420	65.8	37,587	11.7	43,220	13.5	100	----	320,400
1944	23,026	9.4	2,767	1.1	140,255	57.2	27,778	11.2	51,166	21.1	0	0.0	244,992
1945 through June	2,730	8.1	470	1.4	15,658	46.9	6,173	18.5	8,371	25.1	0	0.0	33,402
1940:													
April to June	4,606	4.2	337	0.3	65,440	59.4	10,141	9.2	29,423	26.7	185	0.2	110,132
July to September	4,607	4.8	337	0.3	59,610	61.8	12,787	13.2	19,196	19.8	58	0.1	96,595
October to December	4,606	4.6	337	0.3	65,327	65.6	12,787	12.8	16,501	16.6	103	0.1	99,661
January to March	4,607	4.6	338	0.3	67,606	66.9	12,787	12.7	15,618	15.4	34	0.1	100,990
1941:													
April to June	4,942	4.2	536	0.5	75,573	64.6	12,787	10.9	22,972	19.7	27	0.1	116,837
July to September	4,765	4.6	542	0.5	67,795	65.8	12,787	12.4	17,246	16.7	15	----	103,150
October to December	5,057	4.8	544	0.5	70,888	66.9	12,787	12.3	16,833	15.5	2	----	106,111
January to March	5,631	5.5	543	0.5	69,092	67.2	12,787	12.4	14,871	14.4	4	----	102,928
1942:													
April to June	6,289	5.9	617	0.6	68,500	64.8	12,787	12.2	18,089	16.5	2	----	106,284
July to September	5,784	6.3	639	0.7	59,248	64.3	9,810	10.6	16,681	18.1	4	----	92,166
October to December	6,435	6.6	638	0.7	65,283	66.7	9,810	10.0	15,632	16.0	4	----	97,802
January to March	5,800	6.9	612	0.7	53,964	64.2	9,810	11.7	13,758	16.5	2	----	83,946
1943:													
April to June	6,479	7.0	517	0.6	63,013	68.1	9,810	10.6	12,482	13.6	89	0.1	92,390
July to September	6,143	7.9	551	0.7	50,232	64.7	9,259	11.9	11,444	14.8	3	----	77,632
October to December	6,673	8.5	527	0.7	52,042	66.1	9,259	11.8	10,150	12.9	8	----	78,659
January to March	7,423	10.3	760	1.1	45,133	62.9	9,259	12.9	9,144	12.8	0	0.0	71,719
1944:													
April to June	7,083	8.4	675	0.8	52,699	62.9	9,259	11.1	14,058	16.8	0	0.0	83,774
July to September	5,665	9.5	733	1.2	32,850	55.1	6,173	10.4	14,162	23.8	0	0.0	59,583
October to December	5,521	9.5	680	1.2	30,406	52.3	6,173	10.6	15,320	26.4	0	0.0	58,100
January to March	4,757	10.9	679	1.6	24,300	55.8	6,173	14.2	7,626	17.5	0	0.0	43,535
1945: April to June	2,730	8.1	470	1.4	15,658	46.9	6,173	18.5	8,371	25.1	0	0.0	33,402

[1] Civilian production of nitric acid includes only 98 percent nitric acid, expressed as tons of nitrogen.

[2] Miscellaneous includes ammonium nitrate, dilute nitric acid not converted to ammonium nitrate or to 98 percent acid. The side reaction loss of about 10 percent when ammonia is converted to nitric acid, and as other uses of ammonia.

Source: Chemical Industry Control Association.

[In tons]

Fiscal year and month	Production in home islands [1]	Production in Korea	Total production	Allocated distribution percent of production in home islands		
				Army, percent	Navy, percent	Civilian,[2] percent
1931	79, 640	78, 430	158, 070			
1932	116, 190	63, 870	180, 060			
1933	132, 170	85, 370	217, 540			
1934	152, 350	110, 930	263, 280			
1935	207, 770	124, 380	332, 150			
1936	275, 860	136, 080	411, 940			
1937	303, 900	152, 940	456, 840			
1938	361, 150	164, 830	525, 980			
1939	333, 370	158, 820	492, 190			
1940	375, 800	148, 460	524, 260	0. 9	0. 6	98. 5
1941	414, 580	146, 650	561, 230	1. 2	0. 7	98. 1
1942	372, 340	138, 430	510, 770	1. 4	0. 9	97, 7
1943	328, 240	124, 420	452, 660	1. 8	1. 8	96. 4
1944	238, 410	134, 700	373, 110	1. 6	2. 0	96. 4
1945, April to June	30, 000		30, 000	. 8	1. 0	98. 2
1941:						
April to June	109, 535			1. 0	. 6	98. 4
July to September	100, 155			1. 1	. 7	98. 2
October to December	104, 415			1. 3	. 7	98. 0
January to March	100, 475			1. 5	. 8	97. 7
1942:						
April to June	100, 340			1. 4	. 9	97. 7
July to September	89, 450			1. 4	. 9	97. 7
October to December	97, 450			1. 4	. 9	97. 7
January to March	85, 100			1. 4	. 9	97. 7
1943:						
April	31, 640					
May	31, 620			1. 6	1. 6	96. 8
June	31, 710					
July	28, 650					
August	23, 900			2. 2	2. 2	95. 6
September	25, 940					
October	25, 430					
November	28, 730			2. 3	2. 3	95. 4
December	26, 790					
January	24, 680					
February	22, 690			1. 2	1. 2	97. 6
March	26, 460					
1944:						
April	28, 530					
May	27, 210			1. 2	1. 2	97. 6
June	24, 780					
July	21, 890					
August	17, 270			1. 7	3. 7	94. 6
September	18, 100					
October	17, 810					
November	19, 690			1. 7	1. 7	97. 6
December	17, 970					
January	17, 190					
February	13, 350			2. 0	1. 9	96. 1
March	14, 620					

See footnotes at end of table.

Fiscal year and month	Production in home islands [1]	Production in Korea	Total production	Allocated distribution percent of production in home islands		
				Army, percent	Navy, percent	Civilian,[2] percent
1945:						
April	11,470 ⎫					
May	9,960 ⎬			.8	1.0	98.2
June	8,570 ⎭					

[1] No imports or exports of ammonia from 1931 to 1945. Inventories always very low.

[2] Includes total amount converted by civilian plants to nitric acid. Amount of civilian ammonia consumption going to nonmilitary explosives never exceeded 30 tons per month.

Sources: Ministry of Commerce and Industry (Mr. Tsuda) and Chemical Industry Control Association (Mr. Katsura).

Appendix Table C-64.—*Production and distribution of nitric acid, Japan proper, Korea, and Manchuria, 1931–45*

[In tons]

Fiscal year and month	Production in home islands [1]			Exports	Total	98 nitric acid							50 nitric acid, total production
	Army [2]	Civilian	Total			Allocated distribution of the civilian production			Production in Korea	Production in Manchuria	Total production		
						Army, percent	Navy, percent	Civilian, percent					
1931	1,620	7,056	8,676								8,676		
1932	1,819	10,696	12,515								12,515		
1933	2,149	16,364	18,513								18,513		
1934	2,480	22,918	25,398								25,398		
1935	2,563	25,761	28,324								28,324		
1936	3,142	33,025	36,167						50		36,217		89,726
1937	3,224	47,798	51,022						181		51,203		131,533
1938	3,621	79,897	83,518						551	47	84,116		202,097
1939	4,018	84,724	88,742						662	101	89,505		205,082
1940	4,712	84,575	89,287	2,185	87,102	31.8	29.5	38.7	797	73	90,157		182,928
1941	8,361	90,024	98,385	224	98,161	33.3	29.9	36.8	2,474	251	101,110		227,736
1942	9,759	100,707	110,466	57	110,409	40.1	39.2	20.7	2,828	391	113,685		244,565
1943	8,598	117,370	125,968	451	125,517	43.4	43.3	13.3	2,942	834	129,742		284,185
1944	10,055	102,245	112,300	7	112,393	42.2	42.1	15.7	[4] 2,368	[4] 847	115,514		227,998
1945: April to August	2,194	13,614	15,808	0	15,808				[4] 832	[4] 333	16,973		40,159
1941:													
April	689	7,387	8,076	39	8,037 ⎫								18,881 ⎰
May	689	7,387	8,076	23	8,053 ⎬	32.9	30.2	36.9	611	48	24,887		18,674
June	689	7,387	8,076	63	8,013 ⎭								17,532
July	697	7,141	7,838	48	7,790 ⎫								18,758
August	697	7,141	7,838	0	7,838 ⎬	33.4	29.9	36.7	536	56	24,106		18,602
September	697	7,141	7,838	20	7,818 ⎭								18,954
October	701	7,648	8,349	3	8,346 ⎫								19,105
November	701	7,648	8,349	2	8,347 ⎬	32.3	29.7	38.0	620	68	25,735		19,100
December	701	7,648	8,349	4	8,345 ⎭								19,753
January	700	7,832	8,532	17	8,515 ⎫								19,484
February	700	7,832	8,532	1	8,531 ⎬	34.6	29.7	35.7	707	79	26,382		19,211
March	700	7,832	8,532	4	8,528 ⎭								19,682
1942:													
April	810	8,269	9,079	0	9,079 ⎫								21,097
May	810	8,269	9,079	10	9,069 ⎬	36.5	35.2	28.3	679	98	38,014		21,047
June	810	8,269	9,079	0	9,079 ⎭								20,632

See footnotes at end of table.

[In tons]

Fiscal year and month	Production in home islands [1]			Exports	Total	98 nitric acid						
						Allocated distribution of the civilian production			Production in Korea	Production in Manchuria	Total production	50 nitric acid, total production
	Army [2]	Civilian	Total			Army, percent	Navy, percent	Civilian, percent				
1942:—Continued												
July	828	7,464	8,292	7	8,285	39.3	37.4	23.3	658	88	25,622	19,440
August	828	7,464	8,292	2	8,290							19,033
September	828	7,464	8,292	10	8,282							19,898
October	827	8,779	9,606	7	9,599	41.0	39.4	19.6	753	123	29,694	20,669
November	827	8,779	9,606	11	9,595							21,018
December	827	8,779	9,606	0	9,606							20,968
January	788	9,057	9,845	2	9,843	43.0	44.1	12.9	738	82	30,355	19,800
February	788	9,057	9,845	0	9,845							20,062
March	788	9,057	9,845	8	9,837							20,901
1943:												
April	639	9,920	10,559	396	10,163	41.9	41.5	16.6	780	132	10,863	22,863
May	639	9,218	9,857	0	9,857						10,161	22,078
June	639	9,523	10,162	1	10,161						10,466	23,697
July	645	9,108	9,753	0	9,753	42.8	43.0	14.2	703	138	10,033	23,083
August	645	8,065	8,710	0	8,710						8,990	22,097
September	645	8,249	8,894	17	8,877						9,174	22,471
October	617	9,146	9,763	10	9,753	43.8	43.5	12.7	666	266	10,073	22,904
November	617	10,130	10,747	0	10,740						11,058	24,281
December	617	10,487	11,104	27	11,077						11,414	23,822
January	964	11,092	12,057	0	12,057	45.0	44.9	10.1	793	298	12,421	25,806
February	965	10,461	11,426	0	11,426						11,789	25,382
March	965	11,971	12,936	0	12,936						13,300	25,701
1944:												
April	816	11,256	12,072	0	12,072	43.9	43.8	12.3	586	249	12,350	20,367
May	816	11,055	11,871	7	11,864						12,149	21,853
June	816	8,592	9,408	0	9,408						9,686	20,191
July	894	8,322	9,216	0	9,216	41.8	41.9	16.3	632	198	9,493	19,677
August	895	8,154	9,049	0	9,049						9,325	18,616
September	895	9,342	10,237	0	10,237						10,514	18,841
October	827	7,875	8,702	0	8,702	41.2	40.5	18.3	[4] 600	[4] 200	8,968	17,221
November	827	8,644	9,471	0	9,471						9,738	19,367
December	827	8,299	9,126	0	9,126						9,393	18,706
January	814	8,085	8,899	0	8,899	41.2	41.5	17.3	[4] 550	[4] 200	9,148	19,105
February	814	6,197	7,011	0	7,011						7,261	15,508
March	814	6,424	7,238	0	7,238						7,489	18,546
1945:												
April	504	5,609	6,113	0	6,113	44.8	45.3	9.9	[4] 500	[4] 200	6,346	11,876
May	504	3,857	4,361	0	4,361						4,395	9,510
June	503	2,481	2,984	0	2,984						3,217	8,633
July	683	[3] 1,513	2,196	0	2,196	-------	-------	-------	[4] 332	[4] 133	2,761	6,689
August	0	[3] 154	154	0	154						387	3,451

[1] No imports during periods shown. Inventories were always very low.
[2] Tokyo No. 2 army arsenal for own use. Navy production negligible. Army use of civilian production is in addition to use of its own production.
[3] Calculated from reports of all producing companies.
[4] Assumed. No data available.

Sources: Ministry of Commerce and Industry and Chemical Industry Control Association.

Appendix Table C–65.—*Consumption of crude rubber in Japan, 1931–45*

[In tons]

Calendar year and quarter	Imports			Consumption				
	By civilian agencies	By army and navy	Total	Military	Civilian	Export[1]	Other[2]	Total
1931	48, 500	(3)	48, 500	2, 800	53, 000	1, 900	1, 200	58, 900
1932	62, 800	(3)	62, 800	2, 800	53, 000	1, 900	1, 200	58, 900
1933	77, 200	(3)	77, 200	2, 800	53, 000	1, 900	1, 200	58, 900
1934	79, 400	(3)	79, 400	2, 800	53, 000	1, 900	1, 200	58, 900
1935	66, 100	(3)	66, 100	3, 300	66, 100	2, 200	1, 700	73, 300
1936	70, 500	(3)	70, 500	4, 400	68, 300	2, 200	1, 700	76, 600
1937	70, 500	(3)	70, 500	4, 400	66, 100	3, 300	3, 300	77, 100
1938	45, 200	(3)	45, 200	5, 500	27, 600	3, 900	3, 300	40, 300
1939	52, 900	(3)	52, 900	7, 700	26, 500	5, 000	4, 400	43, 600
1940	32, 700	(3)	32, 700	11, 000	25, 400	3, 300	5, 500	45, 200
1941	39, 700	(3)	39, 700	16, 500	24, 300	1, 100	5, 500	47, 400
1942	37, 500	30, 800	68, 300	22, 000	23, 100	1, 100	5, 500	51, 700
1943	37, 400	46, 400	83, 800	27, 600	18, 700	1, 100	5, 500	52, 900
1944	33, 000	22, 000	55, 000	29, 800	13, 200	1, 100	4, 400	48, 500
1945								
1945: January to September	22, 000	5, 600	27, 600					
1940:								
January to March	8, 600		8, 600					
April to June	8, 000		8, 000					
July to September	9, 600		9, 600					
October to December	6, 500		6, 500					
1941:								
January to March	12, 900		12, 900					
April to June	9, 600		9, 600					
July to September	13, 200		13, 200					
October to December	4, 000		4, 000					
1942:								
January to March	17, 600	7, 700	25, 300					
April to June	9, 000	7, 700	16, 700					
July to September	10, 900	7, 700	18, 600					
October to December		7, 700	7, 700					
1943:								
January to March	9, 400	11, 600	21, 000					
April to June	7, 500	11, 600	19, 100					
July to September	9, 800	11, 600	21, 400					
October to December	10, 700	11, 600	22, 300					
1944:								
January to March	26, 600	5, 500	32, 100					
April to June	5, 300	5, 500	10, 800					
July to September	400	5, 500	5, 900					
October to December	700	5, 500	6, 200					
1945:								
January to March	21, 500	2, 800	24, 300					
April to June	500	2, 800	3, 300					
July to September								

[1] For manufacture of goods for export.

[2] Includes crude rubber for electric wire covering, and crude rubber exported to Manchuria, Kwantung, and China.

[3] No imports.

Source: Rubber Control Association.

APPENDIX TABLE C-66.—*Synthetic rubber production in Japan proper, 1941-45*

[In tons]

Calendar	Mitsui Chemical Industry Co. (Miike)	Mitsubishi Synthetic Industry Co. (Kurosaki)	Nippon Carbide Industry Co. (Uozu)	Sumitomo Chemical Industry Co. (Niihama)	Kanegafuchi Industry Co.[1] (Hyogo)	Nippon Tire Co.[2] (Yokohama)	Total
1941	3.4	0	0	0	0	0	3.4
1942	6.7	0	0	0	0	3.9	10.6
1943	9.3	15.8	3.2	3.4	2.2	5.3	39.2
1944:							
January	2.3	8.3	2.8	1.2	1.1	.4	16.1
February	2.5	8.4	1.4	1.2	1.1	.4	15.0
March	11.0	8.1	2.8	.2	1.7	.4	24.2
April	9.4	7.1	1.6	1.6	1.7	.4	21.8
May	11.0	8.8	1.7	1.5	2.8	.4	26.2
June	4.9	6.2	3.9	1.1	1.7	.4	18.2
July	10.2	6.7	2.0	1.8	1.6	.4	22.7
August							
September	7.2	6.0	4.5	.7	1.6	.4	20.4
October	5.7	4.1	2.4	.7	1.1	.4	14.4
November	6.5	8.9	4.5	.8	1.1	.4	22.2
December	12.4	9.1	.9	.6	1.1	.4	24.5
1945:							
January	11.7	5.3	2.9	.4	1.1	.2	21.6
February	10.0	3.0	0	.3	[3]0	.3	13.6
March	10.8	3.0	0	.3	0	.3	14.4
April	8.4	4.8	0	.9	0	.3	14.4
May	2.6	9.1	.5	.6	.2	.2	13.2
June	1.0	2.9	4.3	.2	0	.3	8.7
July	0	3.6	3.2	.2	0	.3	[1]8.0
August	0	.3	1.3	.1	0	.3	2.0
September	0	0	1.2	0	0	.2	1.4

[1] Kanegafuchi Industry Co. also built plant at Torikai, Osaka, which produced 0.7 ton in July 1945 only. This is included in July total.
[2] Nippon Tire Co. also had a plant under construction at Kurume which was destroyed by bombing before completion.
[3] Bombed.

Source: Ministry of Commerce and Industry.

APPENDIX TABLE C-67.—*Production and consumption of calcium carbide in Japan proper, 1930–45*

[In tons]

Fiscal year and quarter	Inventories (at beginning of period)	Production	Consumption [1]	Inventories (at end of period)
1930	(2)	330, 400	(2)	(2)
1931	(2)	188, 200	(2)	(2)
1932	(2)	257, 800	(2)	(2)
1933	(2)	239, 200	(2)	(2)
1934	(2)	280, 200	(2)	(2)
1935	(2)	428, 700	(2)	(2)
1936	(2)	467, 000	(2)	(2)
1937	(2)	488, 500	(2)	(2)
1938	(2)	459, 700	(2)	(2)
1939	(2)	(2)	(2)	(2)
1940	(2)	(2)	(2)	(2)
1941	13, 845	397, 136	396, 961	14, 020
1942	14, 020	337, 732	337, 401	14, 351
1943	14, 351	331, 950	328, 738	17, 563
1944	17, 563	321, 731	319, 051	20, 243
1945, April to September	20, 243	77, 890	72, 647	25, 486
1941:				
April to June	13, 845	149, 144	143, 137	19, 852
July to September	19, 852	106, 675	108, 492	18, 035
October to December	18, 035	82, 541	85, 600	14, 976
January to March	14, 976	58, 776	59, 732	14, 020
1942:				
April to June	14, 020	138, 766	132, 759	20, 028
July to September	20, 028	80, 555	83, 884	16, 699
October to December	16, 699	83, 051	85, 087	14, 663
January to March	14, 663	35, 360	35, 672	14, 351
1943:				
April to June	14, 351	123, 463	89, 959	47, 855
July to September	47, 855	89, 873	77, 873	59, 855
October to December	59, 855	84, 928	81, 364	63, 419
January to March	63, 419	33, 686	79, 542	17, 563
1944:				
April to June	17, 563	133, 377	100, 552	50, 388
July to September	50, 388	83, 415	83, 892	49, 911
October to December	49, 911	69, 058	82, 266	36, 703
January to March	36, 703	35, 881	52, 341	20, 243
1945:				
April to June	20, 243	63, 973	59, 179	25, 037
July to September	25, 037	13, 917	13, 468	25, 486

[1] Including exports which were always under 1 percent of total.
[2] No data.

Source: Chemical Industry Control Association.

APPENDIX TABLE C-68.—*Production and consumption of superphosphates in Japan proper, 1940–45*

[In tons]

Fiscal year and quarter	Production	Exports [1]	Consumption
1940	1, 846, 800	41, 700	1, 288, 600
1941	1, 058, 800	8, 800	776, 000
1942	671, 900	6, 500	745, 200
1943	515, 700	2, 700	440, 900
1944	56, 800	0	15, 400
1945, April to August	8, 200	([2])	
1940:			
April to June	503, 600	28, 400	
July to September	417, 100	2, 500	
October to December	480, 500	2, 000	
January to March	445, 600	8, 800	
1941:			
April to June	362, 800	3, 100	
July to September	296, 600	100	
October to December	275, 200	1, 300	
January to March	124, 200	4, 300	
1942:			
April to June	137, 400	0	
July to September	163, 600	2, 500	
October to December	201, 100	3, 200	
January to March	169, 800	800	
1943:			
April to June	154, 800	100	
July to September	144, 400	700	
October to December	149, 000	500	
January to March	67, 500	1, 400	
1944:			
April to June	53, 100	0	
July to September	2, 500	0	
October to December	900	0	
January to March	300	([2])	
1945:			
April to June	4, 800	([2])	
July to August	3, 400	([2])	

[1] "Exports" do not include shipments to Korea and Formosa.
[2] No data.

Source: Production: Chemical Industry Control Association. Exports: Import-Export Bureau.

APPENDIX TABLE C-69.—*Production and consumption of carbon disulfide in Japan proper, 1940–45*

[1,000 pounds]

Fiscal year and quarter	Inventory (beginning of period)	Production	Consumption	Inventory (end of period)
1940	5, 300	191, 200	130, 200	66, 300
1941	66, 300	154, 700	103, 000	118, 000
1942	118, 000	96, 800	71, 700	143, 100
1943	143, 100	64, 500	64, 900	142, 700
1944	142, 700	40, 700	32, 100	151, 300
1945, April to June	151, 300	5, 600	5, 500	151, 400
1940:				
April to June	5, 300	42, 700	32, 200	15, 800
July to September	15, 800	45, 000	30, 700	30, 100
October to December	30, 100	51, 400	33, 700	47, 800
January to March	47, 800	52, 100	33, 600	66, 300
1941:				
April to June	66, 300	50, 500	33, 700	83, 100
July to September	83, 100	41, 600	27, 200	97, 600
October to December	97, 600	36, 600	24, 400	109, 800
January to March	109, 800	26, 000	17, 700	118, 100
1942:				
April to June	118, 100	26, 800	17, 900	127, 000
July to September	127, 000	25, 700	17, 600	135, 100
October to December	135, 100	24, 200	16, 200	143, 100
January to March	143, 100	20, 100	20, 100	143, 100
1943:				
April to June	143, 100	17, 900	17, 700	143, 300
July to September	143, 300	16, 800	16, 900	143, 200
October to December	143, 200	16, 800	17, 000	143, 000
January to March	143, 000	13, 000	13, 300	142, 700
1944:				
April to June	142, 700	12, 800	11, 600	143, 900
July to September	143, 900	11, 300	11, 300	143, 900
October to December	143, 900	10, 300	3, 100	151, 100
January to March	151, 100	6, 300	6, 100	151, 300
1945, April to June	151, 300	5, 600	5, 500	151, 400

Source: Chemical Industry Control Association.

APPENDIX TABLE C–70.—*Japanese production, exports and imports of refined naphthalene, 1940–45*

[Thousands of pounds]

Fiscal year and quarter	Production[1]	Imports	Exports
1940: October to March	12, 200	1, 440	910
1941	23, 520	3, 010	1, 800
1942	39, 310	4, 370	570
1943	30, 240	2, 829	720
1944	15, 910	--------	20
1945	--------	--------	--------
1940:			
April to June	--------	540	490
July to September	--------	--------	530
October to December	6, 490	720	370
January to March	5, 710	720	540
1941:			
April to June	5, 320	1, 170	930
July to September	4, 840	810	450
October to December	6, 300	610	300
January to March	7, 060	410	120
1942:			
April to June	7, 800	930	240
July to September	6, 550	1, 350	90
October to December	11, 720	1, 420	190
January to March	13, 240	670	50
1943:			
April to June	8, 810	460	200
July to September	5, 230	1, 000	160
October to December	7, 510	1, 370	120
January to March	8, 680	--------	230
1944:			
April to June	6, 690	--------	11
July to September	3, 490	--------	4
October to December	3, 160	--------	9
January to March	2, 570	--------	--------

[1] Largest producer—Kyushu Chemical Industry Co., destroyed by bombing, together with all records on June 14, 1944. Estimate of its production was made by taking 85 percent of the crude naphthalene production of the Yawata plant of Japan Iron Mfg. Co., Ltd.,(Nihon Seitetsu K. K.) which supplied all the crude naphthalene requirements of Kyushu Kagaku Co.

Sources: Production figures are from Chemical Industry Control Association and plant records. Import and export figures are from Import-Export Bureau.

APPENDIX TABLE C–71.—*Production, imports and exports of acetone in Japan proper, 1940–45*

[Thousands of pounds]

Fiscal year and quarter	Production	Imports	Exports
1940	4, 530	2, 730	--------
1941	5, 600	570	--------
1942	14, 130	--------	--------
1943	11, 830	--------	--------
1944	6, 350	--------	8
1945	--------	--------	--------
1940:			
April to June	1, 150	540	--------
July to September	1, 190	1, 420	--------
October to December	1, 250	440	--------
January to March	940	330	--------
1941:			
April to June	1, 250	570	--------
July to September	1, 430	--------	--------
October to December	1, 420	--------	--------
January to March	1, 500	--------	--------
1942:			
April to June	3, 180	--------	--------
July to September	3, 280	--------	--------
October to December	3, 590	--------	--------
January to March	4, 080	--------	--------
1943:			
April to June	2, 880	--------	--------
July to September	2, 870	--------	--------
October to December	2, 990	--------	--------
January to March	3, 090	--------	8
1944:			
April to June	1, 720	--------	8
July to September	1, 350	--------	--------
October to December	1, 720	--------	--------
January to March	1, 560	--------	--------

Sources: Production: Chemical Industry Control Association. Imports and Exports: Import-Export Bureau.

[Thousands of pounds]

Fiscal year and quarter	Production	Imports
1940	780	1,050
1941	3,910	660
1942	7,690	0
1943	13,210	7
1944	1,570	0
1945	(1)	
1940:		
April to June	140	0
July to September	150	0
October to December	220	0
January to March	270	1,050
1941:		
April to June	710	490
July to September	740	0
October to December	790	110
January to March	1,670	60
1942:		
April to June	1,560	0
July to September	2,010	0
October to December	2,030	0
January to March	2,090	0
1943:		
April to June	4,000	0
July to September	3,270	0
October to December	2,880	0
January to March	3,060	7

Appendix Table C–72.—*Production and imports of butanol in Japan proper, 1940–45*—Continued

Fiscal year and quarter	Production	Imports
1944:		
April to June	340	0
July to September	530	0
October to December	430	0
January to March	270	(1)

[1] No date.

Sources: Production: Chemical Industry Control Association. Imports: Import-Export Bureau.

Appendix Table C–73.—*Production and imports of glycerine in Japan proper, 1940–45*

Thousands of pounds]

Calendar year	Production	Imports
1940	14,820	220
1941	15,780	3,635
1942	11,950	2,935
1943	13,050	895
1944 [1]	8,520	65,500
1945: January to September	2,920	None

[1] 415,000 pounds were exported in 1944.

Sources: Production: Chemical Industry Control Association; Imports and Exports: Import-Export Bureau.

Appendix Table C–74.—*Japanese imports of phosphorite, by source, 1935–44*

[Thousands of tons]

Source	1935	1936	1937	1938	1939	1940	1941	1942	1943	1944
South Pacific Islands:										
Ocean Nauru	43	45	60	44	45	168	0	0	0	0
Christmas	125	131	132	115	140	205	87	0	4	0
Makatea	123	123	154	101	151	172	150	0	0	0
Angaur	86	98	100	115	158	134	148	140	108	29
Others	79	121	36	110	153	140	172	186	84	13
Subtotal	456	518	482	485	647	819	557	326	196	42
Percent of total	44	44	39	53	53	73	71	63	54	26
Other:										
Florida	267	290	313	180	283	252	132	0	0	0
Indochina	0	0	0	0	0	0	23	76	72	3
Haichow	0	0	0	0	0	21	71	83	75	77
Kossier	152	215	223	111	160	3	0	0	0	0
Safaga	142	117	128	99	88	7	0	0	0	0
Gafsa	0	0	23	10	0	0	0	0	0	0
Morocco	26	40	54	22	28	0	3	0	0	0
Others	0	0	0	1	11	20	1	30	24	39
Subtotal	587	662	741	423	570	303	230	189	171	119
Percent of total	56	56	61	47	47	27	29	37	46	74
Total	1,043	1,180	1,223	908	1,217	1,122	787	515	367	161

Source: Fertilizer Section, Fertilizer and Agriculture Bureau.

APPENDIX TABLE C-75.—*Production, imports and exports of ammonium sulfate and calcium cyanamide, Japan proper, 1940–45*

[In tons]

Fiscal year quarter	Ammonium production	Sulfate [1] imports	Calcium production	Cyanamide exports
1940	1, 252, 400	128, 554	233, 487	7
1941	1, 374, 000	60, 511	250, 779	0
1942	1, 189, 300	34, 834	211, 488	1
1943	1, 021, 400	0	169, 823	0
1944	680, 900	1, 034	163, 451	0
1945; April to August	92, 100	0	40, 809	---------
1940:				
April to June	317, 700	62, 152	71, 202	0
July to September	289, 400	38, 503	51, 410	1
October to December	317, 100	15, 935	55, 360	0
January to March	328	11, 964	55, 515	6
1941:				
April to June	366, 800	23, 402	77, 291	0
July to September	329, 100	11, 001	60, 703	0
October to December	324, 700	6, 757	62, 607	0
January to March	335, 400	19, 351	50, 178	0
1942:				
April to June	332, 500	15, 267	71, 442	0
July to September	287, 600	4, 134	57, 747	1
October to December	307, 200	11, 354	46, 442	0
January to March	262, 000	4, 079	35, 857	0
1943:				
April to June	. 305, 900	0	50, 435	0
July to September	243, 800	0	44, 807	0
October to December	252, 600	0	39, 661	0
January to March	219, 100	0	34, 920	0
1944:				
April to June	255, 800	0	59, 360	0
July to September	159, 500	0	43, 727	0
October to December	147, 600	1, 034	41, 812	0
January to March	118, 000	(2)	18, 552	(2)
1945:				
April to June	76, 000	(2)	30, 192	(2)
July to August	16, 100	(2)	10, 617	(2)

[1] Includes byproduct ammonium sulfate.
[2] No data.

Source: Production—Chemical Industry Control Association Imports and Exports—Import-Export Bureau.

Fiscal year-month	Production by causticization	Production by electrolysis	Imports	Total production and imports	Consumption, home islands	Exports to foreign countries [1]	Consumption—actual		Civilian (including) aircraft)
							Army	Navy	
1931	8, 512	40, 851	45, 851	95, 214	99, 340	12			
1932	32, 480	46, 143	31, 068	109, 691	106, 372	3, 503			
1933	60, 180	57, 627	13, 650	131, 457	125, 662	5, 593			
1934	120, 414	61, 936	10, 922	193, 272	179, 675	13, 524			
1935	149, 110	86, 030	21, 975	257, 115	236, 443	19, 286			
1936	194, 638	95, 628	12, 772	303, 038	313, 053	26, 357			
1937	259, 556	116, 075	30, 235	405, 866	399, 789	6, 134			
1938	336, 605	149, 245	293	486, 143	487, 217	12, 803			
1939	387, 994	194, 561	0	582, 555	443, 059	26, 768	1. 9		98. 1
1940	300, 749	154, 743	0	455, 492	540, 127	13, 389	2. 8		97. 2
1941	173, 672	132, 102	0	305, 774	318, 342	8, 619	6. 3		93. 7
1942	120, 618	125, 685	0	246, 303	265, 264	4, 949	17. 7		82. 3
1943	112, 846	126, 523	0	239, 369	249, 025	6, 372	13. 6	7. 5	78. 9
1944	48, 909	106, 062	0	154, 971	142, 250	638	20. 1	10. 4	69. 5
1945 through August	6, 825	21, 543	0	28, 368	[2] 15, 000	6	12. 5	12. 4	75. 1
1941:									
April	18, 192	12, 911		31, 103					
May	21, 132	13, 025		34, 157					
June	20, 837	11, 725		32, 562					
July	13, 369	11, 422		24, 791					
August	16, 547	10, 176		26, 723					
September	11, 668	10, 872		22, 540					
October	12, 290	11, 892		24, 182					
November	12, 545	11, 437		23, 982					
December	11, 719	11, 092		22, 811					
January	12, 072	10, 126		22, 198					
February	11, 562	8, 317		19, 879					
March	11, 739	9, 107		20, 846					
1942:									
April	11, 210	9, 533		20, 793					
May	10, 793	10, 179		20, 972					
June	9, 816	9, 719		19, 535					
July	10, 301	10, 898		21, 199					
August	9, 122	10, 963		20, 085					
September	6, 721	11, 111		17, 832					
October	9, 815	11, 702		21, 517					
November	10, 538	11, 226		21, 764					
December	12, 003	11, 146		23, 149					
January	10, 417	10, 126		20, 543					
February	9, 195	9, 054		18, 249					
March	10, 687	9, 978		20, 665					
1943:									
April	8, 046	11, 274		19, 320					
May	12, 120	12, 243		24, 363					
June	10, 846	11, 741		22, 587					
July	10, 627	11, 388		22, 015					
August	9, 888	10, 346		20, 234					
September	8, 938	9, 433		18, 371					
October	19, 704	10, 609		21, 313					
November	9, 087	10, 287		19, 374					
December	10, 515	10, 258		20, 773					
January	8, 946	10, 121		19, 067					
February	6, 382	9, 162		15, 544					
March	6, 847	9, 661		16, 508					

See footnotes at end of table.

Fiscal year-month	Production by causticization	Production by electrolysis	Imports	Total production and imports	Consumption, home islands	Exports to foreign countries [1]	Consumption—actual Army	Consumption—actual Navy	Civilian) (including aircraft)
1944:									
April	6,942	10,729		17,671					
May	5,863	11,325		17,088					
June	5,220	10,639		15,859					
July	4,248	9,695		13,943					
August	3,164	9,109		12,273					
September	3,597	7,900		11,497					
October	3,989	8,880		12,869					
November	3,430	8,393		11,823					
December	4,049	7,654		11,703					
January	3,287	8,525		11,812					
February	2,798	6,241		9,039					
March	2,422	6,972		9,394					
1945:									
April	2,663	5,006		7,669					
May	1,843	5,926		7,769					
June	1,688	5,111		6,799					
July	631	3,729		4,360					
August	0	1,771		1,771					

[1] Does not include about 5,000 tons per year exported to Korea and an unknown quantity to Taiwan.

Source: Data are from Chemical Industry Control Association (Mr. Endo).

APPENDIX TABLE C-77.—*Production and consumption of chlorine in Japan proper, 1931-45*

[In tons]

Fiscal year and month	Production	Consumption [1]	Planned allocation Army percent	Planned allocation Navy percent [2]	Planned allocation Aircraft percent [3]	Planned allocation Civilian percent	Functional break-down of total consumption— to bleaching powder	to liquid chlorine	to hydrochloric acid	to unclassified uses [4]
1931	36,235	36,190					16,990	2,741	16,459	
1932	40,930	40,680					19,559	3,966	17,155	
1933	51,115	50,398					21,225	5,316	23,857	
1934	54,938	54,982					23,149	9,213	22,620	
1935	76,309	76,365					31,579	13,413	31,373	0
1936	84,822	84,038					32,742	18,785	32,511	0
1937	102,959	102,245					39,311	21,230	41,704	0
1938	132,380	132,380								
1939	173,554	173,554								
1940	126,235	126,235								
1941	117,174	117,174	3.8			96.2	33,165	24,748	51,661	7,690
1942	111,483	111,483	11.7			88.3	27,476	20,590	48,251	15,166
1943	112,224	112,224	11.5	5.4		83.1	24,776	23,314	52,357	10,777
1944	94,076	94,076	8.1	5.4	4.3	82.2	14,750	18,384	34,926	26,016
1945: April to August	19,110	19,110	5.0	4.1	3.8	87.1	2,296	2,056	4,398	10,360
1941:										
April	11,452						8,146	7,031	10,346	
May	11,553									
June	10,400									
July	10,131						8,207	4,651	17,245	
August	9,027									
September	9,643									
October	10,548						11,007	7,272	14,855	
November	10,146									
December	9,836									

See footnotes at end of table.

Fiscal year and month	Production	Consumption [1]	Planned allocation				Functional break-down of total consumption—			
			Army percent	Navy percent [2]	Aircraft percent [3]	Civilian percent	to bleaching powder	to liquid chlorine	to hydro-chloric acid	to unclassi-fied uses [4]
1941—Con.										
January	8, 982									
February	7, 378						5, 805	5, 794	9, 215	
March	8, 078									
1942:										
April	8, 501									
May	9, 029						6, 262	4, 597	11, 465	
June	8, 621									
July	9, 667									
August	9, 723						7, 490	5, 530	12, 972	
September	9, 856									
October	10, 379									
November	9, 957						7, 582	5, 410	13, 925	
December	9, 887									
January	8, 982									
February	8, 031						6, 142	5, 053	9, 889	
March	8, 850						27, 476	20, 590	48, 251	
1943:										
April	10, 000									
May	10, 860						6, 895	5, 935	13, 546	
June	10, 413									
July	10, 101									
August	9, 177						7, 080	6, 975	14, 366	
September	8, 368									
October	9, 409									
November	9, 124						5, 669	5, 957	13, 438	
December	9, 028									
January	8, 977									
February	8, 128						5, 122	5, 447	11, 007	
March	8, 569						24, 766	24, 314	52, 357	
1944:										
April	9, 516									
May	10, 045						4, 793	5, 587	10, 797	
June	9, 437									
July	8, 599									
August	8, 079						4, 949	5, 774	10, 057	
September	7, 007									
October	7, 877									
November	7, 445						2, 812	3, 385	8, 119	
December	6, 789									
January	7, 562									
February	5, 536						2, 216	3, 638	5, 593	
March	6, 184						14, 750	18, 384	34, 926	
1945:										
April	4, 440									
May	5, 257						2, 296	2, 056	4, 398	
June	4, 534									
July	3, 308									
August	1, 571									

[1] Stocks, exports and imports were negligible or nonexistent.

[2] Prior to 1944 requirements for aviation undustry came out of civilian allocation.

[3] Data are from Chemical Industry Control Association (Mr. Endo).

[4] "Unclassified uses" are almost entirely direct orders from the army and navy to the chlorine manufacturers for chlorine compounds made at the plants. Data on such dealings were not reported to the C. I. C. A. This practice assisted in undermining its effectiveness, because these orders were over and above the planned allocations obtained through the C. I. C. A.

APPENDIX TABLE C-78.—*Production of sulfuric acid, Japan proper, 1931–45*

[In tons of 100 H₂SO₄ [1]]

Fiscal year and month	Chamber acid	100 percent H₂SO₄	Contact acid 25 percent oleum	Total contact acid	Total acid
1931					767, 000
1932					961, 000
1933					1, 176, 000
1934					1, 281, 000
1935					1, 507, 000
1936					1, 882, 000
1937					2, 507, 000
1938					2, 240, 000
1939					
1940					2, 493, 000
1941					
1942	1, 110, 800	753, 000	60, 100	813, 100	1, 923, 900
1943	739, 200	814, 500	61, 600	876, 100	1, 615, 300
1944	432, 000	607, 000	60, 600	667, 600	1, 099, 600
1945: April to August	59, 000			118, 800	177, 800
1942:					
April	97, 900	63, 200	5, 100	68, 300	166, 200
May	100, 600	65, 200	5, 000	70, 200	170, 800
June	99, 200	58, 100	4, 900	63, 000	162, 200
July	93, 600	63, 000	5, 600	68, 600	162, 200
August	91, 700	61, 200	5, 100	66, 300	158, 000
September	86, 600	55, 600	4, 800	60, 400	147, 000
October	97, 300	61, 200	5, 600	66, 800	164, 100
November	94, 900	71, 500	4, 800	66, 300	161, 200
December	97, 200	69, 600	4, 100	73, 700	170, 900
January	86, 700	68, 800	4, 500	68, 300	155, 000
February	78, 700	59, 800	4, 500	64, 300	143, 000
March	86, 400	70, 800	6, 100	76, 900	163, 300
1943:					
April	72, 000	77, 000	4, 900	81, 900	153, 900
May	69, 100	75, 200	4, 000	79, 200	148, 200
June	70, 300	69, 100	5, 500	74, 600	144, 600
July	61, 700	68, 100	4, 400	72, 500	134, 200
August	62, 700	62, 300	5, 200	67, 500	130, 200
September	61, 000	52, 600	5, 500	58, 100	119, 100
October	61, 200	57, 300	5, 800	63, 100	124, 300
November	61, 200	67, 900	5, 400	73, 300	134, 500
December	62, 700	73, 500	5, 500	79, 000	141, 600
January	58, 600	76, 200	5, 200	81, 400	140, 000
February	48, 300	65, 500	5, 000	70, 500	118, 800
March	50, 900	69, 800	5, 200	75, 000	125, 900
1944:					
April	50, 500	69, 500	5, 500	75, 000	125, 500
May	50, 500	69, 600	5, 300	74, 900	125, 400
June	48, 900	63, 500	4, 200	67, 700	116, 600
July	41, 700	51, 300	5, 500	56, 800	98, 500
August	32, 700	49, 200	5, 700	54, 900	87, 600
September	29, 100	56, 100	4, 400	50, 500	79, 600
October	32, 800	46, 400	5, 600	52, 000	84, 800
November	32, 800	49, 600	5, 900	55, 500	88, 300
December	33, 100	45, 900	5, 100	51, 000	84, 100
January	30, 500	45, 700	4, 200	49, 900	80, 400
February	24, 200	34, 700	4, 000	38, 700	62, 800
March	25, 300	35, 500	5, 200	40, 700	66, 000

See footnotes at end of table.

APPENDIX TABLE C-78.—*Production of sulfuric acid, Japan proper, 1931-45*—Continued

Fiscal year and month	Chamber acid	100 percent H₂SO₄	Contact acid 25 percent oleum	Total contact acid	Total acid
1945:					
April	18,100	31,600	4,600	36,200	54,300
May	22,030	31,800	4,100	35,900	57,900
June	4,900	21,500	3,300	24,800	29,700
July	8,200	----------	----------	15,700	23,900
August	5,800	----------	----------	6,200	12,000
Postwar:					
September	3,300	----------	----------	1,600	4,900
October	4,500	----------	----------	1,900	6,400

¹ Production was nearly equal to consumption because there were no imports; exports were never over 2 percent of production, and inventories amounted to only 2 or 3 weeks' supply.

Source: Data for 1940 through 1945 are from the Japan Sulfuric and Nitric Acids Controlling Co., a section of the Chemical Industry Control Association. Data for 1931 through 1938 are from Foreign Economic Administration (U. S.) Report JS-28.

APPENDIX TABLE C-79.—*Production of tetraethyl lead in Japan, 1940-45*

[Pounds of tetraethyl lead]

Production year and month	Army	Navy	Total	Production year and month	Army	Navy	Total
1940	35,200	49,900	85,100	1942—Continued			
1941	426,600	398,600	825,200	January	165,600	188,800	354,400
1942	1,599,300	2,036,100	3,635,400	February	169,500	217,000	386,500
1943	2,923,000	3,295,400	6,218,400	March	196,700	240,900	437,600
1944	3,671,200	3,353,200	7,024,400	1943:			
1945 (5 months)	635,900	475,700	1,111,600	April	179,000	226,900	405,900
1940:				May	178,900	256,500	435,400
September	----------	14,000	14,000	June	186,600	217,300	403,900
October	5,600	4,900	10,500	July	200,300	210,100	410,400
November	5,900	4,900	10,800	August	198,500	223,000	421,500
December	7,300	6,700	14,000	September	221,500	263,700	485,200
January	8,300	7,200	15,500	October	233,100	285,800	518,900
February	5,500	5,500	11,000	November	269,800	323,600	593,400
March	2,600	6,700	9,300	December	301,800	309,500	611,300
1941:				January	283,700	308,700	592,400
April	9,500	7,700	17,200	February	289,800	289,400	579,200
May	26,100	5,700	31,800	March	380,000	380,900	760,900
June	15,300	5,800	21,100	1944:			
July	16,400	15,200	31,600	April	423,100	350,600	773,700
August	24,800	23,300	48,100	May	303,200	397,100	700,300
September	36,400	36,200	72,600	June	323,400	310,300	633,700
October	37,900	35,300	73,200	July	305,400	298,000	603,400
November	40,900	42,400	83,300	August	337,600	323,100	660,700
December	54,600	46,200	100,800	September	464,700	369,500	834,200
January	48,400	50,100	98,500	October	334,200	287,700	621,900
February	53,400	59,700	113,100	November	360,800	261,100	621,900
March	62,900	71,000	133,900	December	292,500	299,600	592,100
1942:				January	240,900	219,000	459,900
April	68,200	81,300	149,500	February	125,700	140,800	266,500
May	84,900	101,100	186,000	March	159,700	96,400	256,100
June	90,100	102,000	192,100	1945:			
July	77,500	108,600	186,100	April	106,600	67,900	174,500
August	109,300	138,000	247,300	May	163,000	87,900	250,900
September	118,900	175,000	293,900	June	196,700	132,200	328,900
October	156,600	242,300	398,900	July	110,600	136,400	247,000
November	161,200	225,600	386,800	August	59,000	51,300	110,300
December	200,800	215,500	416,300				

Source: Records from producing plants.

APPENDIX TABLE C–80.—*Production and distribution of toluol, Japan proper, 1931–45*

[Thousands of gallons]

Fiscal year and month	Stocks, beginning of period	Production	Manchuria	Imports from total	Consumption [1]	End of period
1931	(2)	154	(2)	(2)	(2)	(2)
1932	(2)	241	(2)	(2)	(2)	(2)
1933	(2)	363	(2)	(2)	(2)	(2)
1934	(2)	486	(2)	(2)	(2)	(2)
1935	(2)	615	(2)	(2)	(2)	(2)
1936	(2)	696	(2)	(2)	(2)	(2)
1937	(2)	840	(2)	(2)	(2)	(2)
1938	(2)	1, 414	(2)	(2)	2, 200	(2)
1939	(2)	1, 595	(2)	(2)	3, 050	(2)
1940	(2)	1, 869	(2)	(2)	2, 100	304
1941	304	2, 257	218	2, 779	2, 256	523
1942	523	2, 330	146	2, 999	2, 378	621
1943	621	2, 776	275	3, 672	3, 079	593
1944	593	2, 156	25	2, 774	2, 357	417
1945 to August 15	417	355	0	772	620	152
1941:						
April	304	198	42	544	240	304
May	304	224	21	549	237	312
June	312	178	0	490	153	337
July	337	211	0	548	207	341
August	341	202	34	577	215	362
September	362	153	40	555	157	398
October	398	165	2	565	153	412
November	412	168	16	596	204	392
December	92	195	37	624	210	414
January	414	176	0	590	174	416
February	416	162	13	591	118	473
March	473	225	13	711	188	523
1942:						
April	523	213	0	736	212	524
May	524	204	27	755	108	647
June	647	188	0	835	202	633
July	633	200	10	843	259	584
August	584	201	18	803	202	601
September	601	187	26	814	213	601
October	601	198	0	799	118	681
November	681	170	4	855	113	742
December	742	205	20	967	242	725
January	725	177	0	902	210	692
February	692	187	10	889	229	660
March	660	209	31	891	270	621
1943:						
April	621	214	0	835	270	565
May	565	180	15	760	273	487
June	487	220	0	707	331	376
July	376	209	0	585	165	420
August	420	203	92	715	352	363
September	363	183	0	546	109	437
October	437	231	68	736	301	435
November	435	271	0	706	194	512
December	512	250	31	793	230	563
January	563	268	0	831	245	586
February	586	259	0	845	286	559
March	559	288	69	916	323	593
1944:						
April	593	280	0	873	259	614
May	614	220	25	859	251	608

See footnotes at end of table.

APPENDIX TABLE C–80.—*Production and distribution of toluol, Japan proper, 1931–45*—Continued

Fiscal year and month	Stocks, beginning of period	Production	Manchuria	Imports from total	Consumption [1]	End of period
1944—Con.						
June	608	221	0	829	302	527
July	527	191	0	718	218	500
August	500	160	0	660	207	453
September	453	176	0	629	118	451
October	451	172	0	623	142	481
November	481	171	0	652	141	511
December	511	140	0	651	160	491
January	491	178	0	669	135	534
February	534	114	0	648	169	479
March	479	133	0	612	195	417
1945:						
April	417	109	0	526	147	379
May	379	103	0	482	220	262
June	262	84	0	346	143	203
July	203	53	0	256	78	178
Aug. 1 to Aug. 15	178	6	0	184	32	152

Fiscal year and month	Allocated distribution, percent of production in home islands		
	Army,[3] percent	Navy, percent	Civilian, percent
1941	53.0	28.0	19.0
1942	53.0	33.0	14.0
1943	53.0	32.0	15.0
1944	64.0	29.0	7.0
1945	73.0	21.0	6.0

[1] There were no exports in recent years.
[2] No data.
[3] Includes Air Force.
Source: Data received November 24, 1945, from Mr. Fukuzawa of the Coke Oven Products Control Co. (Teisabura Kuga, president), a section of the Chemical Industry Control Association.

APPENDIX TABLE C–81.—*Production and consumption of organic glass in Japan, 1937–45*

[In pounds]

Fiscal year and month	Inventory—beginning of period	Production	Consumption	Inventory—end of period	Factory labor [1]		
					Male	Female	Total
1937					110	100	[2] 210
1938		139,600		39,700	180	150	[3] 330
1939	39,700	608,700	522,100	126,300			
1940	126,300	472,400	518,000	80,700			
1941	80,700	788,900	786,300	83,300			
1942	83,300	1,290,600	1,298,200	75,700			
1943	75,700	1,843,900	1,778,700	140,900			
1944	140,900	2,256,000	2,188,900	208,000			
1945: April to July	208,000	540,700	427,600	321,100			
1940:							
April	126,300	51,700	45,100	132,900	210	162	372
May	132,900	65,700	51,100	147,500	342	180	522
June	147,500	47,800	59,700	135,600	345	180	525
July	135,600	47,200	48,500	134,300	350	180	530
August	134,300	44,100	39,500	138,900	341	182	523
September	138,900	30,300	37,600	131,600	342	183	525
October	131,600	27,400	45,200	113,800	322	183	505
November	113,800	22,600	31,600	104,800	320	185	505
December	104,800	28,900	38,800	94,900	321	185	506
January	94,900	23,400	33,000	85,300	322	185	507
February	85,300	45,000	44,000	86,300	325	188	513
March	86,300	38,300	43,900	80,700	327	189	516

See footnotes at end of table.

Appendix Table C–81.—*Production and consumption of organic glass in Japan, 1937–45*—Continued

Fiscal year and month	Inventory—beginning of period	Production	Consumption	Inventory—end of period	Factory labor [1]			Total
					Male	Female		
1941:								
April	80,700	37,200	46,800	71,100	329	189		518
May	71,100	46,400	42,400	75,100	330	194		524
June	75,100	41,500	37,900	78,700	330	197		527
July	78,700	48,200	61,100	65,800	340	208		548
August	65,800	55,100	43,900	77,000	344	208		552
September	77,000	59,000	37,800	98,200	352	214		566
October	98,200	59,600	67,200	90,600	345	217		562
November	90,600	69,100	63,500	96,200	350	221		571
December	96,200	78,100	96,900	77,400	361	242		603
January	77,400	93,700	76,200	94,900	372	270		642
February	94,900	92,900	116,700	71,100	367	272		639
March	71,100	108,100	95,900	83,300 [3]	365	280		645
1942:								
April	83,300	98,300	103,700	77,900	370	284		654
May	77,900	112,100	95,800	94,200	373	287		660
June	94,200	123,900	143,400	74,700	380	292		672
July	74,700	110,900	113,800	71,800	395	291		686
August	71,800	97,000	94,400	74,400	395	296		691
September	74,400	90,600	56,400	108,600	400	284		684
October	108,600	102,600	143,700	67,500	401	302		703
November	67,500	104,300	124,200	47,600	410	306		716
December	47,600	115,000	89,800	72,800	415	308		723
January	72,800	103,700	107,400	69,100	419	310		729
February	69,100	102,700	108,300	63,500	425	313		738
March	63,500	129,500	117,300	75,700	430	322		752
1943:								
April	75,700	125,900	116,300	85,300	435	337		772
May	85,300	123,400	127,700	81,000	439	339		778
June	81,000	131,300	137,200	75,100	452	351		803
July	75,100	131,300	139,300	67,100	460	359		819
August	67,100	136,100	127,800	75,400	475	373		848
September	75,400	140,600	122,700	93,300	485	384		869
October	93,300	139,700	129,500	103,500	492	387		879
November	103,500	173,800	151,300	126,000	500	395		895
December	126,000	171,500	165,200	132,300	532	420		952
January	132,300	183,900	170,700	145,500	556	435		991
February	145,500	194,100	201,000	138,600	591	465B		1,056
March	138,600	192,300	190,000	140,900	611	483		1,094
1944:								
April	140,900	197,300	200,000	138,200	631	500	130	1,261
May	138,200	201,500	242,500	97,200	627	530	130	1,287
June	97,200	205,200	218,400	84,000	624	534	130	1,288
July	84,000	170,700	188,900	65,800	630	533	130	1,293
August	65,800	199,000	189,100	75,700	637	530	130	1,297
September	75,700	194,900	194,200	76,400	630	535	270	1,435
October	76,400	197,300	144,700	129,000	625	523	270	1,418
November	129,000	170,800	116,300	183,500	618	515	270	1,403
December	183,500	237,200	266,600	154,100	607	510	270	1,387
January	154,100	154,100	171,600	136,600	605	500	290	1,395
February	136,600	157,800	100,500	193,900	587	487	290	1,364
March	193,900	170,200	156,100	208,000	562	441	290	1,293
1945:								
April	208,000	162,300	140,500	229,800	549	410	290	1,249
May	229,800	180,000	69,500	340,300	455	377	290	1,122
June	340,300	115,900	133,400	322,800	435	350	290	1,075
July	322,800	82,500	84,200	321,100	495	339	290	1,124
August	321,100	15,400	----------	----------	416	340	290	1,046

[1] Does not include construction workers.   [2] January, 1938.   [3] January, 1939.   Source: Munitions Ministry—Aviation Chemical Department.

[In thousands of United States gallons]

Fiscal year and month	Inventories (start of period)	Home islands		Total	Consumption [1]	Inventories (end of period)	Korea production	Total production	Allocated distribution for home islands (percent)				
		Production	Imports						Army	Navy	Aviation munitions	Fuel	Civilian
1931	------	[3] 26	[3] 744	770	770	------	------	26					
1932	------	[3] 19	[3] 1, 378	1, 397	1, 397	------	------	19					
1933	------	[3] 18	1, 411	1, 429	1, 429	------	------	18					
1934	------	[3] 697	865	1, 562	1, 562	------	------	697					
1935	16	1, 149	745	1, 910	1, 910	0	308	1, 457					
1936	0	1, 453	807	2, 260	2, 212	48	474	1, 927					
1937	48	2, 203	1, 659	3, 910	3, 742	168	531	2, 734					
1938	168	3, 251	3	3, 422	3, 207	215	520	3, 771					
1939	215	3, 671	2, 014	5, 900	5, 777	123	554	4, 225					
1940	123	4, 252	932	5, 307	5, 157	150	479	4, 731					
1941	150	6, 609	34	6, 793	6, 497	294	471	7, 080					
1942	294	6, 749	0	7, 043	6, 689	354	506	7, 255					
1943	354	7, 598	0	7, 952	7, 361	591	2, 137	9, 735	26. 6	47. 0	0	------	26. 4
1944	591	6, 432	0	7, 023	6, 812	211	4, 328	10, 760	20. 4	27. 5	34. 5	------	17. 6
1945: April to August	211	1, 222	0	1, 433	1, 433	------	------	1, 222	17. 6	20. 4	32. 4	21. 3	8. 3
1941:													
April	150	440	12	602	383	219	43	483					
May	219	506	0	725	303	422	29	535					
June	422	463	22	907	581	326	44	507					
July	328	525	0	851	582	269	36	561					
August	269	562	0	831	533	298	25	587					
September	298	577	0	875	575	300	33	610					
October	300	580	0	880	606	274	29	609					
November	274	583	0	857	521	335	48	631					
December	335	613	0	948	260	688	55	668					
January	688	574	0	1, 262	605	657	43	617					
February	657	624	0	1, 281	815	466	43	667					
March	466	562	0	1, 028	734	294	43	605					
1942:													
April	294	492	0	786	495	290	50	542					
May	290	561	0	851	584	267	50	611					
June	267	581	0	848	553	295	47	628					
July	295	598	0	893	658	235	36	634					
August	235	505	0	740	542	198	39	544					
September	198	524	0	722	502	220	39	563					
October	220	549	0	769	518	251	46	595					
November	251	537	0	788	472	316	37	574					
December	316	623	0	939	528	411	36	659					
January	411	600	0	1, 011	588	423	43	643					
February	423	572	0	995	601	394	43	615					
March	394	607	0	1, 001	647	354	40	647					
1943:													
April	354	572	0	926	644	282	42	614					
May	282	607	0	889	635	254	37	644	26. 4	47. 0	0	------	26. 6
June	254	576	0	830	483	347	32	608					
July	347	585	0	932	592	340	34	619					
August	340	605	0	945	714	231	32	637	26. 2	46. 4	0	------	27. 4
September	231	584	0	815	502	313	31	615					
October	313	607	0	920	511	409	199	806					
November	409	621	0	1, 030	646	384	371	992	26. 2	46. 4	0	------	27. 4
December	384	640	0	1, 024	620	404	325	965					

See footnotes at end of table.

Fiscal year and month	Inventories (start of period)	Home islands Production	Home islands Imports	Total	Consumption[1]	Inventories (end of period)	Korea production	Total production	Army	Navy	Aviation munitions	Fuel	Civilian
1943—Con.													
January	404	717	0	1,121	604	517	306	1,023	28.0	48.2	0	------	23.8
February	517	697	0	1,214	630	584	369	1,066					
March	584	787	0	1,371	780	591	359	1,146					
1944:													
April	591	735	0	1,326	706	620	513	1,248	16.9	29.4	31.5	------	22.2
May	620	761	0	1,381	717	664	440	1,201					
June	664	694	0	1,358	673	685	265	959					
July	685	542	0	1,227	959	268	391	933	19.3	30.0	35.1	------	15.6
August	268	495	0	763	433	330	236	731					
September	330	480	0	810	600	210	406	886					
October	210	508	0	718	491	227	459	967	26.7	23.7	35.3	------	14.3
November	227	586	0	813	624	189	412	998					
December	189	405	0	594	441	153	397	802					
January	153	427	0	580	390	190	312	739	20.5	24.3	38.0	------	17.2
February	190	413	0	603	408	195	241	654					
March	195	386	0	581	370	211	256	642					
1945:													
April	211	354	0	565	409	156	------	354	15.0	18.4	33.3	25.8	8.3
May	156	337	0	493	283	210	------	156					
June	210	288	0	498	221	277	------	288					
July	277	185	0	462	403	59	------	185	20.8	22.9	31.3	16.7	8.3
August	59	58	0	117	117	0	------	58					

[1] From FEA report JS–28.

[2] Production prior to 1934 was by wood distillation alone. From 1934 on, principal production was by synthesis.

[3] During the period 1940–43 about 6,000 gallons of methanol were expected.

Source: Data were obtained from Mr. K. Tersaki, organic synthesis section of Chemical Industry Control Association, Nov. 20, 1945.

APPENDIX TABLE C–83.—*Production and consumption of ethyl-alcohol in Japan, 1941–45*

[In thousands of United States gallons]

Fiscal year	Inventory[1] (beginning of period)	Production Civilian	Production Army[2]	Production Navy[2]	Production Total	Imports[3]	Total	Consumption	Inventory[1] (end of period)
1941	1,190	17,810	--------	--------	17,810	9,460	28,460	26,240	2,220
1942	2,220	17,970	--------	--------	17,970	14,530	34,720	33,050	1,670
1943	1,670	16,060	--------	--------	16,060	13,340	31,070	29,200	1,870
1944	1,870	25,100	5,810	4,760	35,670	8,430	45,970	44,250	1,720
1945	1,720	7,660	6,630	6,370	20,660	--------	22,380	22,060	320

See footnotes at end of table.

APPENDIX TABLE C–83.—*Production and consumption of ethyl-alcohol in Japan, 1941–45*—Continued.

CONSUMPTION

| Fiscal year | Military | | | Civilian | | | | Total |
	Army [3]	Navy [3]	Total	Industrial	Fuel	Miscellaneous	Total	
1941	1,850	1,850	3,700	10,570	10,990	980	22,540	26,240
1942	6,710	4,600	11,310	12,130	8,140	1,480	21,750	33,060
1943	10,570	8,190	18,760	6,870	2,510	1,060	10,440	29,200
1944	18,470	21,660	40,130	3,330	530	260	4,120	44,250
1945, April to August 15	8,450	10,440	18,890	2,250	790	130	3,170	22,060

[1] Civilian only.
[2] Civilian plants built to produce butanol, but shifted to produce ethyl alcohol under the direction of the Army and Navy.

[3] From Formosa, South Sea Islands, and Sakhalin.

Source: Fermentation Industry Section Fuel Bureau, Ministry of Commerce and Industry.

APPENDIX TABLE C–84.—*Production and consumption of soda ash [1] in Japan proper, 1935–45*

[In tons]

Fiscal year and quarter	Production	Imports	Exports	Consumption	Fiscal year and quarter	Production	Imports	Exports	Consumption
1935	218,600				1942:				
1936	237,200				April to June	29,200			
1937	255,300				July to September	29,700			
1938	256,700				October to December	58,000			
1939	280,000				January to March	49,200			
1940	244,700	17,900	1,300	261,400	1943:				
1941	178,400	10,200		188,600	April to June	39,900			
1942	166,100	4,400	600	170,000	July to September	33,400			
1943	139,700	2,600	1,200	141,000	October to December	37,500			
1944	110,200		500	109,700	January to March	28,900			
1945: April to September	26,500				1944:				
1940:					April to June	32,000			
April to June	54,600				July to September	23,300			
July to September	62,200				October to December	26,700			
October to December	72,900				January to March	28,200			
January to March	55,000				1945:				
1941:					April to June	23,000			
April to June	47,500				July to September	3,500			
July to September	47,300								
October to December	46,100								
January to March	37,500								

[1] Does not include soda ash converted to caustic soda.
Source: Chemical Industry Control Association.

APPENDIX TABLE C-85.—*Production, imports, and exports of vegetables and animal fats and oils for Japan, 1938–45*

[Thousands of pounds]

Year	Production [1]	Imports	Exports	Year	Production [1]	Imports	Exports
1938 [2]	----	5,864	111,042	1942	448,039	69,665	21,667
1939 [2]	----	8,114	112,376	1943	298,028	102,182	4,076
1940	403,671	5,991	128,290	1944	204,854	18,989	24
1941	447,788	54,078	68,948	1945: April–September	30,108	----	----

[1] Includes production from copra, oil seeds, etc. imported into Japan.
[2] Calendar year: Others are fiscal years—Apr. 1 to Mar. 31.

Source: Production: Teikoku Oil and Oil Seeds Distributing Co.; Imports and exports: Import-export bureau.

APPENDIX TABLE C-86.—*Production and consumption of sodium cyanide in Japan proper, 1940–45*

[Thousands of pounds]

Fiscal year and quarter	Inventories [1] (beginning of period)	Production	Consumption	Fiscal year and quarter	Inventories [1] (beginning of period)	Production	Consumption
1940	----	5,637	5,083	1942:			
1941	243	9,216	9,018	July to September	71	2,086	2,167
1942	525	8,563	8,956	October to December	----	2,277	1,903
1943	86	10,436	10,217	January to March	324	2,196	2,434
1944	185	7,071	7,420	1943:			
1945: April to August	196	1,495	1,556	April to June	86	2,778	2,452
1940:				July to September	412	2,264	2,249
April to June	----	966	765	October to December	306	2,698	2,421
July to September	201	646	791	January to March	507	2,696	3,095
October to December	55	2,081	1,457	1944:			
January to March	425	1,944	2,070	April to June	185	2,549	2,114
1941:				July to September	538	1,713	1,975
April to June	243	2,623	2,546	October to December	761	1,806	2,083
July to September	399	2,216	1,896	January to March	421	1,003	1,248
October to December	723	2,108	2,149	1945:			
January to March	606	2,269	2,427	April to June	196	1,166	1,146
1942:				July	227	245	291
April to June	525	2,004	2,452	September	139	84	119

[1] Some of the inventory and production figures are incomplete because many of the plant documents were destroyed by fires. Imports and exports approximately balanced over the period covered, and were minor in volume.

Source: Chemical Industry Control Association.

APPENDIX TABLE C-87.—*Production and distribution of benzol, Japan proper, 1940–45*

[In thousands of gallons]

Fiscal year and quarter	Stocks (beginning of period)	Production	Imports	Total	Consumption	Stocks (end of period)
1940	577	8, 441	3, 210	12, 228	10, 554	1, 674
1941	1, 674	9, 077	3, 061	13, 812	11, 529	2, 283
1942	2, 283	9, 102	2, 199	13, 584	11, 171	2, 413
1943	2, 413	10, 317	1, 228	13, 958	12, 290	1, 668
1944	1, 668	7, 437	604	9, 709	8, 696	1, 013
1945: April to September	1, 013	1, 281	----------	2, 294	1, 354	940
1940:						
April to June	577	1, 806	965	3, 348	2, 293	1, 055
July to September	1, 055	2, 107	681	3, 843	2, 825	1, 018
October to December	1, 018	2, 136	976	4, 130	2, 512	1, 618
January to March	1, 618	2, 392	588	4, 598	2, 924	1, 674
1941:						
April to June	1, 674	2, 766	1, 373	5, 813	3, 328	2, 485
July to September	2, 485	2, 291	783	5, 559	2, 779	2, 780
October to December	2, 780	2, 009	184	4, 973	2, 402	2, 571
January to March	2, 571	2, 011	721	5, 303	3, 020	2, 283
1942:						
April to June	2, 283	2, 397	588	5, 268	3, 103	2, 165
July to September	2, 165	2, 136	329	4, 630	2, 386	2, 244
October to December	2, 244	2, 297	718	5, 259	2, 701	2, 558
January to March	2, 558	2, 272	564	5, 394	2, 981	2, 413
1943:						
April to June	2, 413	2, 440	263	5, 116	2, 923	2, 193
July to September	2, 193	2, 303	280	4, 776	2, 620	2, 156
October to December	2, 156	2, 682	419	5, 257	3, 061	2, 196
January to March	2, 196	2, 892	266	5, 354	3, 686	1, 668
1944:						
April to June	1, 668	2, 330	382	4, 380	2, 860	1, 520
July to September	1, 520	1, 808	104	3, 432	2, 260	1, 172
October to December	1, 172	1, 871	118	3, 161	2, 056	1, 105
January to March	1, 105	1, 428	----------	2, 533	1, 520	1, 013
1945:						
April to June	1, 013	1, 041	----------	2, 054	1, 164	890
July to September	890	240	----------	1, 130	190	940

Sources: Imports, Import-Export Bureau; all others, Chemical Industry Control Association.

APPENDIX TABLE C-88.—*Production of rayon pulp in Japan proper, 1930–44*

[In tons]

Calendar year	Production[1]	Imports	Total	Consumption for fiber production[2]	Calendar year	Production[1]	Imports	Total	Consumption for fiber production[2]
1930	16	28, 000	28, 016	22, 500	1938	111, 700	127, 800	239, 500	348, 500
1931	155	33, 600	33, 755	29, 200	1939	157, 500	157, 600	315, 100	323, 900
1932	2, 600	44, 800	47, 400	40, 200	1940	204, 400	156, 800	361, 200	296, 600
1933	9, 500	67, 200	76, 700	56, 500	1941	275, 800	37, 900	313, 700	274, 000
1934	19, 600	100, 800	120, 400	86, 100	1942	220, 700	800	221, 500	158, 600
1935	39, 100	141, 500	180, 600	125, 600	1943	124, 400	0	124, 400	96, 600
1936	56, 400	189, 400	245, 800	163, 600	1944	54, 600	0	54, 600	65, 400
1937	62, 700	325, 400	388, 100	308, 300					

[1] Includes Korea, Formosa, and Karafuto.
[2] Both staple and rayon.

Source: Textile Association.

APPENDIX TABLE C-89.—*Production of oxygen in Japan proper, 1942–45*

[In thousands of cubic feet and thousands of cubic feet per month]

Fiscal year and quarter	Production	Monthly production rate	Fiscal year and quarter	Production	Monthly production rate
1942	1,625,800	135,500	1944:		
1943	1,952,400	162,700	April to June	539,600	179,900
1944	2,041,900	170,200	July to September	506,600	168,900
			October to December	553,900	184,600
1945 April to August	487,700	97,500	January to March	441,800	147,300
1943:			1945:		
April to June	460,300	153,400	April to June	350,000	116,700
July to September	470,100	156,700	July to August	137,700	68,900
October to December	524,900	175,000			
January to March	497,100	165,700			

Source: Oxygen Carbide Department, Chemical Industry Control Association.

Electric Power Tables

APPENDIX TABLE C-90.—*Electric power generation by public utility and railway plants, Japan proper, 1914–45*

[In 1,000 kwh]

Year starting April 1	Hydro-electric	Thermal electric	Total
1914	1,257,950	199,320	1,457,270
1915	1,599,900	211,000	1,810,900
1916	1,862,850	290,290	2,153,140
1917	2,208,140	421,804	2,629,944
1918	2,615,640	490,020	3,105,660
1919	2,868,150	646,870	3,515,020
1920	3,165,810	648,900	3,814,710
1921	3,588,710	660,440	4,249,150
1922			
1923	4,245,760	789,280	5,035,040
1924	5,832,290	824,330	6,656,620
1925	6,741,810	993,060	7,734,870
1926	8,083,800	1,007,410	9,091,210
1927	9,290,500	1,221,400	10,511,900
1928	10,771,300	1,187,200	11,958,500
1929	11,561,500	1,750,400	13,311,900
1930	12,524,990	1,508,700	14,033,690
1931	12,977,670	1,318,150	14,295,820
1932 [1]	14,196,710	1,533,340	15,730,050
1933	15,774,780	2,248,020	18,022,800
1934	16,233,120	3,469,630	19,702,750
1935	18,453,760	3,700,880	22,154,640
1936	19,553,740	4,579,130	24,132,870
1937	21,729,400	4,853,170	26,582,570
1938	23,263,540	5,374,000	28,637,540
1939	22,539,290	7,603,880	30,143,170
1940	23,645,500	6,957,000	30,602,500
1941	28,545,110	5,227,610	33,772,720
1942	26,472,410	7,147,090	33,619,500
1943	28,641,670	6,193,640	34,835,310
1944	28,505,000	3,735,000	32,240,000
1945 (first half)	10,025,000	482,700	10,507,700

[1] Prior to 1932 does not include energy supplied to public utilities by private plants.

Source: Electric Power Bureau, Ministry of Commerce and Industry.

APPENDIX TABLE C-91.—*Japan home islands electric generating capacity*

[In kilowatts [1]]

Year	Public utility			Private			Total all installations		
	Hydroelectric	Thermal electric [2]	Total	Hydroelectric	Thermal electric [2]	Total	Hydroelectric	Thermal electric [2]	Total
1903	9, 442	20, 478	29, 920	3, 682	10, 650	14, 332	13, 124	31, 128	44, 252
1904	11, 347	28, 941	40, 288	5, 062	13, 622	18, 684	16, 049	42, 563	58, 972
1905	11, 963	40, 011	51, 974	6, 584	15, 816	22, 400	18, 547	55, 827	74, 374
1906	13, 925	44, 819	58, 744	11, 270	21, 282	32, 552	25, 195	66, 101	91, 296
1907	25, 691	48, 728	74, 419	12, 931	27, 560	40, 491	38, 622	76, 288	114, 910
1908	44, 341	58, 451	102, 792	15, 780	36, 160	51, 940	60, 121	94, 611	154, 732
1909	57, 126	61, 895	119, 021	16, 381	46, 814	63, 195	73, 507	108, 709	182, 216
1910	79, 271	87, 037	166, 308	33, 661	57, 568	91, 229	112, 932	144, 605	257, 537
1911	116, 331	107, 896	224, 227	27, 500	69, 837	97, 337	143, 831	177, 733	321, 564
1912	199, 180	146, 557	345, 737	34, 159	82, 307	116, 466	233, 339	228, 864	462, 203
1913	285, 752	173, 363	459, 115	35, 844	101, 897	137, 741	321, 596	275, 260	596, 856
1914	376, 936	177, 939	554, 875	39, 650	121, 444	161, 094	416, 586	299, 383	715, 969
1915	395, 156	179, 139	574, 295	54, 064	143, 225	197, 289	449, 220	322, 364	771, 584
1916	420, 271	177, 756	598, 027	49, 363	157, 899	207, 262	469, 634	335, 655	805, 289
1917	454, 333	198, 829	653, 162	56, 757	165, 644	222, 401	511, 090	364, 473	875, 563
1918	512, 344	204, 437	716, 781	84, 780	182, 405	267, 185	597, 124	386, 842	983, 966
1919	576, 259	221, 918	798, 177	134, 670	200, 396	335, 066	710, 929	422, 314	1, 133, 243
1920	658, 726	294, 744	953, 470	166, 661	257, 415	424, 076	825, 387	552, 159	1, 377, 546
1921	759, 141	329, 036	1, 088, 177	1, 155, 603	282, 938	438, 541	914, 744	611, 974	1, 526, 718
1922	914, 457	426, 175	1, 340, 632	155, 603	282, 938	438, 541	1, 070, 060	709, 113	1, 779, 173
1923	1, 136, 089	443, 532	1, 579, 621	171, 617	311, 547	483, 164	1, 307, 706	755, 079	2, 062, 785
1924	1, 295, 858	473, 630	1, 769, 488	178, 499	289, 516	468, 015	1, 474, 357	763, 146	2, 237, 503
1925	1, 562, 959	606, 925	2, 169, 884	250, 549	347, 708	598, 257	1, 813, 508	954, 633	2, 768, 141
1926	1, 670, 340	829, 324	2, 499, 664	295, 630	407, 320	702, 950	1, 965, 970	1, 236, 644	3, 202, 614
1927	1, 791, 918	895, 891	2, 687, 809	319, 169	460, 153	779, 322	2, 111, 087	1, 356, 044	3, 467, 131
1928	1, 887, 016	1, 087, 470	2, 974, 486	403, 335	444, 233	874, 568	2, 290, 351	1, 531, 703	3, 822, 054
1929	2, 061, 077	1, 127, 375	3, 188, 452	520, 872	484, 299	1, 005, 171	2, 581, 949	1, 611, 674	4, 193, 623
1930	2, 271, 040	1, 081, 990	3, 353, 030	526, 597	519, 687	1, 046, 284	2, 797, 637	1, 601, 677	4, 399, 314
1931	2, 368, 420	1, 084, 961	3, 453, 381	688, 516	514, 627	1, 203, 143	3, 056, 936	1, 599, 588	4, 656, 524
1932	3, 013, 728	1, 261, 471	4, 275, 199	92, 202	565, 660	657, 862	3, 105, 930	1, 827, 131	4, 933, 061
1933	3, 086, 312	1, 426, 492	4, 512, 804	82, 393	485, 545	567, 938	3, 168, 705	1, 912, 037	5, 080, 742
1934	3, 170, 615	1, 568, 297	4, 738, 912	98, 219	654, 816	753, 035	3, 268, 834	2, 223, 113	5, 491, 947
1935	3, 309, 437	1, 828, 121	5, 137, 558	98, 560	810, 451	909, 011	3, 407, 997	2, 638, 572	6, 046, 569
1936	3, 651, 547	2, 142, 425	5, 793, 972	107, 787	875, 663	893, 450	3, 759, 334	3, 018, 088	6, 777, 422
1937	3, 851, 615	2, 331, 430	6, 183, 045	125, 981	967, 803	1, 093, 784	3, 977, 596	3, 299, 233	7, 276, 829
1938 [3]	4, 166, 000	2, 454, 000	6, 620, 000	79, 000	861, 000	940, 000	4, 245, 000	3, 315, 000	7, 560, 000
1939	4, 555, 000	2, 695, 000	7, 250, 000	122, 000	942, 000	1, 064, 000	4, 677, 000	3, 637, 000	8, 314, 000
1940	4, 997, 000	2, 885, 000	7, 882, 000	130, 000	1, 075, 000	1, 205, 000	5, 127, 000	3, 960, 000	9, 087, 000
1941	5, 222, 000	2, 968, 000	8, 190, 000	146, 000	1, 122, 000	1, 268, 000	5, 368, 000	4, 090, 000	9, 458, 000
1942	5, 480, 000	3, 011, 000	8, 491, 000	172, 000	1, 145, 000	1, 317, 000	5, 652, 000	4, 156, 000	9, 808, 000
1943	5, 650, 000	3, 006, 000	8, 656, 000	236, 000	1, 110, 000	1, 346, 000	5, 886, 000	4, 116, 000	10, 002, 000
1944	5, 819, 000	2, 964, 000	8, 783, 000	238, 000	1, 099, 000	1, 337, 000	6, 057, 000	4, 063, 000	10, 120, 000

[1] Capacities reported are based on the load carrying abilities of plants, not name plate ratings.

[2] Thermal electric includes Diesel (approximately 100,000 kw in 1944).

[3] Classification between public utility and private plants changed in 1938.

Source: Electric Power Bureau annual reports.

Transportation Tables

APPENDIX TABLE C-92.—*Length of Japanese Government railroad lines as of Oct. 11, 1945*

Route mileage	12, 080. 6
Main track mileage	14, 118
Siding track mileage	5, 850

Private railway companies _____ 145
Tramway companies _____ 67

Total _____ 212

Of this total, 14 companies have suspended operation.

Operating kilometers

Private railway _____ 6,040.9
Tramway _____ 1,778.1

Total _____ 7,819.0

Rolling stock

Locomotives:
    Steam _____ 432
    Electric _____ 161
    Internal combustion _____ 34
Electric motor cars _____ 8,141
Electric trailers _____ 596
Passenger cars _____ 990
Internal combustion motor cars _____ 428
Electric motor _____ 298
Wagons
Freight cars _____ 8,656

Track

	Km.
1.435 meter gage	1,321
1.372 meter gage	422
1.067 meter gage	5,163
1.000 meter gage	1
0.914 meter gage	11
0.762 meter gage	815
0.666 meter gage	14
0.609 meter gage	72
	7,819

APPENDIX TABLE C-94.—*Freight cars of the Japanese railroads*

Fiscal Year	Previous fiscal year	Built and purchased	Obsolete and exported	Total	Fiscal year	Previous fiscal year	Built and purchased	Obsolete and exported	Total
1937	72,579	4,640	2,546	74,673	1942	100,685	4,761	147	105,299
1938	74,673	7,117	2,027	79,763	1943	105,299	7,024	380	111,943
1939	79,763	7,911	844	86,830	1944	111,943	7,561	1,055	118,449
1940	86,830	9,742	143	96,429	March 1945	118,449	(1)	(1)	120,747
1941	96,429	5,269	1,013	100,685					

[1] Not available.

Source: Imperial Government Railways.

APPENDIX TABLE C-95.—*Locomotives of the Japanese railroads*

Fiscal year	Steam				Electric				Grand total
	Previous fiscal year	Built and purchased	Obsolete and exported	Total	Previous fiscal year	Built and purchased	Obsolete	Total	
1937	3,963	217	216	3,964	169	11	2	178	4,142
1938	3,964	353	156	4,161	178	9	4	183	4,344
1939	4,161	337	47	4,451	183	3	_____	186	4,637
1940	4,451	361	15	4,797	186	16	2	200	4,997
1941	4,797	196	113	4,880	200	26	_____	226	5,106
1942	4,880	162	8	5,034	226	13	_____	239	5,273
1943	5,034	349	40	5,343	239	24	2	261	5,604
1944	5,343	458	55	5,746	261	31	_____	292	6,038
August 1945	5,746	None	[1] 185	5,561	292	_____	[1] 5	287	5,848

[1] Air raid damage.

Source: Imperial Government Railways.

Fiscal year	Tonnage (1,000 tons)	Ton-miles (1,000 ton-miles)	Fiscal year	Tonnage (1,000 tons)	Ton-miles (1,000 ton-miles)
1936	107, 584	11, 162, 419	1941	167, 212	20, 460, 536
1937	117, 340	12, 614, 639	1942	174, 201	23, 250, 994
1938	130, 131	15, 005, 408	1943	193, 975	29, 185, 846
1939	144, 863	17, 319, 331	1944	184, 504	29, 597, 146
1940	160, 656	19, 142, 733	1945	[1] 78, 041	11, 534, 183

[1] April through October.

Source: Imperial Government Railways.

Appendix Table C–97.—*Tonnage of the principal commodities carried on the Japanese railroads, 1936–45*

[In 1,000 metric tons]

Commodities	1936	1937	1938	1939	1940	1941	1942	1943	1944	1945 (first quarter only)
Rice	3, 547. 5	3, 540. 7	3, 950. 3	4, 373. 1	3, 593. 0	3, 934. 8	4, 393. 0	4, 593. 8	4, 239. 7	916. 9
Grain	984. 6	1, 189. 4	1, 341. 2	1, 698. 5	1, 537. 2	1, 197. 5	1, 538. 8	1, 276. 7	1, 497. 0	261. 0
Soybeans	360. 1	258. 0	282. 9	357. 4	300. 1	214. 7	513. 2	772. 2	967. 9	507. 1
Potatoes	410. 4	420. 0	481. 3	585. 2	650. 1	830. 0	1, 020. 8	1, 235. 3	1, 230. 5	175. 2
Lumber	8, 008. 9	8, 529. 9	10, 425. 1	12, 223. 7	13, 336. 2	13, 363. 2	12, 453. 4	20, 540. 6	18, 841. 5	4, 359. 1
Firewood and charcoal	1, 661. 6	1, 599. 2	1, 810. 1	2, 152. 8	3, 233. 2	3, 299. 6	3, 633. 0	3, 700. 6	3, 211. 7	831. 6
Coal	31, 460. 7	33, 370. 1	36, 219. 3	39, 346. 1	41, 944. 0	38, 670. 4	38, 566. 2	48, 799. 2	44, 621. 8	10, 423. 5
Coke	351. 7	424. 5	633. 2	817. 9	1, 147. 9	1, 319. 6	1, 804. 4	1, 928. 8	1, 861. 8	514. 7
Ore	2, 273. 0	2, 535. 2	2, 982. 0	2, 994. 2	3, 055. 3	3, 466. 0	4, 576. 3	6, 176. 9	6, 101. 9	1, 334. 3
Limestone	1, 925. 3	2, 169. 9	2, 161. 9	2, 115. 0	2, 393. 2	2, 651. 0	3, 131. 0	3, 457. 3	3, 256. 3	715. 3
Ballast	2, 590. 3	2, 256. 1	2, 663. 7	3, 116. 0	4, 071. 4	4, 963. 6	4, 813. 1	9, 982. 0	9, 986. 3	1, 931. 0
Iron and steel	241. 4	2, 123. 0	2, 395. 4	2, 607. 0	1, 947. 4	2, 090. 7	2, 581. 2	4, 053. 3	5, 969. 6	1, 175. 6
Oil	265. 6	1, 172. 1	1, 181. 0	1, 114. 8	1, 037. 2	840. 6	658. 0	1, 632. 2	1, 625. 4	425. 7
Fish	254. 8	1, 236. 4	1, 451. 4	1, 586. 0	1, 639. 4	1, 744. 9	1, 313. 7	1, 434. 1	941. 3	345. 9
Salt	95. 6	647. 8	730. 8	758. 9	882. 4	838. 9	1, 017. 9	1, 262. 7	1, 029. 4	280. 5
Fertilizer	1, 100. 1	4, 262. 3	4, 352. 9	5, 105. 1	5, 264. 2	4, 281. 3	3, 854. 4	2, 845. 9	1, 967. 8	357. 7
Fiber and fiber products	308. 1	1, 815. 0	1, 772. 6	1, 844. 8	1, 700. 0	1, 556. 9	966. 4	820. 9	820. 9	501. 4
Cement	398. 2	2, 052. 4	2, 136. 8	2, 461. 1	2, 894. 9	2, 902. 9	2, 410. 7	2, 695. 2	2, 279. 8	438. 8
Paper and paper products	281. 9	1, 349. 6	1, 365. 7	1, 461. 1	1, 468. 4	1, 604. 3	1, 494. 3	1, 488. 0	1, 003. 1	216. 8
	56, 519. 8	70, 951. 6	78, 337. 6	86, 718. 7	92, 095. 5	89, 770. 9	90, 739. 8	118, 695. 7	111, 453. 7	

Source: Imperial Government Railways.

Appendix Table C–98.—*Average length of haul and freight train miles*

Fiscal year	Length of haul (miles)	Freight train miles (1,000 miles)	Fiscal year	Length of haul (miles)	Freight train miles (1,000 miles)
1936	103. 7	131, 256	1941	122. 8	198, 202
1937	107. 5	144, 477	1942	133. 5	212, 058
1938	115. 3	167, 647	1943	151. 3	247, 112
1939	115. 6	181, 422	1944	160. 5	269, 798
1940	119. 2	195, 362	1945	(1)	(1)

[1] Figures for 1945 not available.

Source: Imperial Government Railways.

APPENDIX TABLE C-99.—*Japanese merchant marine (excluding tankers) during the war.* (*Combined army, navy, civilian fleets*)

Month	Situation as of first of month							Changes during the month			
	Total tonnage afloat	"A" ships in service of the army	"B" ships in service of the navy	"C" ships shipping control association		A B C consolidated fleet		Captured or salvaged	Built	Converted to tankers[1]	Reconverted to cargo[1]
				Afloat	Serviceable	Inner zone, serviceable	Unserviceable or cut off in southern area				
1941: December	5,421,143	2,150,000	1,556,600	1,714,543	1,513,600			96,101	4,929	------	------
1942:											
January	5,464,992	2,109,176	1,610,294	1,745,522	1,518,604			89,468	23,894	------	------
February	5,503,083	2,108,020	1,597,907	1,797,156	1,595,875			54,243	16,638	------	------
March	5,540,051	2,092,523	1,607,274	1,840,254	1,612,063			54,489	21,250	------	------
April	5,544,877	2,051,044	1,573,714	1,910,119	1,659,893			77,722	5,896	------	------
May	5,591,077	1,959,010	1,564,555	2,067,512	1,788,398			34,598	16,242	------	------
June	5,534,248	1,715,403	1,530,796	2,298,049	1,957,938			38,867	23,081	4,000	------
July	5,569,169	1,550,856	1,522,234	2,496,079	2,111,683			39,424	12,895	5,000	------
August	5,547,609	1,275,958	1,504,292	2,767,359	2,305,210			19,778	33,958	------	------
September	5,507,167	1,220,549	1,464,471	2,822,147	2,370,603			56,490	22,879	15,000	------
October	5,524,025	1,199,717	1,463,063	2,861,245	2,466,393			12,722	21,779	------	------
November	5,390,402	1,156,789	1,434,983	2,798,630	2,387,231			16,218	7,753	------	------
December	5,252,201	1,223,523	1,409,042	2,619,636	2,260,746			19,091	33,478	12,000	------
1943:											
January	5,219,547	1,414,695	1,462,243	2,342,609	1,953,736			15,845	7,309	30,000	------
February	5,087,659	1,342,832	1,434,604	2,310,223	1,993,722			7,889	29,945	40,000	------
March	4,990,454	1,376,614	1,400,253	2,213,587	1,846,132			5,976	91,778	20,000	------
April	4,944,600	1,380,477	1,383,160	2,180,963	1,803,656			14,612	16,838	5,000	------
May	4,862,046	1,168,525	1,339,364	2,354,157	1,963,367			8,498	14,238	5,000	------
June	4,763,634	1,152,767	1,286,364	2,324,503	1,971,179			14,518	31,322	------	------
July	4,702,449	1,173,323	1,274,552	2,254,574	1,839,732			5,969	32,095	------	------
August	4,648,216	1,188,966	1,310,485	2,148,765	1,742,648			3,888	47,118	------	------
September	4,598,417	1,161,378	1,270,765	2,166,274	1,789,342			1,893	45,417	------	------
October	4,475,490	1,160,438	1,261,192	2,053,860	1,682,111			10,835	54,913	------	------
November	4,392,732	1,112,941	1,272,526	2,007,265	1,607,819			4,828	47,857	------	------
December	4,170,825	1,019,164	1,212,194	1,939,467	1,545,755			8,080	95,328	------	------
1944:											
January	4,074,745	1,004,454	1,151,233	1,919,058	1,508,380			6,675	72,342	------	------
February	3,884,120	911,916	1,089,918	1,882,286	1,487,006				84,053	------	------
March	3,560,295	825,977	918,436	1,815,882	1,454,521			4,394	178,419	4,000	------
April	3,558,407	835,946	897,493	1,824,968	1,412,525			4,281	73,075	3,000	------
May	3,509,605	874,050	895,112	1,740,443	1,300,110			830	95,852	3,000	------
June	3,353,961	795,437	843,985	1,714,539	1,275,617				93,322	4,000	------
July	3,204,385	705,154	743,086	1,756,145	1,280,230				51,184	8,000	------
August	3,049,965	625,131	689,426	1,735,408	1,270,319			4,303	73,200	40,000	------

[1] Estimate; low or not reported.

Source: Imperial Government Railways.

September	2,874,564	603,810	664,953	1,605,801	1,167,417			9,082	103,497	60,000	
October	2,601,675	483,033	590,192	1,528,450	1,181,492				75,520	30,000	
November	2,256,873	399,137	499,736	1,358,000	995,414				87,536	30,000	
December	1,978,572	260,568	406,017	1,311,987	896,087				86,913		
1945:											
January	1,925,436	253,638	386,455	1,285,343	892,028				82,404		30,000
February	1,789,097	243,255	367,831	1,178,011	845,812			5,880	99,642		55,000
March	1,908,236	254,638	374,333	1,279,265	908,278				112,823		15,000
April	1,902,734	232,372	325,333	1,345,029	934,795	1,217,706			33,707		89,000
May	1,924,799	223,449	302,417	1,398,933	935,886	1,198,378			66,454		71,000
June	1,857,926	197,952	293,163	1,366,811	892,528	1,139,292			22,481		40,000
July	1,733,627	175,320	272,284	1,286,023	733,033	923,905			44,337		18,000
August	1,587,236	150,000	255,737	1,181,499	594,294	743,286	956,558		12,064		
August 15	1,547,418					590,860					
Total								747,487	2,307,655	(¹)	

177

APPENDIX TABLE C–99.—*Japanese merchant marine (excluding tankers) during the war.* (*Combined army, navy, civilian fleets*)—Continued

Month	Changes during the month			Total weight of ammunition expended by United States against shipping	Principal war developments affecting shipping	
	Requisitioned of army and navy	Released by army and navy	Sunk		Allied action	Japanese action
1941: December	64,936	973	57,181	22		Pearl Harbor, occupation of Manila, Hongkong, Singapore, etc., capture of much foreign ship tonnage.
1942:						
January	26,343	544	75,271	26		
February	26,172		33,913	42		
March	6,838	973	70,913	56		Condition of "Operations of the First Period."
April	4,605	85,157	37,418	29		
May	7,905	202,233	97,669	71	Battle of the Coral Sea	Army begins to release ships.
June	11,225	152,539	33,027	27	Battle of Midway	Japs take Kiska and Attu.
July	23,543	263,618	68,879	32		Navy takes over merchant shipbuilding.
August	31,997	51,965	94,178	80	Guadalcanal landing	
September	18,592		47,511	48		
October	30,467	10,420	168,124	102		Attempts to reinforce Guadalcanal.
November	192,170	17,111	162,172	248		
December	292,201		73,223	286		
1943:						
January	18,519	534	125,042	280		Concentration on reinforcement, southern area.
February	67,407	4,422	95,039	211		
March	87,997		123,608	180	"Battle of the Bismarck Sea"	
April	525	181,321	109,004	291		Ceiling of 1,150,000 tons set on army shipping.
May	77,390		116,148	121	Reconquest of Attu	
June	96,144		107,025	198		
July	24,199	28,337	92,297	387		
August	89,890	4,394	100,805	289		
September	53,334		170,237	304	Submarine offensive stepped up	
October	45,668		148,506	416		
November		10,262	274,592	517		Beginning of Singapore convoys.
December	50,621		199,488	691		
1944:						
January	60,046	1,361	269,642	848		
February	81,434	993	407,878	689	Carrier raid on Truk	
March	152,890	3,044	180,701	688		Peak of cargo ship deliveries.
April	126,940	3,576	123,158	789	Carrier raid on Palau	Reinforcement of inner defense.
May	57,071	1,522	249,326	316		

Month	(12)	(13)	(14)	(15)	Events	Remarks
June	19,492	509	238,898	579	Invasion of the Marianas	Conversion of cargo ships to tankers.
July	23,301	5,289	197,604	707		Reinforcement of Philippines, Formosa, and South China.
August	51,750	------	212,904	441	Pre-invasion carrier raids around Philippines.	200,000 tons civilian shipping diverted to Philippines.
September	19,087	7,961	325,468	997		
October	5,131	2,274	390,322	1,616	Carrier support of Leyte landings	Attempted reinforcement of Leyte.
November	11,056	9,905	335,837	1,411	Carrier screen of Philippines	
December	47,000	5,935	140,049	402		
1945:						
January	50,531	------	248,743	962	Carrier raid, South China Sea.	Reconversion of tankers to cargo,
February	28,861	887	41,383	256	Iwo Jima landing	Termination of Singapore convoys.
March	12,271	------	133,325	2,068	Large scale city raids.	Concentration of food imports.
April	3,084	------	100,642	1,333	B-29 minelaying campaign Okinawa landing.	
May	1,746	4,879	204,327	3,052	Navy privateer planes Korean waters	Consolidation of AB&C shipping.
June	------	------	186,780	3,222	Submarines in the sea of Japan.	Ship repair difficulties.
July	------	547	208,728	3,747	Carrier raids Japanese home waters.	Paralysis of shipping.
August	------	12,361	51,882	1,958	Atom bombs, Russia in war, complete air cover.	Surrender.
August 15	------	------	------	------		
Total			6,928,867			

1 Estimates.

Column 1. Beginning with a figure representing USSBS appraisal of the Japanese merchant fleet on Pearl Harbor Day, subsequent monthly figures are arrived at by adding algebraically columns 8, 9, 10, 11, and 14.

Column 2. Beginning with tonnage known to be in service of the Army on Pearl Harbor Day, this column is arrived at by adding and subtracting known requisitions, releases, and losses by the Army, adjusted slightly to reconcile differences in information.

Column 3. Same for the Navy.

Column 4. Column 1 minus columns 2 and 3.

Column 5. Column 4 minus a figure for tonnage under repair or out of service and in need of repair computed by USSBS from various Japanese sources.

Column 6. Beginning with the known situation at war's end from Japanese sources, working backward from USSBS sources or ship damage, an approximate reconstruction of total tonnage.

Column 7. USSBS compilation of situation as of war's end.

Column 8. USSBS compilation of information from various sources. Where exact date of recommissioning unknown (about 20 percent) ships were apportioned in proportion to known dates of recommissioning of other ships.

Column 9. USSBS Military Supplies Division, Shipbuilding Section. Included are only cargo, cargo-passenger, passenger, and some few special types. Fishing vessels and tugs and barges are not included.

Column 10. Estimates based on changes in the tanker situation.

Column 11. Same source.

Column 12. Sum of Japanese Army and Navy reports of ships requisitioned.

Column 13. Sum of Japanese Army and Navy reports of ships released to civilians.

Column 14. USSBS Ship Sinking List expanded by 2 percent to reconcile discrepancy between Pearl Harbor tonnage, war's end tonnage, and other contributing factors, together with belief that Ship Sinking List is only somewhere between 95 and 98 percent complete.

Column 15. Total tonnage of bombs, mines, and torpedoes from Appendix 5.

APPENDIX TABLE C–100.—*Annual construction of 4 main categories of steel merchant ships in Japanese shipyards, 1931–41*

[In gross tons]

Year	Passenger	Passenger-cargo	Cargo	Tankers	Total	Year	Passenger	Passenger-cargo	Cargo	Tankers	Total
1931	1,038	302	67,384	29,366	98,090	1938	1,781	11,223	294,235	42,540	349,779
1932	4,558	18,094	15,955	236	38,843	1939		49,790	214,145	56,531	320,466
1933	937	13,599	46,627		61,163	1940	3,500	82,194	194,418	12,500	293,612
1934	7,112	15,800	93,839	19,283	136,034	1941		40,397	156,596	13,380	210,373
1935	3,071	20,482	98,389	17,972	139,914						
1936	2,472	35,622	126,031	56,739	220,864	Total	25,944	351,356	1,579,315	286,424	2,242,039
1937	1,475	63,853	271,696	36,877	373,901						

Source: Individual shipyards (98 percent coverage).

APPENDIX TABLE C–101.—*Japanese merchant fleet as of Pearl Harbor Day*

Tons	Kisen (over 500 tons)				Small ships					
	Cargo, No.	Psgr. misc. GRT	Tankers		No.	GRT	Kisen No.	GRT	Kihansen No.	GRT
			No.	GRT						
20–100									15,851	742,935
100–500							841	203,512	2,930	442,163
500–1,000	264	198,036	20	12,770	284	210,806			3	1,710
1,000–3,000	527	1,055,224	10	15,740	537	1,070,964			5	10,543
3,000–6,000	486	2,330,577	13	61,379	499	2,391,956				
6,000–10,000	219	1,603,219	32	253,458	251	1,856,677				
Over 10,000	19	234,087	19	232,117	38	466,204				
Total	1,515	5,421,143	94	575,464	1,609	5,996,607	841	203,512	18,789	1,197,351

Source: Shipping Control Association.

APPENDIX TABLE C–102.—*Japanese merchant ship construction during the war (monthly deliveries in gross tons)*

[Ships over 500 tons]

Month and year	Cargo, passenger, and miscellaneous		Tankers		Total	
	No. ships	Tonnage	No. ships	Tonnage	No. ships	Tonnage
1941: December	3	4,929	1	975	4	5,904
Total	3	4,929	1	975	4	5,904
1942:						
January	4	23,894			4	23,894
February	7	16,638			7	16,638
March	8	21,250			8	21,250
April	3	5,896	1	1,186	4	7,082
May	6	16,242			6	16,242
June	6	23,081			6	23,081
July	5	12,895			5	12,895
August	5	33,958	2	6,416	7	40,374
September	8	22,879			8	22,879
October	5	21,779	1	572	6	22,351

APPENDIX TABLE C-102.—*Japanese merchant ship construction during the war (monthly deliveries in gross tons)*—Con.

Month and year	Cargo, passenger, and miscellaneous		Tankers		Total	
	No. ships	Tonnage	No. ships	Tonnage	No. ships	Tonnage
1942—Continued						
November	3	7, 753			3	7, 753
December	10	33, 478	3	12, 142	13	45, 620
Total	70	239, 743	7	20, 316	77	260, 059
1943:						
January	5	7, 309	1	5, 240	6	12, 549
February	12	29, 945	4	13, 009	16	42, 954
March	24	91, 778	4	16, 666	28	108, 444
April	8	16, 838			8	16, 838
May	5	14, 238	4	17, 077	9	31, 315
June	14	31, 322	3	16, 678	17	48, 000
July	12	32, 095	3	31, 871	15	63, 966
August	19	47, 118	3	15, 365	22	62, 483
September	19	45, 417	8	43, 388	27	88, 805
October	23	54, 913	.4	25, 499	27	80, 412
November	22	47, 857	9	39, 421	31	87, 278
December	37	95, 328	11	30, 713	48	126, 041
Total	200	514, 158	54	254, 927	254	769, 085
1944:						
January	45	72, 342	10	35, 874	55	108, 216
February	39	84, 053	14	40, 849	53	124, 902
March	67	178, 419	22	78, 031	89	256, 450
April	31	73, 075	4	10, 108	35	83, 183
May	40	95, 852	23	66, 387	63	162, 239
June	38	93, 322	18	49, 060	56	142, 382
July	33	51, 184	17	55, 428	50	106, 612
August	36	73, 200	18	28, 688	54	101, 888
September	44	103, 497	22	81, 724	66	185, 221
October	42	75, 520	18	69, 155	60	144, 675
November	43	87, 536	21	62, 295	64	149, 831
December	41	86, 913	17	46, 691	58	133, 604
Total	499	1, 074, 913	204	624, 290	703	1, 699, 203
1945:						
January	33	82, 404	14	31, 015	47	113, 419
February	35	99, 642	11	40, 730	46	140, 372
March	34	112, 823	3	13, 906	37	126, 729
April	14	33, 707			14	33, 707
May	21	66, 454			21	66, 454
June	5	22, 481			5	22, 481
July	13	44, 337			13	44, 337
August	5	12, 064			5	12, 064
Total	160	473, 912	28	85, 651	188	559, 563
Grand total	932	2, 307, 655	294	986, 159	1, 226	3, 293, 814

Source: Individual shipyards (95 percent coverage).

Construction of Kihansen during the war [1]

	70–150 G/T		200–500 G/T		Total	
	No.	G/T	No.	G/T	No.	G/T
1943:						
March	1	100			1	100
April	1	70			1	70
May	5	460			5	460
June	4	420	1	250	5	670
July	22	1, 990	1	250	23	2, 240
August	46	4, 150	9	2, 250	55	6, 400
September	85	8, 690	4	1, 000	89	9, 690
October	96	9, 510	9	2, 150	105	11, 660
November	100	10, 240	1	250	101	10, 490
December	86	9, 480	14	3, 450	100	12, 930
Total	446	45, 110	39	9, 600	485	54, 710
1944:						
January	51	5, 170	7	1, 750	58	6, 920
February	80	7, 130	20	4, 650	100	11, 780
March	65	4, 760	44	9, 200	109	13, 960
April	52	5, 090	7	1, 750	59	6, 840
May	153	17, 160	35	8, 750	188	25, 910
June	320	34, 100	103	25, 050	423	59, 150
July	236	26, 240	88	21, 800	324	48, 040
August	83	9, 460	38	9, 350	121	18, 810
September	75	8, 650	35	8, 750	110	17, 400
October	78	9, 210	27	6, 750	105	15, 960
November	65	7, 390	30	7, 550	95	14, 940
December	61	7, 310	30	7, 500	91	14, 810
Total	1, 319	141, 670	464	112, 850	1, 783	254, 520
1945:						
January	37	4, 600	16	4, 000	53	8, 600
February	36	4, 550	27	6, 750	63	11, 300
March	69	7, 740	35	8, 650	104	16, 390
April	456	7, 300	22	5, 500	478	12, 800
May	24	2, 720	16	4, 250	40	6, 970
June	32	3, 850	17	4, 300	49	8, 150
July	21	2, 370	16	4, 000	37	6, 370
August	6	900	3	750	9	1, 650
Total	681	34, 030	152	38, 200	833	72, 230
Grand total	2, 446	220, 810	655	160, 650	3, 101	381, 460

[1] Kihansen are the Japanese variety of oriental junk, built of wood, equipped with power and seldom exceeding 150 tons. They are to be distinguished from the Kisen which are European style steamships usually of over 500 G/T.

Source: Transport ministry.

Appendix Table C–103.—*Wartime history of Japanese tanker fleet*

Month	Tonnage afloat first of month	In serviceable condition—first	Importing oil into Japan	Servicing the army—overseas	Servicing the navy (not counting fleet oilers)	In local use around Japan	In need of repairs, repairing or converting (estimate)	Converted during month [1]	Built during month	Captured or salvaged	Sunk during month	Tonnage afloat at end of month
1941: December	575,464	510,464	0	13,480	160,000	336,984	65,000	--------	975	10,806	-------	587,245
1942:												
January	587,245	516,116	0	13,480	160,000	342,636	71,129	--------	-------	10,778	-------	598,023
February	598,023	539,070	0	13,480	160,000	365,590	58,953	--------	-------	8,014	-------	606,037
March	606,037	560,647	0	13,480	160,000	387,167	45,390	--------	-------	7,601	8,653	604,985
April	604,985	556,976	0	13,480	160,000	383,496	48,009	--------	1,186	1,158	-------	607,329
May	607,329	579,285	256,140	13,480	160,000	149,665	28,044	--------	-------	-------	904	606,425
June	606,425	554,170	256,140	13,480	160,000	124,550	52,255	+4,000	-------	1,458	-------	611,883
July	611,883	552,793	272,313	13,480	160,000	107,000	59,090	+5,000	-------	7,981	-------	624,864
August	624,864	554,117	294,637	13,480	160,000	86,000	70,747	--------	6,416	-------	-------	631,280
September	631,280	544,828	306,348	13,480	160,000	65,000	86,452	+15,000	-------	2,088	-------	648,368
October	648,368	618,560	402,080	13,480	160,000	43,000	29,808	--------	572	13,416	-------	662,356
November	662,356	594,895	402,080	13,480	160,000	19,335	67,461	--------	-------	-------	-------	662,356
December	662,356	622,335	428,855	13,480	160,000	20,000	40,021	+12,000	12,142	-------	-------	686,498
1943:												
January	686,498	650,029	444,549	13,480	172,000	20,000	36,469	+30,000	5,240	6,197	-------	727,935
February	727,935	677,210	471,730	13,480	172,000	20,000	50,725	+40,000	13,009	-------	-------	780,944
March	780,944	728,972	534,492	13,480	161,000	20,000	51,972	+20,000	16,666	-------	29,448	788,162
April	788,162	740,783	533,833	12,950	174,000	20,000	47,379	+5,000	-------	-------	24,965	768,197
May	768,197	701,921	493,971	12,950	175,000	20,000	66,276	+5,000	17,077	-------	17,604	772,670
June	772,670	712,185	501,235	12,950	178,000	20,000	60,485	-------	16,678	-------	4,197	785,151
July	785,151	747,285	536,335	12,950	178,000	20,000	37,866	-------	31,871	-------	-------	817,022
August	817,022	756,300	551,350	12,950	172,000	20,000	60,722	-------	15,365	-------	-------	832,387
September	832,387	753,131	547,181	12,950	173,000	20,000	79,256	-------	43,388	-------	31,069	844,706
October	844,706	770,560	563,610	12,950	174,000	20,000	74,146	--------	25,499	-------	-------	870,205
November	870,205	815,491	614,541	12,950	168,000	20,000	54,714	-------	39,421	-------	45,673	863,953
December	863,953	811,220	606,270	12,950	172,000	20,000	52,733	--------	30,713	-------	21,596	873,070
1944:												
January	873,070	753,769	558,819	12,950	162,000	20,000	119,301	--------	35,874	6,079	75,447	839,576
February	839,576	787,497	594,547	12,950	160,000	20,000	52,079	--------	40,849	-------	119,918	760,507
March	760,507	728,146	588,196	12,950	107,000	20,000	32,361	+4,000	78,031	-------	48,705	793,833
April	793,833	767,539	643,589	12,950	91,000	20,000	26,294	+3,000	10,108	-------	8,119	798,822
May	798,822	768,625	644,675	12,950	91,000	20,000	30,197	+3,000	66,387	-------	32,851	835,358
June	835,358	770,647	627,697	12,950	110,000	20,000	64,711	+4,000	49,060	-------	51,092	837,326
July	837,326	766,127	633,177	12,950	100,000	20,000	71,199	+8,000	55,428	-------	48,019	852,735
August	852,735	777,957	645,007	12,950	100,000	20,000	74,778	+40,000	28,688	-------	85,541	835,882
September	835,882	762,640	640,690	12,950	89,000	20,000	73,242	+60,000	81,724	-------	105,273	872,333
October	872,333	806,533	693,583	12,950	80,000	20,000	65,800	+30,000	69,155	-------	132,541	838,947
November	838,947	759,881	667,241	2,640	70,000	20,000	79,066	+30,000	62,295	-------	62,280	868,962
December	868,962	803,019	716,379	2,640	64,000	20,000	65,943	--------	46,691	-------	54,682	860,971
1945:												
January	860,971	787,911	700,000	2,640	60,000	25,271	73,060	-30,000	31,015	-------	182,002	679,984
February	679,984	541,245	388,605	2,640	50,000	100,000	138,739	-55,000	40,730	-------	46,966	618,748
March	618,748	522,606	150,000	2,640	35,000	334,966	96,142	-15,000	13,906	-------	55,518	562,136
April	562,136	441,028	100,000	2,640	30,000	308,388	121,108	-89,000	-------	-------	13,059	460,077
May	460,077	351,758	[2]70,000	2,640	27,000	252,118	108,319	-71,000	-------	-------	11,237	377,840
June	377,840	255,893	[2]65,000	2,640	27,000	161,253	121,947	-40,000	-------	-------	13,058	324,782
July	324,782	204,247	[2]50,000	2,640	25,000	126,607	120,535	-18,000	-------	-------	31,257	275,525
August	275,525	101,196	[2]35,000	2,640	25,000	38,556	174,329	--------	-------	-------	8,577	266,948
15 August	266,948	86,287	[2]25,000	------	------	------	------	--------	-------	-------	-------	------

[1] Estimate.   [2] Cut off in the Southern Area.

Source: Shipping Section, Transportation Division, USSBS.

APPENDIX TABLE C–104.—*Japanese merchant marine at the end of the war* (*Kisken*)

Location and condition	100–500 tons		500–1,000 tons		1,000–3,000 tons		3,000–6,000 tons	
	Number of ships	Tonnage	Number of ships	Tonnage	Number of ships	Tonnage	Number of ships	Tonnage
Inner zone (north of Shanghai):								
Damaged and beached			47	40, 880	35	67, 094	7	26, 084
Damaged heavily	1	267	37	31, 435	22	44, 486	4	14, 228
Damaged slightly (but unserviceable)	1	150	47	41, 193	25	52, 336	7	26, 581
Damaged (extent unknown but unserviceable)	16	4, 336	128	109, 431	26	58, 210	4	18, 526
Total damaged	18	4, 753	259	222, 939	108	222, 126	22	85, 419
Total serviceable	141	38, 781	193	160, 295	78	136, 543	20	73, 689
Total afloat	159	43, 534	452	383, 234	186	358, 669	42	159, 108
Outer zone (south of Shanghai):								
Damaged and beached			1	835	1	1, 398		
Damaged heavily	1	494	2	1, 755	3	8, 097	1	3, 252
Damaged slightly (but unserviceable)			1	873	2	4, 817		
Damaged (extent unknown but unserviceable)	2	632	4	3, 528	6	11, 242	4	21, 655
Total damaged	3	1, 126	8	6, 991	12	25, 554	5	24, 907
Total serviceable	14	4, 341	28	22, 054	17	31, 519	5	19, 419
Total afloat	17	5, 467	36	29, 045	29	57, 073	10	44, 326
Grand total:								
Total damaged	21	5, 879	267	229, 930	120	247, 680	27	110, 326
Total serviceable	155	43, 122	221	182, 349	95	168, 062	25	93, 108
Total afloat	176	49, 001	488	412, 279	215	415, 742	52	203, 434

Location and condition	6,000–10,000		Over 10,000		Total		
	Number of ships	Tonnage	Number of ships	Tonnage	Number of ships	Tonnage [1]	Percent
Inner zone (north of Shanghai):							
Damaged and beached_____	9	67, 790	1	10, 241	99	212, 089	12. 5
Damaged heavily_____	20	143, 163	2	20, 650	86	254, 229	14. 9
Damaged slightly (but unserviceable)____	15	102, 174	3	38, 855	98	261, 289	15. 2
Damaged (extent unknown but unserviceable)_____	10	67, 584	3	30, 524	187	288, 611	16. 9
Total damaged_____	54	380, 711	9	100, 270	470	1, 016, 218	59. 5
Total serviceable_____	33	240, 059	4	41, 711	469	691, 078	40. 5
Total afloat_____	87	620, 770	13	141, 981	939	1, 707, 296	100. 0
Outer zone (south of Shanghai):							
Damaged and beached_____	_____	_____	1	10, 240	3	12, 473	6. 8
Damaged heavily_____	5	37, 361	_____	_____	12	50, 959	27. 8
Damaged slightly (but unserviceable)____	_____	_____	_____	_____	3	5, 690	3. 1
Damaged (extent unknown but unserviceable)_____	_____	_____	_____	_____	16	37, 057	20. 2
Total damaged_____	5	37, 361	1	10, 240	34	106, 179	57. 9
Total serviceable_____	0	0	0		64	77, 333	42. 1
Total afloat_____	5	37, 361	1	10, 240	98	183, 512	100. 0
Grand total:							
Total damaged_____	59	418, 072	10	110, 510	504	1, 122, 397	59. 4
Total serviceable_____	33	240, 059	4	41, 711	533	768, 411	40. 6
Total afloat_____	92	658, 131	14	152, 221	1, 037	1, 890, 808	100. 0

[1] Add Kihansen being operated by the Shipping Control Council as of 15 August 1945: 3,105 vessels—241,413 gross tons.

Source: Shipping Division, USSBS.

APPENDIX TABLE C–105.—*Foreign trade of Japan, 1900–1943*

[In 1,000 yen]

Year	Exports	Imports	Total	Year	Exports	Imports	Total
1900	204, 429	287, 261	491, 690	1922	1, 637, 451	1, 890, 308	3, 527, 759
1901	252, 349	255, 816	508, 165	1923	1, 447, 750	1, 982, 230	3, 429, 980
1902	258, 303	271, 731	530, 034	1924	1, 807, 034	2, 453, 402	4, 260, 436
1903	289, 502	317, 135	606, 637	1925	2, 305, 589	2, 572, 657	4, 878, 246
1904	319, 260	371, 360	690, 620	1926	2, 004, 727	2, 377, 484	4, 382, 211
1905	321, 533	488, 538	810, 071	1927	1, 992, 317	2, 179, 153	4, 171, 470
1906	423, 754	418, 784	842, 538	1928	1, 971, 955	2, 196, 314	4, 168, 269
1907	432, 412	494, 467	926, 879	1929	2, 148, 618	2, 216, 240	4, 364, 858
1908	378, 245	436, 257	814, 502	1930	1, 469, 852	1, 546, 070	3, 015, 922
1909	413, 112	394, 198	807, 310	1931	1, 146, 981	1, 235, 675	2, 382, 656
1910	458, 428	464, 233	922, 661	1932	1, 409, 992	1, 431, 461	2, 841, 453
1911	447, 433	513, 805	961, 238	1933	1, 861, 045	1, 917, 219	3, 778, 264
1912	526, 981	618, 992	1, 145, 973	1934	2, 171, 924	2, 282, 601	4, 454, 525
1913	632, 460	729, 431	1, 361, 891	1935	2, 499, 072	2, 472, 235	4, 971, 307
1914	591, 101	595, 735	1, 186, 836	1936	2, 692, 976	2, 763, 681	5, 456, 657
1915	703, 306	532, 449	1, 235, 755	1937	3, 175, 418	3, 783, 177	6, 958, 595
1916	1, 127, 468	756, 427	1, 883, 895	1938	2, 689, 000	2, 663, 440	5, 352, 440
1917	1, 603, 005	1, 035, 811	2, 638, 816	1939	3, 576, 370	2, 917, 666	6, 494, 036
1918	1, 962, 100	1, 668, 143	3, 630, 243	1940	3, 655, 850	3, 452, 725	7, 108, 575
1919	2, 098, 872	2, 173, 459	4, 272, 331	1941	2, 650, 865	2, 898, 565	5, 549, 430
1920	1, 948, 394	2, 336, 174	4, 284, 568	1942	1, 792, 547	1, 751, 637	3, 544, 184
1921	1, 252, 837	1, 614, 154	2, 866, 991	1943	1, 627, 350	1, 924, 350	3, 551, 700

Source: "Diamond" Yearbook, Japan Yearbook, Orient Yearbook.

APPENDIX TABLE C-106.—*Japanese imports of bulk commodities, 1940–45*

Product	1940 Metric tons	1940 Percent	1941 Metric tons	1941 Percent	1942 Metric tons	1942 Percent	1943 Metric tons	1943 Percent	1944 Metric tons	1944 Percent	1945 Metric tons	1945 Percent
Coal	7,011,000	99.9	6,459,000	100.0	6,388,000	100.0	5,181,000	100.0	2,635,000	100.0	548,000	100.0
Iron ore	6,073,000	100.0	6,309,000	100.0	4,700,000	100.0	4,298,000	100.0	2,153,000	100.0	341,000	100.0
Bauxite	275,000	100.0	150,000	100.0	305,000	100.0	909,000	100.0	376,000	100.0	15,500	100.0
Iron and steel	621,000	----	921,000	----	993,000	----	997,000	----	1,097,000	----	170,000	----
Scrap iron	2,104,000	----	246,000	----	50,000	----	43,000	----	21,000	----	12,000	----
Lead	100,100	----	86,530	----	10,990	----	24,880	----	16,810	----	4,000	----
Tin	10,500	----	5,500	----	3,800	----	26,800	----	23,500	----	3,600	----
Zinc	23,500	----	7,900	----	8,500	----	10,100	----	6,100	----	2,500	----
Phosphorite and phosphate	710,400	----	396,500	----	342,100	----	236,700	----	89,600	----	23,000	----
Dolomite and magnesite	409,600	----	506,300	----	468,700	----	437,500	----	287,100	----	65,900	----
Salt	1,728,300	----	1,438,900	----	1,499,800	----	1,425,100	----	989,700	----	386,900	----
Soybean cake	333,900	----	337,700	----	449,500	----	304,500	----	384,700	----	163,400	----
Soybeans	648,500	----	572,400	----	698,800	----	590,600	----	728,800	----	606,900	----
Rice and paddy	1,694,000	----	2,232,700	----	2,629,200	----	1,135,800	----	783,200	----	151,200	----
Other grains and flours	269,300	----	267,400	----	823,300	----	750,100	----	506,600	----	231,400	----
Raw rubber	27,500	----	67,600	----	31,400	----	42,100	----	31,500	----	17,900	----
Total	22,039,600	----	20,004,430	----	19,402,090	----	16,412,180	----	10,129,610	----	2,743,200	----

Source: Shipping Control Association, Ministry of Commerce and Industry, Transport Ministry, control associations for each commodity, Ministry of Agriculture and Forestry.

APPENDIX TABLE C-107.—Quantity and value of Japanese imports of selected commodities, 1936–43

Commodity	Quantity and value in units	1936	1937	1938	1939	1940	1941	1942	1943
Rice and paddy	Picul [1]	923,237	557,622	378,275	729,441	20,815,523	24,014,888	23,034,184	12,539,152
	Yen	5,098,071	4,032,976	2,807,791	6,286,329	196,006,260	265,481,235	242,625,231	126,347,776
Beans and peas	Picul	12,445,184	12,321,144	13,884,618	13,727,012	8,120,562	8,576,096	10,812,637	4,645,449
	Yen	62,601,112	92,547,363	102,175,975	123,575,994	112,756,842	119,489,724	154,150,813	126,505,302
Seeds, oil-yielding	Picul	5,413,458	4,792,176	3,167,080	2,660,999	2,564,990	3,977,730	1,645,688	2,357,928
	Yen	44,873,079	43,612,048	28,790,494	31,981,686	44,317,128	59,234,406	29,255,471	127,973,191
Salt	Picul	22,039,941	28,148,491	23,805,966	31,408,378	28,578,090	24,142,090	23,245,452	20,087,966
	Yen	17,761,167	28,910,743	30,290,099	41,515,318	63,861,315	52,988,267	55,162,243	50,877,282
Hides and skins	Picul	512,714	687,511	489,473	507,473	504,125	624,334	485,402	264,065
	Yen	24,835,752	44,571,498	27,826,209	30,573,244	32,759,036	43,595,919	38,373,939	22,212,363
Oil, hydrocarbon	Picul							361,183	
	Yen				253,625,063	352,460,219	336,247,149	23,988,918	83,959,966
Cotton, raw	Picul	15,211,168	13,764,913	9,378,454	10,093,418	7,758,441	5,967,811	2,029,709	1,544,678
	Yen	850,451,600	851,162,644	436,834,585	462,006,980	504,070,899	392,261,861	224,305,572	266,300,592
Wool, sheep's	Picul	1,640,636	1,953,835	881,889	801,688	770,089	906,924	142,006	58,863
	Yen	200,898,493	298,406,862	94,425,569	72,590,259	105,251,143	124,066,572	25,883,717	7,211,811
Fiber, vegetable	Picul	2,158,219	1,866,653	1,261,597	1,415,946	1,433,331	938,531	645,814	876,227
	Yen	37,300,937	40,994,972	27,305,564	38,266,314	40,688,364	27,756,899	27,525,194	38,813,750
Fiber, waste of old	Picul	332,141	288,226	277,435	296,186	243,694	211,927	142,996	138,290
	Yen	8,130,911	7,835,781	6,371,001	12,073,929	13,187,995	16,973,272	18,667,778	9,305,869
Pulp	Picul	5,528,532	7,901,727	2,434,819	2,834,939	2,933,167	958,133	167,234	31,134
	Yen	67,107,057	116,719,852	42,131,502	56,537,329	16,107,816	23,717,784	3,797,357	708,813
Phosphorite	Picul	13,830,204	15,371,942	9,402,824	13,049,847	11,840,882	6,608,702	1,741,499	1,862,528
	Yen	22,392,699	30,810,382	19,281,443	25,411,705	41,867,628	21,983,387	5,042,850	5,894,184
Coal	L. ton	4,134,352	4,356,465	3,682,531	3,794,710	5,085,013	5,187,771	5,162,826	4,416,636
	Yen	51,055,577	59,224,254	67,217,482	78,363,522	116,731,648	143,025,556	159,556,151	162,386,289
Dolomite and magnesite	Picul	2,564,224	3,588,032	4,501,293	6,498,341	6,295,345	7,223,182	6,561,126	6,042,582
	Yen	2,349,204	3,484,491	6,067,067	9,711,790	18,818,151	19,846,654	22,436,397	26,455,408
Ores	M. ton				5,228,274	5,584,189	5,572,895	8,840,605	4,568,187
	Yen	374,891,804	901,130,824	661,894,693	158,715,007	204,044,034	197,029,434	126,082,883	143,147,966
Iron	Picul	49,529,815	76,517,602	45,448,162	59,679,967	42,461,185	17,013,195	15,037,040	8,149,471
	Yen	192,039,892	563,840,508	321,294,638	380,659,437	385,780,864	157,930,662	161,841,452	118,172,591
Lead	Picul	1,598,533	1,645,410	1,013,149	1,683,350	1,534,834	1,308,865	12,006	53,010
	Yen	26,873,028	41,975,913	17,618,496	29,140,404	32,417,539	29,783,117	423,051	2,449,666
Tin	Picul	115	114,163	145,753	132,738	181,147	91,342	37	161,756
	Yen	15,425	27,228,830	29,165,741	30,579,243	47,102,041	25,315,783	33,363	41,419,905
Zinc	Picul	1,029,569	1,080,164	778,165	1,012,457	391,223	105,315	56,811	57,358
	Yen	16,427,760	24,569,452	16,061,772	17,137,561	12,604,929	4,738,083	3,562,988	4,058,414
Amures	Picul	10,085,783	9,545,378	11,638,347		7,765,088	7,675,591	8,768,196	5,087,682
	Yen	44,028,171	48,120,841	62,712,748	108,095,527	76,864,554	66,994,509	81,139,368	68,439,442
Other	Yen	694,549,738	554,042,056	663,166,579	950,819,724	985,025,366	770,105,050	347,782,254	491,709,647
Total imports	Yen	2,763,681,477	3,783,222,290	2,663,439,448	2,917,666,365	3,402,723,771	2,898,565,323	1,751,636,990	1,924,350,227

[1] A picul is equal to 60 kilograms or 132 lbs.

Source: Shipping Control Association, Ministry of Commerce and Industry, Transport Ministry, control associations for each commodity, Ministry of Agriculture and Forestry.

Appendix Table C–108.—*Japanese imports of coal, 1940–45*

Country of origin	Quantity											
	1940		1941		1942		1943		1944		1945	
	Metric tons	Percent	Metric tons	Percent	Metric tons	Percent	Metric tons	Percent	Metric tons	Percent	Metric tons	Percent
Total, inner zone countries	6,535,000	93.2	6,109,000	94.6	5,967,000	93.4	5,036,000	97.2	2,635,000	100.0	548,000	100.0
Manchukuo	872,000	12.4	650,000	10.1	631,000	9.9	426,000	8.2	512,000	19.4	201,000	36.7
China	3,819,000	54.4	4,128,000	63.8	4,362,000	68.3	3,923,000	75.7	1,863,000	70.7	270,000	49.3
Formosa	284,000	4.1	94,000	1.5	134,000	2.1	30,000	0.6	------	-----	------	-----
Korea	1,560,000	22.3	1,237,000	19.2	840,000	13.1	657,000	12.7	260,000	9.9	77,000	14.0
Total, southern area	431,000	6.1	350,000	5.4	421,000	6.6	145,000	2.8	------	-----	------	-----
French Indochina	431,000	6.1	350,000	5.4	421,000	6.6	145,000	2.8	------	-----	------	-----
Total, other	45,000	0.6	------	-----	------	-----	------	-----	------	-----	------	-----
Grand total	7,011,000	99.9	6,459,000	100.0	6,388,000	100.0	5,181,000	100.0	2,635,000	100.0	548,000	100.0

Source: Coal Control Association, Shipping Control Association, Ministry of Commerce and Industry, Transport Ministry.

Appendix Table C–109.—*Japanese imports of iron ore, 1940–45*

Country of origin	Quantity											
	1940		1941		1942		1943		1944		1945	
	Metric tons	Percent	Metric tons	Percent	Metric tons	Percent	Metric tons	Percent	Metric tons	Percent	Metric tons	Percent
Total, inner-zone countries	1,944,000	32.0	3,359,000	53.3	4,485,000	95.4	4,027,000	93.7	2,057,000	95.5	314,000	92.0
China	1,400,000	23.1	2,500,000	39.7	3,615,000	76.9	3,725,000	86.7	1,457,000	67.6	75,000	22.0
Manchukuo	55,000	0.9	50,000	0.8	93,000	2.0	3,000	0.1	17,000	0.8	3,000	0.8
Formosa	69,000	1.1	51,000	0.8	32,000	0.7	57,000	1.3	------	-----	------	-----
Korea	420,000	6.9	758,000	12.0	745,000	15.8	242,000	5.6	583,000	27.1	236,000	69.2
Total, southern area	3,288,000	54.1	2,136,000	33.9	215,000	4.6	271,000	6.3	96,000	4.5	27,000	8.0
Philippines	[1]1,209,000	19.9	[1]910,000	14.4	55,000	1.2	85,000	2.0	49,000	2.3	------	-----
Malaya	2,032,000	33.4	1,182,000	18.8	97,000	2.0	173,000	4.0	47,000	2.2	27,000	8.0
French Indochina	47,000	0.8	44,000	0.7	55,000	1.2	13,000	0.3	------	-----	------	-----
Siam	------	-----	------	-----	8,000	0.2	------	-----	------	-----	------	-----
Total, other	841,000	13.9	814,000	[2]12.8	------	-----	------	-----	------	-----	------	-----
Grand total	6,073,000	100.0	6,309,000	[2]100.0	4,700,000	100.0	4,298,000	100.0	2,153,000	100.0	341,000	100.0

[1] Basic Materials Division sources give these figures as about 615,000 and 455,000 tons, respectively, for the comparable fiscal years; part of the difference is explained by the fact that the above figures are for calendar years but the figures remain at substantial variance.

[2] Basic Materials Division sources give these figures as 101,000 and 3,058,000 tons, respectively, for the 1941 fiscal year. Most of the difference is explained by the difference in year as most of the imports from India and other sources were stopped early in 1941.

Source: Iron and Steel Control Association, Shipping Control Association, Transport Ministry, Ministry of Commerce and Industry.

APPENDIX TABLE C-110.—*Japanese imports of bauxite, 1940–45*

Country of origin	Quantity											
	1940		1941		1942		1943		1944		1945	
	Metric tons	Per-cent	Metric tons	Per-cent	Metric tons	Per-cent	Metric tons	Per-cent	Metric tons	Per-cent	Metric tons	Per-cent
Total, southern area countries__	[1] 275, 000	100. 0	[1] 150, 000	100. 0	305, 000	100. 0	909, 000	100. 0	376, 000	100. 0	15, 500	100. 0
Netherland East Indies__					211, 000	69. 2	803, 000	88. 3	357, 000	94. 9	15, 500	100. 0
Palau__					94, 000	30. 8	106, 000	11. 7	19, 000	5. 1		
Grand total_____	275, 000	100. 0	150, 000	100. 0	305, 000	100. 0	909, 000	100. 0	376, 000	100. 0	15, 500	100. 0

[1] No break-down available on prewar imports.

Source: Shipping Control Association, Transport Ministry, Ministry of Commerce and Industry.

APPENDIX TABLE C-111.—*Japanese imports of iron and steel, 1940–45.*

Country of origin	Quantity											
	1940		1941		1942		1943		1944		1945	
	Metric tons	Per-cent	Metric tons	Per-cent	Metric tons	Per-cent	Metric tons	Per-cent	Metric tons	Per-cent	Metric tons	Per-cent
Total, inner zone countries_____	621, 000	100. 0	921, 000	100. 0	993, 000	100. 0	977, 000	100. 0	1, 097, 000	100. 0	170, 000	100. 0
Manchukuo_____	450, 000	72. 5	780, 000	84. 7	830, 000	83. 6	542, 000	55. 5	782, 000	71. 3	80, 000	47. 1
Kwantung_____	1, 000	0. 1	1, 000	0. 1	1, 000	0. 1	14, 000	1. 4	2, 000	0. 2	2, 000	1. 2
Korea_____	170, 000	27. 4	140, 000	15. 2	130, 000	13. 1	270, 000	27. 6	250, 000	22. 8	50, 000	29. 4
China_____					32, 000	3. 2	151, 000	15. 5	63, 000	5. 7	38, 000	22. 3
Grand total_____	621, 000	100. 0	921, 000	100. 0	993, 000	100. 0	977, 000	100. 0	1, 097, 000	100. 0	170, 000	

Source: Iron and Steel Control Association, Transport Ministry, Ministry of Commerce and Industry.

Appendix Table C–112.—*Japanese Imports of Scrap Iron, 1940–45*

Country of origin	Quantity											
	1940		1941		1942		1943		1944		1945	
	Metric tons	Per-cent	Metric tons	Per-cent	Metric tons	Per-cent	Metric tons	Per-cent	Metric tons	Per-cent	Metric tons	Per-cent
Total, inner zone countries	17,000	0.8	16,000	6.5	38,000	76.0	19,000	44.2	18,000	85.7	12,000	100.0
Manchukuo	10,000	0.5	10,000	4.1	10,000	20.0	8,000	18.6	5,000	23.8	2,000	16.7
Kwantung					1,000	2.0	1,000	2.3	1,000	4.8		
China					25,000	50.0	10,000	23.3	12,000	57.1	10,000	83.3
Formosa	7,000	0.3	6,000	2.4	2,000	4.0		25.6				
Total, southern area countries	75,000	3.5	49,000	19.9	9,000	18.0	16,000	37.2				
Hong Kong	13,000	0.6					5,000	11.6				
Netherland East Indies	62,000	2.9	49,000	19.9	9,000	18.0	11,000					
Total, other	2,012,000	95.6	181,000	73.6	3,000	6.0	8,000	18.6	3,000	14.3		
Grand total	2,124,000	100.0	246,000	100.0	50,000	100.0	43,000	100.0	21,000	100.0	12,000	100.0

Source: Iron and Steel Control Association, Ministry of Commerce and Industry, Transport Ministry.

Appendix Table C–113.—*Japanese imports of lead, 1940–45*

Country of origin	Quantity											
	1940		1941		1942		1943		1944		1945	
	Metric tons	Per-cent	Metric tons	Per-cent	Metric tons	Per-cent	Metric tons	Per-cent	Metric tons	Per-cent	Metric tons	Per-cent
Total, inner zone countries	8,080	8.1	8,670	10.0	8,720	79.4	16,190	65.9	16,590	98.7	4,000	100.0
Manchukuo	80	0.1	650	0.7	570	5.2	2,920	11.9	1,180	7.0		
Kwantung					150	1.4	240	1.0				
Korea	8,000	8.0	8,000	9.2	8,000	72.8	13,000	52.9	14,000	83.3	4,000	100.0
China			20	0.1			30	0.1	1,410	8.4		
Total, southern area countries	7,880	7.8	9,270	10.7	2,270	20.6	8,390	34.1	220	1.3		
Singapore	510	0.5					8,390	34.1	220	1.3		
Burma	7,370	7.3	9,270	10.7	2,270	20.6						
Total, others	84,140	84.1	68,590	79.3								
Grand total	100,100	100.0	86,530	100.0	10,990	100.0	24,580	100.0	16,810	100.0	4,000	100.0

Source: Light Metals Control Association, Transport Ministry, Ministry of Commerce and Industry.

APPENDIX TABLE C–114.—*Japanese imports of tin, 1940–45*

Country of origin	Quantity											
	1940		1941		1942		1943		1944		1945	
	Metric tons	Percent	Metric tons	Percent	Metric tons	Percent	Metric tons	Percent	Metric tons	Percent	Metric tons	Percent
Total, southern area countries__	10,500	100.0	5,500	100.0	3,800	100.0	26,800	100.0	23,500	100.0	3,600	100.0
Netherland East Indies and Malaya_____	10,500	100.0	5,500	100.0	3,800	100.0	26,800	100.0	23,500	100.0	3,600	100.0
Grand total_____	10,500	100.0	5,500	100.0	3,800	100.0	26,800	100.0	23,500	100.0	3,600	100.0

Source: Light Metals Control Association, Transport Ministry, Shipping Control Association, Ministry of Commerce and Industry.

APPENDIX TABLE C–115.—*Japanese imports of zinc, 1940–45*

Country of origin	Quantity											
	1940		1941		1942		1943		1944		1945	
	Metric tons	Percent	Metric tons	Percent	Metric tons	Percent	Metric tons	Percent	Metric tons	Percent	Metric tons	Percent
Total, inner zone countries_____	--------	-----	1,600	20.2	5,100	60.0	6,500	65.0	5,500	90.2	2,500	100.0
Korea_____	--------	-----	1,600	20.2	5,100	60.0	6,500	65.0	5,400	88.5	2,500	100.0
China_____	--------	-----	--------	-----	--------	-----	--------	-----	100	1.7	--------	-----
Total, southern area countries__	800	3.4	3,000	38.0	3,300	38.8	3,000	30.0	600	9.8	--------	-----
French Indochina_____	800	3.4	3,000	38.0	3,300	38.8	3,000	30.0	600	9.8	--------	-----
Total, other_____	22,700	96.6	3,300	41.8	100	1.2	500	5.0	--------	-----	--------	-----
Grand total_____	23,500	100.0	7,900	100.0	8,500	100.0	10,000	100.0	6,100	100.0	2,500	100.0

Source: Light Metals Control Association, Shipping Control Association, Transport Ministry, Ministry of Commerce and Industry.

APPENDIX TABLE C–116.—*Japanese imports of phosphorite and phosphate, 1940–45*

Country of origin	Quantity											
	1940		1941		1942		1943		1944		1945	
	Metric tons	Per-cent	Metric tons	Per-cent	Metric tons	Per-cent	Metric tons	Per-cent	Metric tons	Per-cent	Metric tons	Per-cent
Total, inner zone countries	16,700	2.4	54,900	13.8	56,000	16.4	55,900	23.6	66,100	73.8	23,000	100.0
China	16,700	2.4	54,900	13.8	56,000	16.4	55,900	23.6	63,300	70.7	20,000	87.0
Manchukuo									2,800	3.1	3,000	13.0
Total, southern area	117,900	16.6	80,000	20.2	285,600	83.5	180,800	76.4	23,500	26.2		
Straits Settlements	82,900	11.7	47,600	12.0			3,500	1.5	2,000	2.2		
French Indochina	20,000	2.8	22,400	5.7	55,000	16.1	48,300	20.4	4,500	5.0		
Malaya	15,000	2.1	10,000	2.5			4,100	1.7	4,000	4.5		
Pacific oslands					230,600	67.4	124,900	52.8	13,000	14.5		
Total, other	575,800	81.0	261,600	66.0	500	.1						
Grand total	710,400	100.0	396,500	100.0	342,100	100.0	236,700	100.0	89,600	100.0	23,000	100.0

Source: Chemical Industry Control Association, Shipping Control Association, Ministry of Commerce and Industry, Transport Ministry.

APPENDIX TABLE C–117.—*Japanese imports of dolomite and magnesite, 1940–45*

Country of origin	Quantity											
	1940		1941		1942		1943		1944		1945	
	Metric tons	Per-cent	Metric tons	Per-cent	Metric tons	Per-cent	Metric tons	Per-cent	Metric tons	Per-cent	Metric tons	Per-cent
Total, inner zone countries	409,600	100.0	506,300	100.0	468,700	100.0	437,500	100.0	287,100	100.0	65,900	100.0
Manchukuo	247,300	60.4	189,000	37.3	191,700	40.9	189,900	43.4	112,500	39.2	39,500	59.9
Kwantung	130,300	31.8	244,300	48.3	202,000	43.1	172,600	39.5	119,600	41.7	9,400	14.3
Korea	32,000	7.8	73,000	14.4	75,000	16.0	75,000	17.1	55,000	19.1	17,000	25.8
Grand total	409,600	100.0	506,300	100.0	468,700	100.0	437,500	100.0	287,100	100.0	65,900	100.0

Source: Chemical Industry Control Association, Ministry of Commerce and Industry, Shipping Control Association, Transport Ministry.

Country of origin	Quantity											
	1940		1941		1942		1943		1944		1945	
	Metric tons	Per-cent	Metric tons	Per-cent	Metric tons	Per-cent	Metric tons	Per-cent	Metric tons	Per-cent	Metric tons	Per-cent
Total, inner zone countries	1,269,800	73.5	1,341,600	93.2	1,476,600	98.5	1,394,100	97.8	989,300	99.9	386,900	100.0
Manchukuo	40,600	2.4	119,900	8.3	89,000	6.0	115,900	8.1	91,300	9.2	29,300	7.6
Kwantung	501,300	29.0	389,900	27.1	313,400	20.9	354,900	24.9	333,300	33.7	158,800	41.0
China	674,200	39.0	779,400	54.2	969,000	64.6	799,500	56.1	496,600	50.1	195,800	50.6
Formosa	53,700	3.1	52,400	3.6	105,200	7.0	123,800	8.7	68,100	8.7	3,000	0.8
Totzl, southern area	19,600	1.1	27,000	1.9	6,900	.5	31,000	2.2	400	0.1		
Philippines							31,000	2.2	400	0.1		
French Indochina	19,600	1.1	27,000	1.9	6,900	0.5						
Total, others	438,900	25.4	70,300	4.9	16,300	1.0						
Grand total	1,728,300	100.0	1,438,900	100.0	1,499,800	100.0	1,425,100	100.0	989,700	100.0	386,900	100.0

Source: Shipping Control Association, Transport Ministry, Ministry of Agriculture and Forestry.

Appendix Table C–119.—*Japanese imports of soybean cake, 1940–45*

Country of origin	Quantity											
	1940		1941		1942		1943		1944		1945	
	Metric tons	Per-cent	Metric tons	Per-cent	Metric tons	Per-cent	Metric tons	Per-cent	Metric tons	Per-cent	Metric tons	Per-cent
Total, inner zone countries	333,900	100.0	337,700	100.0	449,500	100.0	304,500	100.0	384,700	100.0	163,400	100.0
Manchukuo	317,000	94.9	305,600	90.5	341,900	76.1	258,700	85.0	367,900	95.6	160,300	98.0
Kwantung	600	0.2	7,000	2.1	56,600	12.6	17,400	5.7	7,700	2.0	1,600	1.0
China	16,300	4.9	25,100	7.4	51,000	11.3	28,400	9.3	9,100	2.4	1,600	1.0
Grand total	333,900	100.0	337,700	100.0	449,500	100.0	304,500	100.0	384,700	100.0	163,400	100.0

Source: Ministry of Agriculture and Forestry, Shipping Control Association.

APPENDIX TABLE C–120.—*Japanese imports of soybeans, 1940–45*

Country of origin	Quantity											
	1940		1941		1942		1943		1944		1945	
	Metric tons	Percent	Metric tons	Percent	Metric tons	Percent	Metric tons	Percent	Metric tons	Percent	Metric tons	Percent
Total, inner zone countries_____	642, 900	99. 1	572, 400	100. 0	698, 800	100. 0	590, 600	100. 0	667, 000	91. 5	606, 900	100. 0
Manchukuo_____	464, 600	71. 6	492, 800	86. 1	614, 200	87. 9	524, 700	88. 8	628, 900	86. 3	596, 100	98. 2
Kwantung_____	2, 800	0. 4	1, 200	0. 2	1, 000	0. 1	600	0. 1	600	0. 1	_____	_____
China_____	14, 200	2. 2	20, 600	3. 6	33, 600	4. 8	23, 400	4. 0	4, 000	0. 5	_____	_____
Formosa_____	1, 300	0. 2	3, 600	0. 6	_____	_____	_____	_____	_____	_____	_____	_____
Korea_____	160, 000	24. 7	54, 200	9. 5	50, 000	7. 2	41, 900	7. 1	33, 500	4. 6	10, 800	1. 8
Total, southern area_____	_____	_____	_____	_____	_____	_____	_____	_____	60, 000	8. 2	_____	_____
French Indochina_____	_____	_____	_____	_____	_____	_____	_____	_____	60, 000	8. 2	_____	_____
Total, other_____	5, 600	0. 9	_____	_____	_____	_____	_____	_____	1, 800	0. 3	_____	_____
Grand total_____	648, 500	100. 0	572, 400	100. 0	698, 800	100. 0	590, 600	100. 0	728, 800	100. 0	606, 900	100. 0

Source: Ministry of Agriculture and Forestry, Shipping Control Association.

APPENDIX TABLE C–121.—*Japanese imports of rice and paddy, 1940–45*

Country of origin	Quantity											
	1940		1941		1942		1943		1944		1945	
	Metric tons	Percent	Metric tons	Percent	Metric tons	Percent	Metric tons	Percent	Metric tons	Percent	Metric tons	Percent
Total, inner zone countries_____	445, 100	26. 3	791, 800	35. 5	1, 101, 500	41. 9	279, 200	24. 6	709, 300	90. 6	151, 000	99. 9
Formosa_____	385, 100	22. 7	271, 800	12. 2	261, 500	9. 9	207, 200	18. 3	149, 800	19. 1	9, 000	6. 0
Korea_____	60, 000	3. 6	520, 000	23. 3	840, 000	32. 0	72, 000	6. 3	559, 500	71. 5	142, 000	93. 9
Total, southern area_____	1, 144, 200	67. 5	1, 435, 500	64. 3	1, 527, 700	58. 1	856, 600	75. 4	73, 900	9. 4	200	0. 1
French Indochina_____	439, 300	25. 9	562, 600	25. 2	973, 100	37. 0	662, 100	58. 3	38, 400	4. 9	_____	_____
Burma_____	420, 900	24. 8	437, 500	19. 6	46, 600	1. 8	18, 000	1. 6	_____	_____	_____	_____
Siam_____	284, 000	16. 8	435, 400	19. 5	508, 000	19. 3	176, 500	15. 5	35, 500	4. 5	200	0. 1
Total, other____	104, 700	6. 2	5, 400	0. 2	_____	_____	_____	_____	_____	_____	_____	_____
Grand total____	1, 694, 000	100. 0	2, 232, 700	100. 0	2, 629, 200	100. 0	1, 135, 800	100. 0	783, 200	100. 0	151, 200	100. 0

Source: Ministry of Agriculture and Forestry, Shipping Control Association.

Appendix Table C-122.—*Japanese imports of other grains and flours, 1940–45*

Country of origin	Quantity											
	1940		1941		1942		1943		1944		1945	
	Metric tons	Percent	Metric tons	Percent	Metric tons	Percent	Metric tons	Percent	Metric tons	Percent	Metric tons	Percent
Total, inner zone countries	43,800	16.3	53,000	20.0	676,100	82.1	111,000	14.8	151,800	30.0	231,400	100.0
Formosa	500	0.2	1,000	0.4	1,000	0.1	300	0.1	100	0.1	--------	-----
Korea	3,300	1.2	1,000	0.4	600,000	72.9	25,200	3.3	25,200	4.1	15,000	6.5
China	--------	-----	1,000	0.4	2,300	0.3	5,000	0.7	4,500	0.9	3,000	1.3
Manchukuo	40,000	14.9	50,000	18.8	72,800	8.8	80,500	10.7	122,000	24.0	213,400	92.2
Total, Southern area countries	225,500	83.7	214,400	80.0	147,200	17.9	639,100	85.2	355,000	70.0	--------	-----
French Indochina	148,600	55.2	135,200	50.5	124,900	15.2	634,100	84.5	355,000	70.0	--------	-----
Netherland East Indies	76,900	28.5	79,200	29.5	22,300	2.7	5,000	0.7	--------	-----	--------	-----
Grand total	269,300	100.0	267,400	100.0	823,300	100.0	750,100	100.0	506,800	100.0	231,400	100.0

Source: Ministry of Agriculture and Forestry, Shipping Control Association.

Appendix Table C-123.—*Japanese imports of raw rubber, 1940–45*

Country of origin	Quantity											
	1940		1941		1942		1943		1944		1945	
	Metric tons	Percent	Metric tons	Percent	Metric tons	Percent	Metric tons	Percent	Metric tons	Percent	Metric tons	Percent
Total, southern area	27,500	100.0	67,600	100.0	29,700	94.6	40,100	95.2	28,100	89.2	16,500	92.2
Malaya	14,300	52.0	1,400	2.1	14,000	44.6	25,000	59.4	17,200	54.6	16,500	92.2
Siam	2,700	9.8	23,800	35.2	--------	-----	--------	-----	--------	-----	--------	-----
Netherland East Indies	10,500	38.2	20,500	30.3	12,300	39.2	15,000	35.6	6,500	20.6	--------	-----
French Indochina	--------	-----	21,900	32.4	3,400	10.8	100	0.2	4,400	14.0	--------	-----
Total, other	--------	-----	--------	-----	1,700	5.4	2,000	4.8	3,400	10.8	1,400	7.8
Grand total	[1] 27,500	100.0	[1] 67,600	100.0	31,400	100.0	42,100	100.0	31,500	100.0	17,900	100.0

[1] No information on imports from sources outside Asia.

Source: Rubber Control Association, Shipping Control Association, Greater East Asia Ministry.

Capital Goods Tables

APPENDIX TABLE C–124.—*Production of electrical equipment, Japan proper, 1935–45 (1936 prices)*

[In millions of yen] [1]

Fiscal year	Total production	Communications equipment	Electric machinery	Fiscal year	Total production	Communications equipment	Electric machinery
1935	373	45	167	1941	899	172	462
1936	447	67	206	1942	1,021	261	487
1937	578	68	214	1943	1,272	374	491
1938	678	101	285	1944	1,754	772	542
1939	813	143	383	1945 [2]	650	250	200
1940	842	154	354				

[1] Corrected for price changes by the following index: 1936=100, 1937=109, 1938=123, 1939=137, 1940=150, 1941=167, 1942=180, 1943=190, 1944=214.

[2] Projected for entire year based on first 5 months.
Source: Ministry of Commerce and Industry.

APPENDIX TABLE C–125.—*Exports of electrical equipment, Japan proper, 1937–43 (current prices)*

[1,000 yen]

Product	1937	1938	1939	1940	1941	1942	1943
1. Power and lighting equipment	15,774	26,614	34,764	41,262	46,508	50,121	34,134
2. Insulated wire and cable	15,232	19,887	25,806	24,457	13,699	14,975	8,336
3. Telephones	4,086	7,774	7,302	11,126	7,937	4,644	2,868
4. Telegraph instruments	625	1,958	3,128	3,996	4,654	4,083	2,770
5. Medical instruments	3,391	3,330	3,757	5,017	5,715	4,385	4,133
6. Storage batteries	2,262	3,233	3,999	3,851	2,686	2,657	2,068
7. Radios (standard types)	2,577	2,299	4,200	6,269	5,613	3,960	8,130
8. Electric light parts	21,950	14,747	17,744	21,622	16,364	15,798	11,267
9. Signal equipment	689	1,164	857	1,029	784	73	200
10. Electric fans	710	1,144	1,356	1,193	1,424	825	1,237
11. Electric lamps	10,645	14,747	17,747	20,085	16,364	15,797	11,267
Total	77,941	96,897	120,658	139,907	121,748	117,318	86,410

Source: Ministry of Commerce and Industry.

APPENDIX TABLE C–126.—*Imports of electrical equipment, Japan proper, 1937–43 (current prices)*

[1,000 yen]

Product	1937	1938	1939	1940	1941	1942	1943
1. Motors and generators	1,670	2,589	2,089	2,920	736	534	431
2. Transformers	171	177	96	504	969	33	7
3. Insulated wire and cable	148	38	47	65	133	60	52
4. Telephone and parts	1,815	1,883	1,258	685	159	37	821
5. Telegraph and parts	124	1,594	529	3,716	6	2,213	--------
6. Medical equipment and parts	249	129	161	135	124	32	40
7. Batteries	92	45	26	56	11	5	--------
8. Meters	3,263	1,694	2,129	1,811	1,432	130	417
Total	7,532	8,149	6,335	9,892	3,570	3,044	1,768

Source: Ministry of Commerce and Industry.

APPENDIX TABLE C-127.—*Estimated construction volume in Japan proper, 1937–45*

[In millions of yen—current prices]

Year	Army [1]			Navy [2]				Grand total
	Total (1)	Direct (2)	Indirect (3)	Total (4)	Direct (5)	Indirect (6)	Civilian total (7)	(8)
1937	80	na	80	8	1	7	704	792
1938	211	na	211	90	18	72	625	926
1939	261	na	261	141	28	113	1,128	1,530
1940	221	10	211	240	50	190	838	1,299
1941	900	14	886	603	100	503	902	2,405
1942	1,145	22	1,123	913	180	733	694	2,752
1943	1,181	38	1,143	1,038	243	795	1,798	4,017
1944	1,935	322	1,613	1,515	450	1,065	2,012	5,462
1945 [3]	1,595	545	1,050	1,658	600	1,058	972	4,225
Total	7,529	951	6,578	6,206	1,670	4,536	9,673	23,408

[1] Including Korea, Formosa, and Karafuto.

[2] Excluding Korea, Formosa, and Karafuto.

[3] Approximately first 7 months only.

na Not available but presumably negligible.

Source: For columns (1)–(3), War Ministry; for columns (4)–(6), Navy Ministry.

Since no annual figures were available for Japan Proper from the Navy Ministry, the cumulative figure of 6,206 million yen for Japan proper (this is the difference between the total figure of 9,669 and the overseas figure of 3,463 million yen in appendix table A–9) for the period 1937–45 was distributed over the years 1940–45 in the same ratio as average quarterly employment for Japan proper.

Since the amount of construction for the Navy outside Japan Proper Korea, Formosa and Karafuto was probably negligible in the years 1937–39, the volume figures for these three years were repeated from table 3 and the estimates for the remaining years 1940–45 were reduced in direct proportion to their size by the total of the 3 earlier years. The portion of total Navy construction which was accomplished by the Navy's own forces (referred to herein as "direct Navy") was estimated on the basis of employment of Naval officers, enlisted personnel, and a reasonable proportion of laborers (this last being based on estimates supplied by interrogation of Navy civil engineering officers). The difference between total Navy and direct Navy was allotted to indirect Navy.

For columns (7) and (8), the grand total is the sum of columns (2) and (5) above plus column (2) of table 5 in the text. The purely civilian figure in column (7) above is then obtained by subtracting the Army and Navy totals from the grand total.

Since nearly all the basic figures for the above table were originally estimated by the Japanese themselves, the additional estimates made herein to present a complete picture of the construction industry's activity are subject to proportionately larger errors in variation.

APPENDIX TABLE C-128.—*Volume of Japanese Army construction, 1937–45*

[In millions of yen]

Fiscal year	Current prices			Adjusted prices [1]		
	Japan proper [2]	Over-seas	Total	Japan proper [2]	Over-seas	Total
1937 [3]	80	45	125	80	45	125
1938 [3]	211	149	360	211	149	360
1939	261	208	469	261	208	469
1940	221	296	517	221	296	517
1941	900	319	1,219	900	319	1,219
1942	1,145	427	1,572	954	357	1,311
1943	1,181	645	1,826	845	461	1,306
1944	1,935	1,106	3,041	1,210	346	1,556
1945 [4]	1,595	2,800	4,395	798	225	1,023
Total	7,529	5,995	13,524	5,480	2,406	7,886

[1] Based on the following indices of unit costs estimated by War Ministry officials: 100 in 1937–41, 120 in 1942, 140 in 1943, 160 in 1944, and 200 in 1945.

[2] Including Korea, Formosa, and Karafuto.

[3] Partially estimated.

[4] First 6 months only.

Source: War Ministry, Tokyo.

APPENDIX TABLE C-129.—*Estimated volume of Japanese Navy construction in Japan proper and overseas, 1937–45*

[In millions of yen]

Fiscal year	Current value	Adjusted value [1]
1937	8	8
1938	90	90
1939	141	141
1940	248	248
1941	656	656
1942	1,130	1,130
1943	1,947	1,500
1944	3,145	2,100
1945 [3]	[2] 2,304	1,540
Total	9,669	7,413

[1] Based on the following index of unit costs estimated by Navy Paymaster Office representative: 100 for 1937–42, 130 for 1943, 150 for 1944–45.

[2] Including about 200 million yen paid to contractors for compensation at end of war.

[3] First 7 months only.

Source: Navy Ministry, Tokyo.

APPENDIX TABLE C-130.—*Estimated volume of nonmilitary construction* [1] *in Japan proper, 1937–45*

[In millions of yen—current value]

Calendar year	Value of contracts awarded to all contractors	Value of construction completed	
		By all contractors	By 40-odd large contractors
1937	942	791	ne
1938	998	908	ne
1939	1,747	1,502	ne
1940	1,662	1,429	796
1941	2,810	2,291	1,306
1942	3,390	2,550	1,449
1943	5,330	3,736	2,162
1944	7,000	4,500	2,840
1945 [2]	5,170	3,080	2,160

[1] Nonmilitary construction excludes work done by Army or Navy with its own forces, but includes work done for Army and Navy by civilian contractors and their employees.

[2] Approximately first 8 months.

ne Not estimated.

Source: Ministry of Commerce and Industry, and Japanese Architectural Industry Control Association, Tokyo.

APPENDIX TABLE C-131.—*Production of principal building materials in Japan Proper, 1937–45*

[Index numbers based on 1937=100]

Year [1]	Cement		Structural steel [2]		Lumber	
	Thousand metric tons	Index number	Thousand metric tons	Index number	Million board feet [3]	Index number
1937	6,069	100	728	100	8,555	100
1938	5,846	96	644	88	9,587	112
1939	6,161	102	574	79	11,344	133
1940	6,002	99	635	87	11,097	130
1941	5,604	92	578	79	11,560	135
1942	4,237	70	576	79	10,748	126
1943	3,721	61	479	66	12,029	141
1944	2,960	49	277	38	12,795	150
1945 [4]	1,011	17	na	na	8,209	96
Quarter: [5]						
1944 Jan.–Mar.	759	50	114	63	4,419	207
Apr.–June	862	57	134	74	2,972	139
July–Sept.	727	48	55	30	2,744	128
Oct.–Dec.	612	40	54	30	2,800	131
1945 Jan.–Mar.	447	29	33	18	4,279	200
Apr.–June	395	26	na	na	} 3,930 { na
July–Sept.	169	11	na	na		na

[1] Data for cement based on calendar years, and for steel and lumber on fiscal years beginning April 1.

[2] Data includes shapes only.

[3] Converted on the basis of 1 koku=120 board feet. Data supplied in log volume.

[4] First 9 months of calendar year only.

[5] Index numbers based on one-fourth of 1937 figures.

na Not available.

Source: Cement Control Association, Iron and Steel Control Association, and Ministry of Agriculture and Forestry.

APPENDIX TABLE C-132.—*Adjusted capacity rating of cement mills* [1] *in Japan proper, 1941–45*

[In metric tons]

Year	Adjusted capacity
1941	6,855,700
1942	6,403,200
1943	5,221,800
1944	4,209,000
1945	2,077,500

[1] Formerly plant capacity was rated on the basis of kiln capacity alone, but in 1941 the Cement Control Association rerated capacity in more realistic terms, taking into consideration all plant facilities, such as excavating, drying, crushing equipment, storage, etc., as well as kiln capacity. As an example of the difference resulting from the two methods of rating capacity, take 1943; by the old method, capacity was rated as 7,908,500 metric tons, as compared with the adjusted rating of 5,221,800 tons.

Source: Cement Control Association, Tokyo.

APPENDIX TABLE C-133.—*Estimated consumption of cement by principal recipients in Japan proper, 1940–45*

[In thousand metric tons]

Calendar year	Total	Military [1]	Industrial	Nonindustrial [2]	Shipbuilding
(Annually)					
1940	4,934	1,151	1,650	2,016	117
1941	4,900	1,103	1,853	1,814	130
1942	4,039	1,439	1,378	1,092	130
1943	3,605	1,799	949	698	160
1944	3,150	1,754	696	563	137
1945 [3]	980	566	156	199	59
(Quarterly)					
1944:					
Jan.–Mar.	773	480	138	125	30
Apr.–June	971	475	284	181	31
July–Sept.	743	386	150	158	49
Oct.–Dec.	665	414	125	99	27
1945:					
Jan.–Mar.	428	243	79	78	28
Apr.–June	400	255	55	66	24
July–Sept.	152	68	22	55	7

[1] Includes army, navy, and aircraft consumers.

[2] Includes railway, air defense, general civil use, emergency reserve, and miscellaneous.

[3] First nine months.

Source: Cement Control Association, Tokyo.

APPENDIX TABLE C-134.—*Production of cement in principal overseas areas under Japanese control, annually, 1937-44*

[In thousand metric tons]

Year	Total	Formosa	Korea	Manchuria
1937	1, 601	148	665	788
1938	2, 222	142	1, 055	1, 025
1939	2, 361	221	1, 096	1, 044
1940	2, 386	226	1, 143	1, 017
1941	2, 591	212	1, 215	1, 164
1942	2, 942	228	1, 182	1, 532
1943	3, 002	309	1, 190	1, 503
1944	2, 386	245	1, 003	1, 138

Source: Cement Control Association, Tokyo.

APPENDIX TABLE C-135.—*Exports of Japanese Cement, 1940-45*

[In thousand metric tons]

Calendar year	Cement exported
1940	973
1941	692
1942	168
1943	126
1944	32
1945	

Source: Cement Control Association, Tokyo.

APPENDIX TABLE C-136.—*Ordinary rolled steel consumed by army and navy for construction purposes [1] in Japan proper, 1937-45*

[In thousand metric tons]

Fiscal year	Total	Army ground forces	Navy surface forces	Merchant shipbuilding [2]	Air forces
1937	na	na	77. 0	30. 9	57. 7
1938	188. 4	49. 3	64. 2	19. 7	55. 2
1939	213. 0	69. 0	66. 6	20. 4	57. 0
1940	234. 3	80. 8	75. 3	14. 7	63. 5
1941	340. 5	111. 7	109. 5	22. 5	96. 8
1942	310. 6	94. 5	97. 3	33. 8	85. 0
1943	398. 0	122. 8	109. 4	59. 1	106. 7

APPENDIX TABLE C-136.—*Ordinary rolled steel consumed by army and navy for construction purposes [1] in Japan proper, 1937-45—Continued*

Fiscal pear	Total	Army ground forces	Navy surface forces	Merchant shipbuilding [2]	Air forces
1944	294. 5	45. 2	53. 0	87. 7	108. 6
1945 [3]	42. 6	10. 4	6. 0	15. 2	11. 0

[1] Data include structural steel as well as other types of rolled steel.
[2] Includes steel consumed in construction of yards, docks, and associated structures, but excludes steel used in shipbuilding.
[3] First 3 months only.
na Not available.

Source: Iron and Steel Control Association.

APPENDIX TABLE C-137.—*Production, imports, and exports of lumber in Japan proper, 1937-44*

[In million board feet—log volume]

Fiscal year	Production	Imports	Exports	Net available
1937	8, 555	1, 290	722	9, 123
1938	9, 587	483	1, 136	8, 934
1939	11, 344	489	2, 100	9, 733
1940	11, 097	545	1, 463	10, 179
1941	11, 560	291	810	11, 041
1942	10, 748	154	528	10, 374
1943	12, 029	17	162	11, 884
1944	12, 795		197	12, 598

Source: Ministry of Forestry and Agriculture.

APPENDIX TABLE C-138.—*Consumption of lumber by principal uses in Japan proper, 1943-44*

[In million board feet—log volume]

Use	1943	1944
Public works and construction	8, 470	8, 916
Shipbuilding and cartwright	1, 205	1, 063
Mine timber	1, 259	1, 393
Railroad ties	261	222
Telegraph poles	86	88
Pulpwood	504	472
Veneer and plywood	157	79
Other	87	562
Total	12, 029	12, 795

Source: Japan Lumber Company, Tokyo.

TABLE C-139.—*Japan machine-building industry—annual production Japan proper, 1936–45*

Fiscal year	Number of machine tools	Value (1,000 ¥)	Average price	Index of unit production	Index of total value of machine tools	Value of production machinery (1,000 ¥)	Index of total value of machinery production
1936	[1] 15,000	30,668	2,000	33	9.8	1,609,000	43.7
1937	21,888	50,199	2,934	48	16	2,380,000	64.5
1938	67,260	204,085	3,034	146	64	3,589,000	97.4
1939	66,830	274,597	4,108	146	87	3,792,308	103.
1940	58,088	312,979	5,388	126	98	3,256,833	88.3
1941	46,025	317,175	6,891	100	100	3,685,714	100.0
1942	50,997	428,997	8,412	111	135	4,889,473	132.6
1943	60,134	602,913	10,026	130	189	4,976,165	135.0
1944	53,844	723,378	13,434	117	228	5,113,252	138.7
1945 [2]	7,242	127,284	17,575	(63)	(160)	----------	----------

[1] Estimated on basis of yen value of 1936 production and 1937 average price per unit.
[2] First quarter only (of fiscal year).

Source: Yen value annually for production machinery based on sample of industry by the Production Machinery Control Association. Unit production of machine tools is taken from the records of the Precision Machinery Control Association.

APPENDIX TABLE C-140.—*Output, import, export, and domestic sales of machine tools and productive machinery*

[In 1,000 Yen]

Fiscal year	Machine tools				Productive machinery			
	Total output (1)	Import (2)	Export (3)	Domestic sales (1+2−3)	Total output	Import	Export	Domestic sales
1933	10,000	11,339	565	20,774	805,000	----------	----------	----------
1934	16,000	14,485	1,189	29,296	1,082,000	----------	----------	----------
1935	18,750	9,998	1,941	26,807	1,581,000	----------	----------	----------
1936	30,668	16,539	4,907	42,300	1,609,000	----------	----------	----------
1937	50,199	42,512	5,799	86,912	2,380,000	165,800	66,033	2,479,767
1938	204,085	91,738	9,571	286,252	3,589,000	248,968	101,384	3,736,584
1939	274,597	157,166	23,985	407,778	[1] 3,792,308	52,170	122,670	3,721,808
1940	312,979	78,500	22,698	368,781	[2] 3,256,833	45,203	169,351	3,132,685
1941	317,175	[3] 40,363	18,749	338,789	3,685,714	23,753	158,996	3,550,471
1942	428,997	[3] 16,375	13,782	431,590	4,889,473	11,724	138,053	4,763,144
1943	602,913	[3] 16,566	10,970	608,509	4,976,165	6,193	148,336	4,833,995
1944	723,378	----------	3,000	720,378	[4] 5,113,252	----------	----------	----------
1945	127,284	----------	----------	----------	----------	----------	----------	----------

[1] Estimated on basis of 25 percent of production.
[2] Estimated on basis of 33.3 percent of production.
[3] Includes woodworking machines.
[4] Estimated for 1944 on basis of first quarter—1,278,313 yen.

Sources: Output 1933–40, Ministry of Industry and Commerce. Output 1941–45, Precision Machinery and Production Machinery Control Associations. Imports and exports: Ministry of Commerce and Industry.

APPENDIX TABLE C-141.—*Expansion of Japanese machine-tool industry, Japan proper, 1940–45*

Fiscal year	Productive floor space (square feet)	Increase in floor space (square feet)	Index of floor space	Index of productive capacity [1]	Index of production [2]
1940	6,588,000	----------	87	84	98
1941	7,560,000	972,000	100	100	100
1942	10,368,000	2,808,000	137	116	135
1943	11,562,948	1,194,948	153	197	189
1944	13,107,600	1,544,652	173	[3] 335.5	228
1945	----------	----------	----------	170	160

[1] Productive capacity estimated by precision machinery control association. Estimates based on 10-hour 1-shift day, except in 1944 when based on 2 shifts.
[2] Based on yen value of yearly output.
[3] Two shifts. (Index of capacity on single shift in 1944 was 218.4. For Japanese definition of "capacity" see p. 20 of USSBS "Machine-Building Industry" Report.)

APPENDIX TABLE C-142.—*Japanese national inventory of machine tools*

End of fiscal year:

1940:

Civilian industries	606, 550
Army [1]	26, 865
Navy	9, 499.
National railways	3, 690
Total	646, 604

1941:

Civilian	640, 072
Army	34, 505
Navy	10, 591
National railways	3, 995
Total	689, 163

1942	740, 469
1943	801, 162
1944	[2] 854, 785
Civilian [4]	517, 264
Army	84, 981
Navy	17, 363
Aircraft	164, 600
National railways	4, 514
Total	788, 722

1945	[3] 862, 000
Civilian [4]	370, 364
Army	43, 806
Navy	17, 593
Aircraft	163, 568
National railways	4, 539
Total	599, 870

[1] Inventories for army arsenals in 1940, 1941, and 1944 are based on actual inventories of 1942 and 1945 adjusted by yearly purchases and allowing 2% depreciation. Inventories for 1942 and 1945 were furnished by the Machinery and Material Mobilization Branch of the Material Mobilization Section of the Japanese War Department.

[2] Inventories for 1944 and 1945 obtained by adding production and imports less exports to previous year's inventory. The disagreement with break-down of existing machines for the same year should be due to obsolescence and destruction in raids.

[3] It should be noted that the difference between an additive estimate of 1945 inventory and actual count at the end of the war is 262,130 machine tools. Estimates by the Ministry of Industry and Commerce place machine-tool destruction by air raids at approximately 219,000.

[4] Inventories for Civilian Industries in 1944 and 1945 were estimated by the Ministry of Industry and Commerce on the basis of inventories in 50% of Civilian Industries in those years.

APPENDIX TABLE C-143.—*Japanese munitions output*

[Computed in terms of 1945 prices, 1941–45, by months (1,000,000 yen)]

FISCAL YEAR 1941

	April	May	June	July	August	September	October	November	December	January	February	March	Total	Percent
Merchant ships	35.4	32.2	31.1	30.9	33.8	31.5	31.3	31.7	34.4	35.4	37.2	37.6	402.5	7.9
Navy ships	83.8	82.9	87.3	88.1	85.9	84.7	82.4	83.7	84.0	82.1	82.9	86.2	1,014.0	19.8
Navy ordnance	71.6	73.1	71.4	71.7	73.4	75.2	77.9	84.4	91.7	87.4	89.8	104.8	972.4	19.0
Army ordnance	60.3	68.3	73.1	73.0	71.1	78.9	79.8	83.7	92.6	87.8	89.1	98.8	956.5	18.7
Motor vehicles	43.7	46.5	57.4	51.5	55.3	58.0	64.7	73.4	76.9	58.6	54.8	50.6	691.4	13.5
Aircraft	61.9	70.2	72.1	70.5	77.6	84.3	92.4	92.4	113.2	112.7	110.0	123.3	1,080.6	21.1
Total	356.7	373.2	392.4	385.7	397.1	412.6	428.5	449.3	492.8	464.0	463.8	501.3	5,117.4	------

FISCAL YEAR 1942

	April	May	June	July	August	September	October	November	December	January	February	March	Total	Percent
Merchant ships	35.7	38.1	38.8	39.2	37.5	36.1	37.9	45.1	51.5	54.7	63.2	67.0	544.8	8.1
Navy ships	89.0	89.7	87.4	90.7	91.4	86.6	91.7	92.9	96.2	97.1	100.1	99.6	1,112.4	16.5
Navy ordnance	109.2	117.2	120.4	112.1	118.1	129.6	137.7	128.9	133.5	137.2	141.5	154.3	1,539.7	22.9
Army ordnance	74.7	73.0	101.8	96.4	97.6	112.7	110.7	109.6	123.9	105.0	117.5	139.0	1,261.9	18.8
Motor vehicles	36.9	35.4	36.5	40.3	32.1	42.2	44.2	32.2	38.0	28.8	24.1	35.9	426.6	6.3
Aircraft	123.1	129.0	114.5	128.0	115.3	137.0	152.9	168.2	184.7	187.1	191.4	211.5	1,842.7	27.4
Total	468.6	482.4	499.4	506.7	492.0	544.2	575.1	576.9	627.8	609.9	637.8	707.3	6,728.1	------

FISCAL YEAR 1943

	April	May	June	July	August	September	October	November	December	January	February	March	Total	Percent
Merchant ships	64.0	79.4	91.5	97.7	103.0	107.2	115.0	121.2	139.6	170.3	162.3	160.0	1,411.2	12.8
Navy ships	107.8	111.2	113.2	115.2	112.5	115.0	118.4	129.7	133.2	136.1	147.1	137.0	1,476.4	13.4
Navy ordnance	133.4	150.0	156.9	167.6	187.7	205.6	214.7	229.3	254.8	247.1	291.3	312.2	2,550.6	23.1
Army ordnance	102.6	116.2	128.0	117.9	121.3	125.3	132.7	139.1	152.6	149.3	149.7	151.3	1,586.0	14.4
Motor vehicles	28.8	27.2	22.0	30.3	27.5	28.6	23.6	20.3	21.1	22.9	24.3	32.2	308.8	2.8
Aircraft	214.0	224.2	229.4	239.6	268.3	302.3	312.8	354.2	406.6	354.9	372.1	408.5	3,686.8	33.5
Total	650.6	708.2	741.0	768.3	820.3	883.9	917.2	993.8	1,107.9	1,080.6	1,146.8	1,201.2	11,019.8	------

APPENDIX TABLE C-143.—*Japanese munitions output*—Continued

FISCAL YEAR 1944

	April	May	June	July	August	September	October	November	December	January	February	March	Total	Percent
Merchant ships	164.4	164.4	159.9	153.9	161.1	154.5	157.8	145.8	131.0	108.3	98.0	66.3	1,665.6	10.5
Navy ships	175.1	183.2	188.7	194.2	194.5	196.7	181.9	172.8	173.1	157.5	144.0	136.8	2,098.5	13.3
Navy ordnance	349.7	369.7	389.2	297.1	415.1	428.1	425.3	417.0	406.3	375.3	341.9	323.3	4,638.0	29.3
Army ordnance	135.5	142.2	139.5	147.6	192.6	178.9	169.5	171.7	195.1	212.7	218.1	203.4	2,107.0	13.3
Motor vehicles	23.8	36.7	25.7	27.6	20.3	20.1	25.6	28.2	17.9	12.9	15.3	15.6	269.7	1.7
Aircraft	416.0	386.8	465.7	441.5	422.7	452.2	462.9	475.4	428.7	385.8	304.0	382.4	5,024.1	31.8
Total	1,264.5	1,283.0	1,368.7	1,361.9	1,406.5	1,430.5	1,423.0	1,410.9	1,352.1	1,252.5	1,121.3	1,127.8	15,802.9	-----

FISCAL YEAR 1945

	April	May	June	July	August	September	October	November	December	January	February	March	Total	Percent
Merchant ships	55.2	44.6	34.8	30.7	-----	-----	-----	-----	-----	-----	-----	-----	165.3	4.9
Navy ships	110.6	102.4	98.6	92.6	-----	-----	-----	-----	-----	-----	-----	-----	404.2	11.9
Navy ordnance	334.4	317.2	264.4	214.4	-----	-----	-----	-----	-----	-----	-----	-----	1,130.4	33.2
Army ordnance	119.8	114.8	119.1	101.1	-----	-----	-----	-----	-----	-----	-----	-----	454.8	13.3
Motor vehicles	9.1	18.6	3.4	4.9	-----	-----	-----	-----	-----	-----	-----	-----	36.0	1.1
Aircraft	361.2	350.1	279.8	225.5	-----	-----	-----	-----	-----	-----	-----	-----	1,216.6	35.7
Total	990.3	947.7	800.1	669.2	-----	-----	-----	-----	-----	-----	-----	-----	3,407.3	-----

Source: Military Supplies Division, USSBS.

APPENDIX TABLE C–144.—*Monthly indices of Japanese munitions production, based on 1945 prices, 1941–45 (fiscal years)*

[Average 1941 month=100]

FISCAL YEAR 1941

	April	May	June	July	August	September	October	November	December	January	February	March
Merchant ship	105. 6	95. 9	92. 8	92. 3	100. 6	94. 0	93. 4	94. 5	102. 5	105. 4	110. 8	112. 0
Navy ship	99. 2	98. 1	103. 3	104. 3	101. 7	100. 2	97. 5	99. 1	99. 4	97. 2	98. 1	102. 0
Navy ordnance	88. 4	90. 2	88. 1	88. 5	90. 6	92. 8	96. 2	104. 2	113. 2	107. 9	110. 9	129. 4
Army ordnance	75. 6	85. 7	91. 7	91. 5	89. 2	99. 0	100. 1	105. 0	116. 2	110. 1	111. 8	123. 9
Motor vehicles	75. 8	80. 7	99. 6	89. 4	96. 0	100. 7	112. 3	127. 4	133. 5	101. 7	95. 1	87. 8
Aircraft	67. 6	78. 6	80. 4	76. 5	86. 1	92. 6	102. 5	103. 2	126. 0	123. 6	121. 8	141. 1
Total	83. 6	87. 5	92. 0	90. 4	93. 1	96. 7	100. 4	105. 3	115. 5	108. 8	108. 7	117. 5

FISCAL YEAR 1942

	April	May	June	July	August	September	October	November	December	January	February	March
Merchant ship	106. 6	113. 5	115. 8	116. 9	111. 6	107. 3	112. 5	132. 9	150. 4	156. 7	179. 2	186. 4
Navy ships	105. 3	106. 2	103. 4	107. 3	108. 2	102. 5	108. 5	109. 9	113. 8	114. 9	118. 5	117. 9
Navy ordnance	134. 8	144. 7	148. 6	138. 4	145. 8	150. 0	170. 0	159. 0	164. 8	169. 4	174. 7	190. 5
Army ordnance	93. 7	91. 6	127. 7	120. 9	122. 4	141. 4	138. 9	137. 5	155. 4	131. 7	147. 4	174. 4
Motor vehicles	64. 0	61. 4	63. 3	69. 9	55. 7	73. 2	76. 7	55. 9	65. 9	50. 0	41. 8	62. 3
Aircraft	136. 9	146. 1	129. 4	145. 6	130. 5	159. 2	177. 5	199. 0	213. 8	216. 6	222. 4	244. 0
Total	109. 8	113. 1	117. 1	118. 8	115. 3	127. 5	134. 8	135. 1	146. 9	142. 5	148. 8	164. 7

FISCAL YEAR 1943

	April	May	June	July	August	September	October	November	December	January	February	March
Merchant ships	174. 4	217. 3	248. 6	265. 6	277. 9	280. 0	289. 6	301. 2	353. 7	444. 6	417. 9	410. 1
Navy ships	127. 6	131. 6	134. 0	136. 3	133. 1	136. 1	140. 1	153. 5	157. 6	161. 1	174. 1	162. 1
Navy ordnance	164. 7	185. 2	193. 7	206. 9	231. 7	253. 8	265. 0	283. 0	314. 5	305. 0	359. 6	385. 4
Army ordnance	128. 7	145. 8	160. 6	147. 9	152. 2	157. 2	166. 5	174. 5	191. 4	187. 3	187. 8	189. 8
Motor vehicles	50. 0	57. 2	38. 2	52. 6	47. 7	49. 6	41. 0	35. 2	36. 6	39. 7	42. 2	55. 9
Aircraft	247. 4	258. 4	261. 9	272. 8	309. 8	349. 7	361. 1	415. 3	472. 4	464. 1	478. 4	529. 5
Total	151. 2	164. 5	171. 8	178. 1	190. 0	204. 1	210. 8	228. 2	254. 8	248. 3	263. 6	276. 3

FISCAL YEAR 1944

	April	May	June	July	August	September	October	November	December	January	February	March
Merchant ships	424. 0	422. 7	413. 0	408. 6	440. 7	353. 8	364. 1	337. 7	304. 0	251. 0	227. 4	151. 4
Navy ships	207. 2	216. 8	223. 3	229. 8	233. 3	232. 8	215. 3	204. 5	204. 9	186. 4	170. 4	161. 9
Navy ordnance	431. 7	456. 4	489. 4	490. 2	512. 4	528. 5	525. 0	514. 7	501. 5	463. 3	422. 0	399. 1
Army ordnance	170. 0	178. 4	175. 0	185. 2	241. 9	224. 4	212. 6	215. 4	244. 8	266. 8	273. 6	255. 2
Motor vehicles	41. 3	63. 7	44. 6	47. 9	35. 2	34. 9	44. 4	48. 9	31. 1	22. 4	26. 6	27. 0
Aircraft	550. 3	514. 9	580. 3	577. 8	556. 9	628. 2	614. 3	603. 7	565. 7	463. 6	366. 3	457. 7
Total	291. 2	295. 4	315. 8	315. 3	326. 6	332. 5	330. 9	328. 4	314. 9	291. 9	261. 3	263. 1

FISCAL YEAR 1945

	April	May	June	July	August	September	October	November	December	January	February	March
Merchant ships	153. 3	125. 5	98. 3	88. 6	62. 6							
Navy ships	130. 9	121. 2	116. 7	109. 6								
Navy ordnance	411. 6	391. 6	326. 4	264. 7	118. 3							
Army ordnance	150. 3	144. 0	149. 5	126. 8								
Motor vehicles	15. 8	32. 3	5. 9	8. 5								
Aircraft	434. 0	418. 5	334. 9	271. 4	119. 0							
Total	231. 2	221. 6	187. 1	156. 6								

Source: Military Supplies Division, USSBS.

Appendix Table C-145.—Merchant ship yen value input (¥ 1,000), 1941–45

FISCAL YEAR 1941

Ship type	April	May	June	July	August	September	October	November	December	January	February	March	Total
Cargo	18,246	15,811	14,055	13,257	13,445	12,901	13,002	13,377	13,483	13,388	12,502	12,262	165,729
Tanker	1,410	1,203	1,701	1,865	1,712	1,373	1,699	1,699	3,697	5,137	5,137	6,742	33,375
Ore carrier					1,562	1,562	1,562	2,088	2,088	2,436	2,436	2,436	16,170
Passenger	3,827	3,254	3,254	3,634	3,893	3,037	2,701	2,701	2,701	2,701	2,701	2,157	36,561
Ferry					714	715	714	715	714	715			4,287
Fisher	929	490	879	994	904	904	904	742	694	694	694	694	9,522
Tug	660	923	923	834	794	794	794	419	393	393	500	533	7,960
Miscellaneous	951	1,095	940	991	1,345	863	574	574	538	622	2,825	1,443	12,761
Total, new construction	26,023	22,776	21,752	21,575	24,369	22,149	21,950	22,315	24,308	26,086	26,795	26,267	286,365
Repair and conversion	9,393	9,393	9,393	9,393	9,393	9,393	9,393	9,393	10,091	9,276	10,365	11,298	116,174
Grand total	35,416	32,169	31,145	30,968	33,762	31,540	31,343	31,708	34,339	35,362	37,160	37,565	402,539

FISCAL YEAR 1942

Ship type	April	May	June	July	August	September	October	November	December	January	February	March	Total
Cargo	11,061	12,118	13,782	13,209	12,562	12,945	13,464	15,855	20,087	22,070	25,300	24,135	196,588
Tanker	6,659	7,203	6,052	6,052	5,793	5,124	5,902	10,094	10,696	11,911	12,853	16,234	104,573
Ore carrier	3,029	3,029	2,555	2,845	3,006	3,993	3,655	3,307	2,715	4,742	7,284	7,273	47,433
Passenger	1,828	1,828	2,287	2,287	2,287	2,287	2,145	2,145	2,041	1,661	1,084	1,730	23,610
Ferry	636	636	622	622	278	217	217	201	149	149	225	331	4,283
Fisher	699	699	699	722	517	535	337	1,016	911	983	1,077	1,283	9,478
Tug	271	424	424	394	533	615	1,192	2,447	2,995	2,193	2,193	1,434	15,115
Miscellaneous													
Total, new construction	24,183	25,937	26,421	26,131	24,976	25,716	26,912	35,065	39,594	43,709	50,016	52,420	401,080
Repair and conversion	11,563	12,135	12,412	13,087	12,475	10,292	10,819	9,502	10,859	8,870	10,114	10,118	132,246
Grand total	35,746	38,072	38,833	39,218	37,451	36,008	37,731	44,567	50,453	52,579	60,130	62,538	533,326

FISCAL YEAR 1943

Ship type	April	May	June	July	August	September	October	November	December	January	February	March	Total
Cargo	21,413	26,874	31,818	36,679	39,127	43,628	46,024	53,522	66,148	91,480	88,115	88,931	633,859
Tanker	18,798	22,426	25,960	27,938	31,619	27,750	27,707	28,841	28,891	38,665	38,185	36,544	353,324
Ore carrier	5,535	6,266	6,814	8,733	9,811	9,828	8,498	6,151	7,684	4,634	1,150		75,104
Passenger	1,730	1,730	1,798	1,798	1,798	1,157	1,410	1,410	3,490	3,032	3,032	1,103	24,129
Ferry	411	411	687	687	1,157	563	2,192	2,192	1,504	1,504	470	1,052	12,602
Fisher	411	411	411	687	515	563	598	598	829	888	1,372	1,618	8,625

	1	2	3	4	5	6	7	8	9	10	11	12	Total
Tug	786	786	535	572	671	697	806	757	594	560	599	315	7,678
Miscellaneous	749	6,441	6,557	3,334	430	315	231	365	365	365	418	334	19,904
Total, new construction	49,422	64,934	74,580	80,152	85,128	85,736	87,466	93,836	109,505	141,128	133,341	129,897	1,135,125
Repair and conversion	9,086	7,961	8,829	8,939	8,115	8,183	9,680	7,211	9,155	8,028	6,832	7,668	99,687
Grand total	58,508	72,895	83,409	89,091	93,243	93,919	97,146	101,047	118,660	149,156	140,173	137,565	1,234,812

FISCAL YEAR 1944

	1	2	3	4	5	6	7	8	9	10	11	12	Total
Cargo	80,044	72,386	66,597	65,830	75,712	73,198	78,779	81,118	77,903	71,228	69,592	43,647	856,034
Tanker	47,527	52,679	55,246	56,249	55,778	54,263	52,832	38,421	26,876	11,829	5,282	820	457,802
Ore carrier								1,443	1,443	1,443	124	124	4,577
Passenger	1,408	2,509	2,509	2,203	3,284	3,592	3,592	2,489	2,489	1,388	1,388	1,388	28,239
Ferry	1,052	1,894	1,894	842	1,544	1,544	702	702	1,543	2,056	1,513	1,513	16,299
Fisher	1,754	1,689	1,451	1,421	1,356	1,080	963	1,123	1,192	807	793	622	14,251
Tug	315	265	265	291	291	291	291	265	265	265	265	235	3,304
Miscellaneous	250	457	457	637	637	637	520	520	314	314	133	133	5,009
Total, new construction	132,350	131,879	128,419	127,473	138,602	134,605	137,679	126,081	112,025	89,330	79,090	48,482	1,385,515
Repair and conversion	9,874	9,934	10,131	9,608	9,222	7,826	8,911	9,849	10,341	11,703	12,442	12,472	122,313
Grand total	142,224	141,813	138,551	137,082	147,824	142,430	146,590	135,931	122,268	101,034	91,531	60,954	1,508,332

FISCAL YEAR 1945

	1	2	3	4	5	6	7	8	9	10	11	12	Total
Cargo	32,949	25,333	17,910	16,535	10,090								102,817
Tanker	797	797	797	797	797								3,985
Ore carrier	124	124	124	124	124								620
Passenger	307	307	307	307	307								1,535
Ferry	1,513	671	671	671	671								4,197
Fisher	389	389	389	316	316								1,799
Tug	196	232	188	189	167								972
Miscellaneous	133	133	133	133	80								612
Total, new construction	36,408	27,986	20,519	19,072	12,552								116,537
Repair and conversion	15,024	14,100	12,447	10,659	8,450								60,680
Grand total	51,432	42,086	32,966	29,731	21,002								177,217

Source: Military Supplies Division, USSBS.

FISCAL YEAR 1941

Ship type	April	May	June	July	August	September	October	November	December	January	February	March	Total
Cargo	132.1	114.5	101.8	96.0	97.4	93.4	94.1	96.9	97.6	96.9	90.5	88.8	100.0
Tanker	50.7	43.3	61.2	67.1	61.6	49.4	61.1	61.1	132.9	184.7	184.7	242.4	100.0
Ore carrier	—	—	—	—	115.9	115.9	115.9	155.0	155.0	180.8	180.8	180.8	100.0
Passenger	125.6	106.8	106.8	119.3	127.8	99.7	88.6	88.6	88.6	88.6	88.6	70.8	100.0
Ferry	—	—	—	—	200.0	200.0	200.0	200.0	200.0	200.0	—	—	100.0
Fisher	117.1	61.7	110.7	125.2	113.9	113.9	113.9	93.5	87.4	84.4	87.4	87.4	100.0
Tug	99.5	139.2	139.2	125.8	119.7	119.7	119.7	63.2	59.3	59.8	75.4	80.4	100.0
Miscellaneous	89.4	103.0	88.4	93.2	126.5	81.1	54.0	54.0	50.6	58.5	265.6	135.7	100.0
New construction total	109.1	95.5	91.2	90.4	102.1	92.8	92.0	93.5	101.9	109.3	112.3	110.1	100.0
Wooden ships													
Repair and conversion	97.0	97.0	97.0	97.0	97.0	97.0	97.0	94.0	104.2	95.8	107.1	116.7	100.0
Grand total	105.6	95.9	92.8	92.3	100.6	94.0	93.4	94.5	102.5	105.4	110.8	112.0	100.0

FISCAL YEAR 1942

Ship type	April	May	June	July	August	September	October	November	December	January	February	March	Total
Cargo	80.1	87.7	99.8	95.6	91.0	93.7	97.5	114.8	145.4	159.8	183.2	174.8	118.6
Tanker	239.5	259.0	217.6	217.6	208.3	184.3	212.2	363.0	384.6	428.3	462.1	583.8	313.3
Ore carrier	224.8	224.8	159.6	211.2	223.1	296.4	271.3	245.4	201.5	352.0	540.6	539.8	293.4
Passenger	60.0	60.0	75.1	75.1	75.1	75.1	70.4	70.4	67.0	54.5	35.6	56.8	64.5
Ferry													
Fisher	80.1	80.1	78.4	78.4	35.0	27.3	27.3	25.3	18.8	18.8	28.4	41.7	45.0
Tug	105.4	105.4	105.4	108.9	78.0	80.7	50.8	153.2	137.4	148.2	162.4	193.5	119.1
Miscellaneous	25.5	39.9	39.9	37.0	50.1	57.8	112.1	230.1	281.6	206.2	206.2	134.8	118.4
Wooden ships	—	—	.4	.4	.6	3.3	5.8	21.5	40.7	81.1	117.4	168.3	36.6
New construction total	101.4	108.7	110.7	109.6	104.7	108.1	113.4	149.3	170.4	192.1	222.6	238.3	144.1
Repair and conversion	119.4	125.4	128.2	135.2	128.9	106.3	111.7	98.2	112.2	91.6	104.5	104.5	113.8
Grand total	106.6	113.5	115.8	116.9	111.7	107.6	112.9	134.5	153.6	163.1	188.5	199.7	135.4

FISCAL YEAR 1943

Ship type	April	May	June	July	August	September	October	November	December	January	February	March	Total
Cargo	155.1	194.6	230.4	265.6	283.3	315.9	333.3	387.6	479.0	662.4	638.0	643.9	382.5
Tanker	676.0	806.4	933.5	1,004.7	1,137.0	997.9	996.3	1,037.1	1,038.9	1,390.4	1,373.1	1,314.1	1,058.6
Ore carrier	410.8	465.1	505.7	648.2	728.2	729.4	630.7	456.5	570.3	343.9	85.4	—	464.5
Passenger	56.8	56.8	59.0	59.0	59.0	59.0	46.3	46.3	114.5	99.5	99.5	36.2	66.0
Ferry	192.3	192.3	192.3	192.3	323.8	323.8	613.5	613.5	421.0	421.0	131.6	294.5	294.0
Fisher	51.8	51.8	51.8	51.8	64.9	70.9	75.3	75.3	104.5	111.9	172.9	203.9	90.6
Tug	118.5	118.5	60.7	86.3	101.8	105.1	121.5	114.2	89.6	84.4	90.3	47.5	96.4

Miscellaneous	156.0	31.4	39.3	34.3	34.3	21.7	29.6	40.4	313.5	616.6	605.6	70.4	
Wooden ships	556.9	850.0	838.5	801.9	792.7	764.0	675.0	503.1	369.9	326.8	305.1	246.0	209.7
Total	458.0	638.4	651.5	680.1	546.6	477.7	441.2	414.9	397.7	372.0	346.3	303.5	230.3
Repair and conversion	85.8	79.2	70.6	82.9	94.6	74.5	100.0	84.5	83.8	92.3	91.2	82.2	93.9
Grand total	350.5	476.9	483.8	507.7	416.1	361.3	342.7	319.5	307.0	291.3	272.6	236.6	190.9

FISCAL YEAR 1944

Cargo	516.5	316.0	503.9	515.8	564.1	587.4	570.4	530.0	548.2	476.7	482.2	524.1	579.6
Tanker	1,371.6	29.5	189.9	425.4	966.5	1,381.6	1,899.8	1,951.3	2,005.8	2,022.8	1,986.6	1,894.3	1,709.1
Ore carrier	28.3	8.2	9.2	45.6	107.1	107.1	107.1	117.9	117.9	72.3	82.3	82.3	46.2
Passenger	77.2	45.6	45.6	45.6	81.7	81.7	81.7	432.2	432.2	235.7	530.1	530.1	294.5
Ferry	391.9	423.5	423.5	575.5	431.9	196.5	196.5	432.2	170.9	182.8	182.8	212.8	221.0
Fisher	149.6	78.4	99.9	101.7	150.2	141.5	121.3	136.1	43.9	43.9	40.0	40.0	47.5
Tug	41.6	35.4	40.0	40.0	40.0	40.0	43.9	43.9	59.9	59.9	43.0	40.0	23.5
Miscellaneous	39.3	12.5	12.5	29.5	29.5	48.9	48.9	59.9	459.2	638.9	809.6	43.0	840.2
Wooden ships	496.7	203.2	245.2	277.2	327.7	376.0	423.7	459.2	503.1	638.9	809.6	857.0	840.2
Total	538.9	225.7	358.6	405.0	505.7	570.0	623.9	614.9	636.5	604.9	627.7	647.4	647.6
Repair and conversion	105.3	128.8	128.5	120.9	106.8	101.7	92.1	80.8	95.3	99.3	104.7	102.6	102.0
Grand total	413.7	197.7	292.1	323.0	390.5	434.8	470.3	460.7	480.2	458.9	476.7	490.1	490.0

FISCAL YEAR 1945

Cargo	148.9	—	—	—	—	—	—	—	73.1	119.7	129.7	183.4	238.6
Tanker	28.6	—	—	—	—	—	—	—	28.6	28.6	28.6	28.6	28.6
Ore carrier	9.2	—	—	—	—	—	—	—	9.2	9.2	9.2	9.2	9.2
Passenger	10.1	—	—	—	—	—	—	—	10.1	10.1	10.1	10.1	10.1
Ferry	234.8	—	—	—	—	—	—	—	196.6	196.6	196.6	196.6	443.3
Fisher	45.4	—	—	—	—	—	—	—	39.8	39.8	49.9	49.0	49.0
Tug	29.3	—	—	—	—	—	—	—	25.2	28.5	28.5	35.0	29.6
Miscellaneous	11.5	—	—	—	—	—	—	—	7.5	12.5	12.5	12.5	12.5
Wooden ships	71.7	—	—	—	—	—	—	—	14.7	38.4	68.7	94.6	142.2
Total	105.6	—	—	—	—	—	—	—	54.2	84.2	93.6	127.8	16.83
Repair and conversion	125.4	—	—	—	—	—	—	—	87.3	110.1	128.6	145.7	155.2
Grand total	111.3	—	—	—	—	—	—	—	63.8	91.6	103.7	132.9	164.5

Source: Military Supplies Division, USSBS.
For actual merchant tonnage constructed, and number of ships, see this appendix, section on Transportation.

APPENDIX TABLE C–147—*Value of Japanese aircraft production, monthly, 1941-1945, in 1945 prices (1,000,000¥)*

COMPLETED AIRCRAFT

Year	April	May	June	July	August	September	October	November	December	January	February	March	Total
1941____	46. 5	54. 1	55. 3	52. 6	59. 2	63. 7	70. 5	71. 0	86. 7	85. 0	83. 8	97. 1	825. 5
1942____	94. 2	100. 5	89. 0	100. 2	89. 8	109. 5	122. 1	136. 9	147. 1	149. 0	153. 0	167. 9	1, 459. 2
1943____	170. 2	177. 8	180. 2	187. 7	213. 1	240. 6	248. 4	285. 7	325. 0	270. 0	283. 1	303. 0	2, 884. 8
1944____	314. 8	307. 5	341. 9	339. 1	316. 1	361. 6	356. 1	363. 1	337. 8	318. 9	252. 0	314. 9	3, 923. 8
1945____	361. 2	350. 1	279. 8	225. 8									1, 216. 6

COMPLETED AIRCRAFT AND SPARE PARTS

Year	April	May	June	July	August	September	October	November	December	January	February	March	Total
1941____	61. 9	70. 2	72. 1	70. 5	77. 6	84. 3	92. 4	92. 4	113. 2	112. 7	110. 0	123. 3	1, 090. 6
1942____	123. 1	129. 0	114. 5	128. 0	115. 3	137. 0	152. 9	168. 2	184. 7	187. 1	191. 4	211. 5	1, 842. 7
1943____	214. 0	224. 2	229. 4	239. 6	268. 3	302. 2	312. 8	354. 2	406. 6	354. 9	372. 1	408. 5	3, 686. 8
1944____	416. 0	386. 8	465. 7	441. 5	422. 7	452. 2	462. 9	475. 4	428. 7	385. 8	304. 0	382. 4	5, 024. 1
1945____	361. 2	350. 1	279. 8	225. 5									1, 216. 6

Source: Air Ordnance Bureau, Munition Ministry, War and Navy Ministeries.
Note.—For actual number of aircraft produced, see this Appendix, section on aircraft.

APPENDIX TABLE C.-148.—*Value of Japanese naval vessels production, monthly, by fiscal year, 1941–45*

[1,000,000v]

FISCAL YEAR 1941

Type	April	May	June	July	August	September	October	November	December	January	February	March	Total
Battleships_____	5. 40	5. 40	5. 40	5. 40	5. 40	5. 40	5. 40	5. 40	4. 00	2. 60	2. 60	2. 60	55. 00
Carriers_____	23. 11	23. 11	23. 11	23. 11	21. 83	18. 52	16. 62	16. 35	15. 56	15. 56	15. 56	15. 56	228. 00
Cruisers_____	4. 27	4. 27	4. 27	3. 57	2. 86	4. 74	4. 74	5. 81	6. 36	6. 36	6. 36	6. 36	59. 97
Seaplane carriers_____	1. 94	1. 94	1. 94	1. 94	1. 94	1. 94	1. 94	1. 94	1. 94	1. 94	1. 89	1. 01	22. 30
Mine layers_____	3. 40	3. 40	3. 40	3. 62	3. 77	3. 77	3. 42	2. 85	2. 20	1. 92	1. 92	1. 45	35. 12
Destroyers_____	8. 42	7. 06	8. 49	7. 75	8. 04	8. 18	7. 85	9. 05	10. 4	10. 78	10. 33	11. 76	108. 37
Mine sweepers_____	1. 01	1. 01	. 49	. 49	. 65	. 65	1. 32	1. 46	1. 17	. 92	1. 23	1. 29	11. 64
Coast defense_____													
Transports_____													
Submarines_____	11. 36	11. 71	13. 81	15. 08	15. 14	15. 60	15. 75	15. 08	16. 13	17. 01	17. 05	17. 71	181. 43
Subchasers_____	3. 58	3. 68	5. 12	5. 89	4. 99	4. 62	4. 10	4. 52	4. 88	3. 69	3. 90	5. 32	54. 29
Landing craft_____													
Special attack_____													
Auxilliary_____	11. 08	11. 08	11. 08	11. 08	11. 08	11. 08	11. 08	11. 08	11. 08	11. 08	11. 08	11. 08	132. 96
Total_____	73. 57	72. 66	77. 11	77. 93	75. 70	74. 70	72. 22	73. 49	73. 78	71. 86	72. 67	76. 00	891. 49

FISCAL YEAR 1942

Type	April	May	June	July	August	September	October	November	December	January	February	March	Total
Battleships_____	2. 60	2. 60	2. 60	2. 60	0. 44								10. 84
Carriers_____	15. 84	14. 86	13. 28	13. 28	14. 48	14. 48	16. 83	16. 65	17. 48	18. 24	18. 24	18. 24	191. 90
Cruisers_____	6. 36	6. 36	6. 36	6. 36	6. 36	6. 36	6. 36	5. 74	6. 87	6. 87	6. 87	5. 19	76. 06
Seaplane carriers_____	. 97												. 97
Mine layers_____	1. 11	. 80	. 80	. 94	1. 22	. 85	. 85	. 63	. 42	. 42	. 42	. 42	8. 86
Destroyers_____	12. 19	12. 78	11. 07	11. 89	12. 59	10. 22	11. 47	11. 47	11. 25	10. 68	10. 97	11. 35	137. 93
Mine sweepers_____	1. 57	2. 27	3. 02	2. 64	2. 20	2. 20	2. 20	2. 58	2. 78	2. 90	2. 89	2. 82	30. 07
Coast Defense_____	1. 86	2. 25	2. 43	2. 86	3. 07	3. 07	3. 50	4. 59	4. 62	4. 62	5. 07	5. 59	43. 53
Transports_____													
Submarine_____	20. 69	22. 12	22. 77	25. 32	26. 43	25. 29	26. 48	28. 31	29. 88	30. 23	32. 12	32. 96	322. 60
Subchaser_____	6. 10	5. 73	5. 37	5. 10	4. 88	4. 43	4. 28	3. 19	3. 16	3. 40	3. 86	3. 34	52. 84
Landing craft_____													
Special attack_____													
Auxiliary_____	11. 12	11. 12	11. 12	11. 12	11. 12	11. 12	11. 12	11. 12	11. 12	11. 12	11. 12	11. 12	133. 44
Total_____	80. 39	81. 08	78. 77	82. 11	82. 77	78. 00	83. 08	84. 28	87. 57	88. 48	91. 55	91. 02	1, 009. 11

Source: Navy Ministry.

FISCAL YEAR 1943

Type	April	May	June	July	August	September	October	November	December	January	February	March	Total
Carriers	19.49	20.68	22.48	26.67	25.58	25.58	25.58	25.29	23.63	22.85	22.85	21.39	282.07
Cruisers	5.19	5.19	5.19	3.31	3.31	3.19	1.70	1.70	1.70	1.70	1.70	1.70	35.58
Mine layers	.42	.42	.42	.42									1.68
Destroyers	10.82	9.80	9.84	9.76	8.65	9.80	10.07	10.83	10.63	12.31	19.20	17.95	139.66
Mine sweepers	1.77	1.71	1.68	1.40	1.18	1.89	1.79	1.58	2.66	3.11	2.54	2.42	23.73
Coast defense	5.72	5.83	6.48	6.03	6.06	6.87	13.59	23.37	25.93	28.25	33.11	26.62	187.86
Transports							.09	1.11	1.99	2.83	5.17	5.10	16.29
Submarines	33.51	36.07	35.39	35.84	36.18	36.15	34.08	34.26	36.08	34.21	32.44	32.62	419.53
Subchasers	4.25	4.89	5.17	5.22	4.90	4.96	4.96	5.00	3.94	4.21	3.51	2.65	53.66
Landing craft	1.47	1.47	1.47	1.47	1.47	1.47	1.47	1.47	1.47	1.47	1.47	1.47	17.64
Special attack													
Auxiliaries	10.32	10.32	10.32	10.32	10.32	10.32	10.32	10.32	10.32	10.32	10.32	10.32	123.84
Total	92.96	96.38	98.44	100.44	97.65	100.23	103.65	114.93	118.35	121.26	132.31	122.24	1,298.84

FISCAL YEAR 1944

Type	April	May	June	July	August	September	October	November	December	January	February	March	Total
Carriers	20.91	20.91	20.91	20.91	16.62	15.03	13.50	7.28	3.56	3.56	3.56	3.02	149.77
Cruisers	1.70	1.70	1.70	1.70	1.70	1.70	1.70	1.70					13.60
Mine layers											.28	.86	1.14
Destroyers	17.73	19.48	20.36	20.58	20.05	20.94	18.22	21.67	25.67	19.59	17.08	14.21	235.58
Mine sweepers	2.42	2.35	.64	.24									5.65
Coast defense	24.67	30.37	38.15	43.72	48.93	57.06	51.30	47.65	53.00	48.47	39.36	33.45	516.13
Transports	6.33	7.55	8.62	9.58	10.93	9.08	6.48	5.28	3.98	1.70	1.44	1.91	72.88
Submarines	32.46	32.03	29.59	29.66	28.53	25.16	22.91	21.77	19.43	16.74	14.86	15.85	288.98
Subchasers	1.36	1.36	1.28	.31	.31	.31	.28						5.21
Landing craft	9.03	9.03	9.03	9.03	9.03	9.03	9.03	9.03	9.03	9.03	9.03	9.03	108.36
Special attack	17.15	17.15	17.15	17.15	17.15	17.15	17.15	17.15	17.15	17.15	17.15	17.15	205.80
Auxiliaries	20.19	20.19	20.19	20.19	20.19	20.19	20.19	20.19	20.19	20.19	20.19	20.19	242.28
Total	153.95	162.12	167.62	173.07	173.44	175.64	160.76	151.72	152.01	136.43	122.95	115.67	1,845.38

FISCAL YEAR 1945

Type	April	May	June	July	August	September	October	November	December	January	February	March	Total
Carriers	0.08												0.08
Mine layers	.86	0.86	0.86	0.86	0.42								3.86
Destroyers	8.48	5.40	2.10										16.08
Mine sweepers													
Coast defense	20.53	15.81	12.83	9.69	4.39								63.25
Transports	1.53	1.10	.66	.33									3.62
Submarines	17.48	17.50	20.53	20.12	8.78								84.41
Landing craft	3.91	3.91	3.91	3.91	1.87								17.51
Special attack	23.92	23.92	23.92	23.92	11.96								
Auxiliaries	1.80	1.80	1.80	1.80	.90								8.10
Total	78.59	70.40	66.61	60.63	28.32								304.55

Source: Navy Ministry.

[Average month in 1941=100]

FISCAL YEAR 1941

Type	April	May	June	July	August	September	October	November	December	January	February	March
Battleships	118	118	118	118	118	118	118	118	87	57	57	57
Carriers	122	122	122	122	115	97	87	86	82	82	82	82
Cruisers	85	85	85	71	57	95	95	116	127	127	127	127
Seaplane carriers	104	104	104	104	104	104	104	104	104	104	104	55
Mine layers	116	116	116	124	129	129	117	97	75	66	66	49
Destroyers	93	78	94	86	89	91	87	100	116	119	117	130
Mine sweepers	104	104	51	51	67	67	136	145	120	95	127	133
Coast defense											15	51
Transports												
Submarines	75	78	91	100	100	103	103	100	107	113	113	117
Subchasers	79	81	113	130	110	102	91	100	108	82	86	118
Landing craft												
Special attack												
Auxiliaries	100	100	100	100	100	100	100	100	100	100	100	100
Total	105.0	103.2	107.2	107.2	104.1	101.2	97.4	99.3	96.3	91.7	92.4	95.1

FISCAL YEAR 1942

Type	April	May	June	July	August	September	October	November	December	January	February	March
Battleships	57	57	57	57	10							
Carriers	83	78	70	70	76	76	89	88	92	92	92	92
Crusiers	127	127	127	127	127	127	127	115	138	138	138	104
Seaplane carriers	52											
Mine layers	38	27	27	32	42	29	29	22	14	14	14	14
Destroyers	135	142	123	132	139	113	127	127	125	118	121	126
Mine sweepers	162	234	311	273	227	227	227	267	286	299	298	291
Coast defense	51	62	67	79	85	85	96	127	127	127	140	154
Transports												
Submarines	137	146	151	168	175	167	175	187	198	200	213	218
Subchasers	135	129	119	113	108	98	95	70	70	75	85	74
Landing craft												
Special attack												
Auxiliaries	101	101	101	101	101	101	101	101	101	101	101	101
Total	99.0	98.2	94.6	97.7	94.6	88.8	95.6	96.7	100.5	101.7	104.4	103.5

FISCAL YEAR 1943

Type	April	May	June	July	August	September	October	November	December	January	February	March
Battleships												
Carriers	103	109	118	133	135	135	135	133	124	120	120	113
Cruisers	104	104	104	66	66	64	34	34	34	34	34	34
Mine layers	14	14	14	14								
Destroyers	120	109	110	108	96	109	111	120	118	136	213	199
Mine sweepers	182	177	174	145	122	195	185	163	274	321	262	249
Coast defense	158	161	179	166	167	190	375	644	715	779	913	577
Transports							3	34	61	87	160	157
Submarines	222	239	234	237	246	239	226	227	239	227	215	216
Subchasers	94	108	114	115	108	110	110	111	87	93	78	59
Landing craft	100	100	100	100	100	100	100	100	100	100	100	100
Special attack												
Auxiliaries	93	93	93	93	93	93	93	93	93	93	93	93
Total	107.8	111.2	114.7	116.5	115.2	118.1	123.2	140.7	147.1	154.2	178.4	158.9

APPENDIX TABLE C–149.— *Monthly indices of Japanese naval ship production, by fiscal year, 1941–45*—Continued

FISCAL YEAR 1944

Type	April	May	June	July	August	September	October	November	December	January	February	March
Battleships												
Carriers	110	110	110	110	87	79	71	38	19	19	19	16
Cruisers	34	34	34	34	34	34	34	34				
Mine layers												
Destroyers	196	216	225	228	222	232	202	240	284	217	189	157
Mine sweepers	249	242	66	24								
Coast defense	680	838	1,052	1,205	1,349	1,573	1,414	1,314	1,461	1,337	1,085	925
Transports	195	232	266	296	337	280	200	163	123	52	44	59
Submarines	215	212	196	196	189	167	152	144	129	111	98	105
Subchasers	30	30	28	7	7	7	6					
Landing craft	614	614	614	614	614	614	614	614	614	614	614	614
Special attack	100	100	100	100	100	100	100	100	100	100	100	100
Auxiliaries	182	182	182	182	182	182	182	182	182	182	182	182
Total	203.5	218.6	231.0	242.0	246.4	241.8	213.3	194.9	188.7	161.7	145.2	137.6

FISCAL YEAR 1945

Type	April	May	June	July	August	September	October	November	December	January	February	March
Battleships												
Carriers	4											
Cruisers												
Mine layers	29	29	29	29	14							
Destroyers	94	61	23									
Mine sweepers												
Coast defense	566	436	354	267	121							
Transports	47	34	20	10								
Submarines	116	116	136	133	58							
Subchasers												
Landing craft	266	266	266	266	127							
Special attack	139	139	139	139	70							
Auxiliaries	16	16	16	16	8							
Total	77.3	65.6	58.0	49.7	22.2							

Source: Military Supplies Division, USSBS.

Appendix Table C-150.—*Delivered tonnage and number of ships, Japanese navy, by fiscal year 1931-45*

Class	Total prior 1931	Fiscal years							
		1931	1932	1933	1934	1935	1936	1937	1938
Battleships _____ tons__	298,000	--------	19,500	--------	--------	--------	--------	--------	--------
number__	9	--------	1	--------	--------	--------	--------	--------	--------
Carriers _____ tons__	92,500	--------	--------	7,400	--------	--------	--------	10,050	27,000
number__	5	--------	--------	1	--------	--------	--------	1	3
Cruisers _____ tons__	149,000	9,850	29,550	--------	--------	17,000	--------	17,000	8,500
number__	25	1	3	--------	--------	2	--------	2	1
Destroyers _____ tons__	86,050	5,100	8,500	2,736	5,472	--------	6,840	17,340	1,500
number__	73	3	5	2	4	--------	5	12	1
Submarines _____ tons__	48,450	--------	6,869	--------	1,400	6,855	4,755	700	4,755
number__	35	--------	4	--------	1	5	3	1	3
Coast defense _____ tons__	43,090	--------	--------	--------	--------	--------	--------	--------	--------
number__	5	--------	--------	--------	--------	--------	--------	--------	--------
Transports _____ tons__	--------	--------	--------	--------	--------	--------	--------	--------	--------
number__		--------	--------	--------	--------	--------	--------	--------	--------
Minelayers _____ tons__	1,840	--------	1,135	443	886	--------	4,400	--------	720
number__	3	--------	1	1	2	--------	1	--------	1
Mine sweepers _____ tons__	3,690	--------	--------	984	984	492	492	--------	1,260
number__	6	--------	--------	2	2	1	1	--------	2
Sub chasers _____ tons__		--------	--------	600	--------	--------	270	--------	1,450
number__		--------	--------	2	--------	--------	1	--------	5
Gun boats _____ tons__	3,400	--------	--------	--------	--------	--------	--------	--------	--------
number__	9	--------	--------	--------	--------	--------	--------	--------	--------
Torpedo boats _____ tons__		--------	--------	1,581	527	--------	2,380	2,380	--------
number__		--------	--------	3	1	--------	4	4	--------
Landing craft _____ tons__		--------	--------	--------	--------	--------	--------	--------	--------
number__		--------	--------	--------	--------	--------	--------	--------	--------
Special attack [1] _____ tons__		--------	--------	--------	--------	--------	--------	--------	--------
number__		--------	--------	--------	--------	--------	--------	--------	--------
Auxiliaries [2] _____ tons__	203,920	7,600	7,750	17,675	7,500	7,800	8,912	7,890	18,404
Grand total all classes__	929,940	22,550	73,304	31,419	16,769	32,147	28,049	55,360	63,589

See footnotes at end of table.

Class		1939	1940	1941	1942	1943	1944	1945 (April–July)	Total by class 1931–45	Grand total by class
		Fiscal years								
Battleships	tons	--------	--------	64,000	64,000	--------	--------	--------	147,500	445,500
	number	--------	--------	1	1	--------	--------	--------	3	12
Carriers	tons	10,050	9,500	74,000	86,050	60,360	114,500	--------	398,910	491,410
	number	1	1	5	6	3	4	--------	25	30
Cruisers	tons	8,500	11,600	5,800	14,500	16,000	8,000	--------	146,300	295,300
	number	1	2	1	2	2	1	--------	18	43
Destroyers	tons	13,000	16,000	18,160	21,660	30,360	45,600	9,000	201,268	287,318
	number	7	8	9	9	15	31	6	117	190
Submarines	tons	2,180	12,640	21,930	26,676	49,016	53,560	14,930	206,266	254,716
	number	1	6	11	22	40	37	22	156	191
Coast defense	tons	--------	3,440	--------	3,760	26,730	87,730	14,400	136,060	179,150
	number	--------	4	--------	4	32	111	18	169	174
Transports	tons	--------	--------	890	--------	6,840	61,100	6,280	75,110	75,110
	number	--------	--------	1	--------	7	57	5	70	70
Mine layers	tons	3,040	3,760	7,760	2,880	720	--------	--------	25,744	27,584
	number	4	4	5	4	1	--------	--------	24	27
Mine sweepers	tons	1,260	--------	1,260	3,150	3,780	2,520	--------	16,182	19,872
	number	2	--------	2	5	6	4	--------	27	33
Sub chasers	tons	1,160	1,320	5,720	6,600	7,040	1,320	--------	25,480	25,480
	number	4	3	13	15	16	3	--------	62	62
Gun boats	tons	320	1,310	990	--------	--------	--------	--------	2,620	6,020
	number	1	2	1	--------	--------	--------	--------	4	13
Torpedo boats	tons	--------	--------	--------	--------	--------	--------	--------	6,868	6,868
	number	--------	--------	--------	--------	--------	--------	--------	12	12
Landing craft	tons	--------	--------	--------	--------	6,280	38,655	10,420	55,355	55,355
	number	--------	--------	--------	--------	24	1,464	617	2,105	2,105
Special attack [1]	tons	--------	--------	--------	--------	--------	10,508	9,162	19,670	19,670
	number	--------	--------	--------	--------	--------	5,121	1,733	6,854	6,854
Auxiliaries [2]	tons	18,738	35,135	24,649	24,716	22,940	44,909	2,500	257,118	461,038
Grand total all classes		58,248	94,705	225,159	253,992	230,066	468,402	66,692	1,720,451	2,650,391

[1] Special attack vessels include suicide boat, 5- and 2-man submarines, and the "human" torpedo. All special attack vessels were classified under naval ammunition—not ships—by the Japanese Navy. Further details included in this report.

[2] Figures for auxiliary deliveries are estimated.

Source: Over-all table prepared from information received from Japanese Navy Ministry and Japanese Navy Technical Bureau.

APPENDIX TABLE C-151.—*Construction of important Japanese fleet units*

Type of ship	Tonnage	Average yen cost per ton	Average time, keel to launch	Average time, launch to delivery
			Days	*Days*
Battleship	64,000	2,140	1,007	793
Carriers	9,000	3,895	364	338
Do	17,500	3,895	421	315
Do	19,000	3,895	828	311
Cruiser	8,000	5,151	349	379
Destroyers	2,040	3,522	248	120
Do	1,260	3,522	161	80
Do	2,700	3,522	227	97
Submarines	429	8,317	164	210
Do	965	8,317	273	259
Do	1,500	8,317	319	372
Do	1,950	8,317	490	494
Do	2,200	8,317	480	634
Coast Defense	750	5,575	93	56
Do	940	5,575	105	101

Source: Navy Ministry.

APPENDIX TABLE C-152.—*Value of Japanese Army and Navy ammunition production, monthly, 1941–45 in 1945 prices*

[Millions of yen]

Year	Month												Total
	4	5	6	7	8	9	10	11	12	1	2	3	
1941	68.0	69.0	67.3	67.8	67.5	70.5	70.7	76.5	82.2	79.4	80.8	69.4	869.1
1942	93.6	98.0	103.3	95.9	100.8	108.5	117.1	110.4	112.2	113.3	116.9	126.3	1,296.9
1943	101.5	113.9	116.4	121.2	126.2	140.8	137.3	149.0	156.1	153.6	172.4	184.2	1,572.6
1944	211.5	207.2	194.7	208.5	210.4	216.6	213.9	214.0	200.0	191.8	181.1	176.3	2,426.0
1945	148.6	146.6	117.3	87.6									500.1

Sources: Japanese Army arsenals and Navy Ministry.

APPENDIX TABLE C-153.—*Japanese Army ordnance production by years, 1931–45*

[Values in thousands of yen]

	1931	1932	1933	1934	1935	1936	1937	1938	1939	1940	1941	1942	1943	1944	1945
Small arms	1,228	1,820	4,552	3,556	5,899	6,349	10,624	33,512	52,680	80,670	94,888	132,906	181,859	179,537	46,943
Aircraft arms	391	639	647	1,256	1,101	1,026	2,088	3,066	5,491	8,520	18,359	48,888	93,059	206,258	73,903
Artillery	3,048	4,528	11,655	11,536	12,087	21,404	23,840	24,151	40,982	69,705	97,419	124,115	164,770	135,039	29,231
Ground and AA ammunition	13,297	14,931	26,254	29,339	34,775	35,743	76,679	242,192	259,645	289,489	313,761	376,910	365,346	327,957	59,246
Air corps ammunition	210	382	3,249	3,820	4,117	5,120	17,236	47,240	37,927	36,510	50,282	111,321	144,262	273,573	64,729
Combat and tracked vehicles	400	820	580	580	900	2,385	3,015	18,739	52,196	118,273	247,487	307,485	280,112	232,147	54,817
Optical equipment	1,085	1,426	1,831	2,347	3,916	5,081	6,372	10,256	11,188	14,817	44,140	38,988	61,238	100,536	17,774
Radio and communication equipment	484	774	1,225	1,490	1,781	2,063	2,773	3,594	4,315	4,980	19,224	38,841	164,518	243,342	43,370
Marine transport							7,285	15,120	18,715	18,085	34,595	36,863	94,704	247,669	55,460
Miscellaneous	527	1,200	1,230	1,436	387	487	3,731	940	1,809	26,875	36,310	45,625	36,059	15,662	8,794
Balloon bombs															146,223
Total	20,670	26,520	51,223	55,360	64,963	79,658	153,643	398,810	484,948	667,924	956,462	1,261,942	1,585,927	2,108,093	454,767

Source: Japanese Army arsenals.

APPENDIX TABLE C-154.—*Japanese Army ordnance production by years 1931-45*

[Index numbers based on 1941 yearly totals]

	1931	1932	1933	1934	1935	1936	1937	1938	1939	1940	1941	1942	1943	1944	1945
Small arms	1.3	1.9	4.8	3.7	4.2	6.7	11.2	35.3	55.6	85.2	100	140.1	191.6	189.2	148.4
AC arms	2.1	3.5	3.5	6.8	6.0	5.6	11.4	16.7	29.9	46.5	100	266.7	507.5	1,123.3	1,202.7
Artillery	3.1	4.7	12.0	11.9	12.4	22.0	24.5	24.7	42.1	71.9	100	127.4	169.1	138.8	90.2
Ground and AA ammunition	4.2	4.8	8.4	9.4	11.1	11.4	24.6	70.8	82.8	92.5	100	120.3	116.4	104.7	57.1
Aircraft ammunition	.4	.8	6.5	7.6	8.2	10.2	34.3	93.8	75.3	72.5	100	221.5	287.0	544.0	386.0
Combat and tracked vehicles	.2	.3	.2	.2	.4	1.0	1.2	7.6	21.0	47.8	100	124.2	113.8	93.6	64.4
Optical equipment	2.5	3.2	4.1	5.3	8.8	11.5	14.4	23.4	25.6	33.5	100	88.4	139.1	226.6	120.7
Radio and communication equipment	2.5	4.0	6.4	7.7	9.3	10.7	14.4	18.7	22.5	25.9	100	204.2	855.7	1,265.6	728.7
Marine transportation							21.1	43.8	54.1	52.3	100	106.7	273.7	715.8	480.8
Total	2.2	2.8	5.5	5.8	6.8	8.4	16.1	41.9	51.0	70.2	100	132.5	166.5	221.3	143.3

SOURCE: Japanese Army arsenals.

APPENDIX TABLE C–155.—*Japanese naval ordnance—over-all indices of output, 1931–45*

[1941=100]

Year or month	Actual						Plans					
	Total	Guns	Ammunition	Bombs, mines, torpedoes	Optical and navigational	Radio and electrical equipment	Total	Guns	Ammunition	Bombs, mines, torpedoes	Optical and navigational	Radio and electrical equipment
1931	19	19	6									
1932	10	18	8									
1933	15	19	15									
1934	19	21	22									
1935	21	21	25									
1936	24	29	29									
1937	32	32	38									
1938	40	37	48									
1939	45	47	50									
1940	61	60	70	38	62	38						
1941	100	100	100	100	100	100	109	83	102	119	138	136
1942	157	190	151	174	150	158	178	192	158	201	193	220
1943	267	570	221	213	268	311	450	785	457	278	351	419
1944	523	1,508	345	310	464	641	782	1,774	649	474	654	1,031
1945	285	783	182	276	226	404				464	743	753
1941:												
April	88	74	99	72	67	79	103	64	99	106	115	131
May	90	83	97	74	77	89	101	68	96	106	116	131
June	88	80	91	79	87	91	98	67	89	107	119	131
July	89	88	92	80	86	84	101	73	94	107	123	133
August	91	87	91	86	89	95	103	78	96	108	123	136
September	93	94	94	83	96	97	105	80	98	108	132	136
October	96	96	96	85	103	106	107	80	100	113	135	136
November	104	109	104	99	107	107	110	85	104	113	140	137
December	113	128	109	125	134	103	116	92	109	114	142	137
January	108	104	104	135	105	99	117	96	108	134	149	139
February	111	125	106	129	120	103	121	105	108	148	154	140
March	123	131	118	162	131	147	128	109	120	148	154	140
1942:												
April	134	133	137	121	114	140	159	144	142	171	155	216
May	144	145	141	121	118	165	161	150	146	172	157	216
June	148	160	139	121	140	151	164	158	147	177	169	216
July	138	147	129	139	134	156	158	112	139	198	171	216
August	145	153	135	155	130	167	167	164	146	198	176	219
September	159	172	156	155	139	161	182	177	168	199	177	220
October	169	180	172	173	157	161	193	188	181	211	206	220
November	158	199	147	173	164	161	179	196	153	215	211	221
December	164	190	150	173	179	177	181	201	156	217	214	221
January	168	222	161	190	152	147	192	233	168	218	224	224
February	174	276	166	190	181	139	200	279	174	220	225	225
March	189	298	181	190	197	157	205	300	179	217	226	228
1943:												
April	168	281	130	164	180	227	382	399	430	233	252	371
May	189	310	153	181	208	255	394	505	435	230	257	371
June	198	333	163	177	222	261	403	557	444	231	278	375
July	212	358	176	183	243	278	421	664	448	250	301	377
August	237	507	192	199	257	275	428	683	451	257	312	387
September	260	497	225	190	282	309	438	754	455	257	344	390
October	271	512	222	205	301	366	450	789	459	286	364	398
November	290	552	246	230	316	348	465	875	464	288	377	422
December	322	769	264	214	333	363	480	914	469	309	405	454
January	312	760	262	236	337	304	499	1,098	475	325	422	481

Year or month	Actual						Plans					
	Total	Guns	Ammunition	Bombs, mines, torpedoes	Optical and navigational	Radio and electrical equipment	Total	Guns	Ammunition	Bombs, mines, torpedoes	Optical and navigational	Radio and electrical equipment
1943—Continued												
February	268	955	301	307	352	336	518	1, 098	481	351	447	499
March	394	1, 004	325	347	397	340	532	1, 212	486	354	448	499
1944:												
April	475	1, 138	396	396	373	481	680	1, 226	574	425	487	1, 033
May	502	1, 299	374	380	411	646	686	1, 320	572	416	497	1, 038
June	528	1, 439	333	375	439	883	722	1, 447	609	427	513	1, 042
July	539	1, 538	351	386	511	803	747	1, 580	630	439	574	1, 029
August	564	1, 772	342	413	662	797	779	1, 716	640	497	738	1, 022
September	581	1, 735	364	386	656	876	772	1, 807	621	466	743	1, 017
October	578	1, 902	364	358	568	800	813	2, 005	656	502	731	1, 011
November	566	1, 831	368	373	557	746	811	1, 835	680	494	754	1, 014
December	552	1, 659	335	350	591	884	831	1, 933	688	523	749	1, 028
January	509	1, 541	305.	326	505	833	831	1, 921	694	514	683	1, 037
February	464	1, 267	306	281	428	762	859	2, 091	714	542	696	1, 044
March	439	973	299	262	423	808	881	2, 402	712	477	686	1, 048
1945:												
April	389	1, 105	257	291	213	588				480	669	745
May	370	999	267	253	250	522				486	660	755
June	308	897	187	203	306	510				454	800	753
July	250	686	133	166	293	494				452	790	749
August	112	224	67	17	143	290				448	797	763
September												
October												
November												
December												
January												
February												
March												

APPENDIX TABLE C-156.—*Japanese war matériel on hand, 1941–45*

Units: Ammunition—one kaisenbun for one division.
Weapons—equipment for one division.
Motor vehicles—one vehicle.

AMMUNITION

	1941	1942	1943	1944	1945
Stocks at beginning of year	100	118	113	113	94
Production	19	25	25	20	8
Consumption	1	30	25	41	7
Stocks at end of year	118	113	113	94	95

WEAPONS

Stocks at beginning of year	95	109	117	130	116
Production	15	17	24	22	11
Consumption	1	9	11	36	7
Stocks at end of year	109	117	130	116	120

MOTOR VEHICLES (1,000 Vehicles)

Stocks at beginning of year	45	81	83	81	73
Requisitioned	18	2	0	1	0
Production	19	15	14	11	6
Consumption	1	15	16	20	10
Stocks at end of year	81	83	81	73	69

Source: War ministry.

APPENDIX TABLE C-157.—*Japanese production and imports of motor vehicles, by type, 1936–41*

	1936	1937	1938	1939	1940	1941
Light trucks:						
Domestic	5,757	12,669	10,988	6,283	4,818	4,264
Imports	0	0	0	0	0	0
2-ton trucks:						
Domestic	1,180	6,152	13,771	26,334	30,687	39,297
Imports	14,476	17,081	13,817	0	0	0
4-ton trucks:						
Domestic	0	0	1,325	3,357	2,551	2,828
Imports	0	0	0	0	0	0
Light cars:						
Domestic	1,513	4,856	2,308	1,816	1,496	464
Imports	0	0	0	0	0	0
Standard cars:						
Domestic	165	1,437	1,690	807	1,396	995
Imports	14,329	12,950	4,057	0	0	0
Busses:						
Domestic	226	528	798	2,711	1,599	53
Imports	3,370	2,908	719	0	0	0
Total:						
Domestic	8,841	25,642	30,880	41,308	42,547	47,901
Imports	32,175	32,939	18,593	0	0	0
Grand total	41,016	58,581	49,473	41,308	42,547	47,901

Source: Japanese Automobile Control Association.

APPENDIX TABLE C-158.—*Japanese planned and actual production of two- and four-ton trucks, 1940–45*

Year	2-ton truck production			4-ton truck production		
	Planned	Actual	Percent of plan obtained	Planned	Actual	Percent of plan obtained
1940	36,800	30,687	83	3,960	2,551	64
1941	44,800	39,297	88	3,960	2,828	72
1942	43,000	33,129	77	3,240	2,257	70
1943	34,850	21,987	63	3,000	2,013	67
1944	32,750	19,546	60	2,100	900	43
1945 (Apr.–July)	15,300	1,695	11	800	63	8

Source: Japanese Automobile Control Association.

APPENDIX TABLE C-159.—*Value of output of the Japanese motor vehicle industry, in 1945 prices, monthly, 1941–45 (fiscal years)*

[1,000,000 yen]

Year	1941	1942	1943	1944	1945
April	43.7	36.9	28.8	23.8	9.1
May	46.5	35.4	27.2	36.7	18.6
June	57.4	36.5	22.0	25.7	3.4
July	51.5	40.3	30.3	27.6	4.9
August	55.3	32.1	27.5	20.3	_____
September	58.0	42.2	28.6	20.1	_____
October	64.7	44.2	23.6	25.6	_____
November	73.4	36.2	20.3	28.2	_____
December	76.9	38.0	21.1	17.9	_____
January	58.6	28.8	22.9	12.9	_____
February	54.8	24.1	24.3	15.3	_____
March	50.6	35.9	32.2	15.6	_____
Total	691.4	430.6	308.8	269.7	36.0

Source: Japanese Automobile Control Association, Military Supplies Division, USSBS.

APPENDIX TABLE C-160.—*Monthly index of value of output of the Japanese motor vehicle industry, based on 1945 prices, 1941–45 (fiscal years)*

[Average month in 1941=100]

Year	1941	1942	1943	1944	1945
April	75.8	64.0	50.0	41.3	15.8
May	80.7	61.4	57.2	63.7	32.3
June	99.6	63.3	38.2	44.6	5.9
July	89.4	69.9	52.6	47.9	8.5
August	96.0	55.7	47.7	35.2	_____
September	100.7	73.2	49.6	34.9	_____
October	112.3	76.7	41.0	44.4	_____
November	127.4	55.9	35.2	48.9	_____
December	133.5	65.9	36.6	31.1	_____
January	101.7	50.0	39.7	22.4	_____
February	95.1	41.8	42.2	26.6	_____
March	87.8	62.3	55.9	27.0	_____

Source: Japanese Automobile Control Association, Military Supplies Division, USSBS.

APPENDIX TABLE C-161.—*Production of tanks and combat vehicles in Japan proper, 1931-45*

	1931		1932		1933		1934		1935		1936		1937		1938	
	Unit	Value	Unit	Value	Unit	Value	Unit	Value	Unit	Value	Unit	Value	Unit	Value	Unit	Value
Medium tanks	--	--	1	100	1	100	1	100	1	100	--	--	--	--	89	11,636
Light tanks	12	1,100	20	1,820	69	6,740	111	10,480	358	20,200	328	17,985	325	16,119	198	11,257
13-ton tractors	--	--	--	--	20	1,362	18	1,226	4	315	11	866	19	1,495	37	2,812
8-ton tractors	--	--	1	62	--	--	--	--	32	2,179	24	1,634	28	1,907	36	2,451
6-ton tractors	--	--	--	--	--	--	--	--	--	--	--	--	--	--	1	21
4-ton tractors	--	--	--	--	42	1,680	49	1,960	40	1,600	20	800	50	2,000	2	80
Armoured cars	--	--	--	--	20	900	30	1,350	44	1,760	32	1,280	--	--	--	--
Miscellaneous vehicles	--	--	--	--	--	--	--	--	21	999	65	3,469	57	3,762	59	3,145
Total	--	1,100	--	1,982	--	10,782	--	15,116	--	27,153	--	26,034	--	25,283	--	31,402

	1939		1940		1941		1942		1943		1944		1945		Total units	Total value in 1,000 yen
	Unit	Value	Unit	Value	Unit	Value	Unit	Value	Unit	Value	Unit	Value	Unit	Value		
Medium tanks	205	29,873	315	46,116	495	73,296	531	78,322	544	79,971	294	46,680	89	14,800	2,576	381,094
Light tanks	357	23,278	708	46,184	529	38,673	634	46,481	232	17,241	48	3,932	5	477	3,934	261,967
13-ton tractors	15	1,181	77	6,060	110	8,668	139	10,941	61	4,800	--	--	--	--	473	37,138
8-ton tractors	67	4,562	147	10,010	211	14,369	346	23,563	247	16,885	126	8,905	19	1,709	1,322	90,824
6-ton tractors	13	275	82	1,719	398	27,370	587	39,980	222	15,271	425	29,577	147	9,805	1,875	124,018
4-ton tractors	21	840	162	6,480	200	8,156	409	18,804	340	18,280	190	10,200	30	1,460	1,464	68,700
Self-propelled guns	--	--	--	--	--	--	26	3,120	14	1,680	59	6,720	48	4,680	147	16,200
Armoured cars	--	--	--	--	--	--	88	4,671	505	31,437	385	24,599	126	8,049	1,271	75,436
Miscellaneous vehicles	125	6,060	272	16,404	503	28,196	442	22,228	615	42,112	725	47,846	105	6,954	3,039	183,425
Spare parts	--	--	--	--	--	26,800	--	36,600	--	40,800	--	38,400	--	4,055	--	146,655
Total	--	66,069	--	132,973	--	225,528	--	284,710	--	268,477	--	216,859	--	51,989	--	1,385,457

Unit values—medium tank, 1945-44—166.

Source: War Ministry and Japanese Automobile Control Association.

Unit values—medium tank, 1945-44—166.

APPENDIX TABLE C–162.—*Japanese aircraft production all types,[1] by months, January 1941 to August 1945*

Month	1941	1942	1943	1944	1945
January_____	306	564	1, 010	2, 122	1, 836
February_____	339	580	1, 049	2, 199	1, 391
March_____	357	687	1, 147	2, 435	1, 713
April_____	367	646	1, 141	2, 473	1, 567
May_____	420	706	1, 207	2, 318	1, 592
June_____	426	639	1, 217	2, 541	1, 340
July_____	380	705	1, 259	2, 473	1, 131
August_____	435	678	1, 418	2, 346	[2] 496
September_____	462	804	1, 573	2, 572	_____
October_____	510	886	1, 662	2, 371	_____
November_____	514	943	1, 862	2, 220	_____
December_____	574	1, 023	2, 148	2, 110	_____
Total_____	5, 090	8, 861	16, 693	28, 180	11, 066

[1] Types included: Fighter, bomber, reconnaissance, trainer, transport, flying boat, glider, and suicide (except the piloted bomb "Baka" of which 755 were produced between September 1944 and March 1945, and 50 in June 1945).
[2] Less than one-half month.

Source: Air Ordnance Bureau, Munitions Ministry.

APPENDIX TABLE C–163.—*Index numbers of Japanese aircraft production, airframe weight, and numbers of aircraft by months, January 1941 to July 1945*

[Average for 1941=100]

	Airframe weight	Number of aircraft
1941		
January_____	56. 6	72. 2
February_____	65. 0	80. 0
March_____	75. 8	84. 2
April_____	87. 3	86. 1
May_____	99. 9	99. 1
June_____	100. 5	100. 5
July_____	93. 3	89. 6
August_____	104. 9	102. 6
September_____	111. 8	109. 0
October_____	126. 9	120. 3
November_____	126. 3	121. 2
December_____	151. 7	135. 4
1942		
January_____	138. 8	133. 0
February_____	139. 3	136. 8
March_____	161. 1	162. 0
April_____	155. 1	152. 4
May_____	164. 3	166. 5
June_____	142. 5	150. 7
July_____	161. 3	166. 3
August_____	147. 0	159. 9
September_____	178. 6	189. 6
October_____	196. 4	209. 0
November_____	218. 9	222. 4
December_____	2358.	241. 3

APPENDIX TABLE C–163.—*Index numbers of Japanese aircraft production, airframe weight, and numbers of aircraft by months, January 1941 to July 1945*—Con.

	Airframe weight	Number of aircraft
1943		
January_____	234. 2	238. 2
February_____	239. 7	247. 4
March_____	263. 1	270. 5
Apr._____	261. 4	269. 1
May_____	270. 5	284. 7
June_____	273. 5	287. 0
July_____	281. 6	296. 9
August_____	314. 6	334. 4
September_____	345. 7	371. 0
October_____	354. 2	392. 0
November_____	402. 6	439. 2
December_____	465. 7	506. 6
1944		
January_____	447. 0	500. 5
February_____	458. 2	518. 6
March_____	499. 9	574. 3
April_____	530. 9	583. 3
May_____	499. 2	546. 7
June_____	566. 9	599. 3
July_____	569. 7	583. 3
August_____	541. 1	553. 3
September_____	592. 8	606. 6
October_____	569. 7	559. 2
November_____	546. 7	523. 6
December_____	488. 3	497. 6
1945		
January_____	421. 9	433. 0
February_____	324. 4	328. 1
March_____	382. 7	404. 0
April_____	353. 2	369. 6
May_____	342. 5	375. 5
June_____	274. 3	316. 0
July_____	210. 1	266. 7

Source: Air Ordnance Bureau, Munitions Ministry.

APPENDIX TABLE C–164.—*Japanese aircraft production by functional types, by quarters, 1941–45*

Calendar year and quarter	Type of aircraft					
	Fighter	Bomber	Recce	Trainer	Other [1]	Total
1941:						
I_____	199	232	126	380	65	1, 002
II_____	210	340	149	404	108	1, 211
III_____	274	400	169	331	103	1, 277
IV_____	397	489	195	374	143	1, 598
Total__	1, 080	1, 461	639	1, 489	419	5, 088

APPENDIX TABLE C–164.—*Japanese aircraft production by functional types, by quarters, 1941–45*—Continued

Calendar year and quarter	Fighter	Bomber	Recce	Trainer	Other [1]	Total
1942:						
I	507	541	207	478	98	1,831
II	623	582	201	517	68	1,991
III	764	552	229	565	77	2,187
IV	1,041	758	330	611	112	2,852
Total	2,935	2,433	967	2,171	355	8,861
1943:						
I	1,264	827	425	583	107	3,206
II	1,480	973	462	558	92	3,565
III	1,864	1,098	519	684	85	4,250
IV	2,539	1,291	664	1,046	132	5,672
Total	7,147	4,189	2,070	2,871	416	16,693
1944:						
I	3,043	1,331	633	1,532	217	6,756
II	3,518	1,216	528	1,812	258	7,332
III	3,752	1,275	448	1,573	343	7,391
IV	3,498	1,278	538	1,230	157	6,701
Total	13,811	5,100	2,147	6,147	975	28,180
1945:						
I	2,345	960	371	1,135	129	4,940
II	2,353	792	307	977	68	4,499
III [2]	776	182	177	411	81	1,627
Total	5,474	1,934	855	2,523	280	11,066

[1] Others include flying boats, transports, gliders and suicide aircraft.
[2] July and part of August only.

Source: Air Ordnance Bureau, Munitions Ministry.

APPENDIX TABLE C–165.—*Percentage distribution of Japanese aircraft production by functional types, by quarters, 1941–45*

Calendar year and quarter	Percent fighters	Percent bombers	Percent reconnaissance	Percent trainers	Percent transports	Percent other [1]
1941:						
I	19.9	23.2	12.6	37.9	5.4	1.1
II	17.3	28.1	12.3	33.4	7.7	1.2
III	21.5	31.3	13.2	25.9	6.8	1.3
IV	24.8	30.6	12.2	23.4	7.6	1.3
1942:						
I	27.7	29.5	11.3	26.1	3.9	1.4
II	31.3	29.2	10.1	26.0	2.2	1.3
III	34.9	25.2	10.5	25.8	2.4	1.1
IV	36.5	26.6	11.6	21.4	3.1	.9
1943:						
I	39.4	25.8	13.3	18.2	2.5	.8
II	41.5	27.3	13.0	15.6	2.2	.5
III	43.9	25.8	12.2	16.1	1.4	.6
IV	44.8	22.8	11.7	18.4	1.3	1.0
1944:						
I	45.0	19.7	9.4	22.7	1.3	1.8
II	48.0	16.6	7.2	24.7	1.1	2.4
III	50.8	17.3	6.1	21.3	1.3	3.4
IV	52.2	19.1	8.0	18.4	1.0	1.3
1945:						
I	47.5	19.4	7.5	23.0	1.1	1.5
II	52.3	17.6	6.8	21.7	.7	.9
III [2]	47.6	11.2	10.9	25.3	.7	4.3

[1] "Others" include flying boats, gliders and suicide aircraft.
[2] July and part of August only.

Source: Air Ordnance Bureau, Munitions Ministry.

Civilian Supply Tables

APPENDIX TABLE C–166.—*Indexes of quantities of selected goods available for civilian consumption in Japan proper, 1937–45*

Commodity	1937	1938	1939	1940	1941	1942	1943	1944	1945
Cotton cloth	100	68	61	54	28	7	4	4	2
Wool cloth	100	97	33	23	25	16	17	8	1
Silk cloth	100	65	97	99	104	91	57	36	18
Synthetic cloth	100	145	135	96	79	56	31	16	8
Wooden clogs	100	107	187	235	320	236	257	196	75
Rubber footwear	100	86	92	89	79	88	67	31	10
Leather shoes	100	128	84	48	64	108	60	16	0
Furniture	100	100	109	109	109	96	66	55	23
Enameled ironware	100	68	61	26	25	15	10	7	0
Aluminumware	100	75	63	52	39	39	39	19	1
Cast ironware	100	6	5	4	3	1	(1)	(1)	(1)
Mats (tatami)	na	na	na	100	90	57	44	34	na
Rice bowls	na	na	na	100	71	27	11	5	na
Plates	na	na	na	100	69	28	8	4	na
Cups	na	na	na	100	72	31	10	3	na
Cooking braziers	na	na	na	100	133	100	117	67	na
Soap	100	94	132	109	93	35	32	34	4
Umbrellas	100	128	77	63	53	80	90	40	3
Paper products	na	na	na	100	88	66	57	31	10

na Not available.
[1] Less than 0.5 percent.

Source: Control associations; Ministry of Commerce and Industry.

APPENDIX TABLE C-167.—*Index of official retail prices in Tokyo, selected groups of consumer goods, annually 1930–39, monthly 1940–45*—Continued

[Annual average 1937=100]

Year	Food	Fuel and lighting	Cloth-ing	Other	Average
1930	90	99	86	86	88.9
1931	78	86	70	78	77.7
1932	82	75	70	78	78.5
1933	83	84	80	85	83.5
1934	85	86	83	86	85.3
1935	88	86	82	88	86.9
1936	95	90	85	88	91.3
1937	100	100	100	100	100.0
1938	109	125	125	115	114.6
1939	123	128	141	129	128.3
1940	146	136	163	151	149.0
January	145	132	149	137	141.9
February	144	132	149	143	143.8
March	144	134	160	145	146.0
April	145	134	165	149	148.8
May	147	134	168	152	150.7
June	146	134	169	152	150.7
July	150	134	169	153	152.9
August	149	134	169	153	152.0
September	147	137	164	156	151.7
October	144	137	164	156	150.3
November	142	141	163	155	149.6
December	143	141	163	155	149.8
1941	141	142	167	159	150.8
January	141	141	160	155	148.9
February	141	141	160	156	148.9
March	142	141	164	156	149.6
April	142	142	166	156	150.4
May	142	142	168	158	151.3
June	142	142	169	159	151.6
July	141	142	169	159	151.2
August	141	142	169	159	151.2
September	140	142	169	159	150.9
October	141	142	168	159	150.9
November	141	142	168	161	151.2
December	141	142	173	165	153.5
1942	143	142	176	166	155.2
January	141	142	174	165	153.8
February	142	142	174	165	154.0
March	142	142	176	165	154.5
April	142	142	176	165	154.4
May	142	141	176	165	154.5
June	143	141	176	165	154.9

[Annual average 1937=100]

Year	Food	Fuel and lighting	Cloth-ing	Other	Average
1942:—Continued					
July	143	141	176	166	155.1
August	144	141	178	165	155.5
September	144	141	178	165	155.7
October	144	143	178	165	155.9
November	144	143	178	169	157.3
December	143	143	178	169	156.8
1943	147	143	181	188	164.8
January	145	143	178	170	157.4
February	145	143	178	176	159.8
March	146	143	180	179	161.5
April	146	143	180	189	164.7
May	145	143	180	189	164.1
June	145	143	180	192	164.8
July	145	143	182	192	165.0
Aug	146	143	182	191	165.3
September	148	143	182	193	166.8
October	149	144	182	194	167.8
November	152	144	182	194	169.2
December	153	144	182	194	169.7
1944	166	150	184	219	184.4
January	154	144	182	199	171.9
February	154	144	182	199	172.1
March	156	151	185	204	175.1
April	160	151	185	214	180.0
May	161	151	185	214	180.6
June	161	151	185	214	180.6
July	161	151	185	221	182.8
August	163	151	185	222	184.1
September	174	151	185	232	192.1
October	178	151	185	235	194.9
November	183	151	185	239	199.1
December	183	151	185	241	199.7
1945:					
January	195	151	185	246	206.5
February	197	182	192	248	211.6
March	199	182	192	255	214.6
April	201	182	192	271	220.2
May	218	182	192	280	231.0
June	219	182	192	285	232.7
July	221	251	192	291	241.1
August	235	253	192	291	247.4
September	238	253	192	291	249.1

Source: Bank of Japan.

[Unit: 1 Yen]

Item	Unit	Official price	Dec. 1943	Mar. 1944	June 1944	Sept. 1944	Nov. 1944	Mar. 1945	June 1945	July 1945	Nov. 1945
						Prices on the black market					
Rice	1 sho	0. 5	3. 0	7. 0	14. 0	18. 0	22. 0	25. 0	28. 0	35. 0	60. 0
Glutinous rice	1 sho	. 5	2. 5	6. 0	10. 0	18. 0	30. 0	35. 0	38. 0	40. 0	50. 0
Wheat flour	1 kan	1. 5	8. 0	12. 0	22. 0	30. 0	30. 0	35. 0	38. 0	40. 0	90. 0
Soy bean	1 sho	. 4	3. 0	5. 0	5. 5	5. 5	7. 0	10. 0	11. 0	12. 0	13. 3
Red bean	1 sho	. 4	4. 0	5. 0	5. 5	6. 0	10. 0	11. 0	11. 0	12. 0	20. 0
Potato	1 kan	. 5	2. 5	3. 5	·3. 5	7. 0	8. 0	8. 6	12. 0	13. 0	15. 0
Stone leek	1 kan	. 6	2. 5	3. 5	5. 5	6. 5	6. 5	6. 5	10. 0	13. 0	10. 0
Sweetpotato	1 kan	· . 4	4. 0	5. 0	6. 0	6. 0	8. 0	8. 0	8. 5	9. 0	12. 0
Burdock	1 kan	. 9	1. 5	3. 0	3. 0	3. 0	3. 5	5. 0	7. 0	8. 0	12. 0
Niso	1 kan	1. 3	3. 5	3. 5	3. 5	3. 5	3. 5	10. 0	20. 0	40. 0	30. 0
Soy	1 sho	. 8	3. 0	4. 0	5. 0	8. 0	13. 0	15. 0	35. 0	38. 0	50. 0
Edible oil	1 sho	2. 9	15. 0	20. 0	40. 0	90. 0	120. 0	140. 0	180. 0	220. 0	170. 0
Refined sake	1 sho	3. 5	15. 0	35. 0	70. 0	90. 0	120. 0	160. 0	200. 0	200. 0	160. 0
Beer	1 btl	. 9	2. 0	4. 0	7. 5	9. 0	9. 5	10. 0	11. 0	15. 0	30. 0
Dried bonito	1 kan	14. 6	70. 0	84. 0	150. 0	200. 0	220. 0	250. 0	350. 0	520. 0	670. 0
Butter	1 lb	3. 8	6. 5	10. 0	30. 0	50. 0	60. 0	60. 0	60. 0	60. 0	250. 0
Pork	100 momme	1. 0	3. 0	8. 5	14. 0	16. 0	17. 0	19. 0	23. 0	27. 0	25. 0
Beef	100 momme	1. 6	3. 5	8. 0	13. 5	15. 0	20. 0	25. 0	28. 0	30. 0	25. 0
Hen's egg	1 piece	. 1	. 3	1. 0	1. 0	1. 5	1. 6	1. 7	2. 5	3. 5	3. 0
Sugar	1 kan	2. 2	50. 0	100. 0	200. 0	260. 0	300. 0	390. 0	450. 0	530. 0	700. 0
Salt	1 kan	5. 0	30. 0	50. 0	45. 0	48. 0	40. 0	35. 0	35. 0	40. 0	35. 0
Salted salmon	1 kan	4. 4	15. 0	30. 0	33. 0	33. 0	35. 0	35. 0	30. 0	25. 0	15. 0
Cabbage	1 kan	. 5	. 6	. 7	1. 0	2. 0	3. 0				
Mad apple	1 kan	1. 5	2. 0	2. 0	3. 5	7. 0	7. 0				
Saccharin	100 tablets	. 5	3. 0	4. 0	5. 0	5. 0	5. 0	15. 0	28. 0	35. 0	
Bleached cotton	1 tan	2. 5	15. 0	30. 0	35. 0	45. 0	48. 0	120. 0	120. 0	130. 0	120. 0
Cotton towel	1	. 3	1. 0	2. 0	3. 5	6. 0	8. 0	12. 0	13. 0	15. 0	15. 0
Tabi	1 pair	· . 8	3. 5	7. 0	10. 0	12. 0	20. 0	37. 0	· 52. 0	60. 0	65. 0
Umbrella	1	15. 0	40. 0	40. 0	45. 0	155. 09	170. 0	190. 0	200. 0	200. 0	150. 0
Shoes (oxhide)	1 pair	22. 7	100. 0	130. 0	300. 0	350. 0	500. 0	800. 0	1, 000. 0	1, 000. 0	500. 0
Chika-tabi	1 pair	1. 7	5. 0	10. 0	18. 0	20. 0	35. 0	50. 0	70. 0	90. 0	110. 0
Socks	1 pair	. 5	2. 5	4. 0	5. 0	7. 0	10. 0	13. 0	16. 0	18. 0	20. 0
Meisen	1 tan	23. 0	50. 0	70. 0	80. 0	120. 0	140. 0	160. 0	180. 0	220. 0	250. 0
Meisen quilt	1 suit	44. 0	100. 0	150. 0	1, 000. 0	1, 200. 0	1, 000. 0	1, 100. 0	1, 000. 0	1, 300. 0	2, 000. 0
Cotton yukata	1 tan	3. 8	17. 0	30. 0	60. 0	70. 0	90. 0	100. 0	130. 0	150. 0	180. 0
Soap	1 cake	. 1	2. 0	3. 0	5. 0	5. 0	6. 0	15. 0	20. 0	20. 0	22. 0
Match	1 L. box	. 4	1. 0	1. 2	6. 0	18. 0	30. 0	45. 0	60. 0	80. 0	70. 0
Charcoal	1 bag	2. 2	10. 0	25. 0	35. 0	40. 0	80. 0	65. 0	65. 0	85. 0	90. 0
Firewood	1 bundle	. 4	1. 5	3. 5	· 4. 5	4. 5	4. 5	6. 0	6. 0	8. 0	10. 0
Kama	1	7. 6	25. 0	45. 0	50. 0	60. 0	60. 0	120. 0	180. 0	230. 0	270. 0
Nabe	1	3. 1	15. 0	30. 0	40. 0	50. 0	60. 0	90. 0	100. 0	120. 0	135. 0
Bicycle	1	76. 8	225. 0	400. 0	600. 0	800. 0	1, 000. 0	1, 300. 0	1, 500. 0	2, 000. 0	2, 000. 0

Source: Bank of Japan.

1 sho equals 1.80391 litres.   1 momme equals 3.75 grams.   1 tan equals 9.91736 yards.   1 kwan equals 3.75 kg.

APPENDIX TABLE C-169.—*Wholesale prices in Tokyo*

[1931 average=100]

(Oriental Economist Index)

End of—	Average for all items [1]	Average for all items	Cereals	Other food products	Textiles	Textile materials
1943 average	315. 1	259. 1	288. 4	207. 2	344. 4	218. 6
1944 average	332. 8	273. 7	295. 8	226. 3	344. 0	242. 2
1944:						
July	331. 1	272. 3	298. 7	222. 4	344. 0	229. 2
August	337. 2	277. 2	298. 6	228. 3	344. 0	264. 2
September	339. 3	279. 0	298. 6	242. 5	344. 0	264. 2
October	340. 7	280. 2	311. 3	228. 3	344. 0	264. 2
November	344. 5	283. 3	319. 9	242. 5	344. 0	264. 2
December	344. 5	283. 3	319. 9	242. 5	344. 0	264. 2
1945:						
January	348. 3	286. 4	319. 9	247. 4	344. 0	264. 2
February	358. 7	295. 0	319. 9	265. 8	363. 0	264. 2
March	358. 7	295. 0	319. 9	265. 8	363. 0	264. 2
April	360. 2	296. 2	332. 9	265. 8	363. 0	264. 2
1944, April	327. 3	269. 2	298. 1	222. 4	344. 0	229. 2

End of—	Metals	Coal and petroleum	Industrial chemicals	Fertilizers	Building materials	Miscellaneous
1943 average	309. 0	234. 2	227. 7	240. 1	276. 5	231. 6
1944 average	308. 4	236. 7	255. 4	240. 0	294. 2	258. 0
1944:						
July	309. 9	238. 2	255. 1	240. 0	289. 5	265. 9
August	309. 9	238. 2	255. 1	240. 0	289. 5	265. 9
September	309. 9	238. 2	262. 9	240. 0	306. 7	265. 9
October	309. 9	238. 2	262. 9	240. 0	306. 7	265. 9
November	309. 9	238. 2	262. 9	240. 0	306. 7	265. 9
December	309. 9	238. 2	262. 9	240. 0	306. 7	265. 9
1945:						
January	309. 9	238. 2	289. 2	240. 0	306. 7	265. 9
February	323. 7	238. 2	294. 2	240. 0	306. 7	274. 8
March	323. 7	238. 2	294. 2	240. 0	306. 7	274. 8
April	323. 7	238. 2	294. 2	240. 0	306. 7	274. 8
1944, April	309. 9	234. 9	252. 2	240. 0	289. 5	249. 8

[1] January 1913=100.

APPENDIX TABLE C-170.—*Index of salaried worker's living costs in Japan proper, 1937-44*

[July 1937=100]

Month	1937	1938	1939	1940	1941	1942	1943	1944
January		104. 2	113. 5	131. 2	142. 0	148. 2	153. 3	166. 8
February		105. 5	114. 6	134. 6	142. 7	147. 7	155. 7	170. 7
March		106. 3	115. 0	136. 8	143. 0	148. 4	156. 7	172. 1
April		107. 5	116. 8	140. 5	144. 2	149. 7	159. 8	179. 0
May		107. 7	118. 4	141. 2	144. 8	150. 8	160. 7	181. 2
June		108. 4	117. 9	142. 8	144. 8	150. 3	162. 2	
July	100. 0	111. 6	119. 7	147. 2	145. 1	151. 2	162. 9	
August	100. 6	112. 7	121. 2	147. 5	144. 7	151. 4	163. 5	
September	101. 7	112. 6	122. 7	144. 4	144. 8	151. 6	163. 2	
October	101. 8	112. 5	123. 3	140. 9	144. 6	151. 4	163. 2	
November	101. 6	112. 1	126. 8	141. 1	144. 4	151. 3	165. 5	
December	102. 9	112. 6	128. 5	141. 6	146. 8	152. 5	166. 8	

Source: Census Bureau, Cost of Living Section.

APPENDIX TABLE C–171.—*Index of workers' living cost, Japan proper and Tokyo, 1937–45* [1]

[July 1937=100]

Year and month	Food Japan	Food Tokyo	Housing Japan	Housing Tokyo	Fuel and light Japan	Fuel and light Tokyo	Clothing Japan	Clothing Tokyo	Other Japan	Other Tokyo	All items Japan	All items Tokyo
1937:												
August		97.9		100.2		101.3		99.2		103.7		99.8
September		104.2		100.0		102.2		98.9		103.9		102.5
October		102.0		100.1		105.9		100.4		104.0		102.0
November		101.5		100.3		111.9		101.0		104.2		102.2
December		103.6		100.4		112.2		101.5		104.5		103.3
1938	110.3		103.0		116.7		123.1		104.4		110.1	
January		106.4		100.5		112.4		102.5		104.9		104.7
February		107.0		101.0		112.0		109.2		104.6		105.9
March		107.3		101.3		112.3		112.8		105.1		106.7
April		109.7		101.6		112.3		116.2		105.5		108.3
May		108.3		102.0		113.1		117.9		106.0		108.2
June		108.5		102.4		114.4		121.6		106.5		109.0
July		115.0		102.8		114.6		128.8		107.4		113.0
August		116.2		102.9		114.6		128.3		107.0		113.4
September		115.2		102.9		114.5		130.2		107.2		113.3
October		113.2		103.0		114.5		132.9		107.6		112.8
November		111.5		103.0		114.1		134.6		107.5		112.3
December		112.5		103.1		114.0		134.6		107.6		112.8
1939	123.3		107.3		122.6		150.6		106.9		121.2	
January		114.7		103.3		114.1		135.7		108.0		114.0
February		116.0		103.3		114.5		140.0		107.5		115.0
March		115.4		103.6		114.5		140.3		107.7		114.9
April		119.6		103.9		114.7		143.1		108.2		117.2
May		123.0		104.4		114.8		145.5		108.3		119.2
June		120.0		105.0		114.8		146.6		108.2		118.1
July		123.4		105.2		115.0		147.8		108.5		119.8
August		126.0		105.5		115.9		148.9		108.4		121.2
September		128.0		106.5		117.1		152.3		108.7		122.8
October		128.2		107.5		118.3		154.1		109.0		123.4
November		135.6		107.6		123.5		157.4		108.9		127.3
December		136.9		108.2		124.3		163.0		109.3		128.9
1940	152.8	152.1	115.3	113.0	139.9	139.2	185.9	191.0	116.7	119.8	143.4	142.8
January	141.2	142.6	111.1	109.0	130.9	125.7	167.6	168.5	110.2	110.5	133.3	132.5
February	145.5	147.3	112.2	110.3	136.5	140.7	173.2	180.1	111.8	115.5	136.8	138.0
March	147.8	148.8	113.2	111.1	139.1	142.3	177.3	186.3	113.6	118.1	139.1	140.3
April	154.4	153.4	114.4	112.2	139.6	140.6	183.9	191.5	115.0	119.3	143.4	143.2
May	153.6	149.7	115.4	113.2	140.8	140.8	188.3	193.1	116.9	121.1	144.3	142.4
June	154.7	154.5	116.3	113.9	141.1	140.6	191.2	196.0	118.0	121.2	145.5	145.0
July	164.1	165.5	116.3	113.8	140.2	140.1	191.0	195.6	118.2	121.6	149.6	149.7
August	165.0	164.4	116.6	114.3	140.6	140.1	190.2	194.1	118.4	121.7	150.0	149.1
September	157.7	155.0	116.7	114.3	141.3	140.4	190.7	196.3	119.6	122.4	147.2	145.6
October	149.9	147.7	117.0	114.4	142.4	140.6	191.4	196.5	119.3	122.2	143.9	142.5
November	149.5	147.1	117.3	114.5	143.2	139.5	192.0	196.9	119.6	122.1	143.9	142.2
December	149.6	149.3	117.6	114.4	143.3	138.8	193.6	197.4	120.1	122.2	144.4	143.2
1941	152.5	152.9	119.4	116.4	142.3	133.4	202.5	205.7	120.6	122.9	147.3	146.1
January	150.2	149.3	118.1	115.0	141.1	132.2	195.1	198.6	120.1	122.5	144.8	143.2
February	151.1	152.3	118.2	115.3	141.2	132.2	196.3	199.0	120.0	122.1	145.4	144.5
March	151.5	148.5	118.5	115.3	141.0	132.2	198.3	199.4	120.3	122.2	146.0	142.9
April	152.9	154.9	118.9	115.9	141.3	132.2	199.5	200.2	120.3	122.0	146.8	145.9
May	153.7	155.0	119.1	116.1	141.2	132.2	200.7	202.4	120.7	122.5	147.4	146.4
June	154.0	154.9	119.5	116.6	141.0	132.2	201.5	203.3	120.8	122.5	147.8	146.6
July	153.9	154.4	119.6	116.7	141.2	132.2	203.2	206.5	121.2	123.5	148.1	146.9
August	153.4	154.7	119.7	116.8	140.9	132.2	203.6	206.9	120.8	123.2	147.8	147.1
September	152.8	152.7	119.9	116.8	142.5	135.4	205.0	209.4	121.2	123.2	147.9	146.8
October	151.5	149.9	120.0	116.9	145.0	135.6	207.2	213.1	119.6	122.8	147.6	146.1
November	150.8	150.1	120.0	117.1	145.6	136.1	208.5	213.2	120.6	123.1	147.6	146.3
December	154.2	157.8	121.4	118.1	145.4	135.8	211.6	216.5	122.2	124.6	150.1	150.4

See footnote at end of table.

Year and month	Food		Housing		Fuel and light		Clothing		Other		All items	
	Japan	Tokyo	Japan	Tokyo	Japan	Tokyo	Japan	Tokyo	Japan	Tokyo	Japan	Tokyo
1942	156. 3	157. 7	124. 4	119. 2	147. 5	136. 7	216. 5	221. 8	129. 1	130. 8	153. 7	152. 5
January	155. 7	157. 8	122. 6	118. 5	145. 4	135. 5	213. 0	217. 4	124. 7	125. 6	151. 6	150. 8
February	154. 5	156. 9	122. 7	118. 6	145. 2	135. 7	213. 5	218. 9	124. 9	126. 2	151. 2	150. 7
March	155. 3	156. 9	122. 8	118. 6	145. 5	136. 0	214. 3	220. 5	125. 7	126. 4	151. 9	151. 1
April	156. 8	158. 8	123. 4	118. 8	145. 8	136. 2	215. 1	221. 1	127. 1	126. 9	153. 2	152. 1
May	157. 6	158. 0	124. 0	118. 9	145. 9	136. 2	216. 2	222. 4	128. 9	132. 0	154. 0	152. 9
June	155. 7	154. 3	124. 3	119. 0	147. 5	136. 1	217. 0	222. 8	129. 3	132. 1	153. 5	151. 4
July	157. 2	156. 2	124. 8	119. 1	147. 5	136. 1	217. 9	222. 7	130. 0	132. 5	154. 5	152. 3
August	157. 0	157. 9	125. 0	119. 2	147. 6	136. 1	217. 9	222. 9	130. 4	132. 4	154. 5	153. 0
September	156. 9	159. 7	125. 3	119. 5	147. 8	136. 3	217. 8	222. 8	131. 2	133. 1	154. 7	154. 0
October	155. 9	158. 3	125. 7	119. 7	150. 2	138. 4	218. 1	222. 9	131. 8	134. 1	154. 6	153. 8
November	155. 4	157. 4	126. 0	119. 9	150. 5	138. 7	218. 2	223. 2	132. 4	134. 2	154. 6	153. 5
December	157. 7	160. 2	126. 5	120. 0	151. 5	138. 6	218. 8	224. 0	132. 7	133. 8	155. 9	154. 7
1943	170. 9	172. 9	132. 3	123. 3	154. 2	141. 3	228. 3	232. 1	137. 9	140. 0	165. 1	163. 2
January	158. 9	160. 0	127. 4	121. 2	152. 0	139. 7	219. 2	223. 8	133. 0	133. 8	156. 7	154. 9
February	164. 0	166. 3	128. 0	122. 1	152. 1	139. 7	219. 6	224. 0	132. 5	133. 6	159. 0	157. 8
March	164. 2	167. 0	129. 4	122. 1	152. 8	140. 7	224. 5	228. 6	133. 7	134. 1	160. 3	158. 8
April	171. 1	174. 6	130. 1	122. 3	153. 4	141. 0	226. 8	230. 0	134. 5	134. 5	164. 0	162. 4
May	172. 3	174. 8	131. 0	123. 0	153. 7	141. 0	227. 8	231. 7	135. 4	134. 8	165. 0	162. 8
June	173. 0	174. 6	131. 6	123. 2	153. 7	140. 9	228. 6	231. 3	139. 4	143. 4	166. 3	164. 4
July	173. 7	176. 9	132. 9	124. 3	153. 7	140. 9	229. 6	232. 8	139. 7	143. 3	167. 0	165. 8
August	174. 6	177. 2	133. 0	124. 0	153. 7	140. 9	230. 5	234. 2	140. 1	143. 7	167. 0	166. 1
September	173. 2	176. 7	134. 8	124. 1	153. 8	140. 9	231. 5	234. 6	140. 1	143. 8	167. 5	166. 0
October	171. 6	172. 5	136. 1	124. 1	156. 1	142. 9	233. 2	237. 3	140. 6	144. 1	167. 5	164. 7
November	176. 6	176. 8	136. 5	124. 3	156. 5	143. 0	233. 7	238. 3	142. 1	145. 1	170. 1	166. 9
December	177. 9	178. 0	137. 1	124. 8	158. 5	143. 7	234. 4	238. 2	143. 2	145. 6	171. 2	167. 7
1944	200. 0	_____	142. 0	_____	172. 0	_____	243. 0	_____	162. 0	_____	187. 5	_____
January	181. 6	181. 2	137. 4	124. 9	158. 8	143. 7	234. 9	239. 3	143. 9	145. 7	173. 1	169. 2
February	182. 4	184. 2	138. 0	125. 1	159. 0	148. 2	238. 2	244. 1	146. 5	152. 7	174. 6	170. 8
March	183. 7	185. 9	138. 5	125. 1	167. 0	148. 2	242. 3	244. 1	149. 4	152. 7	176. 8	173. 6
April	195. 6	195. 2	141. 9	125. 2	171. 3	152. 9	242. 7	243. 9	158. 3	165. 2	184. 6	180. 0
May	198. 3	198. 7	140. 7	125. 2	172. 5	154. 5	243. 2	244. 7	161. 2	169. 4	186. 3	182. 4
June	199. 5	198. 5	141. 2	125. 2	172. 8	154. 8	243. 7	244. 4	161. 8	168. 9	187. 1	182. 4
July	198. 7	197. 8	141. 7	125. 5	173. 0	154. 8	242. 4	244. 3	162. 4	170. 6	186. 8	182. 3
August	199. 7	_____	143. 7	_____	173. 4	_____	243. 2	_____	165. 8	_____	188. 3	185. 6
September	210. 2	_____	143. 9	_____	177. 0	_____	243. 6	_____	167. 4	_____	193. 6	191. 3
October	212. 9	_____	144. 0	_____	177. 6	_____	244. 8	_____	175. 3	_____	196. 6	196. 9
November	214. 8	_____	144. 3	_____	178. 9	_____	245. 5	_____	179. 3	_____	200. 7	197. 7
December	216. 8	_____	144. 3	_____	179. 0	_____	246. 0	_____	180. 6	_____	201. 7	198. 7

[1] This index is presented merely as an official Japanese estimate of the cost of living during the war.   Source: Cabinet Bureau of Statistics.

Annual average 1937=100]

Month	1937	1938	1939	1940	1941	1942	1943	1944
January	96	104	117	135	154	163	188	218
February	99	106	119	132	150	166	185	218
March	101	108	123	135	154	165	188	223
April	99	107	120	134	152	165	184	222
May	99	107	120	134	151	165	188	223
June	100	109	122	137	152	165	188	231
July	100	110	123	138	152	168	193	na
August	100	109	122	139	154	166	196	na
September	100	110	122	139	155	166	199	na
October	102	112	123	142	157	173	205	na
November	103	114	126	145	157	176	210	na
December	107	120	132	149	163	na	216	na
Average	100	109	123	138	155	167	195	223

na Not available.   Source: Cabinet Bureau of Statistics.

APPENDIX TABLE C–173.—*Monthly index of transport workers' wages, Japan proper, 1937–44*

[July 1937=100]

Month	1937	1938	1939	1940	1941	1942	1943	1944
January	na	na	na	105	111	118	140	158
February	na	na	na	105	111	119	132	161
March	na	na	na	108	114	123	139	160
April	na	na	na	108	116	125	150	172
May	na	na	na	108	114	126	149	175
June	na	na	na	110	115	131	151	163
July	100	na	104	110	117	131	150	na
August	na	na	101	107	117	131	150	na
September	na	na	103	108	118	131	152	na
October	na	na	104	111	121	129	155	na
November	na	na	105	110	118	133	157	na
December	na	na	111	118	127	na	158	na
Average	na	na	105	109	117	127	149	165

na Not available.   Source: Cabinet Bureau of Statistics.

APPENDIX TABLE C–174.—*Monthly index of miners' wages, Japan proper, 1937–44*

[July 1937=100]

Month	1937	1938	1939	1940	1941	1942	1943	1944
January	92	107	125	142	163	169	184	199
February	94	109	126	144	166	172	189	199
March	98	110	130	146	167	172	189	196
April	98	113	130	148	166	172	189	205
May	98	114	131	149	165	174	189	218
June	99	115	133	151	167	175	191	226
July	100	117	133	152	165	174	193	na
August	100	118	133	153	165	177	191	na
September	101	119	136	156	167	177	191	na
October	103	122	138	158	167	181	194	na
November	105	124	140	159	169	184	196	na
December	107	125	141	160	171	na	199	na
Average	99	116	133	152	167	175	191	207

na Not available.   Source: Cabinet Bureau of Statistics.

APPENDIX TABLE C–175.—*Consumption of staple food by coal miners and their families and its effect upon coal output, Japan proper, 1931–45*

	1931	1932	1933	1934	1935	1936	1937	1938	1939	1940	1941	1942	1943	1944	1945	Nov. 1945
Consumption of staple food per worker per day (grams)	1,400	1,400	1,300	1,300	1,300	1,200	1,200	1,200	1,000	1,000	700	700	700	700	700	705
Percentage of rice and barley in staple food	100	100	100	100	100	100	100	100	100	100	100	90	80	80	60	50
Percentage of supplementary food supplied	100	100	100	100	100	100	100	100	100	100	100	100	80	60	40	30
Coal output per man per month (tons)	18	21	26	30	29	28	23	24	23	21	17	16	19	12	8	4
Consumption of staple food by adult members of workers' family, per man per day (grams)	1,026	1,026	1,026	1,026	955	900	900	900	800	800	325	325	325	325	290	325

Note: From 1938 other foods were included in the staple food ration with rice. Before 1938 the staple food ration was only rice.
Source: Mitsubishi Mining Company.

APPENDIX TABLE C–176.—*Imports of major textile raw materials, Japan proper, 1935–45*

[1,000 pounds]

Year	Wool	Cotton	Silk
1935	243,009	1,641,000	1,566
1936	216,569	2,033,000	1,022
1937	257,045	1,850,000	826
1938	116,251	1,254,000	4,160
1939	105,392	1,348,000	2,807
1940	101,652	866,000	3,980
1941	119,714	651,000	6,600
1942	18,882	154,000	3,960
1943	7,824	100,000	660
1944	4,428	31,000	99
1945 (January to August)	1,766	23,000	0

Source: Japanese Textile Control Association, Japan Yearbook, 1943–44, Orient Year Book, 1942–43.

APPENDIX TABLE C–177.—*Civilian production, imports, exports and amounts of textile cloth available for consumption, Japan Proper, 1935–44*

[1,000 square yards]

Year	Total civilian production of cloth	Total imports	Total exports	Net supply [1]
1935	5,824,516	1,885,575	3,309,727	4,400,364
1936	4,944,277	2,250,591	3,396,098	3,798,770
1937	6,354,819	2,107,871	3,302,912	5,159,778
1938	5,014,154	1,374,411	2,693,709	3,694,856
1939	4,580,537	1,456,199	2,893,422	3,143,314
1940	3,925,251	971,612	2,139,385	2,757,478
1941	2,519,014	777,314	1,174,526	2,121,802
1942	1,268,709	176,842	232,064	1,213,487
1943	768,199	108,484	265,183	611,500
1944	422,985	35,527	70,770	387,742

[1] Net supply equals production plus imports minus exports, without adjustment for stocks or changes in stocks.

Source: Japanese Textile Control Association, Japan Yearbook, 1943–44, Orient Yearbook, 1942–43.

APPENDIX TABLE C–178.—*Production of cloth, Japan proper, 1935–45*

[1,000 square yards]

Year	Wool	Cotton	Silk	Synthetic[1]
1935	297,359	4,499,000	561,395	466,762
1936	284,583	3,496,000	418,281	745,413
1937	248,914	4,826,000	475,273	804,632
1938	242,648	3,297,000	309,628	1,164,878
1939	81,840	2,951,000	461,255	1,086,442
1940	57,753	2,624,000	472,013	771,485
1941	62,481	1,329,000	494,752	632,781
1942	39,086	349,000	432,313	448,310
1943	43,072	[2] 200,000	272,999	252,128
1944	19,317	180,274	172,145	131,523
1945 (January to August)	1,171	[3] na	na	na

[1] Includes rayon and Staple Fiber.
[2] Estimate.
[3] Not available.

Source: Japanese Textile Control Association, Japan Yearbook, 1943–44, Orient Yearbook, 1942–43.

APPENDIX TABLE C–179.—*Production, imports, exports and stocks on hand of raw silk, Japan proper, 1935–45* [1]

[1,000 pounds]

Year	Production	Imports	Exports	Stocks on hand
1935	96,413	1,566	73,017	26,880
1936	93,315	1,022	66,446	21,480
1937	92,317	826	62,485	17,520
1938	97,128	4,160	63,026	15,200
1939	93,335	2,807	50,956	16,316
1940	94,644	3,960	39,061	42,600
1941	71,218	6,600	18,974	47,452
1942	62,170	3,960	1,087	38,495
1943	40,777	660	1,664	34,621
1944	18,982	99	1,363	4,826
1945	15,960	0	0	[2] na

[1] 3,300,000 pounds of raw silk is considered indispensable for industrial purposes, medical supplies, and sewing threads.
[2] Not available.

Source: Japanese Textile Control Association, Japan Yearbook, 1943–44, 1944–45, Orient Yearbook, 1942–43.

APPENDIX TABLE C–180.—*Production, imports, exports and stock on hand of silk cloth, Japan proper, 1935–45*

[1,000 square yards]

Year	Production	Imports	Exports
1935	561,395	Negligible	131,000
1936	418,281	...do	121,000
1937	475,273	...do	122,000
1938	309,628	...do	91,000
1939	461,255	...do	60,000
1940	472,013	...do	31,554
1941	494,752	...do	25,409
1942	432,313	...do	12,841
1943	272,999	...do	13,040
1944	172,145	...do	3,784
1945 (January to August)	[1] na	...do	na

[1] Not available.

Source: Japanese Textile Control Association, Japan Yearbook, 1943–44, 1944–45, Orient Yearbook, 1942–43.

APPENDIX TABLE C–181.—*Miscellaneous silk statistics, Japan proper, 1935–45*

Year	Number of workers [1]	Number of looms	Production of cocoons
			1,000 lbs.
1935	290,912	334,845	681,114
1936	310,359	369,319	688,003
1937	294,292	379,214	713,567
1938	304,932	391,286	624,624
1939	[2] na	na	753,631
1940	[3] 29,185	na	726,631
1941	25,907	na	579,746
1942	19,802	341,250	463,563
1943	22,805	127,420	448,200
1944	12,605	117,707	na
1945 (January to August)	na	100,707	na

[1] All workers in silk industry.
[2] Not available.
[3] These figures are only for "Spun silk industry."

Source: Japanese Textile Control Association, Japan Yearbook, 1943–44, Orient Yearbook, 1942–43.

APPENDIX TABLE C–182.—*Production, imports,[1] exports and stocks on hand of raw cotton, Japan proper, 1935–45*

[1 million pounds]

Year	Production of raw cotton	Imports	Exports	Stocks on hand at end of year	Index of imports
1935	Negligible	1, 641	Negligible	307	100
1936	___do___	2, 033	___do___	489	124
1937	___do___	1, 850	___do___	248	113
1938	___do___	1, 254	___do___	223	76
1939	___do___	1, 348	___do___	245	82
1940	___do___	866	___do___	252	53
1941	___do___	651	___do___	234	40
1942	___do___	154	___do___	98	9
1943	___do___	100	___do___	51	6
1944	___do___	31	___do___	32	2
1945 (January to August)	___do___	23	___do___	12	1

[1] Imports of raw cotton for domestic consumption before the war account for 50 percent of all textiles.

Source: Japanese Textile Control Association, Japan Yearbook, 1943–44, Orient Yearbook, 1942–43.

APPENDIX TABLE C–183.—*Production, imports, exports and stocks on hand of cotton cloth, Japan proper, 1935–45*

[1,000 square yards]

Year	Production	Imports	Exports	Stocks
1935	4, 499, 000	1, 530	2, 725, 109	[1] 161, 088
1936	3, 496, 000	1, 423	2, 709, 000	[1] 162, 848
1937	4, 826, 000	960	2, 643, 000	164, 204
1938	3, 297, 000	265	2, 180, 000	161, 500
1939	2, 951, 000	34	2, 445, 000	345, 236
1940	2, 624, 000	39	1, 854, 000	718, 288
1941	1, 329, 000	127	1, 018, 797	854, 188
1942	349, 000	89	166, 612	(2)
1943	[1] 240, 000	51	189, 043	(2)
1944	180, 274	(2)	5, 665	(2)
1945 (January to August)	(2)	(2)	0	(2)

[1] Estimated.
[2] Not available.

Source: The Japanese Textile Control Association, Japan Yearbook, 1943–44, 1944–45, Orient Yearbook, 1942–43.

APPENDIX TABLE C–184.—*Production, imports, exports and stocks on hand of raw wool, Japan proper, 1935–45*

[1,000 pounds]

Year	Production	Imports [1]	Exports	Stocks on hand and of year	Available for consumption
1935	Negligible	243, 009	Negligible	42, 843	[2] na
1936	do	216, 569	do	25, 185	234, 227
1937	do	257, 045	do	35, 958	246, 272
1938	do	116, 251	do	25, 005	127, 204
1939	do	105, 392	do	9, 525	117, 872
1940	do	101, 652	do	na	na
1941	do	119, 714	do	30, 490	na
1942	do	18, 882	do	10, 260	29, 112
1943	do	7, 824	do	3, 517	14, 567
1944	do	4, 428	do	1, 365	6, 580
1945 (January to August)	do	1, 766	do	na	na

[1] Includes tops, raw wool, goat, and camel hair.
[2] Not available.

Source: Japanese Textile Control Association, Japan Yearbook, 1943–44, 1944–45, Orient Yearbook, 1942–43.

APPENDIX TABLE C–185.—*Civilian stocks, production and consumption of woolen cloth, Japan proper, 1935–45*

Year	Civilian stocks on hand (end of year) [1]	Civilian production	Civilian consumption	Index of civilian consumption (1937 = 100)
1934	39, 620	[2] na	na	na
1935	50, 234	297, 359	286, 745	116. 0
1936	44, 334	284, 583	290, 483	117. 6
1937	46, 193	248, 914	247, 055	100. 0
1938	41, 468	242, 648	247, 373	100. 1
1939	25, 442	81, 840	97, 866	39. 6
1940	21, 368	57, 753	61, 827	25. 0
1941	26, 732	62, 481	57, 117	23. 1
1942	13, 438	39, 086	52, 380	21. 2
1943	12, 332	43, 072	44, 178	17. 9
1944	12, 558	19, 317	19, 543	7. 9
1945 (January to August)	7, 131	1, 171	6, 598	2. 7

[1] Civilian mills and warehouses.
[2] Not available.

Source: Textile Bureau, Ministry of Commerce and Industry, Japanese Textile Control Association, Japan Yearbook, 1943–44, 1944–45; Orient Yearbook, 1942–43.

APPENDIX TABLE C–186.—*Production, imports, exports, and stocks on hand of synthetic cloth, Japan proper, 1935–45*

[1,000 square yards]

Year	Production	Imports	Exports
1935	466, 762	Negligible	424, 114
1936	745, 413	do	527, 942
1937	804, 632	do	501, 882
1938	1, 164, 878	do	397, 573
1939	1, 086, 442	do	358, 784
1940	771, 485	do	235, 921
1941	632, 781	do	118, 107
1942	448, 310	do	48, 056
1943	252, 128	do	60, 976
1944	131, 523	do	59, 803
1945 (January to August)	(1)	do	0

[1] Not available.

Source: Japanese Textile Control Association, Japan Yearbook, 1943–45, 1944–45; Orient Yearbook, 1942–43.

APPENDIX TABLE C–187.—*Quantities of footware produced for civilian consumption, Japan proper, 1935–45*

[1,000 pair]

| Year, month, or quarter | Wooden clogs (geta) | Rubberized footwear | | | | Leather shoes |
		Rubberized socks	Rubber shoes and boots	Rubber soled canvas shoes	All rubberized shoes	
1935	33, 700				54, 800	2, 700
1936	42, 200				44, 400	2, 300
1937	60, 700				64, 700	2, 500
1938	64, 900				55, 400	3, 200
1939	113, 400				59, 300	2, 100
1940	142, 700	22, 481	1, 177	33, 684	57, 342	1, 200
1941	194, 400	26, 102	1, 336	23, 368	50, 806	1, 600
1942	183, 500	27, 136	4, 923	24, 303	56, 362	2, 700
I	46, 200					
II	47, 300					
III	43, 800					
IV	46, 200					
1943	156, 200	26, 969	4, 256	13, 047	44, 272	1, 500
I	40, 800					
II	41, 700					
III	39, 200					
IV	34, 500					
1944	118, 700	10, 731	2, 550	6, 601	19, 882	400
I	34, 600					
II	34, 700					
III	28, 500					
IV	20, 900					
1945	45, 300					0
January	6, 500					
February	6, 100				3, 600	
March	5, 800					
April	5, 500					
May	5, 400				1, 000	
June	5, 400					
July	5, 400					
August	5, 200				2, 000	

Source: For wooden clogs and leather shoes, Consumer Goods Bureau, Ministry of Commerce and Industry, figures rounded to even hundreds. For rubberized footwear, Rubber Industry Control Association.

APPENDIX TABLE C–188.—*Imports of furs, hides, skins, leather and leather goods, Japan proper, 1935–45*

[Tons]

Year	Hides and skins	Raw leather	Leather goods	Furs	Total
1935	30, 421	889	5	397	31, 712
1936	30, 763	779	4	246	31, 792
1937	41, 251	2, 413	7	349	44, 020
1938	29, 363	931	1	982	31, 277
1939	30, 448	755	1	3, 325	34, 529
1940	30, 248	410	0	285	30, 943
1941	38, 540	447	0	162	39, 149
1942	29, 124	38	0	143	29, 305
1943	15, 844	41	0	177	16, 062
1944	(1)	(1)	(1)	(1)	(1)
1945 (January to August)	(1)	(1)	(1)	(1)	(1)

[1] Not available.

Source: Hide and Leather Control Association.

APPENDIX TABLE C–189.—*Exports of leather, leather goods and fur, Japan proper, 1935–45*

[Tons]

Year	Leather	Leather goods	Furs	Total
1935	627	143	346	1, 116
1936	1, 057	148	602	1, 807
1937	1, 109	3	379	1, 491
1938	883	19	19	921
1939	159	3	24	186
1940	91	5	23	119
1941	50	6	50	106
1942	20	1	6	27
1943	31	1	12	44
1944	(1)	(1)	(1)	(1)
1945 (January to August)	(1)	(1)	(1)	(1)

[1] Not available.

Source: Hide and Leather Control Association.

APPENDIX TABLE C–190.—*Monthly production of hides and leather, Japan proper, 1935–45*

[Tons]

Month	1940	1941	1942	1943	1944	1945
January	4, 050	3, 900	3, 250	2, 100	1, 800	1, 520
February	4, 280	4, 150	3, 000	1, 980	1, 756	1, 950
March	5, 620	4, 350	3, 050	2, 090	1, 650	250
April	5, 035	4, 225	2, 480	2, 028	1, 890	840
May	5, 100	4, 028	2, 560	1, 998	1, 700	400
June	4, 850	4, 180	2, 750	1, 700	1, 825	340
July	4, 900	4, 200	2, 300	1, 680	1, 600	350
August	4, 335	4, 105	2, 290	1, 890	1, 580	280
September	4, 650	3, 980	2, 250	1, 945	1, 865	870
October	4, 700	4, 395	2, 215	2, 015	1, 928	
November	4, 015	4, 350	2, 300	2, 670	1, 629	
December	4, 355	4, 550	2, 155	3, 000	1, 687	
Total	55, 890	50, 413	30, 600	25, 096	20, 910	6, 800

Source: Hide and Leather Control Association.

APPENDIX TABLE C–191.—*Imports and estimated consumption of crude rubber, Japan proper, 1931–45*

[Metric tons]

| Year | Crude rubber imports | Crude rubber consumption | | | | |
		Military	Export	Civilian	Other[3]	Total
1935 [1]	60, 000	3, 000	2, 000	53, 500	1, 500	60, 000
1936 [1]	64, 000	3, 000	2, 000	53, 500	1, 500	60, 000
1937 [1]	64, 000	3, 000	2, 000	53, 500	1, 500	60, 000
1938	41, 000	5, 000	3, 500	25, 000	3, 000	36, 500
1939	48, 000	7, 000	4, 500	24, 000	4, 000	39, 500
1940	30, 000	10, 000	3, 000	23, 000	5, 000	41, 000
1941	36, 000	15, 000	1, 000	22, 000	5, 000	43, 000
1942	[2] 34, 000	20, 000	1, 000	21, 000	5, 000	47, 000
1943	[2] 34, 000	25, 000	1, 000	17, 000	5, 000	48, 000
1944	[2] 30, 000	27, 000	1, 000	12, 000	4, 000	44, 000

[1] Figures for 1935, 1936 and 1937 are estimated average.
[2] In addition to these imports there were those of the Japanese Army and Navy.
[3] Includes materials for election insulation and rubber exported to Manchuria.

Source: Rubber Industry Control Association.

Item and unit	1940	1941	1942	1943	1944
Footwear_____1,000 pairs__	22, 481	26, 102	27, 136	26, 969	10, 731
Rubber shoes and boots_____do____	1, 177	1, 336	4, 923	4, 256	2, 550
Canvas shoes_____do____	33, 684	23, 368	24, 303	13, 047	6, 601
Automobile tires_____1,000 tires__	378	384	406	264	126
Automobile tubes_____1,000 tubes__	282	331	326	209	111
Bicycle tires_____1,000 tires__	6, 971	5, 348	5, 522	4, 638	2, 014
Bicycle tubes_____1,000 tubes__	5, 937	3, 427	4, 929	4, 785	2, 097
Conveyor and power transmitting belts_____tons__	3, 000	2, 553	2, 735	1, 730	1, 306
V-belts_____do____	3	2	52	112	384
Hoses_____do____	430	490	715	769	650
Rubber cloth for fisheries_____do____	323	308	388	234	167
Robber cloth for general use_____do____	959	898	589	486	145

Source: Rubber Industry Controlling Association.

APPENDIX TABLE C–193.— *Production, imports, exports, and domestic consumption of pulp, Japan proper, 1935–45*

[1,000 long tons]

Year [1]	Kind	Production					Exports	Imports	Domestic comsumption
		Japan proper	Saghalien	Korea	Formosa	Total			
1935_____	[2] R	0	33	0	0	33	0	126	160
	[3] P	377	327	17	0	721	1	144	863
1936_____	R	0	54	1	0	55	0	169	224
	P	394	335	17	0	746	1	157	903
1937_____	R	0	36	21	0	57	0	291	348
	P	434	379	17	0	830	3	176	1, 002
1938_____	R	14	65	23	0	102	0	114	217
	P	458	372	17	5	852	0	30	882
1939_____	R	49	81	27	0	157	0	141	298
	P	516	344	17	20	897	0	27	922
1940_____	R	112	86	33	0	231	0	140	371
	P	518	334	18	35	905	1	33	937
1941_____	R	196	66	29	0	291	0	36	327
	P	558	342	18	48	966	0	21	988
1942_____	R	180	21	26	0	227	0	0	227
	P	472	325	16	39	852	8	9	854
1943_____	R	85	0	6	0	91	0	0	91
	P	434	233	25	28	720	0	0	720
1944_____	R	42	0	0	0	42	0	0	42
	P	258	178	19	14	469	0	0	468
1945, April–June_____	R	7	0	[4] na	na	7	0	0	7
	P	41	25	na	na	66	0	0	66

[1] Data on a fiscal year basis, 1 Apr.-31 Mar.
[2] R=Rayon pulp.
[3] P=Paper pulp, including that for chemical and mechanical uses.
[4] Not available.
Source: Paper Control and Distributing Corporation.

APPENDIX TABLE C-194.—*Production, imports, exports, and domestic consumption of all types of paper, Japan proper, 1935-45*

[1,000,000 pounds]

Year	Japan proper	Saghalien	Korea	Formosa	Total	Imports	Exports	Consumption
1935	2,264	407	56	7	2,734			
1936	2,428	386	59	7	2,880			
1937	2,872	422	61	N. A.	3,355			
1938	2,529	372	60	23	2,984			
1939	2,900	395	60	37	3,392			
1940	2,864	466	34	41	3,405	4	314	3,095
1941	2,814	452	34	39	3,339	1	244	3,096
1942	2,201	428	25	26	2,680	(¹)	165	2,515
1943	1,614	332	23	34	2,003	0	45	1,958
1944	867	327	19	21	1,234	0	11	1,223

¹ Less than 0.5.

Source: PapoCntroler and Distributing Corporation.

Food Tables

APPENDIX TABLE C-195.—*Supply, consumption, and exportation of staple foods, 1937-45* [1]

[1,000 metric tons]

Year of consumption (Nov.-Oct.)	Carry-over ;from previous year	Production in previous year	Imports				Quantity of current harvest consumed before Nov. 1
			Foreign	Korea	Formosa	Total	
1937	1,335	11,223	48	1,123	809	1,980	
1938	1,252	11,053	25	1,692	829	2,546	
1939	1,416	10,978	26	948	660	1,634	
1940	677	11,494	1,331	66	464	1,861	
1941	726	10,047	1,638	551	328	2,517	99
1942	1,178	9,082	1,457	873	284	2,614	218
1943	392	10,911	880		302	1,182	423
1944	435	10,059		583	217	800	417
1945	384	9,366		237		237	467

Year of consumption (Nov.-Oct.)	Food substituted in ration				Special reserve for bombing	Total supply	Ration consumption			
	Wheat and barley	Domestic potatoes and other grains	Miscellaneous imported grains	Total			Farmers	Urban	Military	Total
1937						14,538	(²)	(²)	(²)	13,178
1938						14,851	(²)	(²)	(²)	13,337
1939						14,028	(²)	(²)	(²)	13,224
1940						14,031	(²)	(²)	(²)	13,148
1941						13,389	4,058	7,807	179	12,044
1942	393			393		13,486	4,233	8,513	231	12,977
1943	633	67	43	743		13,649	4,415	8,296	374	13,085
1944	917	406	512	1,835		13,535	4,025	8,558	503	13,086
1945	1,243	533	493	2,269	245	12,992	3,792	8,175	826	12,793

See footnotes at end of table.

Year of consumption (Nov.–Oct.)	Exports	Total consumption and exportation	Carry-over	Percentage of imports	Percentage of substitute foods	Year of consumption (Nov.–Oct.)	Exports	Total consumption and exportation	Carry-over	Percentage of imports	Percentage of substitute foods
1937	108	13,286	1,252	--------	--------	1942	117	13,094	392	20.6	2.0
1938	99	13,435	1,416	--------	--------	1943	129	13,214	435	9.3	5.6
1939	128	13,352	677	--------	--------	1944	75	13,161	384	10.0	13.9
1940	157	13,305	726	14.0	--------	1945	67	12,860	133	5.9	17.6
1941	167	12,211	1,178	20.6	--------						

[1] Carry-over, production, and import figures apply only to rice. Substitute foods appear only as that quantity used in the staple ration.
[2] No rationing.

Source: Data submitted to the Japanese Diet at the end of the war by the Minister of Agriculture and Forestry.

APPENDIX TABLE C-196.—*Domestic production of principal foods, Japan proper, 1931–45*

[1,000 metric tons]

Year	Rice	Wheat	Barley	Naked barley	Soy beans	Sweet potatoes	Potatoes	Vegetables	Fruits
1931	9,202	889	801	904	357	2,790	907	6,080	955
1932	10,065	902	813	910	344	2,898	987	6,331	1,076
1933	11,604	1,098	751	742	401	2,968	1,352	6,281	1,082
1934	8,640	1,295	730	855	309	2,509	1,249	6,329	1,045
1935	----------	1,323	791	919	323	2,855	1,231	6,635	1,299
1936	11,223	1,228	690	810	376	3,160	1,651	6,725	1,124
1937	11,053	1,369	747	827	406	3,243	2,033	6,668	1,286
1938	10,972	1,228	687	710	385	3,159	1,818	6,624	1,275
1939	11,494	1,659	844	933	349	2,874	1,852	6,639	1,416
1940	10,146	1,794	817	869	314	2,910	1,618	6,809	1,440
1941	9,181	1,461	706	936	230	3,377	1,934	5,956	1,450
1942	11,129	1,386	733	918	296	3,079	1,935	5,940	1,492
1943	10,481	1,095	572	732	307	3,951	2,032	6,269	1,441
1944	9,778	1,385	781	912	267	4,282	1,973	5,831	1,026
1945	6,600	895	501	685	339	5,572	2,398	5,396	718

Source: Ministry of Agriculture and Forestry.

APPENDIX TABLE C-197.—*Expansion and contraction of arable land, Japan proper, 1933–43*

[Acres]

Year	Total land expansion	Dry fields	Rice fields	Total land contraction	Dry fields	Rice fields	Total gain or loss	Dry fields	Rice fields
1933	147,568.9	118,754.4	28,814.5	71,946.7	44,301.1	27,645.6	75,622.2	74,453.3	1,168.9
1934	121,043.2	98,437.6	22,605.6	95,534.8	48,803.7	46,731.1	25,508.4	49,633.9	−24,125.5
1935	133,271.4	100,194.2	33,077.2	82,420.7	47,309.0	35,111.7	50,850.7	52,885.2	−2,034.5
1936	124,768.2	99,467.8	25,300.4	60,830.8	37,800.3	23,030.5	63,937.4	61,667.5	2,269.9
1937	93,419.2	75,664.1	17,755.1	58,492.5	36,184.3	22,308.2	34,926.7	39,479.8	−4,553.1
1938	79,247.4	63,346.9	15,900.5	115,095.1	70,702.3	44,392.8	−35,847.7	−7,355.4	−28,492.3
1939	77,716.9	57,399.1	20,317.8	75,831.9	48,470.3	27,361.6	1,885.0	8,928.8	−7,043.8
1940	75,133.2	53,391.4	21,741.8	84,447.4	52,556.7	31,890.7	−9,314.2	834.7	−10,148.9
1941	65,489.5	53,177.0	12,312.5	112,068.2	81,922.4	30,145.8	−46,578.7	−28,745.4	−17,833.3
1942	70,645.5	53,701.3	16,944.2	141,630.6	109,522.4	32,108.2	−70,985.1	−55,821.1	−15,164.0
1943	53,282.3	42,750.5	10,531.8	163,613.9	104,753.7	58,860.2	−110,331.6	−62,003.2	−48,328.4
Totals	1,041,585.7	816,284.3	225,301.4	1,061,912.6	682,326.2	379,586.4	−20,326.9	133,958.1	−154,285.0

Source: Statistical Annual, Ministry of Agriculture and Forestry, 1944.

APPENDIX TABLE C-198.—*Total arable land, acreages in various crops, and total cultivated acreage (including double cropping), Japan proper, 1931-44* [1]

[1,000 acres]

PART 1. FOOD CROPS

Year	Total arable land	Rice	Barley	Naked barley	Wheat	Oats	Soybeans	Sweet-potatoes	Potatoes	Vegetables	Fruits	Total in food crops
1931	14, 578	7, 963	931	1, 176	1, 225	294	858	637	270	1, 348	(360)	15, 062
1932	14, 678	7, 987	931	1, 176	1, 250	319	833	662	270	1, 397	(360)	15, 185
1933	14, 754	7, 767	851	1, 072	1, 510	314	800	666	319	1, 450	(360)	15, 109
1934	14, 780	7, 767	813	1, 040	1, 589	295	831	657	343	1, 463	(360)	15, 158
1935	14, 830	7, 840	838	1, 077	1, 626	300	822	681	343	1, 491	(360)	15, 378
1936	14, 890	7, 865	835	1, 077	1, 688	308	807	698	368	1, 489	(360)	15, 495
1937	14, 928	7, 889	809	1, 052	1, 775	300	812	708	417	1, 461	(360)	15, 583
1938	14, 892	7, 889	876	1, 016	1, 776	337	808	690	392	1, 427	(360)	15, 571
1939	14, 894	7, 816	867	1, 004	1, 827	303	795	681	417	1, 440	(350)	15, 500
1940	14, 886	7, 791	835	992	2, 061	297	802	675	417	1, 424	(350)	15, 644
1941	14, 839	7, 796	876	1, 150	2, 023	341	760	762	445	1, 378	335	15, 866
1942	14, 769	7, 752	969	1, 247	2, 115	356	777	792	475	1, 338	345	16, 166
1943	14, 658	7, 620	938	1, 189	1, 984	332	766	804	501	1, 276	305	15, 715
1944 [2]	13, 629	7, 320	1, 049	1, 245	2, 058	-------	-------	-------	-------	-------	292	-------

[1] Figures in parentheses are estimated.
[2] Data for 1944 are incomplete.

Source: Compiled from data furnished by the Ministry of Agriculture and Forestry.

APPENDIX TABLE C-198.—*Total arable land, acreages in various crops, and total cultivated acreage (including double cropping) Japan proper, 1931-44* [1]

[1,000 acres]

PART 2. NONFOOD CROPS

Year	Mulberry	Miscellaneous grains	Industrial crops	Feed crops	Green manure crops	Other	Total cultivated acreage	Ratio cultivated to arable land	Percentage of food crops to total cultivated acreage
1931	(1, 625)	(975)	(590)	(150)	(1, 200)	(325)	19, 927	1. 37	75. 6
1932	(1, 600)	(975)	(600)	(150)	(1, 200)	(325)	20, 035	1. 37	75. 8
1933	1, 568	976	613	(150)	1, 208	(325)	19, 949	1. 35	75. 7
1934	1, 526	989	657	(150)	1, 238	(325)	20, 043	1. 35	75. 6
1935	1, 427	954	703	(160)	1, 212	(325)	20, 159	1. 36	76. 3
1936	1, 387	943	725	(170)	1, 221	(325)	20, 266	1. 36	76. 5
1937	1, 375	923	720	(175)	1, 195	(350)	20, 321	1. 36	76. 7
1938	1, 346	901	749	192	1, 189	(375)	20, 323	1. 36	76. 6
1939	1, 307	837	754	223	1, 153	(400)	20, 174	1. 35	76. 8
1940	1, 308	854	768	247	1, 267	(440)	20, 528	1. 38	76. 2
1941	1, 211	850	849	205	1, 239	480	20, 700	1. 39	76. 6
1942	1, 011	821	785	242	1, 270	529	20, 824	1. 41	77. 6
1943	892	854	541	276	1, 126	649	20, 053	1. 37	78. 4
1944 [2]	-------	-------	-------	-------	-------	-------	-------	-------	-------

[1] Figures in parentheses are estimated.
[2] Data for 1944 are incomplete.

Source: Compiled from data furnished by the Ministry of Agriculture and Forestry.

APPENDIX TABLE C–199.—*Per acre yields of rice, wheat, barley, and naked barley, Japan proper, 1931–44*

[Metric tons per acre]

Year	Rice	Wheat	Barley	Naked barley
1931	1. 16	0. 73	0. 86	0. 77
1932	1. 26	. 72	. 88	. 77
1933	1. 49	. 73	. 88	. 69
1934	1. 11	. 81	. 91	. 82
1935	1. 22	. 81	. 94	. 85
1936	1. 43	. 73	. 83	. 75
1937	1. 40	. 77	. 92	. 78
1938	1. 39	. 69	. 78	. 70
1939	1. 47	. 91	. 97	. 93
1940	1. 30	. 87	. 98	. 88
1941	1. 18	. 72	. 81	. 81
1942	1. 44	. 66	. 76	. 74
1943	1. 38	. 55	. 61	. 62
1944	1. 34	. 67	. 74	. 73

Source: Ministry of Agriculutre and Forestry.

APPENDIX TABLE C–200.—*Rice imports from Korea and Formosa, Japan proper, November 1944–October 1945*

[Metric tons]

Month and year	Korea	Formosa
1944:		
November	22, 642	24, 582
December	16, 827	7, 122
1945:		
January	13, 387	6, 661
February	17, 788	0
March	26, 626	0
April	31, 931	2, 295
May	24, 179	0
June	27, 997	0
July	31, 549	0
August	12, 607	0
September	373	0
October	0	0
Total	225, 906	40, 660

Source: Ministry of Agriculture and Forestry.

APPENDIX TABLE C–201.—*Net imports of sugar, Japan proper, 1931–45*

[Metric tons]

1931	818, 200
1932	774, 000
1933	611, 800
1934	654, 300
1935	874, 700
1936	894, 500
1937	940, 500
1938	841, 000

APPENDIX TABLE C–201.—*Net imports of sugar: Japan proper, 1931–45*—Continued

1939	903, 300
1940	811, 800
1941	678, 000
1942	719, 100
1943	529, 200
1944	432, 900
1945	116, 000

Source: Ministry of Agriculture and Forestry.

APPENDIX TABLE C–202.—*Food stocks on hand at specified periods, Japan proper, 1931–45* [1]

[Metric tons]

	Rice	Other grains [2]	Canned foods	Sugar
1931	1, 523, 374		25, 612	177, 437
1932	1, 484, 571		31, 236	299, 250
1933	1, 501, 266		38, 224	180, 750
1934	2, 738, 481		46, 955	49, 200
1935	1, 656, 023		52, 033	73, 620
1936	1, 344, 416		61, 155	57, 270
1937	1, 251, 955		78, 953	69, 603
1938	1, 451, 550		91, 147	63, 631
1939	676, 900		102, 642	55, 381
1940	726, 124	2, 642, 431	64, 721	66, 693
1941	1, 178, 377	2, 264, 042	73, 721	89, 744
1942	392, 000	1, 855, 614	47, 224	167, 159
1943	435, 333	1, 543, 092	61, 014	105, 956
1944	384, 167		50, 128	11, 272
1945	133, 000			4, 583

[1] Figures for rice represent stocks on hand as of 31 October; figures for other grains represent stocks on hand as of 30 June; figures for canned foods and sugar represent stocks on hand as of 31 December.
[2] Barley, naked barley, and wheat. Since these figures are as of 30 June they are not carry-over figures to the next crop year.

Source: Compiled from data furnished by the Ministry of Agriculture and Forestry.

APPENDIX TABLE C–203.—*Quantity of foods allotted to the armed services, Japan proper, 1942–45*

[Metric tons]

	1942	1943	1944	1945
Rice	230, 600	374, 300	502, 500	666, 600
Barley	41, 800	23, 000	25, 900	63, 800
Naked barley	139, 000	75, 100	90, 100	130, 200
Wheat	3, 100	3, 700	6, 900	18, 100
Wheat flour	na	na	100, 000	122, 900
Miso	28, 300	38, 750	67, 650	66, 370
Shoyu	23, 050	30, 750	56, 500	55, 650
Total	[1] 465, 850	[1] 545, 600	849, 550	1, 123, 020

na Not available.
[1] Does not include wheat flour, if any.

Source: Ministry of Agriculture and Forestry.

APPENDIX TABLE C–204.—*Production, imports and consumption of marine products, Japan proper, 1939–45*

[Metric tons]

Year	Production		Total	Percentage of 1939	Imports	Total supply
	Overseas	Coastal				
1939	167, 188	4, 626, 240	4, 793, 428	100	1, 223, 805	6, 017, 233
1940	137, 534	4, 351, 360	4, 488, 894	94	1, 060, 510	5, 549, 404
1941	122, 449	3, 616, 089	3, 738, 528	78	786, 991	4, 525, 519
1942	89, 622	3, 200, 130	3, 289, 752	69	42, 139	3, 331, 891
1943	81, 638	2, 891, 230	2, 972, 868	62	37, 649	3, 010, 517
1944 [1]	43, 872	2, 450, 780	2, 494, 652	52	----------	2, 494, 652
1945 [2]	16, 706	2, 062, 510	2, 079, 216	43	----------	2, 079, 216

Year	Consumption		Percentage of 1939	Food [3]	Percentage of 1939	Fresh fish included in food	Percentage of 1939
	Exports	Fertilizer and feed					
1939	1, 388, 252	1, 510, 478	100	3, 018, 234	100	1, 280, 050	100
1940	1, 162, 136	1, 360, 791	90	3, 217, 817	107	1, 360, 790	106
1941	708, 972	544, 770	36	3, 271, 795	108	1, 052, 345	82
1942	97, 070	291, 663	19	2, 942, 937	98	1, 040, 098	81
1943	55, 792	141, 069	9	2, 814, 116	93	855, 030	67
1944 [1]	----------	121, 110	8	2, 373, 673	79	514, 833	40
1945 [2]	----------	102, 059	7	1, 976, 776	65	171, 913	13

[1] 1944 data submitted by Japanese is based on partial estimates.
[2] 1945 data based on Japanese estimates.
[3] Frozen, canned, salted and fresh fish.

Source: Data submitted by the Ministry of Agriculture and Forestry.

APPENDIX TABLE C–205.—*Proportions of food derived from production and imports, on a caloric basis, Japan proper, 1931–40 average; annually, 1941–45*

[Percentages]

	1931–40 average		1941		1942		1943		1944		1945	
	Production	Imports	Production	Imports	Production	Imports	Production	Imports	Production	Imports	Production	Imports
Rice	83	17	78	22	81	19	90	10	92	8	97	3
Wheat	79	11	99	1	99	1	99	1	100	0	100	0
Barley	100	0	100	0	100	0	100	0	100	0	100	0
Naked barley	100	0	100	0	100	0	100	0	100	0	100	0
Soybeans	33	67	28	72	32	68	34	66	27	73	29	71
Potatoes	100	0	100	0	100	0	100	0	100	0	100	0
Sweetpotatoes	100	0	100	0	100	0	100	0	100	0	100	0
Vegetables	100	0	100	0	100	0	100	0	100	0	100	0
Fruits	100	0	100	0	100	0	100	0	100	0	100	0
Fish [1]	96	4	97	3	97	3	97	3	98	2	99	1
Sugar	16	34	18	82	17	83	21	79	23	77	44	56
Other grains and beans	63	37	48	52	66	34	76	24	54	46	65	35
Other foods	95	5	96	4	97	3	99	1	100	0	100	0
Weighted average	81. 0	19. 0	79. 7	20. 3	81. 3	18. 7	87. 3	12. 7	87. 9	12. 1	90. 6	9. 4

[1] Production, coastal fishing, imports, overseas fishing.

Source: Compiled from data furnished by the Ministry of Agriculture and Forestry.

UNITED STATES STRATEGIC BOMBING SURVEY

LIST OF REPORTS

The following is a bibliography of reports resulting from the Survey's studies of the European and Pacific wars. Certain of these reports may be purchased from the Superintendent of Documents at the Government Printing Office, Washington, D. C. Permission to examine the remaining reports may be had by writing to the Headquarters of the Survey at Gravelly Point, Washington 25, D. C.

European War

OFFICE OF THE CHAIRMAN

1 The United States Strategic Bombing Survey: Summary Report (European War)
2 The United States Strategic Bombing Survey: Overall Report (European War)
3 The Effects of Strategic Bombing on the German War Economy

AIRCRAFT DIVISION

(By Division and Branch)

4 Aircraft Division Industry Report
5 Inspection Visits to Various Targets (Special Report)

Airframes Branch

6 Junkers Aircraft and Aero Engine Works, Dessau, Germany
7 Erla Maschinenwerke G m b H, Heiterblick, Germany
8 A T G Maschinenbau, G m b H, Leipzig (Mockau), Germany
9 Gothaer Waggonfabrik, A G, Gotha, Germany
10 Focke Wulf Aircraft Plant, Bremen, Germany
11 Messerschmitt A G, Augsburg, Germany { Over-all Report / Part A / Part B / Appendices I, II, III
12 Dornier Works, Friedrichshafen & Munich, Germany
13 Gerhard Fieseler Werke G m b H, Kassel, Germany
14 Wiener Neustaedter Flugzeugwerke, Wiener Neustadt, Austria

Aero Engines Branch

15 Bussing NAG Flugmotorenwerke G m b H, Brunswick, Germany
16 Mittel-Deutsche Motorenwerke G m b H, Taucha, Germany
17 Bavarian Motor Works Inc, Eisenach & Durrerhof, Germany
18 Bayerische Motorenwerke A G (BMW) Munich, Germany
19 Henschel Flugmotorenwerke, Kassel, Germany

Light Metal Branch

20 Light Metals Industry of Germany { Part I, Aluminum / Part II, Magnesium

21 Vereinigte Deutsche Metallwerke, Hildesheim, Germany
22 Metallgussgesellschaft G m b H, Leipzig, Germany
23 Aluminiumwerk G m b H, Plant No. 2, Bitterfeld, Germany
24 Gebrueder Giulini G m b H, Ludwigshafen, Germany
25 Luftschiffbau, Zeppelin G m b H, Friedrichshafen on Bodensee, Germany
26 Wieland Werke A G, Ulm, Germany
27 Rudolph Rautenbach Leichmetallgiessereien, Solingen, Germany
28 Lippewerke Vereinigte Aluminiumwerke A G, Lunen, Germany
29 Vereinigte Deutsche Metallwerke, Heddernheim, Germany
30 Duerener Metallwerke A G, Duren Wittenau-Berlin & Waren, Germany

AREA STUDIES DIVISION

31 Area Studies Division Report
32 A Detailed Study of the Effects of Area Bombing on Hamburg
33 A Detailed Study of the Effects of Area Bombing on Wuppertal
34 A Detailed Study of the Effects of Area Bombing on Dusseldorf
35 A Detailed Study of the Effects of Area Bombing on Solingen
36 A Detailed Study of the Effects of Area Bombing on Remscheid
37 A Detailed Study of the Effects of Area Bombing on Darmstadt
38 A Detailed Study of the Effects of Area Bombing on Lubeck
39 A Brief Study of the Effects of Area Bombing on Berlin, Augsburg, Bochum, Leipzig, Hagen, Dortmund, Oberhausen, Schweinfurt, and Bremen

CIVILIAN DEFENSE DIVISION

40 Civilian Defense Division—Final Report
41 Cologne Field Report
42 Bonn Field Report
43 Hanover Field Report
44 Hamburg Field Report—Vol I, Text; Vol II, Exhibits
45 Bad Oldesloe Field Report
46 Augsburg Field Report
47 Reception Areas in Bavaria, Germany

EQUIPMENT DIVISION

Electrical Branch

48 German Electrical Equipment Industry Report
49 Brown Boveri et Cie, Mannheim Kafertal, Germany

Optical and Precision Instrument Branch

50 Optical and Precision Instrument Industry Report

ECONOMIC STUDIES

Aircraft Division

15 The Japanese Aircraft Industry
16 Mitsubishi Heavy Industries, Ltd.
    Corporation Report No. I
      (Mitsubishi Jukogyo KK)
      (Airframes & Engines)
17 Nakajima Aircraft Company, Ltd.
    Corporation Report No. II
      (Nakajima Hikoki KK)
      (Airframes & Engines)
18 Kawanishi Aircraft Company
    Corporation Report No. III
      (Kawanishi Kokuki Kabushiki Kaisha)
      (Airframes)
19 Kawasaki Aircraft Industries Company, Inc.
    Corporation Report No. IV
      (Kawasaki Kokuki Kogyo Kabushiki
      Kaisha)
      (Airframes & Engines)
20 Aichi Aircraft Company
    Corporation Report No. V
      (Aichi Kokuki KK)
      (Airframes & Engines)
21 Sumitomo Metal Industries, Propeller Division
    Corporation Report No. VI
      (Sumitomo Kinzoku Kogyo KK, Puropera
      Seizosho)
      (Propellers)
22 Hitachi Aircraft Company
    Corporation Report No. VII
      (Hitachi Kokuki KK)
      (Airframes & Engines)
23 Japan International Air Industries, Ltd.
    Corporation Report No. VIII
      (Nippon Kokusai Koku Kogyo KK)
      (Airframes)
24 Japan Musical Instrument Manufacturing Company
    Corporation Report No. IX
      (Nippon Gakki Seizo KK)
      (Propellers)
25 Tachikawa Aircraft Company
    Corporation Report No. X
      (Tachikawa Hikoki KK)
      (Airframes)
26 Fuji Airplane Company
    Corporation Report No. XI
      (Fuji Hikoki KK)
      (Airframes)
27 Showa Airplane Company
    Corporation Report No. XII
      (Showa Hikoki Kogyo KK)
      (Airframes)
28 Ishikawajima Aircraft Industries Company, Ltd.
    Corporation Report No. XIII
      (Ishikawajima Koku Kogyo Kabushiki
      Kaisha)
      (Engines)
29 Nippon Airplane Company
    Corporation Report No. XIV
      (Nippon Hikoki KK)
      (Airframes)
30 Kyushu Airplane Company
    Corporation Report No. XV
      (Kyushu Hikoki KK)
      (Airframes)
31 Shoda Engineering Company
    Corporation Report No. XVI
      (Shoda Seisakujo)
      (Components)
32 Mitaka Aircraft Industries
    Corporation Report No. XVII
      (Mitaka Koku Kogyo Kabushiki Kaisha)
      (Components)

33 Nissan Automobile Company
    Corporation Report No. XVIII
      (Nissan Jidosha KK)
      (Engines)
34 Army Air Arsenal & Navy Air Depots
    Corporation Report No. XIX
      (Airframes and Engines)
35 Japan Aircraft Underground
    Report No. XX

Basic Materials Division

36 Coal and Metals in Japan's War Economy

Capital Goods, Equipment and Construction Division

37 The Japanese Construction Industry
38 Japanese Electrical Equipment
39 The Japanese Machine Building Industry

Electric Power Division

40 The Electric Power Industry of Japan
41 The Electric Power Industry of Japan (Plant Reports)

Manpower, Food and Civilian Supplies Division

42 The Japanese Wartime Standard of Living and Utilization of Manpower

Military Supplies Division

43 Japanese War Production Industries
44 Japanese Naval Ordnance
45 Japanese Army Ordnance
46 Japanese Naval Shipbuilding
47 Japanese Motor Vehicle Industry
48 Japanese Merchant Shipbuilding

Oil and Chemical Division

49 Chemicals in Japan's War
50 Chemicals in Japan's War—Appendix
51 Oil in Japan's War
52 Oil in Japan's War—Appendix

Overall Economic Effects Division

53 The Effects of Strategic Bombing on Japan's War Economy (Including Appendix A: U. S. Economic Intelligence on Japan—Analysis and Comparison; Appendix B: Gross National Product on Japan and Its Components; Appendix C: Statistical Sources).

Transportation Division

54 The War Against Japanese Transportation, 1941–1945

Urban Areas Division

55 Effects of Air Attack on Japanese Urban Economy (Summary Report)
56 Effects of Air Attack on Urban Complex Tokyo-Kawasaki-Yokohama
57 Effects of Air Attack on the City of Nagoya
58 Effects of Air Attack on Osaka-Kobe-Kyoto
59 Effects of Air Attack on the City of Nagasaki
60 Effects of Air Attack on the City of Hiroshima

MILITARY STUDIES

Military Analysis Division

61 Air Forces Allied with the United States in the War Against Japan
62 Japanese Air Power
63 Japanese Air Weapons and Tactics
64 The Effect of Air Action on Japanese Ground Army Logistics
65 Employment of Forces Under the Southwest Pacific Command
66 The Strategic Air Operations of Very Heavy Bombardment in the War Against Japan (Twentieth Air Force)
67 Air Operations in China, Burma, India— World War II
68 The Air Transport Command in the War Against Japan
69 The Thirteenth Air Force in the War Against Japan
70 The Seventh and Eleventh Air Forces in the War Against Japan
71 The Fifth Air Force in the War Against Japan

Naval Analysis Division

72 The Interrogations of Japanese Officials) Vols. I and II)
73 Campaigns of the Pacific War
74 The Reduction of Wake Island
75 The Allied Campaign Against Rabaul
76 The American Campaign Against Wotje, Maloelap, Mille, and Jaluit (Vols. I, II and III)
77 The Reduction of Truk
78 The Offensive Mine Laying Campaign Against Japan
79 Report of Ships Bombardment Survey Party—Foreword, Introduction, Conclusions, and General Summary
80 Report of Ships Bombardment Survey Party (Enclosure A), Kamaishi Area
81 Report of Ships Bombardment Survey Party (Enclosure B), Hamamatsu Area
82 Report of Ships Bombardment Survey Party (Enclosure C), Hitachi Area
83 Report of Ships Bombardment Survey Party (Enclosure D), Hakodate Area
84 Report of Ships Bombardment Survey Party (Enclosure E), Muroran Area
85 Report of Ships Bombardment Survey Party (Enclosure F), Shimizu Area
86 Report of Ships Bombardment Survey Party (Enclosures G and H), Shionomi-Saki and Nojima-Saki Areas
87 Report of Ships Bombardment Survey Party (Enclosure I), Comments and Data on Effectiveness of Ammunition
88 Report of Ships Bombardment Survey Party (Enclosure J), Comments and Data on Accuracy of Firing
89 Reports of Ships Bombardment Survey Party (Enclosure K), Effects of Surface Bombardments on Japanese War Potential

Physical Damage Division

90 Effect of the Incendiary Bomb Attacks on Japan (a Report on Eight Cities)
91 The Effects of the Ten Thousand Pound Bomb on Japanese Targets (a Report on Nine Incidents)
92 Effects of the Atomic Bomb on Hiroshima, Japan
93 Effects of the Atomic Bomb on Nagasaki, Japan
94 Effects of the Four Thousand Pound Bomb on Japanese Targets (a Report on Five Incidents)
95 Effects of Two Thousand, One Thousand, and Five Hundred Pound Bombs on Japanese Targets (a Report on Eight Incidents)
96 A Report on Physical Damage in Japan (Summary Report)

G–2 Division

97 Japanese Military and Naval Intelligence
98 Evaluation of Photographic Intelligence in the Japanese Homeland, Part I, *Comprehensive Report*
99 Evaluation of Photographic Intelligence in the Japanese Homeland, Part II, *Airfields*
100 Evaluation of Photographic Intelligence in the Japanese Homeland, Part III, *Computed Bomb Plotting*
101 Evaluation of Photographic Intelligence in the Japanese Homeland, Part IV, *Urban Area Analysis*
102 Evaluation of Photographic Intelligence in the Japanese Homeland, Part V, *Camouflage*
103 Evaluation of Photographic Intelligence in the Japanese Homeland, Part VI, *Shipping*
104 Evaluation of Photographic Intelligence in the Japanese Homeland, Part VII, *Electronics*
105 Evaluation of Photographic Intelligence in the Japanese Homeland, Part VIII, *Beach Intelligence*
106 Evaluation of Photographic Intelligence in the Japanese Homeland, Part IX, *Artillery*
107 Evaluation of Photographic Intelligence in the Japanese Homeland, Part X, *Roads and Railroads*
108 Evaluation of Photographic Intelligence in the Japanese Homeland, Part XI, *Industrial Analysis*